Training and Development

FOR DUMMIES
A Wiley Brand

by Elaine Biech
CPLP Fellow

Foreword by Tony Bingham
President and CEO, Association for Talent Development

FOR DUMMIES
A Wiley Brand

Training and Development For Dummies®

Published by:
John Wiley & Sons, Inc.,
111 River Street,
Hoboken, NJ 07030-5774,
www.wiley.com

For general information on our other products and services, please contact our Customer Care Department within the U.S. at 877-762-2974, outside the U.S. at 317-572-3993, or fax 317-572-4002. For technical support, please visit www.wiley.com/techsupport.

Wiley publishes in a variety of print and electronic formats and by print-on-demand. Some material included with standard print versions of this book may not be included in e-books or in print-on-demand. If this book refers to media such as a CD or DVD that is not included in the version you purchased, you may download this material at http://booksupport.wiley.com. For more information about Wiley products, visit www.wiley.com.

Library of Congress Control Number: 2015937669

ISBN 978-1-119-07633-9 (pbk); ISBN 978-1-119-07642-1 (ebk); ISBN 978-1-119-07615-5 (ebk)

Manufactured in the United States of America

C10014307_092719

Contents at a Glance

Table of Contents

Foreword

. . . .

Great organizations exist because of great people. Helping those people reach their potential is the work of talent development professionals.

These professionals commit themselves to developing the knowledge, skills, and abilities of others that help the organization achieve its strategic goals and objectives. They hold many titles: trainers, instructional designers, knowledge managers, coaches, subject matter experts, facilitators, and talent developers. Their work is delivering greater impact than ever before. More than just providing training events, these individuals are learning facilitators, collaborators, and partners in helping others achieve their full potential.

While many of these practitioners enter into this profession intentionally, we know that many others are "accidental trainers," or serve a training role in addition to other responsibilities they have in their company. For both groups, a handy resource like this is important to have. I am so pleased that Elaine Biech agreed to update this book — her expertise is beyond compare, and I can think of no one better to boil down "training and development" to its most essential components.

Training & Development For Dummies is a comprehensive — and fun — look at what comprises the important work of developing others. I encourage you to invest the time to really absorb all Elaine is sharing here. And I hope you'll also take advantage of the deep resources that our organization — The Association for Talent Development (formerly ASTD) — has to help you grow and strengthen your skills in the field. We serve a global community of practitioners and are committed to providing you great content, a supportive community, and robust tools that will benefit you in your work.

Creating a world that works better is the vision that drives the work we do. We're glad you're a part of our community.

— Tony Bingham, President and CEO, Association for Talent Development (formerly ASTD)

Introduction

Training is the best profession in the world. The training professional touches almost everyone every day. Whether you're experiencing a golf lesson, taking a virtual course to learn to use new computer software, working with Leaders Beyond Boundaries in Ethiopia, trying a new recipe, or being coached by your boss, you're learning something new and experiencing training. You and your trainer don't even need to be in the same room or on the same schedule.

What other career affords you the opportunity to increase an organization's bottom line, improve your country's productivity level, and enhance individuals' lives around the globe, all at the same time? It is truly a privilege to be a trainer, yet it's also a responsibility.

Training is a profession on the move, and those moves are ones to be proud of. As I finished this book, the Association for Talent Development (ATD), the trainers' professional association, is almost a year into its new name; has opened an office in China; is designing two new trainer tool apps for virtual learning and a global approach to learning; and is introducing CTDO, a publication to serve senior leaders who develop talent. We are a profession on the move, and this book shows you why.

About This Book

It's been ten years since the first edition *of Training For Dummies* was published. Now with a slightly updated name, *Training and Development For Dummies* incorporates several new elements that mirror the growth of the training and development (T&D) profession.

Training and Development For Dummies is both practical and fun. It has been written in a logical sequence and is loaded with practical ideas. It is designed to take you through a training cycle from start to finish, and in sequential order. So, if you want to, you can start at the beginning of this book and move through to the end. If you're interested in finding only specific information, however, you can also use the index at the back of the book or the Table of Contents near the front.

This book is fun to read, but don't let the conversational tone fool you. It is jam-packed with technical knowledge about the training profession as well as tips, tricks, and techniques for honing your training skills.

The most exciting part is that several leaders in the T&D profession have agreed to contribute snippets of content that focus on their areas of expertise. So, as you read *Training and Development For Dummies,* be sure to check out what experts say — like Michael Allen on agile-based design, Jennifer Hofmann on virtual classrooms, Karl Kapp on gamification, and Thiagi on facilitation.

Foolish Assumptions

While writing this book, I imagine you, the reader, sitting next to me and telling me what you want to read about. And what did I hear you saying? "Practical. Make it practical." So I did.

I assume you fall into one of two categories: Either you're interested in becoming a trainer, or you're already a part of the T&D profession and want to hone your skills. Perhaps you're even interested in obtaining professional certification from ATD.

I also assume that you've been a participant in training and that some of those training sessions have been life-changing, while others have been a waste of your time. And I assume that you want to know how to conduct more of the former and none of the latter.

I assume that you know how important the training profession is to corporations' bottom lines, individuals' development, happiness, and well-being, as well as your country's productivity.

Finally, I make one other assumption: And that is that you love (or will grow to love) the T&D profession as much as I do!

Icons Used in This Book

Throughout this book, you find icons in the left margins that alert you to information you need to know. You will find the following icons in this book.

Quick tips and tricks to make your job easier and ideas to help you apply the techniques and approaches discussed.

Important information that is critical to being a professional trainer.

A few words that impart wisdom you can rely on.

Many people have made the profession what it is today, and their names and notions are a part of the foundation that trainers rely on to deliver success.

Specific thoughts and ideas that guide what you need to know about the ATD certification.

Beyond the Book

In addition to the material in the print or e-book you're reading right now, this product also comes with some access-anywhere goodies on the web.

Check out the free Cheat Sheet at www.dummies.com/cheatsheet/traininganddevelopment for additional helpful tips on what to do and not do, the seven sins of trainers, ensuring participation, fostering learning, and more.

There were also more goodies than would fit between these pages. You can access these extras at www.dummies.com/extras/trainingand development. There you will find articles on humor in the classroom, fast-tracking Millennials to leadership, how to save time in your classroom, how to facilitate a remote training session, and ways to use social media to help transfer learning — plus an extra Part of Tens chapter only available online.

Where to Go from Here

You can approach this book from several different angles. You can, of course, start with Chapter 1 and read straight through to the end. But you may not have time for that. Check out some other approaches:

- ✔ If you're brand-new to the training scene, you may wish to start with Part I. It grounds you in the topic.

- ✔ If you're looking for ways to enhance your skills in either the design or the delivery area, go directly to Part II or Part III.

- ✔ If you're looking for several fast ways to improve your training delivery or enhance your training session, check out the Part of Tens, where you'll find 50 ideas. You can also skim through the rest of the book and look for the Tip icons, reading each one.

- ✔ If you're thinking about beginning a professional certification process, you may want to go directly to Chapter 16 and read all about it.

No matter where you start reading in this book, you'll find practical ideas. So my advice is to just start!

Part I
So You're Going to Be a Trainer

getting started

with

Training &
Development

In this part . . .

- Introducing you to the world of training and development
- Exploring why adults learn
- Getting to know the training cycle

Chapter 1

What's Training and Development?

So you want to be a trainer — a talent development professional. Or perhaps you already are in the field, and you've picked up this book to enhance your skills. In either case, this chapter helps you understand the profession and what's expected of those who develop others.

Having a role in training and development (T&D) is one of the most exciting jobs anyone can have. Although a trainer's role has changed substantially over the past decade and is currently going through another metamorphosis, many of the positive aspects always remain with the job. First, as a trainer you impact the work of many people — not only the learners with whom you work but also supervisors, senior management, clients, vendors, and perhaps even your company's board of directors. As a trainer, you have access to many people and can develop a broader picture of your organization's needs. Trainers are usually good communicators with good information. People listen to you.

In addition, training is exciting because it is a job that is an integral step in an organization's efforts toward change and improvement. You may be a part of defining the organization of today, envisioning the organization of the future, and helping to incorporate the changes necessary to create the new organization. As a trainer, you have the opportunity to influence the direction your organization takes and how it gets there.

Take a proactive stance in shaping your career. To be the most effective trainer, find out all you can about the organization in which you work. What are the primary issues and priorities it faces? Partner with those who lead your organization and find out how you can help them. Where are the pressure points that affect the bottom line? Identify how your work can positively impact the bottom line, given that you're in a unique position to impact others. At the same time, remember to also take the opportunity to impact your career.

In this chapter, you answer three big questions.

- ✔ What is training and development and who uses it?
- ✔ What do trainers do?
- ✔ Do you have what it takes to be a trainer?

What Is Training and Development?

We've all been in training since the day we were born. You have been learning and changing into the knowledgeable, skilled adult you currently are. Everyone has received training, and we have also all developed others. If you ever demonstrated the phone system to a new employee, advised your boss regarding changes in your department, or explained a shortcut for completing a task to a colleague, you were conducting training.

Training is about change. It is about transformation. It is all about learning. Training is a process designed to assist an individual to learn new skills, knowledge, or attitudes. As a result, individuals make a change or transformation that improves or enhances their performance. These improvements ensure that people and organizations are able to do things better, faster, easier, and with higher quality.

What forms does T&D take?

Learning is acquired in many forms. You may have experienced some of these. You may have a one-on-one session with your supervisor to learn the benefits of a new product your company produces. You may attend a class to upgrade your negotiating skills. You may take an asynchronous online course to learn how to use a new computer program. You may take a golf lesson to learn how to improve your use of long irons. You may be coached by someone in your company to learn to be more politically savvy. You may register for a Massive Open Online Course (MOOC) to learn leadership skills. The key word in each of these examples is "learn." The reason training is provided is so that someone (or many people) learns something in order to make a change.

Is there really a difference between the words *training* and *development*? It seems all professionals in the business have their own definitions, and we aren't going to resolve a mutual definition in this book. Both concepts are paths to learning and performance. In general people view training as those learning options that include someone who facilitates the learning in a formal setting: classroom, workshop, seminar, virtual instructor-led, or synchronous online. Development, on the other hand, is viewed as more self-directed and informal: coaching, mentoring, reading, self-study, social learning, on-the-job learning, and asynchronous online learning. And there is no denying that learning also occurs during water cooler discussions, in cubical conversations, and at conferences. Trainers are involved in all of these training and development alternatives.

Read that last sentence again and remember it. It doesn't matter what your official title is or how you deliver learning and performance. Trainers may be involved in *all* activities where people are learning knowledge and developing skills. Yes, you may design or deliver training in a traditional or virtual classroom. But you may also coach supervisors about the best way to develop their employees or advise leaders of corporate changes required to support desired performance — or even recommend budgets for social media to augment training. In this book I use the title *trainer* to describe all these roles.

Trainers are necessary in every industry, from aardvark ranches to zipper manufacturers. Trainers have jobs in private industry, education, not-for-profit organizations, and government.

Trainers work with people in all positions and at all levels in an organization: executives, managers, supervisors, secretaries, production workers, scientists, artists, doctors, lawyers, security guards, salespeople, teachers, firefighters, authors, custodial workers, waitstaff, and you. Even this book is a form of training — self-directed training as you learn your way through its pages.

The training profession's evolution

Training has been around since the Stone Age. It's not likely that train-the-trainer seminars existed in 2000 B.C. Yet without some natural way to transfer skills and knowledge, people would never have progressed from the first wheel on a muddy road to the computer chips that guide our exploration of outer space. Probably the first documented training occurred in the 18th century, when artisans and craftsmen formed apprenticeships that utilized a demonstration-practice-feedback-practice-again process.

It wasn't until 1944 that training was organized under one banner, The American Society for Training Directors. The association later changed its name to The American Society for Training and Development (ASTD).

(continued)

(continued)

Two influential professionals helped to shape the early years of the profession. In the 1960s, Malcolm Knowles advanced the idea of *andragogy*, a learning theory for adults, distinct from *pedagogy* for children. This tipped the scale toward a more learner-centered approach as opposed to a content-centered approach. Len Nadler coined the term *Human Resource Development* and added structure and organization to the field.

The 1990s reinforced the critical role trainers played in helping organizations achieve their business goals. In the "Why is training necessary?" section in this chapter, I mention the importance of aligning the four requirements of the organization when budgeting for training: business, performance, learning, and environmental needs. Trainers ensure that performance, not just learning, occurs to support the bottom line. The field embraced a *Workplace Learning and Performance* perspective, encouraging some organizations to call their trainers "workplace learning and performance professionals." Quite a mouthful! With the advent of workplace analytics, or "big data" as it is sometimes called, businesses are finding ways to measure the effects of training on the business.

But another role clarification was in the making. As we move well into the 21st century, it is clear that training and development professionals continue to accept a greater role that impacts the total organization's success. Today this broader role includes change management, coaching managers to develop their people, succession planning, engagement and retention efforts, and implementing organizational assessments. This broader role deserved a more impactful name.

During this time, ASTD had become the world's leading association for training and development. The name American Society for Training and Development no longer represented the expanded role of the profession, nor the global reach of the association. Therefore, in 2014 the professional group that represents training and development became the Association for Talent Development (ATD).

Why is training necessary?

Every year, most organizations budget money for training — over $70 billion in the United States and over $130 billion worldwide. The volume of money and effort suggests that corporations believe training is important. What do they know about training that justifies this much investment? For starters, training plays an important role in developing a productive workforce and finely tuning processes to increase profits. Training also helps people and organizations manage change. Because organizations are continuously changing techniques, goals, equipment, people, and locations, all members of the workforce require training to support these changes.

There are four critical aspects of a coordinated comprehensive training approach. In the most efficient organizations, the four are aligned toward the same corporate goals.

✔ **There is a business need or requirement.** This is the starting point. Effective training starts with the clarification (or creation) of organizational goals. This enables the T&D department to provide a strategic approach to the services it offers the organization. Examples of business needs include increasing customer satisfaction, increasing market share, and improving quality.

✔ **There is a need to improve or change performance.** Performance is usually tied to a specific job and a task or set of tasks within that job. It is what the employee must do to achieve the organizational goal. For example, if improving quality is a business goal, each employee must know what process to use to ensure delivery of a quality product or service.

✔ **There is a need to gain knowledge or to learn new skills.** In order to change performance, employees may need to learn something new. This learning may take many forms such as coaching, classroom training, computer-based training (CBT), on-the-job training (OJT), or self-study.

✔ **There is a need for change in the environment.** At times, employees may possess the skills and knowledge required to change their performance, but some aspect of the environment either prevents or discourages individuals from making the change. For example, if an organization's goal is to improve quality, there will be little change if the reward system focuses on quantity, not quality.

Trainers are involved in providing services that address all these aspects. If you're a beginning trainer, you'll most likely start with interventions that deliver knowledge and new skills (the third bullet in the preceding list). This is the traditional "training" role. However, as you grow professionally, you will be required to provide learning or all of the other needs that affect an organization. You will create and deliver formal and informal learning, instructor-led and self-directed learning, and synchronous and asynchronous training. You will do this in a classroom, online, and on the job. For ease of reading, I identify all these roles using the traditional name trainer.

What do organizations expect to accomplish by investing in training efforts? They desire change in performance of employees in order to:

✔ Reduce employee turnover

✔ Maintain current customers

✔ Create new customers

✔ Increase customer satisfaction

✔ Reduce errors

✔ Reduce expenses

✔ Save time

✔ Add dollars to the bottom line

There are many reasons people require training in the workplace. Some of these reasons are to:

✔ Orient new employees

✔ Provide long-term professional development

✔ Upgrade knowledge required for the job

✔ Introduce new skills to experienced employees

✔ Change career paths due to job elimination

But won't trainers run out of people to train? Not likely. Organizations are required to continually make changes. Technology advances continue to influence how trainers do their jobs. The skilled labor pool continues to shrink worldwide. Thousands of new employees enter the workforce or change jobs every week. That keeps at least a few trainers busy.

Is training just for business?

You experience training in other parts of your life in addition to the workplace. For example, you may decide you want to play the piano or practice yoga. You may want to find out more about your ancestors or Italian artists. If so, you'll likely locate someone who teaches these subjects at your local college, community center, or online. In this way, individuals seek training for a variety of reasons outside the workplace to:

✔ Learn new skills (try a new hobby such as painting or growing bonsai)

✔ Enhance skills you already have (take a tennis lesson to improve your game or a gourmet-cooking lesson to learn new techniques)

✔ Acquire knowledge about a subject that intrigues you (attend a class about African history or investing in the stock market)

✔ Gain information you require due to a life change (attend a class to learn to care for your elderly parent or learn how to prepare for retirement)

Training is available for all areas of your life.

What Do Trainers Do?

The trainers' roles, they are a-changing, and many new roles are currently being defined in the T&D arena. The following list provides just a sample of the trainer roles and titles that are emerging.

- Career coach
- Chief learning officer
- Competency expert
- Computer-based training designer
- Continuous learning coach
- Corporate trainer
- Courseware designers
- Curriculum development specialist
- Employee development specialist
- Executive coach
- Facilitator
- Global T&D facilitator
- Instructional designer
- Instructional technologist
- Instructor

- Knowledge manager
- L&D specialist
- Leadership trainer
- Manager of strategic initiatives
- Media designer
- Multimedia engineer
- OD consultant
- Organizational effectiveness specialist
- Performance analyst
- Performance consultant
- Performance technologist
- Talent development professional
- Technical trainer
- Virtual facilitator
- Workforce diversity director
- Workplace learning and performance professional

Even though the preceding list uses wildly different words and appears to be quite diverse, all of these roles play a part in ensuring that people gain knowledge or skills, or change attitudes. In the "Why training is necessary" section in this chapter, I mention that beginning trainers usually start with interventions that design and deliver knowledge and new skills. This traditional "training" role remains the mainstay of the profession. For ease of my writing and your reading, I refer to all roles as training.

The 2014 *ATD State of the Industry Report* says that almost 70 percent of learning involves a trainer, and this is unchanged from previous years. Fifty-five percent occurs in an instructor-led classroom, nine percent utilizes an online instructor, and five percent is led remotely by an instructor.

The two roles (design and delivery) can be further subdivided into two main categories. All training professionals are involved with designing and/or presenting a learning experience. Whether you design, deliver, or do a bit of both, you have two aspects to master: content and process.

- ✔ **Content:** Whether you're designing or presenting, you need to truly understand what others need to know about the topic. Get inside the topic and find out more than what's offered in your trainer's manual. Ask more questions of more people if you're designing. Talk to *subject matter experts,* often called *SMEs* in the profession. The content is based on your organization's needs.

- ✔ **Process:** Both design and delivery have methods that you incorporate into your training task. Design methods incorporate skills such as designing participant materials, incorporating adult learning principles, and selecting methods for the perfect blended learning program. Delivery methods incorporate skills such as facilitating group process, presentation skills, and managing disruptive participants. This is true for both face-to-face and online learning.

This book provides tips and techniques for both content and process.

Assessing your training potential

Every career has its own set of characteristics that increase the chances that someone will enjoy the job and have a natural aptitude for the work that is done. The following list identifies a number of those characteristics for a trainer.

- ✔ Approachable
- ✔ Articulate
- ✔ Assertive and influential
- ✔ Both logical and creative
- ✔ Builds trust
- ✔ Confident and poised
- ✔ Customer-focused
- ✔ Enjoys helping others learn
- ✔ Enthusiastic
- ✔ Excellent communicator
- ✔ Flexible and spontaneous
- ✔ Global mindset
- ✔ Good listener

- ✔ Impartial and objective
- ✔ Lifelong learner
- ✔ Patient
- ✔ Process-oriented
- ✔ Self-sufficient
- ✔ Sense of humor
- ✔ Solution- and results-oriented
- ✔ Strong business sense
- ✔ Team player and partners well
- ✔ Technologically literate
- ✔ Tolerant of ambiguity
- ✔ Well-organized

Examine the list of characteristics. Which of these are natural for you? Which do you need to work harder at to be a successful and satisfied trainer?

Take stock of your skills

In addition to natural aptitude, every job also requires a specific skill set. The skills required of a trainer are many and varied. The ATD Competency Model identifies the roles, competencies, areas of expertise, and skills that are required of a talent development professional. Certification is available for those practicing in the field. This is beneficial because it provides the credentials to support the training field and adds credibility to the professional trainer. ATD has administered the certification process since 2005. Details for how you can be certified as a Workplace Learning and Performance professional are on ATD's website at www.TD.org. I tell you more about the competency model and certification in Chapter 16.

The Knowledge and Skills Inventory that follows incorporates the skills found in the competency model. Complete the Knowledge and Skills Inventory in Table 1-1 to identify your current strengths and the skills you need to improve to perform your job effectively. This activity assists you in setting specific objectives for your professional development. Complete this inventory by evaluating your ability to perform each skill using two rating scales. You evaluate each skill from two perspectives. In Column 1 you rate your ability, and in Column 2 you rate the importance of the skill to your particular job.

Evaluate your ability by completing column 1 using this rating scale:

5 Outstanding ability (one of my talents)

4 Above-average ability

3 Average or moderate ability

2 Minimal ability

1 No experience or training in this area

Describe the importance of each skill to the job you currently have:

5 One of the most important aspects of the job

4 Above-average importance

3 Average importance

2 Occasional importance

1 Minimal importance

0 No importance

Table 1-1	Training Knowledge and Skills Inventory		
Professional Foundation			
Skills	**Column 1** Your Ability	**Column 2** Importance on the Job	**Column 3** Difference (Col 1–2=3)
Communicates effectively and demonstrates emotional intelligence			
Continuous learner, improving and updating professional skills and knowledge			
Establishes trust and professional credibility			
Promotes collaboration, partnerships, and teamwork throughout the organization			
Thinks strategically; is knowledgeable about the organization's vision, goals, business issues, and culture			
Assessing Needs			
Skills	**Column 1** Your Ability	**Column 2** Importance on the Job	**Column 3** Difference (Col 1–2=3)
Designs a plan for assessing needs using appropriate methodologies			
Identifies customer expectations			
Conducts a needs assessment			
Analyzes needs to align with organizational priorities			
Ability to determine whether training or some other intervention is required			
Assesses learning and performance before and after to measure training effectiveness			

Designing Learning			
Skills	*Column 1* *Your* *Ability*	*Column 2* *Importance* *on the Job*	*Column 3* *Difference* *(Col 1–2=3)*
Establishes effective learning objectives			
Selects, adapts, or creates a design that is appropriate and results-oriented			
Selects and sequences content and instructional methods appropriate for the project and learners' diversity			
Designs blended learning solutions that incorporate online, classroom, on-the-job, self-paced, and other options			
Incorporates media and technology options appropriately			
Aligns learning solutions with organizational and learner needs			
Applies adult learning theory and principles in developing a curriculum			
Develops and evaluates instructional materials and media support			
Designs participant-oriented learning activities			
Understands legal and ethical issues relevant to designing training			
Uses various techniques to prepare for training delivery			
Facilitating Training Delivery			
Skills	*Column 1* *Your* *Ability*	*Column 2* *Importance* *on the Job*	*Column 3* *Difference* *(Col 1–2=3)*
Establishes credibility appropriately			
Prepares physical or online environment for optimal learning			

(continued)

Table 1-1 *(continued)*

Facilitating Training Delivery

Skills	Column 1 Your Ability	Column 2 Importance on the Job	Column 3 Difference (Col 1–2=3)
Creates a positive learning environment			
Aligns objectives and learning with business and participant needs			
Demonstrates effective presentation and facilitation skills			
Demonstrates effective questioning skills			
Uses a variety of learning methodologies			
Stimulates and sustains learner motivation and encourages participation			
Uses technology effectively			
Demonstrates understanding of group dynamics			
Manages difficult participants			
Manages unexpected events in the classroom and learning environment			
Promotes transfer of knowledge and skills to the workplace			

Evaluating Learning Impact

Skills	Column 1 Your Ability	Column 2 Importance on the Job	Column 3 Difference (Col 1–2=3)
Applies learning analytics to demonstrate results and impact			
Develops evaluation instruments such as questionnaires, tests			
Incorporates feedback and data for future recommendations			
Analyzes evaluation results against organizational goals			
Uses the four levels of evaluation appropriately			
Totals			

Your self-assessment

So how did you do? Perhaps you do not know what some of the skills mean. That's okay for now. Each is more clearly defined throughout the book.

Take a few minutes to review the inventory you completed. First put a plus (+) next to the items for which you rated yourself at 5. These are the talents that form a foundation for your role as a trainer. Circle your three strongest in Table 1-1.

Next total column 1. The maximum score is 200. In general, a score of 150 or more indicates a well-rounded, proficient trainer. Not there? Not to worry. That's what this book is all about.

Next subtract Column 2 from Column 1 for each of the 40 skills. Write the difference in Column 3. Note that you have a negative number if Column 2 has a larger number than Column 1. If the difference is negative, it means that the task is important in your job and your skill level may not measure up. These areas clearly need improvement. Put squares around them in Table 1-1. If you have no negative numbers, identify those items that have the lowest numbers.

Your results provide you with a general direction for skills and knowledge you may wish to acquire.

The 2013 ATD Competency Study provides a more extensive discussion of the skills and an explanation of the different competencies required for other roles in the training and development profession. ATD offers classes and other learning opportunities for those new to the profession or others desiring to brush up on their skills.

How do you become a trainer?

There are as many paths to a career in training and development as there are types of training. Many trainers, like me, can tell you they "came in the back door." I was a trainer for over a year before I realized that training was a profession in its own right. Because training became a collateral duty to the "real" job I had, I didn't consider that someone may have studied the training process to ensure effectiveness! It was only after I started messing around with the curriculum and experimenting with various training methodologies that my research led me to an entire body of knowledge. Until then, I thought I was inventing Adult Learning Theory! I must admit, I was a bit disappointed when I first discovered Malcolm Knowles!

Many trainers work for organizations in other departments. They may drift over to the learning and development department or the human resources department and apply for a job. Sometimes they have taken a class and decide they want to be at the training end of the classroom rather than the learner end. In other cases they may have been tapped to conduct training on a new product, service, or procedure. Enjoying the experience, they followed up on how to do it full time. Some individuals enroll in adult learning degree programs.

No matter how you have gotten to this point in your career, and whether you're a part-time trainer, full-time trainer, or wannabe trainer, remember that a professional certification is available to you through ATD, providing you with the foundation for becoming a skilled professional.

The Many Hats of a 21st Century Trainer

The 21st century trainer wears many hats, so every day is different. Here's a typical "atypical" day for one trainer:

> Jose has been with Honesty Parts and Services (HPS) for several years. He started out in the marketing department but enjoyed one of his inter-personal communications classes so much that he decided to apply for a job as a trainer in the learning and development department.
>
> Jose's director reports to the Chief Learning Officer, who works with other leaders in the organization to determine a strategic direction and goals. Everything that the department does is aligned with the organization's strategic direction. When one of the department heads contacted Jose's director requesting the department design a training program, she first checked to ensure organizational alignment. Next she conducted a performance assessment. After she determined that training was the solution, she turned the project over to Jose and a team that included an instructional designer, a subject matter expert, and a computer-based training designer.
>
> Jose and his team spent the last few weeks designing a blended training program that would meet the needs of the department. The team started with the assessment results and clarified the requesting department head's expectations. They conducted additional research on the topic, and interviewed people in the department. They considered the content, time available, the audience, and the locations. As a result, they designed a pre-work assignment that included short video clips; a classroom module that included participant materials and a PowerPoint presenta-tion; follow-up self-paced e-learning content; a coaching checklist for participants' supervisors; and a job aid. Jose put in long hours during the

design and development stage and he learned a great deal. Jose also met with participants' immediate supervisors to provide suggestions about how to coach employees to implement the new behaviors.

The program pilot, a trial run, for the classroom module has been scheduled for today. Yesterday Jose and his team finalized the session materials, set up the room, checked out the audiovisual equipment, and arranged for lunch to be brought in from the cafeteria.

This morning, Jose arrived at the training site an hour before the session so that he could be certain everything was ready to go. Participants started arriving 45 minutes before the sessions started. As he introduced himself to individuals he learned that many of them were uncertain of the location and that this was a first training opportunity for a few. The early arrivals did not give him any time to himself, so Jose was glad that he spent the past week preparing for the session. He had practiced the materials out loud, conducted a dry run with his team, tried out the activities with his peers, and even delivered some of the content to his family. He felt ready.

Jose had told his wife that he would be late getting home tonight. Following the session, which ends at 4:30, his team will meet to critique the day and to determine whether any adjustments need to be made in the agenda or the content for the next day.

Following the two-day session, he and his team will make any minor modification to the session based on feedback from the participants, ensure that participants use the follow-up materials, follow up with the department head, and begin to schedule the other classes locally and at remote sites. He will travel overnight for several of the sessions but is looking forward to seeing some of the organization's branch offices.

Now, at 7:59 a.m. Jose looked out to the participants before starting. He felt satisfied that he was in a position to contribute to HPS's bottom line and that he had a job that gave him so much pleasure and satisfaction. With those thoughts on his mind, he smiled at the group and said, "Good morning!"

Do You Have What It Takes?

Although training may seem like a glamorous profession to an observer, like any other profession, it has its hidden challenges. Having the skills to be a trainer is only one prerequisite. A much more difficult requirement for a successful trainer is to have strong mental and emotional composure. Training is a demanding profession. It requires constant energy output. If you tire quickly, become discouraged easily, or become frustrated if things do not go according to plan, training may not be for you. Here are some aspects to consider about training:

✔ **Are you willing to work longer than an 8-hour day?** Even though an Instructor-Led Training (ILT) program may be scheduled from 9 to 5, you may find yourself going to the training room much earlier than 9:00 a.m. and staying much later than 5:00 p.m. A well-prepared training session takes thoughtful room and material setup. If you arrive at the training room at the same time as the trainees, you will feel disorganized and unprepared. You may even start late because of last-minute preparations. If you lead a virtual training program with participants halfway around the world, you may start your day at 9:00 p.m.

✔ **Are you also willing to stay later than your official "ending" time?** The same principle applies after the training program has ended. It is usually the trainer's responsibility to ensure that all items you used for the training are removed from the training room. You may need to replace tables and chairs the way you found them. Many participants stay after the program is over so that they can ask questions they did not wish to ask in front of the rest of the participants. They expect the trainer to be there cheerfully ready to answer their questions. In addition, you may have many details to wrap up at the end of the day: Add notes to your training manual, review your PowerPoint presentation for the next day, revise your schedule, complete administrative tasks, or file your materials in order. If you have completed an online course, you may need to do similar tasks plus send additional resources to participants as follow up.

✔ **Can you go with the flow?** No amount of preparation can equip a trainer for everything that can happen in a training session. In a virtual classroom, participants may discover they have an incorrect link to join the session or the audio connection may stop working. You may find that the majority of online participants have not completed the foundational pre-work required to comprehend the module. In a traditional classroom, the trainer must be prepared to respond to unexpected questions and events. A trainer must be flexible. Sometimes, the planned agenda doesn't fit the needs of the audience. A good trainer adjusts the agenda and changes the material so that it meets the needs of the audience. An effective trainer also reads the audience and adjusts the level of the training to fit the level of the audience.

✔ **Can you cope with multiple logistic and technology details?** In a virtual setting, this means ensuring that all participants have their own computer connections, getting links and passwords to everyone who needs them, helping participants troubleshoot technical problems prior to the class, and of course having a qualified producer to troubleshoot when issues arise. In a traditional classroom it may be someone else's responsibility to make room and equipment arrangements; it becomes the trainer's problem if something is not right. Are you prepared to deal with malfunctioning equipment, rooms that are not set up, materials that do not arrive, materials that are incorrect, or any mess-up in general? Today's trainer is technologically astute and takes full accountability for ensuring that all logistics are in order.

✔ **Can you perform even when you feel lousy?** Whether face-to-face or online, trainers don't often have the discretion to call in sick. When a session is scheduled, it often has been scheduled long in advance, and often learners travel from long distances to attend training. Therefore, trainers must be able to facilitate enthusiastically even when they are a little under the weather. The show must go on!

✔ **Are you prepared to constantly give of yourself without expecting to receive anything in return?** Trainers are often viewed by others as "healers" — those people who always have the answers and who can perform "magic." Conversely, trainers are not often perceived as people who have their own needs. As a result, participants may use your sessions to get some bad feelings off their chests. Giving may extend to time as well, such as having time for breaks and lunch that may be used by participants wanting to discuss their personal situations.

✔ **Can you be the perfect role model all the time?** It is a trainer's job to teach the "right" way to do things. You must also be prepared to practice what you preach. Trainers run the risk of losing their credibility if they are not perceived to be a perfect example of what they teach. And, because no one is perfect, trainers must also admit it when they make a mistake. Trainers cannot allow participants to leave a learning session with incorrect information.

✔ **Are you prepared to encourage your participants even when there is a lack of management commitment?** Sometimes, people are sent to training because their managers think that it is "a good thing to do." There may be little serious commitment to support and encourage these employees when the training is completed. Can you provide support and understanding in the absence of managers' commitment? Can you follow up with the managers and help them see the importance to the organization as well as coach them to reinforce the new skills?

✔ **Can you deliver hard feedback?** Your participants will not learn effectively if during the process they are not given honest and candid feedback. Are you able to give this feedback, even when it is not positive and even if it may impact an employee's job?

✔ **Are you able to process failure, identify solutions, and make improvements?** Not every training program is a smashing success. In fact, some are downright bad. Successful trainers are those who analyze what went wrong in the bad sessions and then design changes in the program so that it improves the next time around.

Many of the preceding questions are certainly not meant to discourage you, but rather to introduce the reality of a sometimes glamorous-appearing job. It may be challenging. It usually requires a great deal of work. And it can be riddled with problems. However, you forget all the difficulties when former participants tell you that you changed their lives. Or that you inspired them. Of course this doesn't happen on a weekly basis, but it does happen often enough to make it all worthwhile.

Yes, training is a demanding, sometimes hectic, often ambiguous job. There is never a dull moment. It is exciting. It is the catalyst for improvement. It is the process to the future. Training exists to facilitate change and to encourage transformation for a better future. The late Christa McAuliffe, teacher and NASA astronaut, summed it up this way: "I touch the future; I teach."

Chapter 2
Why Adults Learn

Think back to the past 60 days. What is one thing you learned?

Before reading ahead, try to recall what you learned and why you learned it. Perhaps you learned to play racquetball because you always wanted to learn to play the game. Perhaps you had a flat tire on the way home, and you had to learn to change the tire because you had to do it. You didn't want to, but you had no choice.

If you're like most adults, you learn to do most things as an adult because you *want* to learn it or you *need* to learn it.

This chapter explores adult learning theory, how people learn, and how trainers can assist participants to learn in the classroom.

Adult Learning Theory

Trainers are most successful when they understand conditions under which adults learn best. Therefore, it is important to understand the difference between why adults learn and how adults are traditionally taught.

The traditional style of teaching is based on a didactic model, a synonym for lecturing. Generally this model is teacher-led and content-centered. Another word used is *pedagogy*, which literally means the art of teaching children.

In the introduction to this chapter, you read that most adults learn things because they *want* to or *need* to. Children do, too. However, children's formal learning is usually led by someone else and is based on learning specific tasks to prepare them to learn additional, more complicated tasks.

For example, you learned to count to 100 in kindergarten, so that you could learn to add and subtract in first grade, so that you could learn to multiply and divide in third grade, so that you could learn algebra in eighth grade, so that you could learn trigonometry in high school, so that you could learn calculus in college.

Most people have experienced the pedagogical model of learning. It has dominated education for centuries and assumes the following.

- ✔ The instructor is the expert. Because the learner has little experience it is up to the instructor to impart wisdom.

- ✔ The instructor is responsible for all aspects of the learning process, including what, how, and when the learners learn.

- ✔ Learning is content-centered. Objectives establish goals, and a logical sequence of material is presented to the learners.

- ✔ Motivation is external, and learners learn because they must reach the next level of understanding, pass a test, or acquire certification.

Does this sound familiar? It should. Unless you had an atypical learning situation, it is most likely how you were taught starting in kindergarten and through college. Some schools are changing however. Although the lecture method is still used, it is frequently enhanced with other learning methods. This suggests that someone has identified a better method for teaching.

Who is Malcolm Knowles?

Malcolm Knowles is considered the father of adult learning theory. Because pedagogy is defined as the art and science of teaching children, European adult educators coined the word *andragogy* to identify the growing body of knowledge about adult learning. It was Dr. Knowles's highly readable book, *The Adult Learner: A Neglected Species,* published in 1973, that took the topic from theoretical to practical. Table 2-1 compares the differences between andragogy and pedagogy. Trainers and adult educators began to implement practical applications based on Dr. Knowles' six assumptions.

The following list summarizes Malcolm Knowles' six assumptions and adds a practical application from a trainer's perspective. Although there is some duplication of ideas, I have presented all six assumptions as Knowles identified them. Some authors distill the six to five, four, and even three.

- Adults have a need to know why they should learn something before investing time in a learning event. Trainers must ensure that the learners know the purpose for training right from the start.
- Adults enter any learning situation with an image of themselves as self-directing, responsible grown-ups. Trainers must help adults identify their needs and direct their own learning experience.
- Adults come to a learning opportunity with a wealth of experience and a great deal to contribute. Trainers are successful when they identify ways to build on and make use of adults' hard-earned experience.
- Adults have a strong readiness to learn those things that help them cope with daily life effectively. Training that relates directly to situations adults face is viewed as relevant.
- Adults are willing to devote energy to learning those things that they believe help them perform a task or solve a problem. Trainers who determine needs and interests and develop content in response to these needs are most helpful to adult learners.
- Adults are more responsive to internal motivators such as increased self-esteem than external motivators such as higher salaries. Trainers can ensure that this internal motivation is not blocked by barriers such as a poor self-concept or time constraints by creating a safe learning climate.

Table 2-1 Andragogical and Pedagogical Training: A Comparison

Andragogy	*Pedagogy*
Learners are called "participants" or "learners."	Learners are called "students."
Independent learning style.	Dependent learning style.
Objectives are flexible.	Objectives are predetermined and inflexible.
It is assumed that the learners have experience to contribute.	It is assumed that the learners are inexperienced and/or uninformed.
Active training methods, such as games and experiential learning, are used.	Passive training methods, such as lecture, are used.
Learners influence timing, pace, and location in a learner-centered approach.	Trainer controls timing, pace, and location.
Participant involvement is vital to success.	Participants contribute little to the experience.
Learning is real-life problem-centered.	Learning is content-centered.
Participants are seen as primary resources for ideas and examples.	The trainer is seen as the primary resource who provides ideas and examples.

Applying adult learning theory to training

I don't know whether Malcolm Knowles had this in mind when he presented his adult learning theory to the world, but it seems that he is talking about responsibility. Furthermore, whether you're the trainer or the learner, you have responsibility to ensure that the training is successful, that learning occurs, that change takes place, and that improved performance is transferred to the workplace.

If you're the trainer

✔ Create a learning environment that is safe both online and in a classroom.

✔ Be organized, have well-defined objectives, and establish a clear direction for your session based on the participants' needs. Be so well organized that it is easy to be flexible when the participants' needs are different from what you anticipated.

✔ Ensure that your content is meaningful and transferable to the learners' world.

✔ Treat your learners with respect, understanding, and genuine concern.

✔ Invite learners to share their knowledge and experiences.

If you're the learner

✔ Be an active learner, participating in the interactive exercises.

✔ Be critical of poorly defined sessions, an unprepared trainer, or processes that prevent your learning; provide constructive feedback to the trainer.

✔ Ensure your personal success by encouraging feedback from the trainer.

Delivering constructive feedback is a key action expected of all professional trainers. Learners have a right to receive feedback from their trainers.

✔ Recognize that you're responsible for your own learning, so ensure that all your questions are answered, whether in a traditional or virtual classroom.

✔ Contribute to your own success by clearly identifying a learning plan for yourself; then do your part to achieve your objectives.

Trainers beware! Note that I encourage learners to be critical of you if you're not prepared or the session doesn't meet their needs. Why? Professional trainers profess to build on the foundation of adult learning theory. If something is not working, step back, determine why, and fix it. If you're not doing that, you're not practicing good adult learning principles. You may need another trainer to guide you.

How Do People Learn?

The adult learning theory presented in the previous section provides a foundation of principles of adult learning. However, there are additional considerations to enhance results when training adults. In the following sections, I examine them.

Three types of learning: KSAs

Trainers address three types of learning: knowledge (K), skills (S), and influencing attitude (A). Trainers frequently shorten this to the KSA acronym. (If you want the research to support this, it is called *Bloom's Taxonomy*.)

Knowledge (Bloom called this *cognitive*) involves the development of intellectual skills. Examples of knowledge include understanding the principles of accounting, knowing the stages of childhood, understanding how interest rates affect the economy, or knowing how to get a book published.

Skills (Bloom called this *psychomotor*) refer to physical movement, coordination, and the use of the motor-skills area. Examples of skills you may learn include the ability to use a 3D printer, operate a backhoe, supervise staff, listen effectively, or kick a soccer ball.

Attitude (Bloom called this *affective*) refers to how you deal with things emotionally, such as feelings, motivation, and enthusiasm. Although attitude is not "taught," training may affect it. Trainers cannot change attitudes, but they frequently have the opportunity to influence attitudes.

Trainers sometimes discuss whether it is the learner's skill or will that prevents topnotch performance following a training session. This refers to the fact that an employee may have learned the skill but is unwilling to use it. Therefore, the real reason an employee may not be using what was learned may not be skill-based at all. It may be that the employee won't use the skill that was learned.

Knowing that there are three types of learning means that you need to use different methods to address each. I discuss this in more depth in Chapter 5 when I address design.

Bloom's Taxonomy

In the early '60s, Benjamin Bloom and a university committee identified three learning domains: cognitive, psychomotor, and affective. Because the project was completed by university folks, the terms may seem a bit abstract.

Trainers typically use knowledge (cognitive), skills (psychomotor), and attitude (affective) to describe the three categories of learning. In addition, trainers frequently refer to these three learning categories as the KSAs. You may think of these as the ultimate goals of the training process — what your learner acquires as a result of training.

Bloom's group further expanded on the domains. They created a hierarchical ordering of the cognitive and affective learning outcomes. Their work subdivided each domain, starting from the simplest behavior to the most complex: Knowledge, Comprehension, Application, Analysis, Synthesis, and Evaluation. Each of these levels builds on the earlier one. For example, knowledge must occur prior to comprehension; comprehension must occur before application. Each level of learning identified the desired specific, observable, and measurable result.

This work is known as *Bloom's Taxonomy*. The divisions are not absolutes, and other systems and hierarchies have been developed since then. Bloom's Taxonomy, however, is easily understood and may be the most widely applied. The following table explains what it means.

Behavioral Levels	Skills	Examples
Knowledge	Define, list, name, recall, repeat knowledge or information	Can name six levels of Bloom's Taxonomy
Comprehension	Translate, describe, explain information in one's own words	Can compare and explain Bloom's six levels
Application	Apply, demonstrate, use knowledge in new situations	Can apply Bloom's theory to write learning objectives
Analysis	Analyze, compare, question, break knowledge into parts	Can compare and contrast aspects of Bloom's model
Synthesis	Arrange, create, plan, prepare a new whole from parts	Can design a new learning model
Evaluation	Appraise, assess, judge, score information based on knowledge	Can evaluate and defend the benefits of Bloom's Taxonomy

It is interesting to note that although the committee actually identified three domains of learning, they applied the six levels to only the cognitive and affective learning domains. They did not elaborate on psychomotor (skills). Their explanation for this was that they had little experience teaching manual skills at the college level.

Brain-based learning: It's a no-brainer

Research into how the brain works best has received lots of publicity recently. Brain imaging has given researchers the ability to see the brain as learning occurs. Even though cognitive neuroscience appears to be a hot topic, it is really confirming what Malcolm Knowles, Howard Gardner, Robert Gagne, and others told us decades ago: Adult learning principles are important.

What practical information have we learned from cognitive neuroscience that can help us as trainers? Here is just a sample:

- A learning atmosphere can affect learning.

- Chunking information into two to four smaller bites allows the brain to process the information in the hippocampus (the brain's holding tank) better.

- Movement gives the brain a cognitive boost.

- Participation such as writing, talking, activities, or involvement of any kind enhances learning.

Recent research by a couple of Princeton University and University of California professors found that college students who take notes on paper learn significantly more compared to their laptop-tapping peers. The research found that laptop users type almost everything they hear, but they do not process the meaning of it. When students take notes by hand, they can't write every word so they listen, summarize, and gain meaning through the process.

- Pictures, stories, metaphors, or other images increase learning and memory.

You will find ideas to implement these concepts in this book.

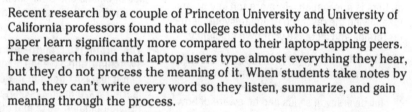

Many people have theories about how humans learn best. David Kolb, for example, presents four learning styles: the converger, the diverger, the assimilator, and the accommodator. Another theory was developed by W. E. (Ned) Herrmann. His research shows brain specialization in four quadrants and that each quadrant has its own preferred way of learning. Ned's daughter Ann Herrmann-Nehdi continues to expand her father's work. Current authors David Rock, Patricia Wolfe, Eric Jensen, and David Sousa write about how the brain learns.

Brain science resonates strongly with the learning and development community. Over 50,000 neuroscientists publish studies every year, and the studies sometimes contradict each other. It is a complex field, and we still have lots of exciting things to uncover about cognitive neuroscience. In the meantime, we all need to stay in touch with new research and implement what we learn in our online and traditional classrooms.

Get sticky! Engage your learners' brains for lasting results

by *Ann Herrmann-Nehdi*

It's often reported that our knowledge of the brain doubles every ten years; the recent explosion of research and methods means we may be learning much more, much faster.

In some ways, this has been a mixed blessing for training professionals. Although learning is a mental activity, and understanding how people think and process information is essential to engaging them and getting long-term results, I've heard more than one leader say, "It's all very interesting, but what do I *do* with it?"

Scientific theories are helpful, but what really matters is application. Here are ten key points for applying the research to engage your learners' brains and increase your own efficiency:

- **Every learner's brain is unique, specialized, and situational.** We all have preferred modes of learning and thinking. Plan for a full diversity of styles and be aware of how your own preferences impact you as the designer or trainer. The more important the learning points, the more important it is to bring in a "tapestry" of approaches that appeal to all the thinkers in your group.

- **Mindsets frame how we see the world and can interfere with learning.** To overcome the brain's resistance to change, use a "whole brain" approach: Provide context, engage emotions, introduce novelty, create meaty challenges, and provide time for processing and practice.

- **The brain looks for patterns, and those patterns form the way we think.** The brain will "fill in the blanks" based on prior experiences, so you can use this to your advantage to accelerate learning — but be careful of the mindset trap.

- **The greater the mental stretch, the more energy it takes to learn.** To make sure learners are mentally prepared for the challenge, prepare the brain by providing context and aligning design with the learner's needs.

- **Learners need stretch, not stress.** Stress alters neuron growth. As you challenge learners, watch for too much stress, which will shut learning down.

- **Learners don't pay attention to boring things.** Particularly now, when there is almost an addiction to the constant stimulus of emails and other interruptions, if the brain doesn't have an array of different activities to engage in, it becomes bored.

- **The brain isn't multi-tasking, it's task switching**, and a wealth of research shows that it just isn't good at it. But face it: Your learners *are* multi-tasking, so plan for it. Provide email breaks and other options to keep them focused during the training.

- **Memories strengthen during periods of rest, even when we're awake.** Staggered training and breaks help the learner retain information they just learned.

- **What isn't rehearsed doesn't stick in long-term memory.** For critical content that must be processed and moved to long-term memory, make sure there is adequate learning, practice, and reinforcement time.

- **The brain is wired to be social.** Take advantage of online collaboration tools, and don't forget the traditional methods like mentoring and group work challenges.

Other considerations for learning

How do you gain information? Hearing? Seeing? Do you also touch? Smell and taste, too? You bet you do. We all gain information through our five senses. The highest percent of information usually comes through seeing and hearing.

You've probably also heard about learning styles, the concept that individuals learn differently based on the mode the content is presented: visual, auditory, or kinesthetic. Perhaps you've used one of the instruments by David Kolb or others to determine your participants' learning styles. Unfortunately, there is no solid evidence that individuals have a preferred learning style. I know this may come as a surprise to you, because the approach boasts widespread popularity. In 2008, four professors from four different U.S. universities concluded that there is a lack of evidence to support the concept.

Does this mean you should forget about how people learn? Definitely not. Most people use a combination of all three modalities, and you will encounter a variety of learners in every training session. So what does a trainer do? Do what all good trainers do:

✔ Accept that people learn in different ways.

✔ Use different methods that facilitate learning for different preferences.

✔ And finally, when designing or delivering training, strive to create a variety of approaches that utilize techniques and activities from all learning preferences.

You can also augment your design and delivery to ensure that you incorporate each of the main ways we learn:

✔ Visually, you would include pictures, diagrams, graphics, illustrations, props, or flowcharts. Provide written directions when possible. Help participants visualize a process using video, demonstrations, or role plays to "show" how.

✔ Auditorally, you can ensure that your spoken directions are clear and use discussions, debates, panels, interviews, and other verbal methods for transferring knowledge. Plan for buzz groups, small group discussion, teach-backs, and presentations that allow participants to talk through the information.

✔ Kinesthetically, you could provide physically active learning opportunities or experiential hands-on learning activities. Provide things for participants to touch and "play with," such as Play Doh, tactile toys, koosh balls, and crayons. Take frequent breaks and allow informal movement during the session that doesn't disturb other participants. Build in activities such as making models, role playing, scavenger hunts, relay races, and other active review and practice methods.

Helping Adults Learn in the Classroom and Online

You may have a difficult time finding practical advice to ensure that your classroom — whether traditional or virtual — maximizes adult learning. However, in 35 years of experience, I've discovered practical tips for applying Malcolm Knowles' principles to ensure that participants learn. I've grouped them in four categories for you.

- Create a safe haven for learning.
- Create a comfortable environment.
- Encourage participation.
- Facilitate more than you lecture.

In the following sections, I examine each of these and help you decide how you can address them.

Create a safe haven for learning

It would be great if everything you did as a trainer went just the way it is supposed to, but it won't. Trust me. Some learners may arrive thinking that training is punishment. Others may arrive with memories of past learning experiences in mind, such as a boring webinar or failing tests. Yet others may arrive bringing their daily burdens with them. You can build trust with your learners and create a safe haven for learning for everyone by using some of these ideas in your traditional or virtual classroom:

- Be prepared early enough so that you can welcome participants as they arrive, learn their names, and allow time for them to learn something about others.
- Share the learning objectives early, prior to the session, if possible.
- Let participants know how they will benefit from the information — it's the old WIIFM (what's in it for me).
- Demonstrate your respect for each individual.
- Ensure confidentiality and encourage participants to chat with you in private if necessary.
- Remember that your participants always come first. Respect their time, their opinions, and their expertise.

✔ We all like to hear our names, so use your learners' names early and with sincere reinforcement throughout the training to build rapport. Use cues to help you remember names.

Use names in a traditional classroom

I like to use table tents on which participants write their names as a cue in a traditional classroom. Some facilitators prefer to use name badges. Whatever your choice, be sure that you can read them. For example, ask participants to use a marker to write their first names large enough front and back so that everyone can read them from across the room. If you use preprinted table tents, ensure that the type size is bold and can be read from 40 feet.

Use names in a virtual classroom

Keep a list of all participant names next to you. Even if you have a host or administrative person who "opens" the classroom by checking audio connections and other tasks, you, the facilitator, should welcome participants. This begins to build rapport. In Chapter 7, I suggest you should encourage participants to join ten minutes early. Greeting each person by name is one of those reasons. Add a short comment such as "welcome back" or "what is your location?" This helps build rapport early. Call on people by name during your virtual session too.

Create a comfortable environment

I prefer to arrive early enough so that I am organized and can welcome the learners as my guests. As a trainer, be sensitive to the mood of your classroom — created by both the physical aspects as well as each participant's demeanor. To create a comfortable environment, consider these before your next training session:

In a traditional classroom

✔ Turn the lights on bright. There is nothing more depressing to me than walking into a ballroom where the lights have been left on romantic dim from the party the night before.

Ask for a room with natural light. Even on a sunless day, natural light is more pleasant than any artificial lighting.

✔ Learn how to adjust the thermostat for the most comfortable level for most of the participants. Remember you never please all of them all the time. Do your best.

✔ Ensure that the environment "looks" comfortable. Hide empty boxes. Chairs should be straight. Place materials neatly and uniformly at each seat. This order tells the learners that you care and went to the trouble of getting ready for them.

✔ Ensure that you and your visuals can be seen and heard by all learners. Go ahead try it out. Sit in their seats. Will all participants be able to see your visuals and hear you?

✔ Arrange to have the most comfortable chairs available.

✔ Arrange the tables to be conducive to learning. Chapter 7 provides a number of suggestions.

✔ Ensure that everyone has adequate personal space.

✔ Have extra supplies, pens, and paper available.

✔ Have coffee, tea, and water, waiting in the morning.

In a virtual classroom

✔ Use a pre-class communication to connect with your participants to reassure them that you are there to help facilitate their learning.

✔ Confirm that participants received any handouts or other materials they need before the class.

✔ Ensure that your learners know how to set up their computers prior to the day of your virtual class. They may not have experience with the specific virtual classroom platform you will use.

✔ Help participants manage the environment in which they will attend the virtual session.

✔ Do whatever it takes to put all learners at ease about participating in your virtual classroom.

Breaks are required to ensure a comfortable environment. In both virtual and traditional classrooms, ensure that you plan for ample breaks. The rule of thumb is to take a break every 90 minutes. Few virtual classrooms go beyond 90 minutes, but if yours does, a break midway is imperative.

Encourage participation

I believe that creating active and ample participation is the most important thing you can do to enhance learning. You find this thread running through the entire book. Here are a couple of thoughts to get you started whether you are in a virtual or traditional classroom:

✔ Use small break-out groups to overcome any reluctance to share ideas or concerns. In a virtual classroom, this means using break-out rooms.

✔ Call on specific participants no matter what kind of class you are facilitating.

✔ Use body language in a traditional classroom to encourage participation; positive nods, smiles, eye contact all show that you're interested in others' ideas. In a virtual classroom, you can still encourage participation with an enthusiastic voice and verbal reinforcement. In some instances, you may want to use a webcam for short periods of time.

✔ Ask questions — a show of hands is a good way to start out, and in a virtual setting you have a feature called a poll.

✔ Encourage participants to ask questions. In a virtual setting, encourage them to use chat.

✔ Share something of yourself to begin a trusted exchange of ideas.

✔ Learn and apply techniques to get learners to open up. You discover numerous ideas later in this book.

Facilitate more than you deliver

There are few times when straight delivery or lecture is required. Perhaps when rules or laws must be imparted word for word, when safety is an issue, or when your learners have no knowledge of the subject. But for the most part facilitating experiential activities and discussions lead to the same end, enhancing learning for everyone.

✔ Create discussion. Not just between you and the learners, but among the learners. Encourage the use of chat and breakout rooms in a virtual setting.

✔ Get opinions and ideas out in the open before you deliver your message. You may be surprised at how much "training" the learners can do for you. A virtual classroom can be an advantage here because polls are usually anonymous.

✔ Share personal experiences and stories to build rapport and trust.

✔ Provide opportunities for participants to evaluate their own learning throughout the session. A self-scoring quiz, perhaps or online a multiple choice or true/false quiz in a poll where all responses are combined.

✔ Create experiential learning activities in which the learners discover the learning on their own.

One Last Note: Who's Who and What's What

What is the difference between facilitators, trainers, teachers, instructors, and others? What distinguishes learners, participants, trainees, and students? How about the difference between training, educating, and instructing? And last, what's the difference between learning, knowledge, skills, and performance?

Who's who?

You've probably noticed that I use both *trainer* and *facilitator* in this book. What's in a name? Even though our profession has debated over the years about what to call ourselves, what you *do* is much more important than what you call yourself. This book was not written to resolve the issue of the best title, but to ensure that you do the best job to help others learn and develop. So what's in a name? First, examine those who deliver the training:

- ✔ **Facilitators:** Title given adults who ensure learners are taking an active role in their learning; sometimes interchangeable with trainers but more often used when little knowledge or skill is dispensed. Often used for describing a person who conducts team-building or strategic-planning sessions.

- ✔ **Trainers:** Title given to adults who are the learning catalysts so other adults may learn new skills and knowledge, and of course, interchangeable with facilitators. A good trainer *is* a facilitator.

- ✔ **Presenters:** Title given adults who deliver speeches at conferences or to larger groups; minimal emphasis on two-way communication.

- ✔ **Instructors:** Title used for teachers in academia. May also be used for specific skill sets, such as tennis instructors or flight instructors.

- ✔ **Teachers:** Title most often given those who are instructing children; pedagogical.

How about those who are receiving the training?

- ✔ **Learners:** A neutral term that can be used for anyone gaining information.

- ✔ **Participants:** A general term used by facilitators and trainers to refer to anyone in a learning or intervention session; a learner.

- ✔ **Trainees:** Synonymous with participants; most recently has been replaced by "learners" or "participants."
- ✔ **Students:** Used for young children; pedagogical.

To project respect for your learners, avoid using the word "student" when discussing them. *Learners* or *participants* best define the adults you're training.

You will find that I use facilitator or trainer and learner or participant most often.

What's what?

The activity that occurs between the two *whos* in the preceding section may be called any of these:

- ✔ **Facilitating:** May be interchanged with the term "training." Usually refers to taking less of a leading role and being more of a catalyst.
- ✔ **Training:** The activity conducted by adults who are learning new skills. Knowledge is generally put to immediate use. Hands-on practice is included.

  I was once given a great bit of advice that I pass on to you. To be the most successful trainer/facilitator, don't be a sage on stage, but be a guide on the side.

- ✔ **Instructing:** Allows participants to generalize beyond what has been taught. Minimal hands-on practice. Sounds too much like a college class to me.
- ✔ **Educating:** Imparting knowledge generally in a broader context with delayed implementation. Little hands-on practice.

The results of the activity just discussed may be called some of these:

- ✔ **Learning:** Gaining knowledge and skills to make change.
- ✔ **Knowledge:** Gaining cognitive competence and information assimilation.
- ✔ **Skill development:** Gaining psychomotor competence.
- ✔ **Attitude:** Willingness to change based on new knowledge.
- ✔ **Performance:** Implementing the knowledge and skills that have been gained.

You may find other labels for these roles and what occurs, and as the profession grows and changes you're likely to find even more. What you call yourself is not nearly as important as the significant work you accomplish: Helping adults learn so they can improve their performance.

Again, why do adults learn? Because everyone wants or needs to learn. We are all trainers, all learners. Carl Rogers said, "The degree to which I can create relationships which facilitate the growth of others as separate persons is a measure of the growth I have achieved in myself."

Chapter 3

The Training Cycle

In This Chapter

▶ Introducing The Training Cycle

▶ Defining training jargon

▶ Ensuring learning occurs in The Training Cycle

T he most widely used method for developing new training programs is called *Instructional Systems Design (ISD)*. ISD was originally developed by and for the military to effectively create training programs. There are about 100 different ISD models and as many names, but most are based on four to seven steps represented by the acronym ADDIE.

✔ Analysis

✔ Design

✔ Development

✔ Implementation

✔ Evaluation

These steps are logically sequenced and ensure a practical approach to designing a training program. Some ISD models are linear; some are circular. They all accomplish the same purpose: Designing a training program that gets results. The Training Cycle presented in the next section represents the ISD model that guides you through the rest of the book.

This chapter is dedicated to understanding The Training Cycle, its background, its moving parts, and how learning fits into it.

The Training Cycle: An Overview

Anytime you participate in a training program, whether it is in a virtual or a traditional classroom, whether it was off-the-shelf or developed from scratch, whether it was taught by someone inside your organization or an external vendor, whether it was a program teaching management development skills or word processing skills, chances are that the program was designed by following a specific process, or a representative ISD model. I refer to this process as *The Training Cycle*. The Training Cycle begins long before the training program is conducted and continues after the program has been completed. Figure 3-1 is an illustration of the five stages of The Training Cycle. In this chapter, you get a brief overview of each stage of the Cycle. Subsequent chapters provide the depth you need to begin to implement each stage yourself.

It is critical for all trainers to be well rounded and understand the training process from start to finish. The Training Cycle provides you with a big picture of the process. You can fill in the details as you move through this book.

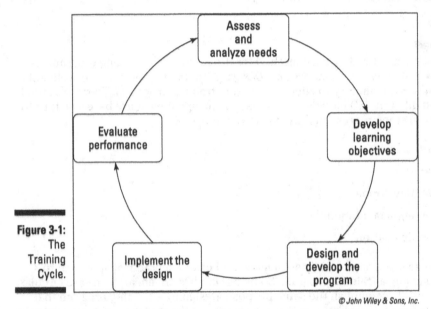

© John Wiley & Sons, Inc.

Figure 3-1: The Training Cycle.

Assess and analyze needs

This stage of The Training Cycle is called *analysis* in the ADDIE acronym. Generally, you need to conduct an assessment and analyze the data, to identify specific needs. There are two main reasons for completing an assessment and analysis.

> ✔ First, you want to make sure there is a reason to conduct training. You may discover that after conducting the analysis the relevant issue can be addressed by something other than training. For example, you may

be able to do on-the-job coaching, online content may exist that could be delivered either asynchronously or synchronously, or you may feel that an article in the company newsletter alerts employees to the information needed.

✔ Second, if you do determine that training is necessary, the analysis should tell you exactly what (content) should be taught and how (by what methodology) it should be taught in the training session. It will also help determine your training objectives.

There are many ways to conduct assessments. You can use a formal instrument that measures a person's skill or knowledge, or one that simply measures a person's preference. You can use written questionnaires or you can use personal interviews with employees or supervisors. If you use interviews, you can meet with individuals one-on-one, or you can conduct small focus groups. Another way to assess a need is to observe an employee working or to take a work sample. You can also use records or reports that already exist, such as performance assessments

Your goal in collecting this data is to determine the gap between a job requirement and an individual's actual skill or knowledge. Bottom line is to determine what is preventing the desired performance. You use this information in the next stage of The Training Cycle.

Develop objectives

After you have determined that there is a legitimate training need, your next step is to state exactly what you want the training to accomplish. You do this by writing objectives. There are two kinds of objectives from two perspectives used in training:

✔ **The learning/performance objective:** This is a statement of the performance (knowledge or skill) that is desired after the training has been conducted. Whether you call them learning or performance objectives doesn't matter, as long as you realize that the purpose is to demonstrate what your participants have learned and can perform. What behavior changes did they make? Learning objectives should be based on the information you discovered during the analysis step. For example, at the end of this training session, "Participants will be able to design participant-focused learning activities."

✔ **The training objective:** This is a statement of what the instructor hopes to accomplish during the training session. This may be an outcome, or it may be a description of what the instructor plans to do in order to accomplish the learning objectives. For example, "This session will create a positive learning climate that encourages participants to get involved and to ask questions."

Some trainers include both learning and training objectives in their design. Learning objectives are a required step in every good training design. Training objectives help the trainer to focus on designing and delivering a first-class training program by setting targets for the trainer to achieve.

Learners are told what the learning objectives are at the beginning of a training session. And preferably at the same time they are told about the training. But wait, I am getting ahead of myself. I have not yet begun the design process! That's what the next stage of The Training Cycle is all about.

Design and develop the program

After you determine the objectives, you can begin the program design. This is the stage of The Training Cycle that I like best. You decide exactly what you're going to do to accomplish the objectives you set. There are many things to consider in designing a training program.

If you haven't already, you will decide the type of delivery that will be the focus to achieve the best results: onsite classroom, virtual classroom, self-paced e-learning, performance support tools, self-study, or a combination of these and others in a blended learning solution. What questions will help determine the location of the training?

- How many participants need new knowledge and/or skills?
- Where are participants located?
- How much time is required?
- How much consistency is needed?
- When is training required?
- How many participants will be in each class?
- What level of trainer expertise will be required?

You may also decide whether to design the content at all. Given thousands of products available, you may decide instead to purchase pre-designed off-the-shelf content and customize it. Whether you design or customize, consider who your audience is; what the best training techniques are; how to provide opportunities to practice; what will be meaningful; how they will implement learning in the real world; how it will improve performance; how to add creativity to the program; in addition to ensuring that learning objectives are met. You also build in methods to ensure that the learning is applied back on the job, and a process to evaluate the program's effectiveness.

Serious e-learning design

by Julie Dirksen

When I went to graduate school for instructional design, I felt like I learned a lot about Analysis and Development and Evaluation, but when it came to Design, it was frequently just a step in the process called "Design the Intervention," which was like saying "Magic happens here!"

Much of my professional life since then has been about trying to understand more about what good learning design looks like. A few years ago, Michael Allen, Clark Quinn, Will Thalheimer, and I sat down and tried to create a statement of what we understood to be the best principles for e-learning design, putting it into a document called the Serious eLearning Manifesto (http://elearningmanifesto.org). This document is available freely online as a resource to the community, with an open Creative Commons license so people can use in any way that's helpful to them.

The document focuses on some of the core principles of instruction — basically that learning should have or be the following:

- Performance focused
- Meaningful to learners
- Engagement-driven
- Authentic contexts
- Realistic decisions
- Individualized challenges
- Spaced practice
- Real-world consequences

The manifesto presents additional supporting principles and more detail about how each of these ideas should be realized. These aren't our unique ideas, but rather a distilling of the best knowledge that we have about how people learn.

One important point: Part of developing any good design is trying it out. The manifesto is a starting point, but it's also important to pilot-test any designs and get feedback on them. No solution is perfect out of the box, no matter what guidelines are followed. When I teach instructional design, I encourage people to pair the manifesto principles with evaluation measures during development using both quantitative measures (the Kirkpatrick Levels) and qualitative measures (Brinkerhoff's Success Case Method).

If you design it, a big task ahead of you is developing the materials. What participant materials do the learners need? What audiovisual materials and equipment will you use? If it is an online course, what technical support will you require? Will your learners require job aids — either paper or online? While this stage can be exciting, it can also be exhausting.

Implement the design

This is The Training Cycle stage where you actually conduct the program. A trainer completes a huge amount of preparation before the program. Even after an excellent job of preparing, there is no guarantee that the program will go off without a hitch. That's why some trainers pilot a program with a group of pseudo-learners who provide feedback before the session is ready for prime time.

You use both presentation and facilitation skills in both a traditional and virtual classroom. I discuss the variations in skills throughout the book. As a trainer, you're a presenter and a facilitator:

- **Presenters provide more information.** If much of the information is new or technical, you may need to present. The preferred role, however, is as a facilitator.

- **Facilitators play more of a catalyst role and ensure learners' participation.** A good trainer is often synonymous with the term "facilitator."

Excellent delivery skills are required whether you are facilitating a virtual or traditional classroom. While you're conducting the training, you want to constantly read your learners to see whether you're meeting their needs. If you see that an approach isn't working, stop and try another. Don't be afraid to stray from the agenda if that seems to be the audience's need. This is the stage where platform experience and good facilitation skills are required.

Evaluate performance

When it's over, it's not over. The evaluation stage is an important part of The Training Cycle for three reasons.

- First, the evaluation tells you whether or not the objectives were accomplished.

- Second, information from the evaluation stage should be fed into the assess-and-analyze stage. It is used to improve the training program should it be conducted again. This is why this model is circular.

- Finally, evaluation information serves as the basis for determining needs for future programs or other changes an organization may need to make.

Thus the cycle is complete and the process starts all over again. I examine each of the five stages in depth starting in Chapter 4.

If you want to achieve a goal, start with the end in mind. In this case it means that you start with the Evaluation stage. What do you want to accomplish? What does your stakeholder expect? How will what is learned enhance the organization's goals? What will success look like? Your evaluation must be a part of the thought process as you begin the design at the Analysis stage.

Other options to ADDIE

ADDIE is certainly the traditional approach; however, many T&D developers use other agile approaches, such as the Successive Approximation Model (SAM — see the sidebar). Each methodology has strengths and weaknesses. ADDIE has many detailed steps that many people feel is burdensome. The more agile models are more iterative, conduct less analysis and produce a fasterdesign.

Three keys to successful SAM

by Dr. Michael Allen

The development of quality instructional products is not an easy task. There are many factors that interact with each other to determine success, including but not limited to: experience of the designer(s), time allowed, range of learner preparedness, content availability and structure, stakeholder views and involvement, development tools and experience with them.

SAM, The Successive Approximation Model, is an iterative, agile-based learning development process for creating serious instructional events within ever-present project constraints. It takes small repeated steps, called *iterations,* rather than risky, giant steps that may prove unfortunate. Design correction and improvement in SAM is fundamental, producing multiple, evolving, usable, and testable versions or prototypes. In these iterations, SAM focuses more on learning experiences, learner engagement, and learner motivation than it does on content organization, presentation of information, and summative posttests. These other elements fall in place as needed.

SAM works. But even the best development process will return less than hoped for results if key elements are ignored. Three requirements will ensure your successful implementation of SAM.

Assemble a mixed team

The first three iterations, which occur in the Savvy Start — the initial brainstorming of SAM — can usually be accomplished within one or two days. Sometimes many more than three iterations can be accomplished in that time period, but at least three need to be taken to have confidence in the chosen design. For at least the first three iterations, it's important to have assembled the right team which should include as many of the following as viable: budget maker, owner of the performance problem, supervisor of learners, subject matter expert (SME), potential learners, recent learners, project manager, instructional designer, and prototyper.

A large team can make the Savvy Start meeting difficult to manage, but not having key stakeholders represented can make the whole project difficult to manage later on. The discussions during the Savvy Start set the tone, reveal expectations and biases, and let you know who is really in charge. That information will be of considerable help when you have to work without direct involvement of some of these people. By having attended the Savvy Start, recipients of your updates will have an easier appreciation of reports and the progress being made.

(continued)

(continued)

Work backward

Begin with the last instructional experience you would deliver before concluding an individual's instruction. What do you want learners doing before they attempt to work on their own? The answer, of course, is doing something that's as similar as possible to the required performance under the range of conditions the learner will encounter. This activity will define goals in functional specificity. There should be little interpretive variance going forward and therefore no problematic surprises.

After learning experiences have been designed to assure readiness of learners to perform the most challenging skills, design attention backs up to consider prerequisite needs for that final learning experience. When those preparatory learning events have been designed, another back up is to consider prerequisites for them. The backing-up process continues until a learning experience is designed for which all expected learners are ready.

Ask "Why shouldn't we do this?"

It's easier to have a constructive conversation about why a proposed design wouldn't work than it is to consider all possible alternatives.

In SAM, we gather easy-to-obtain information and get going with initial prototypes. Some of the most helpful information is about:

- Learners — entry skills and variances, motivation
- Performance needs — what exactly are learners expected to do after training and to what degree of perfection
- The conditions under which learners are expected to perform
- The frequency with which they will perform the task
- Previous instructional successes and failures, if any

If any of this information proves difficult to gather, it's okay to guess. Speed is more important than accuracy for this exercise. Evaluation of prototypes, which is essentially asking the question, "Why shouldn't we do this?" will correct faulty guesses and do so with helpful specificity.

Note: For more information about SAM, check out Michael's book *Leaving ADDIE for SAM* (ASTD Press, 2012).

T&D Jargon

Is it soup yet? Alphabet, that is. If you associate with training types, I am sure you may at times think they are speaking in a foreign tongue.

Perhaps it is time to introduce a few of the acronyms and technical terms you hear in the training field:

- **Active training:** An approach that ensures participants are actively involved in the learning process.
- **ADDIE:** This is the classic model of a training design process. The acronym is formed by the steps in the process: Analysis, Design, Development, Implementation, and Evaluation.

- **Andragogy:** A term developed in Europe to describe the art and science of adult learning. Malcolm Knowles is sometimes incorrectly credited with coining the word. He actually introduced and promoted it through his work and writing. Typically refers to adults' capacity to direct and motivate their learning, utilize past experience and knowledge, and evaluate the relevance of training content to their personal needs.

- **Assessment:** Refers to a questionnaire, exam, test, or other evaluation process.

- **Asynchronous training/learning:** Typically a self-paced, online tutorial that doesn't require the trainer and learner to participate at the same time; could also be a self-paced learning module using worksheets or books.

- **Audiovisuals:** Any medium used to deliver information that enhances the presentation through auditory and/or visual means, for example, PowerPoint presentations, video clips, flipcharts, recordings; frequently abbreviated as AV.

- **Blended learning:** The practice of using several mediums in one curriculum. Typically refers to a combination of classroom and self-paced computer training.

- **Bloom's Taxonomy:** A hierarchical ordering of learning outcomes developed by Benjamin Bloom and a university committee. The three learning outcomes cognitive (knowledge), psychomotor (skills), and affective (attitude) are frequently referred to as the KSAs.

- **Breakout groups:** Private meetings where participants have discussions and collaborate on tasks. In an in-person classroom, it may occur in separate physical rooms or different places in the classroom. In a virtual classroom, the facilitator creates a breakout as a whiteboard or chat.

- **CBT:** Computer Based Training, a generic term for any learning delivered via a computer.

- **Chunking:** Separating learning information into small sections to improve learner comprehension and retention.

- **Cognitive neuroscience:** Also called brain research, the science of how we learn.

- **CPLP: (Certified Professional in Learning and Performance):** The professional credential offered by the ATD Certification Institute.

- **Criterion referenced instruction:** A system of training developed by Bob Mager where the results are measured by the learner's ability to meet specified performance objectives (criterion) upon completion.

- **Delivery method:** The way training is provided to learners — for example, virtual classroom, videoconference, CD-ROM, audio tape, classroom.

- **Design:** The formulation of a plan or outline for training.

- **Development:** The stage of creating a training program in which the materials are created and training methods are finalized.

- **E-Learning:** Inclusive set of electronic computer delivery methods of every kind.

- **Evaluation:** The final step in The Training Cycle used to measure results.

- **Experiential learning:** Occurs when learners participate in activities, identify useful knowledge/skills, and transfer learning to the workplace.

- **Facilitate:** Interchangeable with training, maximizing guidance and support of the learner.

- **Flipped classroom.** A form of blended learning when new content is learned independently first and is followed by interaction with a trainer.

- **Gamification:** Applying the essence of games to real-world scenarios.

- **Icebreaker:** An activity conducted at the beginning of a training program that introduces participants to each other, may introduce content, and in general helps participants ease into the program.

- **ILT:** An acronym that trainers toss about in every discussion. It stands for Instructor-Led Training.

- **Informal learning:** Gaining knowledge or skills outside a structured program, such as reading, peer feedback, discussion, and on-the-job observation.

- **ISD:** Instructional Systems Design, a process used to analyze, design, develop, implement, and evaluate training. Hey, isn't that the ADDIE model? It is also The Training Cycle, discussed in this chapter.

- **Job aid:** A tool to provide on-the-job direction for a specific task; may be in paper, tablet, laptop, or mobile device format.

- **KSA:** Knowledge, skills, attitude — the three learning categories based on Bloom's Taxonomy.

- **Learning objective:** A clear, measurable statement of behavior that a learner demonstrates when the training is considered a success.

- **SME:** Subject Matter Expert, the most knowledgeable person regarding specific content for a training program; pronounced "smee."

- **Social learning:** Occurs by interacting with others. It's usually informal and unconscious, but can be designed into a training event.

- **Soft skills:** Term used to describe a type of nontechnical training, for example, communication, leadership, listening, stress management.

- **Task analysis:** The process of identifying the specific steps to correctly perform a task.

✔ **Virtual classroom:** An online learning space where learners and trainers interact.

✔ **WIIFM:** Acronym for What's In It For Me? — to remind trainers to always ensure participants know how the learning benefits them.

Perhaps this short trip through my trainer's dictionary answers questions you may have had up to this point and prepares you for the rest of the book.

Learning and The Training Cycle

The Training Cycle is so orderly and straightforward, it seems like it would be impossible to miss anything important. That's true, but keep in mind that training is really about the learner.

Adults learn differently. In Chapter 2, I briefly mention several bright minds that have all arrived at various models for learning preferences. Although they do not agree on any one measure or model, they do agree that learners have different preferences for recognizing and processing information. If the experts can't arrive at one model for how people learn, how can you be expected to train people with vastly different learning preferences in the same group? You can!

Variety and flexibility

You can successfully get in touch with all learning preferences in your group if you remember two things:

✔ **Add variety.** Lots! Research suggests that varying your delivery methods and using different training methods enhances learning for everyone. In fact, most recent research goes even further to say that training that affects more than one preference actually has a greater impact than focusing on the one preference for each specific learner (as if you could do that, anyway!) Lots of variety has a greater payoff. Therefore, you should also vary the delivery itself, changing pace, control, complexity, and timing.

✔ **Be flexible.** Just as your learners have a preference for learning, you also have a preference for training. You may prefer small group activities or informal discussion or even lectures. You may tend to be more people focused or content focused. You may prefer to be entertaining or professorial, coaching, or directing. Whatever your preference, be flexible. Move outside your comfort zone at times to improve learner comprehension and retention.

Conditions of learning

Before leaving this discussion about incorporating learning into The Training Cycle, I must mention Robert Gagne and his Conditions of Learning. He identified nine instructional events. Applying these events to your training helps to ensure learning occurs. Here are Gagne's Instructional Events:

- ✔ Gain the learners' attention.

- ✔ Share the objectives of the session.

- ✔ Ask learners to recall prior learning.

- ✔ Deliver the content.

- ✔ Use methods to enhance understanding — for example, case studies, examples, graphs.

- ✔ Provide an opportunity to practice.

- ✔ Provide feedback.

- ✔ Assess performance.

- ✔ Provide job aids or references to ensure transfer to the job.

If you've been around the training field for a while, you know that these events are commonplace and are assumed to be a part of any effective training program.

As a trainer, you're responsible for doing everything you can to ensure that learning takes place: Use a theory-based design model like The Training Cycle presented in this chapter, adapt to learners' preferences, and incorporate conditions of learning. Yet remember these words from Galileo Galilei (1564–1642), an Italian astronomer and physicist: "You cannot teach a man anything. You can only help him discover it within himself."

Part II
Designing the Best Darn Training in the World

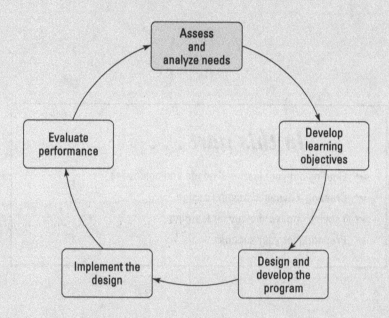

Get some great tips for preparing for a remote training session in a free online article at www.dummies.com/extras/traininganddevelopment.

In this part . . .

- Figuring out your learners' needs and objectives.
- Creating a dynamic training design.
- Tapping into technology for learning.
- Preparing for your success.

Chapter 4

Assessing Needs and Developing Learning Objectives

. . . .

In This Chapter

▶ Describing how to conduct needs assessments

▶ Determining whether it is a training need

▶ Gathering data about your audience

▶ Demonstrating how to write learning objectives

. . . .

*I*f you remember nothing else about training from this book, remember this: It's all about the learner.

In this chapter, I begin the design of a training program *for the learner*. The design follows the five stages in The Training Cycle presented in Chapter 3. This chapter addresses the first two stages of the cycle:

✔ Assess and analyze needs

✔ Develop learning objectives

Conducting Needs Assessments

Designing training may be like planning a sightseeing tour in a strange country. You have lots of things you would like to do, many things you would like to learn, but you have no idea how far apart any of these things are, what the people will be like, how long it will take, what attire is appropriate, or which activities should be higher priority.

When you plan a sightseeing tour, you most likely read a travel guide or two, contact a travel agency and other experts, talk to people who live where you will travel discuss the possibilities with others who have taken a similar tour, and check out the Internet to get the greatest bang for your buck.

You want answers about why to go, how to go, what to see, when to go, and with whom you should confer. You collect data about a potential tour. Next, you analyze that data and make a decision. You may consider the cost, required time, and your safety. Your analysis may suggest that the tour you had hoped for is not a good idea, and you may stop planning. On the other hand, the data may suggest that you modify your original ideas. In any case, you have to make a decision about what to do next.

You have just followed the steps of conducting a needs assessment:

1. **Identify a need or reason to investigate a problem (you need information about a tour).**

2. **Determine a plan for gathering data (decide whom you will contact and what to read).**

3. **Gather the data (talk to people, read books).**

4. **Analyze the data you collected (can you afford it, is the timing right?).**

5. **Make a decision (decide to go or not; if yes, use the data to create a travel plan.**

The why, how, who, and when of needs assessment

Like your sightseeing tour, a trainer wants to get the most bang for the buck. That means conducting a needs assessment and analyzing the data. What's the root cause of the problem? Is training even the issue? Figure 4-1 highlights the first stage of The Training Cycle.

Why conduct a needs assessment?

Why a needs assessment? The ultimate goal of a needs assessment is to determine the current and the desired performance. The difference or the gap between the two is the learning that must occur and the basis for a good training design.

Supervisors and managers may approach trainers and request that they conduct training because of some incident that has happened. For example, your hospital cafeteria is getting an unusually high number of customer complaints. Because of this, the trainer may be asked to develop a customer service skills program. Although it may be tempting to quickly put together

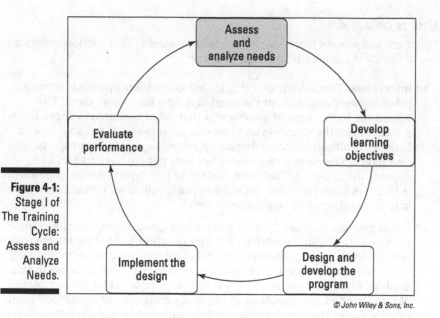

Figure 4-1: Stage I of The Training Cycle: Assess and Analyze Needs.

a customer service training program, it would be much wiser to first determine whether there is really a need for it. An assessment can help you make such a determination. When you invest time, ask good questions, and follow the questioning line to the real reason (root cause analysis) your assessment and analysis glide right into the next step and become the design. Reasons for conducting a needs assessment include at least these:

✔ Determine whether there is a training requirement.

✔ Ensure the training will be linked to organizational needs.

✔ Determine root causes of poor performance.

✔ Determine desired performance (training results).

✔ Provide baseline data.

✔ Identify what to measure and how to measure it.

✔ Identify content and scope of training including examples of what works.

✔ Provide content to turn some of the war stories you hear into role plays, mini case studies, and examples.

✔ Gain participant and organizational support. (Often, folks get on board when they have involvement from the start.)

The bottom line is that an assessment helps you pinpoint the problem, confirm the problem, and seek solutions.

How to collect data?

There are many ways to conduct a needs assessment. This section covers a few of the most commonly used approaches:

- **Interviews:** The trainer uses this technique to identify people who can provide information about the need and then interviews them. The advantage to this type of interview is that you can obtain in-depth information about the situation and you can get others' ideas about how to handle the situation. If you do end up providing a training program, you also have some early commitment because people have had input in shaping the program. The disadvantage to this type of needs assessment is that it is labor intensive. By the way, although it isn't ideal, interviews may be conducted by telephone as well.

- **Focus groups:** Another approach is a focus group. Somewhat like the interview, the trainer identifies key people who can provide information about the need. However, instead of interviewing them individually, the trainer interviews them in groups. There are two advantages to this method. First, the trainer can interview more people in a shorter period of time. Second, the members of the focus group can piggyback off each other's ideas. The disadvantage to this approach is that a quiet person may not give his/her point of view. The result may be that the trainer has information provided only by the outspoken members of the group.

- **Questionnaires:** A tool is used when a trainer wants to collect specific information from a large group or a widely dispersed group. The advantages are that you can include many people, and the results are clear-cut. The disadvantage is that questionnaires may not allow for free expression or unanticipated information; therefore, the trainer may miss some critical data points. Assessment tools such as SurveyMonkey, QuestionPro, Zoomerang, or others can be an easy solution.

   Your data is only as good as the questions you create. You probably want to test a new questionnaire on a small group of people to determine what works and what doesn't. Sometimes, questions can be misinterpreted. Sometimes, questions ask for things they never intended. Sometimes, typos prevent collection of good data also.

- **Observation:** This is a good needs assessment technique in two circumstances. First, it is useful when a trainer is assessing the need for skill-based training. Second, it is a good technique to use when a trainer is asked to conduct a program that changes behavior (for example, customer service, giving constructive feedback, flipping flapjacks, welding an I-beam). The most important advantage to this technique is that it provides the trainer with a realistic view of the situation. The disadvantages are that it takes a long time and is labor intensive. In addition, observation can only indicate behavior, not the reasons behind the behavior or action.

✔ **Performance data reviews:** This technique is used when performance criteria are clear and there is sufficient data available to measure the performance criteria. The advantage to this approach is that the training topics and goals are easy to determine. The trainer need only look at the gap between the criteria and the actual performance. The disadvantage to this approach is that the data may be confounded by other variables, such as equipment downtime or external expectations.

✔ **Informal discussions:** In this approach, the trainer gathers data about training needs through informal conversations with other employees, supervisors, and managers in the organization. The advantage of this approach is that the trainer can get candid information that may help to select a more formal needs assessment approach. The disadvantage is that it may be biased due to its unsystematic approach. These discussions are, however, a great way to gather ideas for practice sessions or role plays.

✔ **Knowledge tests:** Tests are beneficial in helping trainers identify what to include in a knowledge-based program. The advantage to a test is that it measures knowledge versus attitude. A potential disadvantage is that the items on the test may not actually reflect the knowledge used on the job.

Note that you may use a combination of the tools listed. Every assessment is different. You don't use the same assessment you use to plan your foreign tour to determine how to remodel your bathroom. You may not use the same needs assessment and analysis tools for two training programs, either.

What criteria will be used to select a data gathering method?

Many factors determine which method you use. The following list provides an idea of what you, your department, or the organization will consider.

✔ **Time:** What is your turnaround time?

✔ **Cost:** How much money is available for the assessment? Hiring someone from the outside to conduct focus groups can be costly.

✔ **Comfort level and trust:** What is the climate within your organization? Can you rely on the data?

✔ **Size of the population to be surveyed:** How many people need to be involved in the assessment?

✔ **Confidentiality required:** Is confidentiality an issue for individuals in the organization?

✔ **Reliability and validity needed:** To what extent is this critical? How will the assessment methodology affect reliability and validity?

✔ **Culture of the organization:** What are employees accustomed to and how will different methods be perceived? What about the culture? For example, an open organizational structure may encourage focus groups, whereas a hierarchical organization is more likely to administer anonymous surveys.

✔ **Location of those to be surveyed:** Are a large number of people located remotely?

Who will be trained?

As important as it is to determine whether there is a training need, it is equally important to learn as much about your participants as you can. You discover much about your audience in the data-gathering part of your needs assessment.

However, in some instances, someone else will have completed the assessment and the analysis. Your job may be to just deliver the program. At those times, you may find it useful to gain additional information about your participants before the training occurs.

Use the following questions as a starting point to find out more about your participants. It is doubtful that you would ever need to know all the information. Consider it a data smorgasbord. Select those that you want to know more about:

✔ **Background**

- Why were you asked to provide training for them?
- Have they had other training on the same topic?
- What do they know (and need to know) about you?
- How many of the participants are personally acquainted with you?
- Are they aware of the level of expertise or experience you bring to the situation?
- Who are the key players in their department and organization?

✔ **Demographics**

- How many will attend your session?
- Is their attendance voluntary? Required? Requested? Invited?
- Where are they located? Locally? Globally?
- What training experiences have they had?
- How do they prefer to learn?

- What is the demographic make up of the participants? Age? Gender? Other descriptive factors?
- What information sources do they depend upon? Internet? Magazines? TV? Books? Newspapers? Blogs?

✔ **Level of expertise**

- How familiar are they with the subject matter?
- What do they want to know?
- What problem do they want you to help them solve?
- Are all individuals at the same skill and knowledge level about the topic?
- Who are the experts in the group?
- What is their level of responsibility or authority?
- How does their level compare to yours? Does it determine the subject level or delivery style?

✔ **Attitudes**

- Are they interested in the subject? Should they be interested?
- What successes and issues have they encountered?
- What are their attitudes and beliefs relevant to the topic?
- Do they know why they are coming to training?
- May their minds already be made up?
- What are their opinions about you?
- Will they be friendly? Hostile? Raise objections?

✔ **Design considerations**

- How can you use technology to deliver content?
- What follow-up options exist to reinforce the training? Mentoring? Peer groups? Coaching? Social-learning options?
- Did the participants and their managers help to identify the objectives of the training?
- Are you aware of anything that may antagonize them? Hot buttons? Taboo words or subjects? Gestures? Past experiences?
- What is special about these participants?
- Is there anything special about the location where you will be presenting?
- Is there anything unusual about the date or timing of your training — for example, vacation, recent performance appraisals, downsizing effort?

✔ **Expected results**

- How can you meet their needs?
- How does this training benefit the learners and the organization?
- May there be disadvantages to the participants?
- What changes do their supervisors expect as a result of the training?
- Does the organization's culture encourage participants to use what they learn in training? What may get in the way of learners' applying their new knowledge or skill?

When do you begin the needs assessment?

As quickly as you can!

You want as much time as possible designing and developing the training. It's a big job.

No matter how extensive and complete your assessment and analysis are, it is always a good idea to conduct a mini needs assessment at the beginning of each session. I like to chart responses to the question, "What are your hopes and fears for this session?" Other trainers simply ask for each participant's expectation. This does two things:

✔ It helps you determine immediately whether your design is on the mark.

✔ It gives participants an opportunity to state their expectations.

Besides, it's a great way for people to start participating early using the subject as the topic.

Note that you may uncover a few misperceptions. You may also need to make a few slight modifications to meet all the needs. This is all in a day's work for a trainer. Even if participants have expectations that you cannot meet during this session, you can discuss this with them at the first break to determine how you may help them.

Potential questions to ask

Each needs assessment is different. Questions you may consider asking include the following:

✔ What performance gap needs to be addressed?

✔ Is training the best solution?

✔ What type of training is required?

✔ What other solutions have been considered?

✔ How is the performance impacting the organization?

✔ What knowledge or skills need to be addressed?

✔ What are the specific job requirements?

✔ What instruments, materials, and equipment are used by the employees?

✔ Who needs the knowledge or skills?

✔ What is the skill level for these individuals? (may include a list of specific skills)

✔ What materials should be included in the training instruction?

✔ How do these individuals (employees, participants) feel about their performance?

✔ How do these individuals perceive an impending training? What value is it to them?

✔ How supportive are the participants' direct supervisors? Others in management?

✔ What resources are available for the training?

Potentially thousands of questions may be asked. As a trainer, you need to determine what is most important and what you need to know so that you can recommend a learning solution that is most beneficial to the participants as well as the organization. Note that I did not say so that you can design and conduct a training session. One of the most important reasons for conducting a needs assessment and analyzing the data is to determine whether training is the answer. It could be that mentoring or peer-to-peer coaching or even a discussion with someone in another department is needed.

What trainers should know about performance

by Dana Robinson

Learning and performance — what's the difference? Learning and performance are not the same. Learning experiences build capability in people so they can perform. Performance is when people apply this enhanced capability in the workplace, accomplishing results for the organization. People can acquire skills to do many things yet never apply those skills on the job. When this occurs, the investment made to build capability is lost as there is no result or benefit to the employee or to the organization.

Why do people build capability and not use that capability on the job? Geary Rummler said it best: "When you pit a good employee against a bad system, the system will win most every time." The work environment of an employee is "the system" surrounding employees; it must be supportive of the performance that is anticipated following development of capability.

(continued)

(continued)

Examples of work environment include the reward system, efficient work processes, clarity of roles, access to information and data required to perform, sufficient coaching, and a supportive culture — just to name a few. Learning converts to doing when people are supported by the work environment in which they are to operate. Enhanced capability will extinguish in less than 60 days if this is not the case.

Who is responsible for converting learning into doing? Both management and the trainer have accountabilities to ensure this conversion process occurs. Let's begin with management's role. There are two levels of management to consider. The first level is the direct supervisor. This person has the greatest influence on whether employees do or do not apply skills and knowledge to the job. This person can encourage employees through day-to-day coaching and provide guidance when an employee is experiencing difficulty. Involve a higher-level management, often referred to as the "clients" for an initiative. They are senior-level managers who have the authority to make certain that the work environment is supportive at a broad level. For example, they can take actions to ensure that all those whose capability has been enhanced have the tools and information they require to perform as needed.

What motivates senior leaders to work as "clients"? For a leader to engage, there must be a direct and strong linkage between the capability to be developed and the business results that are required. How will the skills people acquire in a specific learning experience benefit the organization? The greater the alignment between development of capability and the business goals, the more likely leaders will take actions needed to ensure skills do convert into desired performance.

And what is the trainer's role to ensure learning converts into doing? There are multiple responsibilities for those who provide learning experiences to others:

- Develop a deep understanding of the business goals and challenges of leaders. Form trusted partnerships with the leaders who "own" these business results. Then ensure that the learning experiences designed and delivered are directly related to, and will benefit, one or more of these goals.

- Before implementing any learning experience, assess the work environment to ensure it is ready to support the enhanced capabilities that will be evident following a learning experience. In other words, identify any *causes* why skills will not convert into doing. Then discuss with clients the barriers, forming actions to address them.

- Include content and experiences in the learning design that are job-relevant. Ensure participants know the WIIFM factor (What's In It For Me) to learn, and then apply, these skills.

- Measure the results obtained from a learning experience — the on-the-job performance change that is evident some weeks following the learning experience as well as the impact to the business that is being realized. Share result information with clients. When results are disappointing, partner with clients to determine reasons and what actions need to be taken.

It is vital to keep in mind that solutions and results are not the same thing. Learning is a solution; performance change is a result. Business dials do not improve because of what people *know* — they improve because of what people *do* with what they know. As a trainer, assessing how to build capability is where your job begins; converting learning into doing is where your job ends.

Is it training?

It isn't over until you know whether it is a training need. These three quick questions help you pinpoint the answer:

- ✔ Does the individual have the skill to do the job?
- ✔ Does the individual have the will to do the job?
- ✔ Is the individual allowed to do the job?

If the answer to the first question is no, training may be a solution, but not necessarily. If the answer to all the questions is yes, it is definitely not a training solution.

Well, what else could it be?

- ✔ A no to the second question means you may have a motivation problem; training doesn't solve that.
- ✔ A no to the third question means there is probably a procedure or policy problem; training doesn't solve that.
- ✔ A yes to all three questions could mean that it is an equipment problem that prevents individuals from producing quality on time.
- ✔ Even a no to the first question doesn't necessarily mean training is required; perhaps coaching is a solution. In other instances, individuals may not have received feedback and may not even know they are doing something incorrectly.

Before anyone jumps to the assumption that a performance problem requires training, consider that it may be due to dozens of other things: inadequate materials, tools, or workspace; unreliable equipment; unclear expectations; inappropriate consequences or incentives; lack or feedback or coaching; inappropriate job assignment; work environment; or others.

Before you finalize your needs assessment, be certain to know whether training is the solution. Don't make the mistake of presupposing that training is the solution to a performance issue prior to completing your needs assessment.

If your time is limited

You may want to believe that The Training Cycle is always followed and that a thorough needs assessment is always completed. That just isn't the real world. If you've been in the training field during the past few years, you know that timelines are shorter, demand is more frequent, and expectations are higher. Although training should start with the business goal, it doesn't always.

So what can you do? You could skip the needs assessment stage completely, but later, you may wish you hadn't. I've done all of these at one time or another. Although they are not the same as a complete needs assessment, one or two can provide you with some basic information so that you can better understand the situation. Some trainers call this *targeted audience analysis*.

- ✔ Get as much information from the contact person as possible. This at least gives you a foundation.

- ✔ Talk to several participants. If I need information fast, I ask the contact person to line up a couple of phone interviews for me. I ask each person several of the questions discussed in the "The why, how, who, and when of needs assessment" section in this chapter.

- ✔ Email a simple questionnaire to all the participants. You get a better response if you attach it to a friendly note from you that welcomes the participants to the training, informs them of the objectives, and lets them know what they may expect, for example, practical, hands-on; ten ways to express your creativity; action-packed day filled with tips you can implement immediately.

- ✔ Save time by using one of the quick assessment tools available, such as SurveyMonkey, QuestionPro, Zoomerang, SurveyGizmo, or others.

- ✔ Ask your contact to provide any materials that may be relevant for the session, for example, meeting agendas and notes, survey results.

- ✔ If you know others in the organization, you may want to contact them for any inside scoop.

- ✔ Contact other trainers or colleagues who may have worked with this group in the past. Do this especially if you're filling in for someone.

- ✔ If you really have no time, you probably want to add opening activities that help you gain information about the group. You may ask about their expectations, their hopes and fears for the session, their greatest problem and greatest success as it relates to the content, or any other activity that helps to fill the needs assessment gap.

- ✔ I may also pack a few backup materials and activities in case the session takes a turn for something different from what I had planned.

Do what you can. An hour or two on the telephone with knowledgeable people makes a huge difference. That way, at least you have some data.

Walking in with even a small amount of data in your hip pocket is always better than walking into a big void.

 Check with your local college or university. Frequently, marketing classes are looking for assessment or survey design projects. You need to allow time for both the design as well as educating the group or individual about you and your organization. If you have time but a minimum amount of money, this can be an elegant solution.

Writing Objectives

After you complete the needs assessment, analyze the data, and ascertain the need for training, you develop the objectives for the training. Figure 4-2 shows that developing objectives is the second stage of The Training Cycle.

Learning objectives are written for the learner. You may also choose to write training objectives that are for the design and development of the training. Learning objectives are a requirement. Many trainers do not write training objectives.

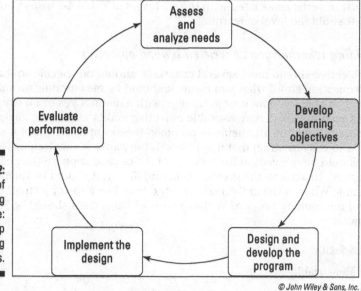

Figure 4-2:
Stage II of
The Training
Cycle:
Develop
Learning
Objectives.

© John Wiley & Sons, Inc.

What objectives should do

Learning objectives are written to specify the performance (knowledge or skill) that is desired after the training has been completed. The following sections spell out the four elements you want to include in your learning objectives.

Specifying exactly what the learner will be able to do

In Chapter 2, you can read about Bloom's Taxonomy, the hierarchy of learning outcomes. Now we are at the point in The Training Cycle where Bloom's Taxonomy comes in handy: specifying exactly what the learner will know or be able to do at the end of the training experience.

Do you want the learners to have knowledge about the subject? Comprehension? Be able to apply the information? Analyze or synthesize it? Or do you want them to be able to make judgments about the information.?

Because the goal of most training that you conduct is to improve skills, you most often select verbs from the application column. However, there are other objectives to training programs that may not require application, but merely comprehension. And, of course, there are also times when you want the learner to go beyond application.

The list of verbs associated with the six levels in Table 4-1 helps you select a verb that fits the level of learning.

Deciding whether you've written a good objective

An objective should meet several criteria: It should be specific so that there is no question about what you mean. It should be measurable, meaning you should be able to count it or determine with a distinct yes or no whether it was accomplished. A measurable objective makes evaluation easier. An objective should be attainable — no pie-in-the-sky statement, yet it should not be so easy to attain that it isn't worth the paper it's written on. An objective should be relevant to the mission of the organization, to the change that is desired, to achieve the greater goal. And finally, it should be time bound, meaning: When is the individual expected to achieve the objective? By the end of the training session? Within a month? Objectives should be SMART, as follows:

- ✔ Specific
- ✔ Measurable
- ✔ Attainable, yet a stretch
- ✔ Relevant
- ✔ Time-bound

Table 4-1

Bloom's Cognitive Domain

Knowledge	Comprehension	Application	Analysis	Synthesis	Evaluation
Recall information	Interpreting information in one's own words	Applying or generalizing knowledge to new situations	Breaking knowledge into parts and showing relationships	Bringing together parts of knowledge to form a new whole	Making judgments based on given criteria
Arrange	Describe	Apply	Analyze	Arrange	Appraise
Cite	Differentiate	Calculate	Appraise	Assemble	Assess
Define	Discuss	Choose	Categorize	Collect	Compare
Duplicate	Explain	Classify	Compare	Combine	Conclude
Label	Express	Complete	Contrast	Compile	Critique
List	Generalize	Compute	Criticize	Compose	Defend
Match	Identify	Demonstrate	Detect	Construct	Estimate
Memorize	Indicate	Dramatize	Diagram	Create	Evaluate
Name	Locate	Employ	Differentiate	Design	Grade
Order	Paraphrase	Illustrate	Discriminate	Formulate	Judge
Outline	Recognize	Interpret	Examine	Generate	Justify
Recall	Report	Modify	Experiment	Manage	Measure
Record	Restate	Operate	Group	Organize	Predict
Relate	Review	Practice	Inventory	Plan	Prescribe
Repeat	Select	Prepare	Question	Prepare	Rank
Reproduce	Sort	Schedule	Subdivide	Propose	Rate
Select	Tell	Sketch	Summarize	Rearrange	Recommend
State	Translate	Solve	Test	Set up	Score
Tabulate		Use		Synthesize	Select
Write				Write	Support
					Validate
					Value

Getting additional guidance

Use these additional ideas for writing objectives:

- Be brief and to the point; include only one major item in each objective.

- Use an *observable* action verb to describe the expected result. You can see (or hear) "list," "demonstrate," and "calculate." You *cannot* see someone "remember," "believe," or "learn."

- Specify a time frame or target date of completion; generally, this occurs at the end of the training session.

- Specify resource limitations (money, personnel, equipment) as appropriate.

- Describe the participants' expected performance.

- Specify results to be achieved in measurable or observable terms.

- Choose areas over which you have direct influence or control; don't write objectives for which your training program has no accountability.

- Make objectives realistic in terms of what can actually be accomplished in the training as well as in terms of resources you have available to you.

- Include enough challenge in the objective to make it worth formulating.

- Indicate the minimum level of acceptable performance.

- Specify the conditions (if any) under which the action must be performed.

- Specify degree of success if less than 100 percent is acceptable.

- Select objectives that are supportive and consistent with overall organization missions and goals.

Using this formula to easily write objectives

A correctly written objective includes four components, sometimes called the *ABCD*s of a good objective:

- Audience (who)
- Behavior (will do what)

✔ Condition (by when or some other condition, such as with assistance)

✔ Degree (how well, if not 100 percent of the time)

To easily write an objective, fill in the blanks. Use this formula to help you out.

Who will do what, by when, and how well?

_____ will _____, by _____, _____.

"You will be able to write appropriate learning objectives, by the time you finish this chapter, 100 percent of the time."

Is it a SMART objective?

✔ Specific? Yes, I can see you "write objectives."

✔ Measurable? Yes, 100 percent.

✔ Attainable, yet a stretch? Yes, but not that much of a stretch for you!

✔ Relevant? Yes, that's what this chapter is about.

✔ Time-bound? Yes, depending upon how fast you read.

Trainers design the training based on the learning objectives. Typically, trainers also post the objectives at the beginning of their sessions. They may word the objectives less clinically and begin them with, "By the end of this training. . . ." If the learners are expected to be able to do the task 100 percent of the time, the trainers may not include it in the objective because it is "assumed." This is sometimes an organizational preference. Therefore, the objective may be rewritten.

"By the end of this training, you will be able to write learning objectives using the SMART guidelines."

Task analysis

At some point in your career you're likely to find folks who are involved in task analysis. In its simplest form, *task analysis* breaks a job (task) down into observable steps. It also reveals the knowledge and skills the employee needs to complete each step. At times task analysis may be used to determine training needs. It may be a part of the analysis completed during the needs assessment. Learning objectives may be written based on the task analysis.

I understand, for example, that the task of tying a shoe can be broken down to 214 steps! Task-analysis steps are completed to determine which aspects of the job to include in a training program:

1. **Identify tasks that are required for performing the job.**

2. **For each task, list the exact steps that a person must do to complete the task. List every step from start to finish in order, no matter how small the step.**

3. **When listing the steps, make them as clear as possible. Even the smallest assumption can create confusion in the actual performance of the task.**

4. **After you have completed all steps for every task, go back and identify each step in one of three ways:**

    • **Common knowledge:** Trainee will know how to do this step because of common knowledge. No training is necessary for this step.

    • **On-the-job training:** The step is simple enough that the trainee can learn it on the job. No training is necessary for this step, but you may want to consider developing a job aid such as a check sheet or a list of procedures.

    • **Training topic:** The trainee will not know how to do this step without training. Your technical training program should be based around these topics.

5. **Ask a subject matter expert (SME) to review your task analysis to see whether you have analyzed the job(s) correctly.**

6. **Design your training program around those topics you identified as requiring training.**

7. **If you also develop job aids, make sure they are integrated into the training program so that trainees know they are available and so that they can ask questions, if they have them.**

Task analysis and training objectives are used prior to designing the training program. Both are critical steps between conducting the needs assessment and designing the training program. Both play a part in setting the goals of the training session and ultimately achieving them. As David Campbell says, "Aim at nothing and you'll hit it every time."

Chapter 5

Developing the Training Design

● ●

In This Chapter

▶ Creating a supportive learning environment

▶ Designing materials to ensure that learning occurs

▶ Examining the pros and cons of presenting information

▶ Identifying a variety of activities

▶ Considering the purpose for using visuals

▶ Wrapping up an effective training session

● ●

*T*raining is serious business. Or is it?

Educators know that children learn from play. Adults do, too. This chapter addresses the design and development of training. While the design and development of a training program is a lot of work, you should remember throughout to ensure that the design creates training that is learner-focused. That is, the participant learns all the KSAs (knowledge, skills, attitudes — remember?) while enjoying the process along the way.

This chapter discusses the third stage of The Training Cycle, design and development (see Figure 5-1). The training you design and develop is built on a foundation formed by two important aspects: adult learning principles and the learning objectives.

> ✔ The adult learning principles, developed by Malcolm Knowles and dis-
> cussed in Chapter 2, are the basic characteristics that distinguish adult
> learning from how children learn.
>
> ✔ The learning objectives, created as a result of the needs assessment and
> analysis are discussed in Chapter 4; what the participant knows or does
> as a result of the training.

You may discover that some training designers create a distinct split between the "design" and the "development" of a training program. The distinctions for these folks focus on a couple of things.

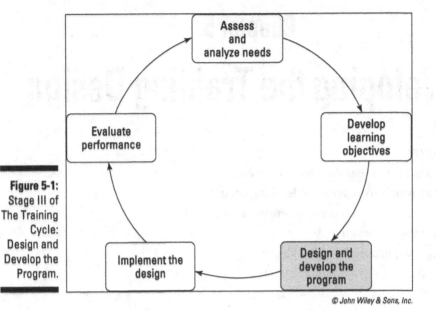

© John Wiley & Sons, Inc.

✔ Design focuses on preparing the designer for selecting and writing the materials. Actions include writing objectives, deciding on the sequence of content, identifying documentation, and planning the evaluation.

✔ Development focuses on selecting and creating the materials. Actions include selecting and writing materials for the participants' and the trainer's use, documentation, and the evaluation of materials.

Do you see the similarities and the small difference? Other than writing the objectives, the design stage provides direction for what to do in the development stage. At any rate, this model combines the two.

In this chapter, I divide the design of training into three segments: what you need to accomplish at the beginning of the training, what you need to accomplish in the middle of the training, and what you need to accomplish at the end of the training. Beginning, middle, end. That makes sense.

✔ **Beginning:** An opening that establishes a climate conducive to learning.

✔ **Middle:** A body that ensures learning occurs.

✔ **End:** A conclusion that provides a sense of closure to the training and anticipation for applying what was learned after the training experience.

Are you ready to begin the design and development process? Remember to have some fun along the way.

Instructional Design is one of the Areas of Expertise identified in the Association of Talent Development (ATD) Competency Model updated in 2014. It is one of the areas that trainers may name as an area of emphasis in their certification.

How Do I Begin?

Your training design starts with the end first: the expected improved change or performance of each participant. The learning objectives act as your guide to the design. List the objectives in the order in which you will teach them. You want to break some of the objectives down to the more specific skills and knowledge each person will acquire to improve their performance. Can you see an outline taking shape? That's exactly what you need to begin the design process! Consider the following abbreviated outline of the topics used for a train-the-trainer session.

I. Opening and Introduction

II. Overview of The Training Cycle

    A. Define training and trainers' roles

    B. Training cycle five stages

III. Stage I: Needs assessment and analysis

    A. Conducting needs assessments

    B. Data collection methods

    C. Analyzing the data

IV. Stage II: Learning objectives

    A. Types of objectives

    B. Writing effective objectives

V. Stage III: Design and Development

    A. Adult learning theory

    B. Sequence and structure

    C. Learning methods and activities

    4. Utilizing technology

VI. Stage IV: Facilitate the Design

    A. Trainer preparation

    B. Difference between presenting and facilitating

C. Group dynamics

D. Technology delivery skills

E. Conducting activities

VII. Stage V: Evaluation

A. Kirkpatrick's four levels of evaluation

B. Ensuring transfer of learning

C. Designing evaluation instruments

D. Using the data

VIII. Training session follow-up

IX. Closing and wrap-up activities

How do you turn an outline into a training session? Entire books are written on the subject of designing a training program. Some designers want you to use a specific model, identify confirming and corrective feedback, identify the rationale, create task listings, list the resources (a.k.a. *markers*), determine a task criticality rating, develop a process map, identify evaluation criteria, identify units, create an information map, compare to an organizational scheme, on and on. I don't know about you, but I can't keep that many concepts in my head all at once.

What I *can* do is organize the content in a logical flow and figure out the best way to assist the participants to acquire the skill or knowledge required to achieve the desired performance. And that's what you need to focus on for now. If you want to go into more depth, I suggest you contact your local chapter of ATD to recommend a design course.

Online or classroom

Oh, and one more thing. Before you continue too far with the design process, you need to find out how the training will be delivered. Someone else will most likely make that decision. The choices include Instructor-Led Training (you will see this referred to as ILT) in a virtual or traditional classroom, on-the-job training (OJT), self-paced, or technology-based training. ATD's 2014 *State of the Industry* report announced little change in the past ten years. ILT continues to be the most often used learning method at about 70 percent. Of that, 55 percent is in face-to-face classrooms, 9 percent is in virtual class-rooms, and 5 percent is led remotely (trainer in one place and the partici-pants in another). Asynchronous and self-paced training are growing slightly each year. Blended learning is a combination of two or more delivery meth-ods. What are the advantages of online learning?

- ✔ Reduces travel and travel costs
- ✔ Enables training anytime and any place
- ✔ Asynchronous enhances the ability for just-in-time training
- ✔ Enables developing a global workforce
- ✔ May be more time responsive

What are the disadvantages of online learning?

- ✔ Requires learners to adapt to new technology and learning methods
- ✔ Requires more time and resources to develop
- ✔ May not be suitable for all content

Blended learning

Blended learning is a solution to the either/or dilemma. Blended learning is particularly effective when the best of both worlds is used — that is, the best features of online and the best of a face-to-face classroom. It is a "blend" of many activities to achieve a learning outcome. For example, it could begin with a traditional classroom, followed by asynchronous online work and self-study, and a 90-minute virtual classroom and self-assessment to wrap up. Mentoring or peer support could provide additional support.

Both participants and the organization benefit. Less time may be spent attending classes when content can be learned by reading or self-study. This can be completed at the learner's pace and at a convenient time. Time in the face-to-face classroom is spent in building relationships that enhance peer feedback and also provides an opportunity for skill practice.

Flipped classroom

Flipped classrooms were first popularized by Khan Academy. Participants study and explore concepts, data, and information through reading, watching videos, or viewing a lesson online prior to attending the face-to-face classroom. Time in the classroom is spent on role plays, practice activities, case studies, and exercises related to using the skills in the real world. The facilitator does less presenting of new concepts and spends more time coaching the participants.

Jane Bozarth reminds us that when we separate "'traditional' and 'virtual' classrooms, we suggest that they are entirely different undertakings. We need to remember that many activities used in traditional face-to-face training translate very easily to other environments." She suggests that if you are mostly engaged in live-classroom work, you start paying attention to the times you conduct activities that are social and collaborative. Consider which activities can easily be translated to a virtual classroom or social learning.

Let's design

Most of the rest of this book focuses on the ILT delivery method. Because over half of all training is held in a face-to-face traditional classroom, this book focuses on that design and delivery method. However, you will use the same fundamentals to design virtual ILT.

You have been asked to develop a training program. What's next? These are the steps I use to design and develop a learning experience. I think you will find them easy to follow.

Before you dive in to design and develop the training program, obtain a clear definition of the limitations. Many a training session has been headed in a direction only to learn that resources are not available in the form of time, money, or people. Clarify the limitations first.

1. **List all the learning objectives for the session. This is the basis for the content.**

2. **If you need to break the objectives down to smaller, more manageable units, do so now.**

3. **Arrange the learning objectives into a logical learning sequence. The sequences that are most often used include these:**

    • Chronological

    • Procedural order

    • Problem/solution

    • Categories

    • General to specific

    • Simple to complex

    • Less risky to more risky

    • Known to unknown

4. **Determine content ensuring that you have enough, but not too much. What do your learners need to know? Need to do? What specific knowledge and skills will help them achieve the learning objectives?**

5. **Identify the best methodology — for example, role play, discussion, practice — to use to transmit the content to the learner.**

6. **Develop or purchase the support material you need to go along with what will happen during the learning experience. This includes some or all of these.**

    • Participant materials, for example, manual, handouts, job aids, texts

- Visual and media support, for example, PowerPoint slides, videos, software

- Activity support, for example, role-play cards, scripts, exercises, props, case studies

- Trainer materials, for example, trainers' guide, markers

- Administrative support, for example, agenda, roster, supply checklist, evaluations

7. Conduct a pilot to determine what needs to be changed or improved to achieve success.

If you need to play with the sequence of the learning objectives, you can do it on your laptop of course. Another possibility is to write each objective on a separate index card. Lay the cards on a table and move them around until you achieve what you're looking for.

The rest of this chapter is devoted to how you fill in the gaps of the design outline you have created. It is divided into the three different parts of the session: the beginning, middle, and the end. (How's that for a logical sequence?)

This chapter also discusses some of the methodologies you may use: lecturettes and over 50 types of activities. It provides you with tips for designing media and visual materials.

Designing a Dynamic Opening

The first five to ten minutes of your training design may be the most important of the entire session. A successful opening should accomplish several things:

- Establish a participative climate
- Introduce participants and foster relationships
- Introduce the agenda
- Clarify the participants' expectations
- List objectives of the training
- Build interest, curiosity, and excitement
- Learn something about the participants
- Determine some minimum rules of engagement and ground rules
- Establish your credibility

All about icebreakers

Have you ever attended a training session when someone droned on for the first 15 minutes about the procedure for completing the sign-in sheet, where the bathrooms are located, how to get to the cafeteria, how to get your parking pass stamped, and on and on? Really got you excited about the training session, I'll bet!

I like to start my sessions with something that surprises or shocks the participants. For example, after being introduced, I have started by walking in with a large shopping bag full of T-shirts and saying, "They say you can't tell a book by its cover. But I believe you can tell a person by her T-shirt!" I proceed to pull T-shirts out of the bag and read the funny sayings to the group. I hand them a bright sheet of paper (several different colors are used) with the outline of a T-shirt and ask them to use the crayons on the table to draw a picture or write a slogan on the T-shirt that represents their motto or what they stand for.

When participants have all finished designing their T-shirts — and it may take some prodding — I ask them to get up and find all the other participants whose paper is the same color as theirs, to introduce themselves to each other, and to explain their T-shirts (about 5 minutes). I ask them to sit down and have each person introduce themselves and their T-shirts to the rest of the group. At the end I have them all hang their T-shirts on the wall.

You discover in the "Selecting activities" section in this chapter how I use the T-shirt theme throughout the session. But for now, what have I done?

- ✔ Grabbed their attention
- ✔ Established a participative climate, instant involvement
- ✔ Set the pace — fast
- ✔ Put people at ease (including the trainer)
- ✔ Initiated personal interaction and individual introductions
- ✔ Heard everyone's names
- ✔ Had everyone speak once in the large group
- ✔ Started to define the group's personality (trainer observation)
- ✔ Started to identify the individual personalities
- ✔ Everyone learned something about each other (shortens the path to find other participants with similar interests)
- ✔ Established a transition to the content

What!?! The content? Yes. I use this icebreaker for the train-the-trainer course that I teach, and after the final introduction, the class begins to process the icebreaker itself. And this is where I slip in a reference about my credibility: "As a trainer for the last 30 years I. . ." or "As the training director for. . ." or "As I discuss in my last book. . . ."

By the way, you should accomplish every one of these with your opening in a virtual classroom, too. If your virtual group will meet multiple times — as is often the case — the time you invest upfront during your icebreaker will pay dividends over and over.

As I write this I am staring at a quote written by someone who published an article in a training journal: "Icebreakers have nothing to do with course content, but they're essential if you want people to work together." Right on the last part, but absolutely *wrong, wrong, wrong* on the first part. With a little planning you should be able to design an icebreaker that introduces the content. See the "Design content-related icebreakers" sidebar for further information.

Design content-related icebreakers

Icebreakers should have something to do with the content. These four ideas show you just how easy it can be. And yes, heeding Jane Bozarth's advice from earlier in this chapter, with very little adjusting every one of these ideas can be used in a virtual classroom. For example, in the last bullet you could post pictures of the same items.

- ✔ When participants introduce themselves, ask them to state their names, which department (or company) they are from, and to add one piece of information that relates to the session content. For example, if the topic is problem-solving skills, ask them to identify one example of how they hope to use the skills they are about to learn.

- ✔ Ask participants to get into small groups (three to four people), to introduce themselves to each other, and as a group to decide on the biggest challenge they have that relates to the session content.

For example, if you're teaching listening skills to front desk hotel personnel, you may ask them to decide the biggest challenge they face where listening skills may be useful.

- ✔ In any training session you can ask them to identify their expectation for the class.

- ✔ You can always bring in a box of "things" (dollar stores are great places to find "things") and have them select one "thing" and relate it to the content. For example, if you're training team-building skills, you can provide a box of tools (tape measure, hammer, ice scraper, measuring cup, pancake turner, wire whip, level, scissors, stapler, calculator). Pass the box around and ask each person to select a tool. When they introduce themselves they are to complete the statement "As a team player I am like a _____ because," filling in the blank with the tool they selected.

If a group is composed of people who know each other well, an icebreaker may not be necessary for getting acquainted; there are other opening activities you may need to conduct. The first five to ten minutes is a very important time for your session. A well-designed opening and icebreaker establish a climate that is conducive to learning.

What else will your participants expect in your design?

Your participants will expect you to design several orientation tasks to get the session started. If I am facilitating a session that lasts at least one full day, I generally allow about an hour for the opening activities. I find that investing time up front prevents other problems from happening later on. Okay, so how do I plan for that time?

- ✔ **Icebreaker:** 15 minutes

- ✔ **Introductions:** 20 minutes (1 minute per person)

- ✔ **Review agenda:** 2 minutes

- ✔ **Mini needs assessment:** 3 minutes

- ✔ **Introduce learning objectives:** 10 minutes

- ✔ **Clarify their expectations:** 10 minutes

- ✔ **Establish ground rules:** 7 minutes

- ✔ **Housekeeping information:** 1 minute

Remember these are estimates. Sometimes, the icebreaker takes longer or participants get wordy with their introductions. Build some slippage in the rest of the morning. Believe me this opening time is worth it. Of course, if this is a 90-minute virtual ILT, you will adjust it and you can shave time off of each of these steps. Notice I said, "shave time" off of each, not "eliminate." For example, you can save time in your virtual classroom by sending the agenda, objectives, and ground rules prior to your session. At the same time you could do a mini needs assessment. You could also use a quick poll to learn about your participants. You could ask participants to introduce themselves by posting their pictures or a video introduction to the group's website discussion board or other location before the session.

If you examine this list of opening activities, what must be developed?

- ✔ You need to design the icebreaker, and if you need a handout (see information about Bingo in Chapter 24), you need to develop it.

✔ You most likely want table tents (cardstock folded in half lengthwise) on which participants write their names; use markers with a broad tip so that participants' names can be seen from all places around the room.

✔ You want an agenda either printed on paper or accessible on their tablets.

 I do not put specific times on the agenda. Participants get nervous if they see that you're behind by 30 minutes. They don't understand that you may be currently covering something that was planned for later or that you know that what they are addressing now is much more important than something later and that you can decrease time on another activity.

 I print my personal agenda on brightly colored paper with time required for each activity. I use bright paper so that I can see it if it gets lost under hand-outs tossed about in your space. I need to have those times so that I keep the class on track. I like to allow flexibility to meet participants' needs, but I also need to take full responsibility for achieving the learning objectives.

✔ You need to know what information you need for the mini needs assessment. In the case of the train-the-trainer, I wanted to know how long they had been trainers, whether they had ever attended a train-the-trainer, whether they had designed training, and finally whether they thought that training was their destined profession.

✔ You may want to post the learning objectives and hang them on the wall after you discuss them, keeping them visible.

✔ You need a way to annotate participants' expectations and the ground rules — perhaps compiled on a slide or flipchart pages. I do not dictate ground rules. The groups establish their own. I find that they buy in and follow them better that way.

Finally, be creative. Think about ways that you could use Instagram, Twitter, or other social media tools for introductions. That wraps up the design for the opening.

Designing the Body to Ensure Learning Occurs

You have designed an opening for the training session that meets the requirements to establish a climate that is conducive to learning. Now get started on the middle, which is the bulk of the training. It requires that you design factors into the session that ensure that learning occurs. The purpose of the body is to ensure that your participants

- Accomplish the stated objectives.
- Learn all the concepts presented.
- Practice the skills.
- Acquire feedback.
- Understand the application to the job or beyond the training experience.

Lectures

You know how important it is for learners to be actively involved in the training. Yet there may be times when you need to deliver new information; a lecture may be unavoidable. In that case, you need to present the information. Even so, I never use the word "lecture." I use a made-up word, *lecturette,* for these special times. It gives the illusion of being less tedious and a bit more playful! And that's exactly what I am recommending you do with your lecturettes. Make them playful and learner-centered.

Problems with a lecture

"So what's so bad about a lecture?" you may ask. You've probably heard hundreds of lectures in school, and you survived that. It's not that a lecture is bad, but there are better ways. First, consider some of the problems with a lecture.

- It doesn't involve the participants.
- Ignores participants' experience.
- It rarely stimulates excitement and involvement.
- The trainer, due to minimal feedback, has no way of knowing whether participants understand the concepts.
- It is one-way communication, often resulting in passive learners who do not have an opportunity to clarify material.
- People may leave with incorrect information.
- It may be physically uncomfortable.
- Can be dull and boring.
- It is impossible to hold individuals' attention for long periods of time.
- Success is dependent upon speaking ability.
- It doesn't account for various learning styles.

✔ It creates a poor transfer of learning.

✔ It is difficult to reinforce an audience.

Can you think of other problems with lecturing?

Some appropriate times for a lecture

On the other hand, there may be times when it is best for you to lecture. Perhaps you have been in situations like these:

✔ A short presentation of less than ten minutes followed by another activity can be appropriate for introducing key conceptual ideas.

✔ When used in conjunction with a variety of activities, a lecture can be a refreshing way for participants to just listen while they learn.

✔ If you need to disseminate a large amount of information in a short period of time, a lecture may be appropriate. However, it should be accompanied by a job aid or some other materials for future reference.

✔ A lecture may be appropriate if you need to maintain control of the group and reduce verbal resistance.

✔ A lecture is appropriate when specific information must be disseminated that affects ethics, legal aspects, safety, and so on.

✔ A well-prepared, humorous lecture may stimulate a group.

✔ Guest speakers, who are known for their expertise in a given content area, may be admired for their lecture. This can backfire, however, if the speaker loses the group.

✔ You may use a lecture when a group is so large that participative methods would be chaotic.

Are there other times when lecture may be appropriate?

If you must use a lecturette, make it participative

How in the world can you design a participative lecturette? Try these suggestions. Most are practical and easy to design in to any presentation.

✔ Design pop quizzes in the middle.

✔ Plan to ask questions regarding predictions or recall of information.

✔ Create a conversation between trainer and participants.

✔ Intersperse tasks or demonstrations.

✔ Develop a guided note-taking page in the form of questions or fill in the blanks.

✔ Develop handouts with a key-word outline of the presentation with room to write.

✔ Design visuals to go with the presentation so that participants can follow your words visually.

✔ Stop midstream at various points to ask whether everyone is with you.

✔ Design a partial story at the beginning and complete the story after the end of the lecturette.

✔ Find ways to interject humor, such as creating a cartoon to match the content you present.

Present content if you must, but build in participation.

Countless alternatives to lecture

There are hundreds of alternative methods you can use to replace a presentation. Recognize that many of these methods usually take longer than a lecturette, but a well-constructed activity enhances learning because the participant experiences the learning by being personally involved. For example, in the classic NASA "Lost on the Moon" exercise participants experience the power and value of group decision making.

Why would you use an activity anyway?

✔ **Activities are energizing.** Use games in your design to give people a break, time to stretch (their brains, as well as their bodies), to relieve stress, and to just get energized.

✔ **Activities get people working together.** Build rapport among participants to increase the amount of knowledge floating around the room. More learning occurs when everyone is sharing and learning from each other. As the trainer/facilitator you have a body of knowledge, but the compiled knowledge of your group far outweighs what you know.

✔ **Activities promote learning by doing.** Your participants retain the knowledge better if you can engage as many of their senses as possible.

✔ **Activities provide you with a way to reinforce information.** It would be pretty boring if you stated the same things over and over in the same way, even though you know that repetition is good. Activities allow participants to experience the same information in another way.

✔ **Activities are motivational.** Learners respond because they are actively involved. It is a pleasant way to learn.

Thousands of activities, games, and exercises exist. Or you can create your own. One of the best resources for games is *The Games Trainers Play* series by Ed Scannell and John Newstrom (published by McGraw-Hill). If you are looking for activities for your virtual ILT, start with these authors: Michael Allen, Jane Bozarth, John Chen, Darlene Christopher, Cynthia Clay, Margaret Driscoll, Jennifer Hofmann, Cindy Huggett, Karl Kapp, Becky Pluth, Kella Price, Clark Quinn, Patti Shank, and others.

Presentation variations

Presentations refer to any method that gives information to the participants with less interaction than many of the other methods.

- ✔ **Panel:** Participants, managers, customers, or top executives, provide a unique opportunity for an intimate discussion or a Q&A session.

- ✔ **Tour:** Visit someplace in the organization where a host guides you through the information you need to know, for example, the corporate library, to demonstrate how to retrieve information.

- ✔ **Guided note taking:** Create handouts that have spaces available to add information during a lecturette, watching a role play, or viewing a video.

- ✔ **Storytelling:** Telling an event (true or fictitious) that has a moral or lesson, or demonstrates consequences. The punch line leaves the listener inspired, influenced, or improved, without explaining the learning point.

- ✔ **Debate:** Two teams address two different sides of an issue to explore perspectives from both sides.

Experiential learning activities

Experiential Learning Activities (ELAs), sometimes called *structured experiences,* are in a category of their own. ELAs are activities that are specifically designed for inductive learning through the five-stage cycle associated with them: experiencing, publishing, processing, generalizing, and applying. Details for ELAs can be found in Chapter 8. ELAs are especially useful in a change-management situation, or when attitudes are an issue.

Demonstrations

Demonstrations typically involve someone showing the participants a process or modeling a procedure.

- ✔ **Instructor role play:** Role play by two instructors to demonstrate a technique or make a point, followed with discussion.

- ✔ **Field trips:** Visit the location where the action takes place. If you're teaching customer service, visit your call center and listen in on a few live calls to discuss technique.

- ✔ **Video, DVD:** Use clips from training or commercial videos or sites such as YouTube as a basis to identify issues, solve problems, or consider examples to use as application options. Be sure to follow copyright laws.

- ✔ **Magic tricks:** Use magic tricks to help you make an analogous point within the training session.

- ✔ **Coaching:** Sometimes conducted outside a training event, it could be used as participants practice a particularly difficult skill. Participants coach each other in pairs during role plays or other skill practice.

- ✔ **Interviews:** Participants ask questions of a resource person who attends the training session at a designated time. Purpose is to obtain another perspective, hear from the expert, or add knowledge.

- ✔ **Props:** Oh my gosh! So many possibilities! Bring tools: "As a team player I am most like a _____." Bring chunks of two by fours for participants to write the skills they have acquired and "build" the final structure. Bring packets of seeds and use as a metaphor for the "seeds of communication." Well, you get the idea.

Reading

Reading refers to any method pertaining to interacting with the printed word.

- ✔ **Read ahead:** Materials provided to participants to read prior to the session.

- ✔ **Letters to each other:** Participants write letters to each other to provide feedback or as a summary of what each has learned in the session, or as follow-up after the session.

- ✔ **Story starters:** Participants are given a partial situation and complete it practicing the skills and knowledge they are learning in the session.

Drama

Drama refers to methods that require the participants or the facilitator to act out a role.

- ✔ **Skits:** A short presentation by small groups to demonstrate skill or knowledge learned.

- ✔ **Survival problem solving:** Usually used as a team-building activity in which a team is placed in a role that represents danger. The team works together to make decisions and uncover their strengths and weaknesses.

- ✔ **Costumes:** Can be used by the trainer to make a point or play a role. Partial costumes, hats for example, could be analogies for the different roles (hats they wear) people play on the job.

- ✔ **Writing a script:** Participants can script a role play for other participants based on the content.

Discussions

Discussion methods refer to two-way discussions that occur between participants and/or the facilitator.

✔ **Buzz groups:** Two people "buzz" for one to two minutes about a topic before sharing their ideas with the larger group.

✔ **Round robin:** Trainer gets opinions from everyone in the session. Discussion or rebuttal is held until everyone's ideas have been stated.

✔ **Brainstorming:** A process for generating a large number of ideas without judgment.

✔ **Nominal group technique:** A problem-solving tool where ideas are initially generated in silence, then weighted, and prioritized.

✔ **Fishbowl:** Group is divided with half the participants sitting in a circle (the fishbowl) discussing a topic. The other half of the group sits around the perimeter and can coach during the discussion, can silently motion to replace someone, or can offer feedback at the end. Several variations.

✔ **Develop a theory:** Participants make up a theory related to the knowledge or skills they are learning.

Cases

Cases generally refer to learning methods in which the participants are presented with scenarios requiring analysis and suggestions for improvement.

✔ **Case studies:** A real or fictional situation is presented to the participants to analyze and recommend solutions. If an actual situation was presented, the facilitator usually shares the actual outcome.

✔ **In-baskets:** Items are given to participants that replicate problems, messages, and tasks that could actually show up in someone's inbox. Participants must make decisions, manage their time, and establish priorities as they address the items.

✔ **Critical incidents:** A short version of a case study, which focuses on the most vital aspects of a problem situation.

✔ **Sequential case studies:** Participants are given a portion of a case study. Depending on the decision they make on the first portion, a second, third and perhaps even a fourth set of data are distributed. All groups may end up in different places.

✔ **Problem-solving clinic:** Participants bring real-world problems for the rest of the group to solve.

Art

Art entails more creative methods involving drawing, design, sculpting, or other nonword events.

- ✓ **Portraits:** Participants create portraits of themselves being successful at learning the content of the session or as an opening activity to introduce themselves to the group.

- ✓ **Cartoons:** Can be used as energizers or to reinforce knowledge or skills that are being taught. Be sure to abide by copyright laws.

- ✓ **Posters:** Participants create posters to make a point, summarize information, and so on.

- ✓ **Draw how you feel about _____:** Exactly what it says, draw how you feel about whatever the topic is. Can be reworded such as draw a logo that represents teamwork.

Playlikes

Playlikes are learning methods that are similar to dramatizations but less serious and more open ended.

- ✓ **Role plays:** Participants act out roles, attitudes, or behaviors that are not their own to practice skills or apply what they have learned. Frequently an observer provides feedback to those in character.

- ✓ **Role reversals:** Participants assume the role of the person with whom they interact daily, for example, their bosses.

- ✓ **Video feedback:** Participants are recorded during a role play or presentation. They view their own tapes and complete a self-critique.

- ✓ **Outdoor adventure learning:** Sometimes called *ropes courses;* used for problem solving and team building.

- ✓ **Improv:** Short for *improvisation*, actors create a skit without a script. Input and ideas are gleaned from the audience.

- ✓ **Simulations:** A training environment that closely represents the real environment to allow participants to practice skills.

Games

Games refer to any board, card, television, computer, or physical event that leads to learning or review of material. A game requires a challenge, rules, and feedback resulting in a measurable outcome.

- ✓ **Crossword puzzles:** Computer software can take a list of terms from the session and arrange clues and words into a crossword puzzle.

- **Relays:** Teams set up in a relay to compete to be the first to complete a set of instructions. Good for review of concepts to test skill acquisition.

- **Card games:** As many variations as there are cards! Various pieces of data can be placed on cards to solve a problem.

- **Computer games:** Good for reinforcing skills back at the workplace after the session.

- **Any board-game adaptation:** Many board games such as Trivial Pursuit can be adapted to the content of the training.

- **Any game-show adaptation:** Game shows such as *Jeopardy!* can be adapted to the content of the training.

Participant directed

The method refers to situations where participants take the leadership role in the delivery of training to others, or the analysis of their own learning.

- **Social learning:** Though it is usually considered informal and unconscious, it can be designed into a training event using social media tools: wikis, blogs, Instagram, Facebook, Twitter, LinkedIn, and others.

- **Skill centers:** Several areas are set up around the training room to practice skills or test knowledge. Participants move from one area to another selecting the ones most appropriate for them to master.

- **Teaching teams:** Participant pairs select a topic from the agenda and teach the rest of the group.

- **Digital storytelling:** Participants create a 1–2 minute video to capture examples or viewpoints related to the topic. Effective for virtual and traditional classrooms.

- **Self analysis:** Usually a series of questions with correct answers to review knowledge. May also be a set of thought-provoking concepts or questions that allow participants to examine their personal attitudes.

- **Teach backs:** Participants are given a small portion of content which they study and "teach back" to the rest of the participants. This can be conducted in small groups or the larger group.

- **Journaling:** Participants keep a written record of thoughts, feelings, reactions, successes, plans, and action items.

- **Research:** Challenge given in the classroom for participants to track down the correct answer between sessions. Can be used to locate information during the session on the Internet.

Participant events

Participant events refers to learning methods that have a specific placement in a training session.

- ✔ **Icebreakers:** A structured activity usually used at the beginning of a training session to initiate participation and introductions.
- ✔ **Energizers:** A brief activity, exercise, or brain teaser offered to "energize" the group.
- ✔ **Closers:** Group activity used at the end to bring closure to the session, make commitments, review key points, plan application actions, and celebrate success.

As you peruse this list, you can see that with some adaptation almost all of these activities can also be used in your virtual ILT. Right? Some, such as videos and reading, can be used as preliminary work. Journaling, in-baskets, coaching, and self-analysis can be used as follow-up reinforcement. Most of the rest can, with slight adaptation, be used during the virtual classroom. Think Skype for a tour or prepping a couple of learners to complete a role play or a teach back.

Engaging participants every three to five minutes in a virtual ILT session seems to be the expectation.

Hey! What about gamification? Gamification uses game-based elements to motivate or engage people or promote learning. The "games" in our list may be the basis for that to occur. Gamification utilizes gaming elements to ensure a change in behavior and the transfer of learning to the workplace.

Looking for more information about gamification? One of Karl Kapp's books such as *The Gamification of Learning and Instruction* (Pfeiffer, 2012) is just what you need.

Selecting activities

Okay, you're exhausted just looking at a few of the activity possibilities. How do you know which activities to select? Use two criteria. First think about the learning objective. In which learning category does it fit? Is it *knowledge, skill, or attitude?* Match the learning category to the activity. The examples discussed in this section show what I mean. Some of the activities can be used for more than one category of learning. Don't try to perfect this step. This just gets you started.

Next, consider other aspects of the activity. But first, examine the learning category examples.

Getting started with gamification

by Karl M. Kapp

The underlying principle of gamification is not to turn learning into a game. Rather it is to take the elements of games that are engaging, motivating, and challenging and weave those elements into the design of instruction. The focus is not on fun but engagement, activity, and immersion. To gamify instruction, you need to think like a game designer.

So my advice to someone who wants to gamify instruction is to play games. You cannot think about gamification or be comfortable implementing gamification techniques if you do not play games. And I don't just mean play the games — I mean play and analyze those games. Figure out why one game was deeply engaging while another turned out to be boring. Determine how the scoring system drove you toward mastery of the game (or away from it). Playing games with a critical eye is important to learning to incorporate gamification in learning.

Also, don't just play one genre of games. Play many genres. Don't just play first-person shooters; also play puzzle games or adventure games. Playing a variety of games will lead to a greater understanding of how you can apply game mechanics and game thinking to learning.

If the process of gamification were easy, everyone would do it. It's not easy to think like a game designer while creating instruction. Game design is action oriented. Instructional design, on the other hand, tends to be content oriented.

To think like a game-designer and to create gamified instruction, think about what you want the learner to *do*, not just what you want the learner to *know*. This seems like a little shift, but it is actually a large change in thinking about designing and delivering instruction. Read more about gamification in Karl's book *The Gamification of Learning and Instruction* (Pfeiffer, 2012).

Strategies for different learning needs

How do you know which type of activity to select? Remember the three categories of learning? Use them as a guide. There will still be some crossover, but it is a place to start.

Different types of learning require different strategies. Match the strategy (type of activity) to the learning objective. Here are a few examples for you.

Knowledge

If you want people to gain knowledge about something, furnish them with information through these activities:

- Articles
- Short presentations
- Diagrams

✔ Audiotapes

✔ Buzz group

Skills

If you want people to be able to do something and acquire a new skill, help them experiment by using these activities:

✔ Case studies

✔ Demonstrations

✔ Role playing

✔ Videos and practice

✔ Exercises

✔ Worksheets

Attitude

If you want people to change their values or priorities, assist them to inquire into and observe the old versus the new by using these:

✔ Instruments

✔ Role plays

✔ Debates

✔ Structured games

✔ Exercises

✔ Self-analysis

Considerations for selecting activities

What other questions should you ask when selecting activities?

✔ **What is the purpose?** Be sure that the design actually accomplishes what the learners need. If they need practice, don't provide a word-match game or a demonstration.

✔ **How well does the activity assist with accomplishing the learning objective?** Sometimes, a learning objective is broken down into smaller segments. Be sure that the time you invest in activities represents the most critical of objectives as well as covers the most of each.

✔ **How much time does the activity take? How much time to debrief?** If you don't know how much time, better try it out with a group prior to the session. Don't skimp on time if the knowledge or skill is important.

Also, don't try to save time by skipping the debrief. Participants leave an activity without a debrief wondering "What was that all about?" If you do not have time for the debrief, don't do the activity. Also consider how rigid the time restraints may be for the activity and know what you can do if you run short of time.

✔ **Is the time investment worth the amount of learning that will occur?** Concepts can be taught in many ways. Activities provide a hands-on opportunity for participants to master knowledge or skills that may be harder to master through discussion. Because activities take more time, it is important to be certain that the concepts are related to the most important learning objectives.

✔ **Is it fun — at least stimulating and interesting?** All activities don't need to be grins and giggles, but if they aren't at least interesting, learners will find something else to do — or think about. You know it's true with virtual ILT! Admit it. Your mind drifts during virtual events!

✔ **Do all the participants have the minimum skills to contribute and learn from the experience?** Or are skill levels uneven among participants? Speaks for itself. You may not know about everyone in the session; that's why you're constantly observing and learning about your group. If you suspect that someone will have difficulty, determine how you can offer support without being obvious. It may be in whom you pair the person with, what you assign the individual, or how you offer nonchalant sideline coaching. Sometimes, activities can be created in which those with higher skill level deliver the content.

✔ **How comfortable does the activity seem?** Your needs assessment should provide information about what is culturally acceptable in general. In addition, build up to riskier activities as the group is together longer. For example, role plays tend to be more acceptable later in the training sequence.

✔ **Is the activity appropriate for the size of the group?** Some activities that focus on creativity or mental imagery may seem threatening in small groups. On the other hand, some groups may be too large for certain activities or there may not be enough space to have small groups spread out to complete the activity. In a virtual classroom, ensure that there will be time to hear from all groups.

✔ **Does this activity maintain the tone and climate the participants need?** If you're trying to build teamwork, it may not be wise to interject an activity that tears apart what you've built. If you're encouraging participation, you may think twice about an activity that the quieter people may deem threatening.

✔ **Does the activity have enough real-world relevance for this group?** If not, you may wish to find another, or add the relevance that is missing.

✔ **How flexible is the activity?** Mold the activity so the participants are able to easily relate to the situation.

✔ **Will you be able to easily provide clear, succinct directions?** The easier the better. Remember you may have 20, 30, or more participants in your session. If the directions are complex and you still think the activity is worth it, plan for how you can ensure the directions are followed. For example, you could have the directions printed so groups can read them or you could dispense the directions in small doses.

✔ **Will the learning that occurs be straightforward?** If participants end the activity requiring much explanation, you will frustrate the learners. Better skip it.

✔ **What is the timing and the sequencing of the activity?** Avoid conducting two similar activities back to back. Think about the time of day, as well. Incorporate activity and movement immediately after lunch. Increase risk as you move through the day.

✔ **How may logistics affect the design?** If you need to travel, you may not want to lug lots of props. It may be difficult to conduct a relay if the room is not large enough. If two trainers are available you may be able to include demonstrations or role plays. Equipment availability also shapes the activities you select. If your participants haven't experienced virtual classrooms, placing them in a chat may take more time.

✔ **Will the experience and the debrief provide participants with the skill or knowledge they need to acquire from the activity?** Will you be able to easily relate it to the previous as well as the next training module? Finally, how will you evaluate the effectiveness of the activity you chose or designed?

It may seem like a lot of questions. If you're new to design, go through each one. Trust me when I say that eventually, this will become second nature to you. You will read a learning objective and immediately have an idea of what activity type will work best.

One last word about activities

Activities can be fun to design and to plan into your training. Remember that balance is the key. To be most successful with activities or games in your session you must be sure to do the following:

✔ **Have a purpose.** Don't plug a game into a training session just because you have a space. Design it in by linking it to a learning objective. Ensure that you include plenty of practice opportunities.

✔ **Know the activity.** During the design stage, try out any activities on a small group to see whether they accomplish the purpose for which you have selected the activity.

✔ **Think variety.** As you design the training program, include different types of activities. It is unlikely, for example, that you would use more than one case study in a day when you have so many different activities from which to choose and so many learners with different learning preferences. Satisfy visual preferences through color, charts, pictures, and video clips. Satisfy auditory preferences with debates, discussions, and stories. Satisfy kinesthetic preferences through role plays, games, and practice.

✔ **Create a consistent theme.** As you design a training program, think of a theme that you could use throughout, or an early event that you could return to, to create consistency. In the "All about icebreakers" section earlier in this chapter I shared my T-shirt icebreaker. I continue to use the T-shirts that participants created during the icebreaker throughout the training program. How did I do that?

The group was in the team-formation stage, so I used it as a team-building exercise. Throughout the three days, participants wrote on each other's T-shirts completing these statements:

- Something I learned about you today is. . . .
- One thing we could do together is. . . .
- Something I'd like to know about you is. . . .

Finally I used the T-shirts to bring closure to the session by having participants write on at least two other participants' shirts with a request to "stay in touch" and add their contact information.

Adding Zest with Visuals

I can't imagine facilitating a training session without visuals. They are so useful! Here's what's available:

✔ PowerPoint, Prezi, or other slide type visuals

✔ DVD players

✔ Interactive white boards, SMART Boards

✔ Flipcharts, posters, or graphics

✔ Blackboards, whiteboards, and felt boards

✔ Participants' own devices and laptops

✔ Props

Knowing why you need visuals

Why use visuals? The benefits far outweigh the problems they cause and the time it takes to create them. The first bullet is the most important one on the list.

- Participants grasp the information faster, understand it better, and retain it longer
- Clarifies a point (a picture is worth a thousand words)
- Adds variety
- Communicates message both visually and aurally (through your presentation)
- Emphasizes a point
- Makes you more persuasive
- Helps you be more concise
- Enhances a transition to change the focus
- Adds color
- Keeps you organized and on track (visuals cue you about content and what's next)

You're sold on using visuals. Now what do you need to know during this design stage?

Creating effective visuals

As you design the visuals that will support your training, ensure that you remember what makes them effective. Visuals are most effective when

- They are relevant to the subject (obvious, but I had to say it!)
- They are visible and understandable.
- Page orientation is consistent, using either landscape or portrait.
- Words are large enough to read.
- They are oriented to the listener: "Here are four ideas you will. . . ."
- Color is used appropriately.
- The typeface varies in boldness and size.
- The print is in both upper- and lower typeface.
- The typeface enhances the readability (usually a san serif font).

✔ Bullets set off each point.

✔ They enhance your performance rather than replace it.

✔ The visual becomes an extension of you and your message.

✔ They are tied together with a common theme — for example, a sketch, graphic, background color.

✔ They are customized for the group.

Designing slide presentations

Most trainers use PowerPoint as their visual design tool of choice. PowerPoint is an efficient tool, but when used incorrectly it loses its effectiveness. Prezi has gained some support since its cloud-base allows you to present from your browser, desktop, iPad, or iPhone.

✔ Keep the limited flexibility in mind because it is not easy to change the slide order or to add content while you present.

✔ Use a graphic theme and stay with it for the most part; try something other than the canned PowerPoint formats.

✔ Use a template that has a fresh look and one that uses a minimum percent of the screen.

Follow the 8 x 8 rule; this refers to the number of lines down and words across a visual; 6 x 6 is better for larger groups.

✔ When presenting a list, design it so you can reveal text one line at a time.

✔ To further emphasize the line item you wish to discuss, change the color of the newest item or have the previous items fade subtly.

✔ Headings should be 36 to 44 points (pt) and body 28 to 32 pt, but no less than 24 pt.

✔ Select one primary transition throughout the content for each module.

✔ Fade to black to signal a new module or if you want to pause for discussion or an activity. Practice using your "B" key while presenting.

✔ Use a subtle background.

✔ Ensure that there is enough contrast between typeface and background.

✔ Use clip art sparingly. Excellent stock photos are better. Check with your graphics department for availability.

✔ If you use animation, select one type and use throughout a module or content section.

✔ I don't recommend sound effects, but if you use them, keep them brief, and make sure they add impact.

Designing or selecting DVD or video clips

A video clip adds a surprise element to a training session. To be effective follow a few guidelines.

✔ Develop program objectives first and then select the best clip to meet your need.

✔ Be sure to consider asking participants to use their own devices, laptops, tablets, or phone to look up videos from sites such as YouTube.

✔ Show only the portion required to make the point; provide a brief explanation about what happens up to this point.

✔ Provide an introduction that includes the title and tells why you're showing the film.

✔ Preview before showing.

✔ Devise open-ended questions that clarify the objectives of the film and create discussion following it.

✔ Media should be proportionate in length to your session.

Designing flipcharts

Design flipcharts? You've got to be kidding! No, I'm not. Planning an effective flipchart page is just as important as a PowerPoint slide. I usually sketch out the design and words on paper so that when it comes time to actually put the words on the chart paper, I know what I want it to say.

✔ Plan the order of the charts and remember to include blank pages for participant ideas and brainstorming.

✔ Plan for clear and descriptive headings.

✔ Consider using a box, cloud, underline, or other graphic to set off the heading, especially if you may use more than one page for one topic.

✔ Identify the specific words you will use.

✔ Know whether you will want to leave space to add information during the session.

✔ Plan for letters that are 1 to 3 inches high, and ten or fewer lines per page.

✔ Plan sketches ahead.

If you have a model or drawing that you like, but you're not an artist, trace it. Create the flipchart ahead or take a copy to the training setup with you for tracing. If you use a model more than once and participants do not interact or write on the chart, you may wish to have it designed professionally as a poster.

✔ A design that includes bullets can help guide learners.

- Numbers suggest a process, sequence of events, or priority.

- Bullets suggest a list without priority.

- Boxes suggest something that may be checked off after it is complete; for example, learning objectives for the session.

✔ Design the colors of markers; for example, two different colors for every other idea on a list, dark colors for words and bright colors for highlighting.

Implement evidence-based training in your design

by Ruth Clark

Evidence-based training involves your consideration of current best evidence during the design, development, and deployment of learning environments. Although you will need to consider budgets, technology, and time constraints, incorporate evidence of what works to your list of decision factors. These prescriptions are based on experimental evidence accumulated over the past 15 years. More details can be read in my book *Evidence-Based Training Methods:* 2nd Edition (ATD Press, 2014).

Use relevant visuals to illustrate your content. This is especially critical for learners who are new to that content.

Keep visuals simple depending on your goal. If a simple line drawing can show the concept, don't add unnecessary details.

Explain complex visuals. Animations or detailed stills may need to be accompanied with a brief audio narration by you.

Illustrate tasks with step-by-step examples. Accompany each step with questions that force learners to carefully review the examples. Your examples may be high-structure examples such as mathematical problems, social-modeling examples such as a best-practice sales video, or cognitive modeling, illustrating problem-solving processes.

Space practice exercises. To ensure that skills are learned, they must be practiced. Schedule them within and among lessons.

Write your lessons using first- and second-person constructions. Evidence shows that a more personalized approach improves learning.

Avoid seductive stories or visuals. Evidence shows that stories or visuals that may be related to the topic but not related to the instructional goal distract from the point of the lesson

Design games in which moves and rewards align with learning goals. Add proven methods such as feedback to maximize the benefits of games and minimize extraneous content.

Designing handouts or participant books

Participant handouts should not be just a page full of words. You can ensure that handouts and other printed participant materials are effective if you consider these ideas:

- Know how the handout will function in terms of note taking, exercise, and as a future resource.
- Use heads and subheads in a variety of type sizes and degrees of boldness.
- Don't mix too many typefaces.
- Experts recommend that you use a serif typeface which makes the letters appear to flow from one to the next.
- Use graphics and sketches.
- Use bullets, dashes, borders, indentations, and margins for ease of reading.
- Number the pages.

Designing a Finale That Brings Closure

It's 4:25 and your session is scheduled to end. Do you just say "That's all folks. Goodbye!"?

Well, of course not. Although it is a small portion of the training session, it is an important one to ensure transfer of learning beyond the classroom Just how long is this part of the training? If it is a half-day session, you need at least 15 minutes. If it is a two-or-more-day session, plan on at least 30 minutes. If it is a 90-minute virtual session, allow 5 to 10 minutes. If you test participants before they leave, add time to complete the test. Remember these are just guidelines from my experience. You may have a unique situation.

The conclusion should provide a sense of closure for the learners. It should also create anticipation for applying what was learned. So what can you include in the design to bring about closure?

- Ensure that expectations were met.
- Provide a shared group experience.
- Evaluate the learning experience.
- Request feedback and improvement suggestions.
- Summarize the course accomplishments and gain commitment to action.
- Send them off with a final encouraging word — or two.

Ensuring that expectations are met

One of the easiest ways to do this is to design time into the agenda to go back to the participants' expectations they shared at the beginning of the session. Did you accomplish all that was expected?

Providing a shared group experience

You may wish to design a closer for your session. It may be used to state a commitment about next steps, review key points of the training, plan for the next actions, or identify how to apply what was learned. It may also be used to celebrate success.

If the group has bonded, you may also wish to do something that helps keep people in touch with each other if they work in different departments, at different locations, or even at different companies. A list of names and emails is an easy perk to supply.

I usually design a large group send-off experience. An old favorite goes like this. Have all the participants stand in a circle. Ask each to state what they are going to do as a result of the training within the next ten days. I like this for two reasons. First, each statement gives other participants ideas of other things they could implement. Second, this call to action helps participants bridge the distance back into the real world.

Evaluating the learning experience

You will want to develop an evaluation for the session. Remember that you may need to evaluate at a couple of different levels. Chances are that if you're new to designing training, someone else will assist you with the evaluation for the session. You will find additional information about evaluation in Chapter 13.

Requesting feedback and suggestions

You may also wish to design time into the agenda to obtain verbal feedback and suggestions from the participants about how to improve the session before you offer it again.

Yes, you may ask some of those questions on the paper evaluation that you design. On the other hand, the group discussion often provides more useful ideas because they can be clarified.

Accomplishments and commitment to action

I usually build this into the shared-group experience in some way to save time. You may wish to use a game, or if time is critical, you may wish to conduct a brief large-group discussion at the close of the session. Examine the expectations and the learning objectives to ensure they were all accomplished. Then ask for volunteers who could talk about how they intend to implement what they learned back on the job.

In the case of the train-the-trainer, presented throughout this chapter, participants wrote a memo to themselves regarding two performance improvements they intend to make. When most people were finished, I asked for volunteers to share one of their improvements with the rest of the group. They placed the memo inside an envelope and addressed it to themselves. I collected them, and one month later, mailed the memos to each trainer.

Jenn Labin suggests that a good closing activity is to have participants send a calendar appointment to their supervisors to meet and discuss outcomes of the session. This is a great way to ensure transfer of learning and to obtain the supervisor's support for new performance.

Sending them off with an encouraging word

One last thing I like to do is to put up a cartoon, a quote, or some inspiring thought that is both rewarding to the learners and pertinent to the next action they must take. In the case of the train-the-trainer session, I did two things. The first thing I did was to use a mind-teaser.

✔ They were concerned about how they would remember all that they had learned. I have a slide that I put up in cases like this. The slide can be interpreted two ways — with exactly the opposite meanings. Therefore, I ask people to read it out loud as soon as they see it. The slide says: "OPPORTUNITYISNOWHERE"

   • Some read this as "opportunity is nowhere."

   • Others read it as "opportunity is now here."

✔ I explain that just as the letters are the same and can be interpreted two different ways, they are leaving the session with an experience that can be interpreted by them in two ways. They have an opportunity to believe they will be successful, or to believe they will not be successful. And no matter what they believe, they will be right. It is really about attitude. The right attitude goes a long way with skills that are maturing.

The second send-off was that I asked them to take their T-shirts with them. I encouraged them to take them home and hang them on their refrigerators. This is a super activity, especially if they have children. Mommy and Daddy are bringing home their school work! It opens discussions at home about what happened in the training. The T-shirt motto is an interesting discussion point, but it is the comments that colleagues wrote on the shirt that is even more interesting to families.

Lastly, stand at the door, shake participant's hands, wish them luck, and say goodbye.

Be sure to design enough time into the plan to include a proper send-off. Nothing is more discouraging than to have the training session fall apart during the last hour because it is behind schedule or that the design is not as tight as the rest of the session.

The schedule for the last half hour of the train-the-trainer looked like this:

- ✔ **Reviewed expectations on wall chart:** 5 minutes
- ✔ **Self memo (two performance improvements I will make):** 10 minutes
- ✔ **Volunteers shared with larger group:** 5 minutes
- ✔ **Evaluated the learning experience:** 10 minutes
- ✔ **OPPORTUNITYISNOWHERE:** 2 minutes
- ✔ **T-shirts and goodbye:** 3 minutes

Selecting Off-the-Shelf Materials

You may decide to purchase off-the-shelf materials instead of designing them yourself. However, you most likely still want to customize them for your organization. In that case, ideas throughout this chapter can help you with that task.

Will off-the-shelf meet your needs?

At first glance, purchasing materials that have already been designed and that are packaged, tested, and ready to implement may appear to be a perfect solution. Here are some possibilities for pre-packaged training:

- ▌ Presenters and speakers from consulting firms, speakers' bureaus, and universities.

✔ Asynchronous content or videos on almost any training topic.

✔ Your company's corporate Learning Management System (LMS) and its learning vendor are ready resources.

✔ Public seminars offered regularly by training and consulting firms; some are on a regular travel schedule presenting in most large cities.

✔ There is an explosion of MOOCs (Massive Open Online Courses) offered by universities and other providers.

✔ Packaged training programs include the participants' materials, a trainer's guide, media and visual support, computer support and programs, and even the job aids, the "cheat sheets" that participants take back to the workplace to remind them of what they learned.

✔ Customized training packages designed by training and consulting firms but created to your specifications; most start with a needs assessment.

Adapting the design

Buying a training program isn't always as easy as it sounds. To ensure that the design achieves what it needs to, you will most likely need to adapt the design to your organization:

✔ Circulate the off-the-shelf program to key managers and participants. Ask for their suggestions to make it a perfect match for your organization.

✔ Review the program well in advance of the training. Make notes in the margins using company examples, anecdotes, policies, and so on that bring the topic home.

✔ Weave your organization's core themes and philosophies into every part of the program. The skills and behaviors taught may be generic, but the way your organization applies them is not.

✔ If a technical process or procedure is being taught, add or delete steps to be consistent with the way the process is performed in your organization.

✔ If a behavioral skill is being taught, add comments that reflect your organization's management beliefs and philosophy regarding the behavior.

✔ If you've chosen a MOOC or other predetermined course, you can create introductory and follow-up materials so that the learners' managers can discuss the differences with them.

So, make or buy? That's the question. If you've decided to buy an off-the-shelf program, find out as much as you can about the package and the company before you buy. What exactly are you buying? What do others say about the product? What kind of support will you receive? How consistent is the content with your needs and your organization's culture? How much will it cost?

Pulling It All Together

At some point you need to capture your design on paper. Most designers use a simple matrix to organize their scheme. Later, a trainer's manual may be written with much more detail. But for now, something simple will serve you well. The design guide that I use has four columns like the one you see in Table 5-1. Think of the design guide as a blueprint if you were building a house. Use it to capture your plans. You see that it has just enough information so that you can capture the flow of content from a big-picture perspective. You identify the knowledge or skill and the activity or method you intend to use. List also the support materials (participant handout, media or visual, prop) required and how long it will take. If you're like most trainers, you have too much in your initial design. You may have 7 hours of available face-to-face time with your learners, and your design is twelve hours long. Trust me, that's normal.

Table 5-1   **Design Guide**

Module _____ Time _____

Objectives:

*

*

*

Time	Knowledge or Skill	Activity or Learning Method	Support Materials and Media

Before you begin filling the blanks, think about the factors that affect your design and the strategies you may consider. The next two sections present you with these considerations.

Factors that affect a design

Every training design you create will be different. That, of course doesn't mean that you cannot use aspects of a design, or modify a design for two different purposes. You can. If you design often, take care that you do not fall into a rut of doing the same things over and over. Try something new. It keeps your designs fresh and keeps you inspired and interested.

Think of these factors as the big-picture items you should think about before putting design pen (or keystroke) to paper.

✔ **Content:** How do you determine content? Content should be a natural off shoot of the learning objectives. Include what the participants need to know — not what would be nice to know. If you're a subject matter expert (SME in trainer jargon), you may have most of the information you need. However, if not, or if you need additional facts, you can start here.

   • **Research:** Start with the Internet or your organization's library.

   • **Brainstorm:** Get a group of people from your department together to identify resources and materials that may already be available.

   • **SME:** Identify the subject matter experts and ask what you need to include. Be sure that they understand who the target audience is and their skill and knowledge level.

SMEs on your side

Subject Matter Experts (SMEs as they are commonly called) are focused on the content and are not overly involved or interested in the other aspects of the training design. A SME is brought into the process to provide content knowledge and to ensure that the details are current and accurate. The best SMEs are experts on the topic, and can also communicate the basics that someone new to the job needs to know. In addition, they are excited about being a SME.

You've found the perfect SME. She has all the experience you need. How to you ensure that the relationship is productive and positive? Start by providing a clear definition of roles and responsibilities. Who will do what? How? Provide clearly written objectives. When is it due? Try to plan this together to begin to build a positive working relationship. Pay close attention to the SME's needs. Do your own homework, like learning the SMEs' terminology and the basic concepts. Be respectful of a SME's time. The more you can work around your SME's schedule, the better.

Communicate frequently with your SME. Keep the person informed and follow up regularly. Integrate the SME on your design team to build a shared feeling of commitment, accountability, and appreciation. Speaking of appreciation, remember to say thank you — often! Few people get too much appreciation at work. Email the SME's supervisor to share positive comments about the SME. Finally, celebrate. Celebrate at the end of the project with your SME.

The bottom line is that you want to find the best SME available to you. Once you find your SME, do everything you can to build and maintain a positive and productive working relationship.

✔ **Time available:** How much time will be allowed for the training? The amount of time available for training has been decreasing as organizations find they cannot spare people away from the worksite.

✔ **Participants:** If you did not gather this information during the Needs Assessment stage, find out now the number of participants, how familiar they will be with each other, their level in the organization, and their knowledge level of the content.

✔ **Culture:** Determine anything unique about the culture of the organization or the department that may be a concern as you develop the materials.

✔ **Cost:** Find out how much money has been budgeted for the design and development.

✔ **Trainer's experience and expertise:** Assess your skills and knowledge. Do you have the ability to develop your own activities and participant handouts? Perhaps you need to rely on purchased off-the-shelf materials.

Strategies for a good design

Of course you want to design the best darn training possible. The following guidelines help you determine how to do just that.

✔ **Variation:** Use as many different methods and types of activities as possible.

✔ **Timing:** Plan for high level of activity after lunch, decide on the best time for breaks, increase risk slowly, and ensuring a mix of high and low energy activities.

✔ **Participation:** Design activities to keep participants involved and engaged.

✔ **Sequence:** Content should build on itself.

✔ **Application:** Design activities that relate directly to the learner's real-world needs, ensuring that they have ample practice opportunities.

✔ **Lecturettes:** Remember, present when you must, but keep it short and involve the participants.

Table 5-2 is a sample of one module of the design guide I developed for the train-the-trainer session you read about in this chapter.

Table 5-2		Sample Completed Design Guide	

Module <u>Facilitation Skills</u>   Time <u>155 minutes</u>

Learning Objectives:

* Participants will list ten ways they will prepare to facilitate a group.

* Participants will identify their preferred training style using a self-assessment.

* Participants will provide feedback to another facilitator, identifying what went well and what could be improved.

Time	Knowledge or Skill	Activity or Learning Method	Support Materials and Media
30 min	Preparation for facilitation	Intro with ten-minute interactive discussion: "what ifs" Small-group guided discussion (Find someone on the other side of the room you have not worked with yet — groups of five.)	PowerPoint Worksheet
45 min	Identify training style	Complete self-assessment. Share in pairs to identify personal strengths and weaknesses.	Training style instrument Assessment sheet
60 min	Co-facilitating skills Note: critical new skill	Role play with observers. Three rounds with different person as observer each time. Role plays get progressively more difficult. Summarize in large group: what worked, what didn't?	Role play card Observation sheets Team trainer checklist
20 min	Apply co-facilitating skills to personal situation	Write memo to co-facilitator: more of, less of, continue doing.	Handout: Memo

As you examine the sample guide, can you see some of the strategies I planned into the design?

✔ Sequencing of topics to build on each other as well as difficulty within the role play

✔ Variation in types of methods

✔ Variation in pace from moving around to sitting alone for self-assessment

✔ Variation in grouping size: pairs, five, self, large group

✔ High level of participation

✔ Variety in who participants are learning with

✔ Critical skill receives more time

✔ Minimal amount of time spent "telling"

Developing materials

Materials support the training you have designed. You either develop or purchase these materials, which supplement and support each learning experience. Materials may include some or all of these:

✔ Participant material that includes at least the handouts and/or manual with information and note-taking space.

✔ Media or visual support such as a PowerPoint presentation to guide a mini-lecturette.

✔ Activity support that the participants may need for the activities such as role-play cards, self-assessment instruments, or checklists.

✔ A trainer's manual to guide your facilitation or for others who may facilitate the session.

✔ Administrative support that you use in order to keep yourself organized or to complete the administrative requirements of the session. It may include an agenda, roster, supply checklist, certificates, and evaluations.

When developing the participant materials, don't try to include everything on paper. The activities you design tap into the knowledge, experience, and expertise of the participants. Participants should have a place to capture ideas they may want to use after the session. Allow space for note taking.

Do consider job aids, performance-support tools, checklists, reference cards, and other guides that can be used after the completion of the session. Investing time to develop these materials, especially for tasks that are done infrequently or for complicated tasks, is a good decision. You still include these tasks in the design, but you free up some classroom time instead of increasing the amount of practice time for tasks that may not be completed very often.

Essential components

As you design participant materials, begin by knowing what content you will include and how participants will use them. Will they be assigned reading prior to the session? Read during the session? Basis for an exercise? Backdrop for taking notes? Future resource? What else should you remember?

- ✔ Make it easy to read and quick to find information by breaking up the text with heads and subheads in a variety of type sizes and degrees of boldness.
- ✔ Use short paragraphs and wide margins, leaving space for taking notes.
- ✔ Use bullets, dashes, borders, indentations, and margins to enhance each page.
- ✔ Write in a conversational tone.
- ✔ Use graphics and sketches, even just lines and boxes, to set off key concepts and to add interest.
- ✔ Number the pages.

How about a trainer's manual?

Your trainer's manual may be anything from your notes written on the participant handouts to a complete manual with references to the training plan, facilitation tips, time use, media and visual list, and masters for the participant materials. A well-designed trainer's manual

- ✔ Uses icons
- ✔ Has plenty of room for writing notes
- ✔ Identifies everything you need to know at a glance (what visual you're using, what page participants should be on, what materials you require, and so on)
- ✔ Provides you with either a lead-in statement, a transition statement, or both

For now, I suggest that you allow someone else to worry about writing a trainer's manual. The preparation chapter provides a few ideas for what you can do to personalize your manual.

Whew! That's all, folks! As you can see, the design and development stage of The Training Cycle requires lots of work — whether it is a virtual or face-to-face classroom. If you are focused on the virtual classroom, take a look at Chapter 6, which takes you a little deeper into e-learning considerations.

The design and development of training is a big job, but don't forget to have fun and to build fun into your design. You can do it. I pass on Henry Ford's advice: "Whether you believe you can or you can't, you will prove yourself correct."

Chapter 6
Nuances of Using Technology for Learning

. . . .

In This Chapter

▶ Defining key technology terms

▶ Exploring the benefits and drawbacks of e-learning

▶ Determining what it takes to deliver successful virtual learning

▶ Summarizing the role of new technology

. . . .

Regina McMichael CSP, CET, chapter co-author

Essentially, we can break e-learning into two categories: not-too-complicated and complicated. The not-too-complicated option for e-learning, online training, virtual instructor led training (ILT), or synchronous programs involves using simpler software programs or platforms that can be mastered if you adopt computer skills easily. PowerPoint, videos, web conferencing, and more can all be a part of your e-learning initiative.

The complicated option includes the super-charged versions of the not-too-complicated options, known as rapid e-learning software, like Adobe Captivate and Articulate. Rapid e-learning software can do amazing things for your learners and you, but you must be ready to learn new software and computer language to make it worth it your efforts.

This chapter touches on a bit of both: the not-too-complicated and the complicated.

 New to online learning design? Explore what rapid e-learning software can do for you. Imagine advanced interactions from drag-and-drop learning confirmations. How about adding an animation-based scavenger hunt to find all the tools or a correct answer you want your audience to master? These and many other things are available to you with rapid e-learning software.

Technology Basics

The field is still evolving for the Talent Development profession. This means you will find various definitions for the same tool, delivery mechanism, and even your professional title. In this chapter, both *webinar* and *virtual ILT classroom* reference the online training event itself. Your role title is the facilitator. More about that later. Let's examine a few other words and how they define what you will do. The terms are presented in order of complexity, not alphabetically. So if you are an old hand at this, you can skip the first few — or perhaps, all of them.

- ✔ **E-Learning:** Typically the "e" stand for electronic, but let's expand that to mean more, let's take a risk and say it also means exciting, effective, and even — easy.

- ✔ **Asynchronous:** Typically a self-paced, online tutorial that doesn't require the trainer and learner to participate at the same time; your learners can access it anytime because it is stored to access 24/7.

- ✔ **Synchronous:** Training delivered in real time when the learner can interact with you, even if only via chat or message boxes; also called a webinar or virtual training.

- ✔ **M-Learning:** Materials designed specifically to use on mobile devices; think smaller in viewing size and shorter attention spans.

- ✔ **LMS:** Your *learning management system* (LMS) can be as simple as a spreadsheet but generally it is a computer-based storage system for your training records.

- ✔ **LRS:** *Learning record systems* (LRS) are a newer concept born from the idea that learning is more than just courses assigned and tracked in an LMS. An LRS is typically associated with the Tin Can API (more later) and seeks to track and monitor all types of learning opportunities, from a voice-recorded synopsis of some behavior coaching to an article relevant to job performance read on the Internet by a learner. The concept is simple: If we are constantly learning, shouldn't we track it in a LMS?

- ✔ **LCMS:** *Learning management content systems* are one step more sophisticated than LMS or LRS, allowing multiple developers to store content and reuse, repurpose, or rebuild materials instead of re-creating them.

- ✔ **Webinars:** Usually synchronous training when interaction between you and your learners is possible.

- ✔ **Webcasts:** Usually asynchronous training or a very large session where individual interaction is not feasible; if a webinar is recorded for later listening by those who may have missed the live version, it may be called a webcast.

✔ **Platform:** Pre-existing environment software; typical platforms include hardware architecture, an operating system (OS), and runtime libraries; often used when referring to what kind of computer systems a certain software program will run on, such as Windows or Macintosh.

✔ **Portal:** Web supersite that delivers services such as web searching, news, free email, discussion groups, and links to other sites; initially general-purpose sites, now often references sites that offer services to a particular industry, such as marketing, banking, or insurance.

✔ **SCORM and Tin Can API:** *Sharable content object reference model (SCORM)* is the standard that allows publishing e-learning materials consistently across many LMS. Tin Can or Experience API is the newly adopted model that advances what can be recorded and what defines learning.

Have you ever been in an e-learning discussion like the following? "*Since I don't want to use AICC anymore, let's make sure the new Articulate modules are output in both SCORM 1.2 and Tin Can with the 508 compliance requirements fully met. Oh, and let's be sure we plan for dashboard data on the learner access of the three elements.*" If you are new to e-learning, all the jargon may seem overwhelming. Well, it is! It is often a different language, and like learning any language, until you use it, it probably won't make much sense.

Get some experience. Sit in on several webinars if you haven't already. Compare what each facilitator does. Ask questions. Lots of questions. And *do*. We all know the best way to learn is by doing. So, design and deliver your own. Start small, whether it is a video or webinar. Limit your time and your learners to a sympathetic group who will give you valuable feedback to make your program better. You know the drill. Experience is the best teacher.

Exploring E-Learning's Benefits and Drawbacks

You might imagine that a chapter about the nuances of e-learning might present only the advantages and ignore its disadvantages. Not so. Before you or your organization venture into the virtual world of delivering learning solutions, you will want to explore both sides.

Benefits of e-learning

Some of the obvious benefits of e-learning include worldwide access to the materials and trainers without the need to put learners on planes or even leave their desks in some cases. It is beneficial when just-in-time information must be distributed. It is valuable to be able to share current information and ensure that learners have the ability to ask questions immediately. These benefits add up to real money savings. Shorter perceived contact time may also be seen as a benefit, but take care that all valuable content is available.

Drawbacks of e-learning

Although it might seem like a simple jump, from a well-prepared face-to-face training program to an equal online presentation, usually the success lies in the preparation and adaptation of your materials, delivery style, and expected outcomes. You've probably heard, "Let's convert our eight-hour onsite training program into online training." The concept of thoughtful program development using an ADDIE-like model is still critical to training success — no matter what the delivery vehicle.

Ultimately, you are better off using the existing programs as a resource from which to develop a new e-learning program. However, don't just convert it. Test your e-learning on your platform, preferably by representatives of the target audience. As with other forms of training, multiple rounds of reviews and revisions are required. However, with e-learning, updates can be a bit more complex, because they can require the creation of new audio, animations, or other features.

The beauty of e-learning is in the pre-supposed shortened content length. Whether your content time is actually shorter than face-to-face training varies with training developers. But just threatening an eight-hour online training program is an incentive to keep materials simple, relevant, and to the point. E-learning, regardless of the delivery system, can bring fear to the heart of many learners, because there is a wide range of computer expertise.

Sadly, the worst drawback to e-learning is, well, that it's e-learning. It has a bad reputation. Too many people just jumped in early without thinking, and as a result, many of us have experienced the equivalent of death by PowerPoint on the phone. If you have seen bad e-learning, this is your chance to leap into the techno world and prove that you can do better.

We aren't there yet. The wide variations in software, operating systems, web platforms, and screen resolutions still create challenges in the wonderful world of virtual learning.

Overcome drawbacks for your success

Your success will be born from using the other skills in this book and then making them fit your e-learning initiative. Also, consider your learners' prior exposure to e-learning. Their experience will influence the design and level of detail of your project. If your learners have very little exposure to an e-learning platform, or even the content material, you will need to go into more detail with basic information, like navigation instructions at the beginning of your session.

Make the move to the virtual classroom

by Becky Pike Pluth, M.Ed., CSP

There are many compelling reasons to move a classroom-based workshop onto a digital platform: time savings, convenience, and reduced budgets. But can online learning be as effective as classroom training? Absolutely!

Here are nine steps you can take to transition to a virtual classroom.

1. Involve key decision makers and stakeholders and include them in the decision to create online workshops. Use compelling arguments about the cost savings, the availability of just-in-time trainings, and the new flexibility for different time zones and markets to make your case.

2. As you convert your content to the new platform, anchor everything to the strategic plan or business direction. This will help ensure you are able to measure the return-on-investment.

3. As you modify your content for maximum effectiveness, keep visuals and participant engagement a priority. Bob Pike Group research shows that learners start doing other things (checking email, surfing Facebook) if they are not engaged every four minutes. So plan a shift in the learning often: Text chat, breakout rooms or share thoughts aloud through their microphones.

4. Create a checklist of what content needs to be covered so all facilitators and producers can be successful.

5. Run a pilot, or a trial run, of the program to practice and enhance the existing curriculum before the "go live" date.

6. Keep the stakeholders and the other facilitators in the loop. Good communication will help ensure better buy-in.

7. Evaluate everything! Determine ahead of time what needs to be evaluated. Then have checklists for the trainer, participant, and producer so they can evaluate effectiveness.

8. Launch the program!

9. Prioritize which additional courses will have the greatest impact by being transitioned to an online setting and move forward.

Although I am a staunch advocate for online training, there are times when this may not be appropriate. If you can't test the skill online, or if safety or money is at risk, don't teach it online.

Note: Becky's book *Webinars with WoW Factor* (Pluth Consulting, 2010) offers tips on how to convert classroom content to an online training environment.

Delivering Webinars and Virtual Classes

Conducting a webinar or virtual ILT requires the same skill set as conducting a face-to-face ILT. In a face-to-face classroom you need to prepare yourself, your participants, and the environment. You need to open with a BANG, create a supportive environment, get to know your participants and meet their needs, conduct activities that help learners experience the content, and manage group dynamics. You'll need to do those exact same things in your virtual classroom.

Jane Bozarth says it best: "Sometimes the idea of separating *classroom* and *virtual* activities suggests that they are really entirely different. Many activities used in traditional face-to-face classrooms translate very easily to other environments. Experienced trainers have the skills needed to facilitate these: starting and redirecting conversations, facilitating activities for an answer or outcome, drawing out quieter participants, harnessing more dominant ones. If you are mostly engaged in live classroom, start paying attention to the times you already conduct activities that are social and collaborative — group work at small tables, games, debates, role plays, case studies, group discussions — and think about how you might make them work in another environment."

It's not that difficult to deliver a stellar webinar or virtual session. Yes, there are a few new skills focused on learning the software and helping your learners master it, too. The most important step, however, is to get it out of your head that success means just sharing a PowerPoint and talking. It is quite the opposite. You will rely on your traditional classroom skills more than ever! Online, synchronous learning requires that you almost constantly re-engage your learners. Some software packages even tell you when your learner has drifted away from the screen and you can gently guide them back with well-chosen words, actions, or imagery.

Translate the skills you use in face-to-face ILT to be successful in virtual ILT. Do you ask for a show of hands in a face-to-face? Use the raise hand feature. Ask open-ended questions? Use chat. Write on a flipchart? Use the whiteboard. Conduct verbal quizzes? Use polls. Put learners into small groups? Use breakout rooms. Call on learners? Open the microphone and call on them in your virtual classroom, too.

What about software?

There are several free and subscription-based webinars and online presentations software packages. Your IT department will have recommendations and restrictions about the software choice. If your organization already has a system, you will need to learn how to work within the scope of service you have. If your organization allows shareware, free downloads, and has a small audience per program, the world is your oyster. The choices are almost limitless. You will discover this once you enter "free web conferencing programs" into a search engine.

If you are in search of a particular program, consult with your IT department for assistance. Many organizations lock down their system to prevent unauthorized downloads by users and to keep viruses under control. Do your research about which option in which programs are right for your delivery needs and fit the organization's security requirements. Meet with the right staff members to present your case. Once you have approval to move forward, you will still need to decide whether you will download and install a free copy or a trial copy or just move forward to purchase the software. On the other hand, Table 6-1 lists many of the fabulous and free products that your favorite search engine will find.

Table 6-1	Freebees IT Will Never Tell You About	
Product	*Download Required*	*Cool Thing It Does*
Screenr	No	Web-based screen recording for showing how to navigate new software or a website. Limited to a 5-minute screen capture (pure genius!) and no edits allowed; get it right or better yet, enjoy your errors and imperfections.
Camstudio	Yes	Simple, intuitive program that records screen activity and allows editing.
Audacity	Yes	Best, simplest audio editing; great for beginners!
Skype	Yes	Screen sharing; free or darn cheap phone worldwide.
Articulate.com	No	Even if you don't use the product, these folks share so much helpful information you have to check it out.
Evernote	No, but you can	Store everything, and we mean everything, in one place. Web-clipping tool and phone and tablet synching.
Screencast	No	Storage for huge multimedia files. Allows downloads, comments, and viewer count.

You'll need your IT team's help throughout the entire process. It is best to develop a respectful relationship early on to ensure they stay aligned with your needs to deliver great learning options. By the way, it never hurts to bring cookies to the first meeting either.

Employ some basic rules for webinars and other online presentations — first, to ensure everyone has the same output expectations and second, to keep yourself in check.

Technical preparation

Get in the habit of practicing a few basic guidelines in every situation. This ensures that everyone has the same output expectations and will also help remind you of everything that needs to be completed before delivering a virtual session. In fact, it is a great idea to create your own checklist that you can refine after each event. You may be tempted to skim this section. After all, it is just about preparation. Ho-hum. However, ignore preparation and your program is likely to fail despite a great design. Preparation of any learning session is so important that this book dedicates Chapter 7 to the topic. These tips will assist with preparation from a technical perspective:

✔ Use a producer. If your system locks up, people need help getting online, or a side conversation needs to occur, the producer can address each one while you continue to train.

Cindy Huggett, one of ATD's star virtual trainers, states that it is most common, and a best practice, to have two people: a facilitator who leads the learning and facilitates the session, as well as a producer who helps with the behind-the-scenes technology and assists participants with any tech issues. However, real-world discussions suggest that organizations often don't have resources for a producer, and so more often than not, it's just one person (the facilitator) who is running the entire production. On the other hand, if you are hosting a webcast with a super large audience, you might expect to have a host, a featured speaker, and a behind-the-scenes producer. You also might have a third person if it is a global audience with needs for language translation.

✔ Plan to acknowledge your producer as part of the team at the beginning of the presentation. When you need to call on your producer during the session, your learners won't be confused about a new person who has suddenly become a part of the program delivery.

✔ Test your audio, video, and any URL links every time, even if you did a presentation yesterday. If you plan on jumping from a PowerPoint presentation to a website with links or video, pre-load everything and have it waiting for you while you are delivering.

✔ Use your phone for audio. Cellular telephone reception is a risky choice; use a landline if possible. If you are using Voice over IP (VoIP), your audio and visual presentation will both be cut off the moment you lose Internet connection.

✔ Print your presentation and notes. If an Internet failure happens, you can continue training if you still have audio via the use of a telephone.

✔ Dry-run your program as many times as needed. Technology can still make a fool of a great trainer. Your confidence in both the content and the delivery platform is key to staying cool under pressure.

✔ Practice using a headset to free your hands to juggle all the other things you need to do.

✔ Take care using videos and other animations. Despite guarantees from the delivery platform providers, video and animations are risky. Learner web access, location, Internet provider, and computer can all affect the quality of your presentation, and you often have no power over any of it. If you can use still images and still train effectively, it may be the most reliable option.

✔ Practice using breakout sessions, whiteboards, and advanced annotations until you are competent in these transitions.

You will want water by your side to stay hydrated. Use a glass with a lid to avoid spills that could signal disaster for your laptop.

Before you dive into webinars as the miracle solution to training, remember: One epic failure on a webinar is hard for your audience to forget, so be sure your first attempt is dynamite. Start well before the content development occurs. Your organization should have a successful marketing, delivery, and registration plan in place. It should also have a vendor to host the webinar, like WebEx or GoToMeeting. If you are reading this book you are probably going to be the facilitator, so you will need to oversee the success of the program. A key to success is ensuring that all involved know their roles. Use the upcoming checklist as a start.

Training alone? A webinar of one requires a commitment to practice and simplicity. Wow them with simple engagement options like slide changes and the tone of your voice. If you work solo, avoid videos, complex quizzing or polls, and choose your chat opportunities wisely. Convince admin to help with tech issues during initial sign-in; that will keep your stress manageable.

Regina McMichael, webinar expert and co-creator of this chapter, has seen it all. She has had the opportunity of delivering webinars with a team of three and has had to do it alone. She says, "It is a great luxury to have a three-person team facilitating a webinar and sometimes it is necessary. In the case where you are facilitating in the technology or regulatory world, a third person, the expert, is critical; for example a chemical engineer who explains the clean-out protocols for a petrochemical plant's new process. This expert may not know (and doesn't want to learn) how to facilitate or produce a webinar; however, they really know their technical stuff!"

Defining the roles for a great webinar production

Before the webinar — Facilitator

Develop and design all the materials, keeping content tight and engagement high.

Collaborate with all the right people.

Develop at least four questions to seed learner participation.

Print a list of the participants' names.

Print a copy of the slides and your facilitator's guide as backup.

Practice all content, keeping stories short but valuable.

Ensure all registrants or learners receive all the relevant information.

Before the webinar — Producer

Ensure acceptable delivery and software compatibility for everyone; if contracts must be signed it may take more time than anticipated.

Practice the audio via VoIP and using the telephone.

Practice breakout sessions, annotation plans, and video components.

Leverage help from the software provider who may offer free support the first time.

During the webinar — Facilitator

Focus on facilitating an amazing webinar.

Keep learners on track and use a variety of tools and tactics to keep engagement high.

Stay on time and on task.

During the webinar — Producer

Deal with technical problems: sign in, connectivity, loss of audio.

Cue facilitator of issues that must be managed.

Inform participants how to contact you if they lose connection, text open the chat option.

Fix anything that breaks.

Have a plan for complete failure including rescheduling

After the webinar — Facilitator

Breathe.

Thank your producer and conduct a post webinar discussion to improve future offerings.

Follow up with anything your participants expect.

After the webinar — Producer

Manage follow-up emails as needed.

Send evaluations to attendees.

Provide evaluation data to the facilitator.

Permanently fix whatever went wrong so that it doesn't happen again.

Encouraging engagement

Engagement in a webinar? Yep. It's probably more important than in a face-to-face classroom. Your learners will be bombarded by distractions. Here are a few ideas to keep your learners engaged. A rule of thumb is to introduce a change at least every three minutes to maintain your learners' attention:

✔ Tell your learners the length of the session and never go longer — never. You will learn that they have already tuned out anyway, even if they have not officially hung up.

✔ For large groups, mute all attendees before they come into the presentation. Tell them they are muted and unmute them for active discussions. Allow for a chat or questions box and actively use it. If you are doing a presentation that requires conversation, unmute the participants once you have completed your part of the program.

✔ Grab participants' attention right up front. Give learners annotation rights at the very beginning. One way is to display a picture of the world or country where the participants are located and ask them to mark where they are on the map. It allows them to see where others are physically and it may also help you adjust your content if needed. It also helps get them engaged early and shows that they have some basic understanding of the software they are using.

✔ Use individuals' names and as a courtesy be sure to tell them up front that you will do so. Having an attendance list nearby will help you with the names.

✔ Monitor and respond to your chat box. Be sure you or your producer keeps a keen eye on the interaction and redirect questions or comments as needed.

✔ Also ask questions and invite learners to use the chat box.

Darlene Christopher, author of *The Successful Virtual Classroom* (AMACOM, 2015) encourages you to use your chat content to: Convert chat comments to FAQs; download poll results; identify improvements for the next session; select follow-up materials to email to the learners or as a facilitation team debrief agenda.

✔ Use polls, quizzes, or surveys and keep them simple. It is about keeping learners engaged, not tricking them for the answer.

✔ Use your producer as necessary to encourage engagement by managing questions and ensuring that everyone can see and hear the session. Your producer can also turn annotation rights on and off during your training.

Tools to engage your learners

You have some practical tools available to engage your learners and increase participation.

Annotation: Drawing and pointer tools that allow you and your learners to graphically mark up the screen when a slide or whiteboard is displayed.

Breakouts: Available in most synchronous software packages that allow you to divide a large group into smaller groups; learners interact in a smaller group and rejoin the large group to share their conclusions.

Chat: A function that allows synchronous text conversation between learners; chat dialogues may be saved for later reference.

Discussion board: A function that allows learners to post messages for other learners; unlike chat, they are not real-time discussions.

Poll/Survey: A function used to obtain feedback from learners in the form of true/false, multiple-choice, or others.

Status indicators: A feature that allows learners to raise their hand (visually) for quick responses, yes/no polls, or to signal when learners finish a task ("Use the raised hand when you have completed the activity)."

Whiteboard: Similar to a flipchart page, this synchronous feature can be written, highlighted, drawn, or typed upon using the annotation tools.

You may want to create a couple of starter questions in case participants are shy early on and don't ask any. This is one advantage of not being able to see each other. It can kick start a Q &A session, demonstrating that you really want questions at any point during the session.

The Technical Stuff

Of course, there is much more to learn, but don't let the technical stuff hold you back from developing your own repertoire of skills.

Choosing a learning management system

Learning management systems (LMS) maintain a record of all training and development activities. The two primary types of LMS programs for purchase usually base pricing either on how many learners you have or how much content you have. If you have 1,000 learners with only a ten-minute video to watch and track, you would want to pursue an LMS that charges by how much content you post, not by how many logins are recorded. The converse is also true, if you have a five-person team who must go through numerous programs, you may want to pay per learner.

Generally, your IT department will play a key role in which LMS to purchase, but your learning and development department and others need to be involved, so it should be a joint decision. Before deciding, consider several features that will be critical for your organization:

✔ **Customer support:** Will the LMS vendor's tech support help set it up and ensure you can administer it throughout the life of your contract, or do you have an IT team who will assist you?

✔ **Learning product support:** Some LMSes offer free or add on materials with the contract, but you must use their proprietary program to develop and deliver your content. It is easier, but if you think you may want to leverage other e-learning development tools, it may not be the right one.

✔ **Tracking tools:** Remember, this is the primary value of the LMS, so be sure your choice does what you need. Does it allow test-recording options, tracking on time and success of learners while reviewing the training? Can it provide metrics to support continuous learning to meet performance expectations? What reports will be required to meet compliance and audit requests?

✔ **Long-term training goals:** Do you see your LMS as a way to prove ROI for your training or do you just want to check a box that all learners logged in? Do you need to maintain certain records for government or certification purposes? Will you need to run dashboard reports and review learner data to maintain your department's budgets and purpose?

Your LMS can help you with many of the administrative challenges of data and learner tracking, but be sure you know what you want before you sign a contract. Most LMS companies will not only let you test drive their products, but allow you to "play in their virtual sandbox" to ensure you can use their products effectively before you buy.

What is HTML5 and why should you care? HTML5 is a core technology markup language of the Internet used for structuring and presenting content for the World Wide Web. As of October 2014, this is the fifth revision of the HTML standard of the World Wide Web Consortium (W3C). Okay, that is a bit scary and makes no sense to most of us. What you need to know is: HTML5 allows you to produce one product that works across all web delivery platforms. You must have the newest hardware and software to make it happen magically. If not, you need to implement workarounds to ensure anyone around the globe can use the HTML5-developed e-learning products. For more information, see http://en.wikipedia.org/wiki/HTML5.

SCORM, Tin Can, and 508 compliance

The platform your organization will use to align and publish e-learning should be determined before you choose an LMS provider. SCORM is the current gold standard, and making sure your LMS can deliver SCORM compliance materials is key. Tin Can is an exciting publishing and data management system that tracks different types of learning opportunities — not just those created and entered into your LMS (one of SCORM's limitations). It can include training moments as diverse as informal coaching or articles read on a relevant topic. In both of these cases, the learner or the coach needs to be diligent about entering the data.

Tin Can data is usually tracked in a Learning Record System (LRS), which is a subset of your full LMS. Tin Can is new territory for most organizations. With the constant enhancement of software and ideas, it may be a while before trainers and other learning professionals adopt the opportunity. Even if you don't adopt formal LMS or LRS, it is a good idea to at least remain current with the latest ideas and advancements.

If you are doing any work for the U.S. government, it is likely you will be required to ensure 508 compliance with the Workforce Rehabilitation Act. Unfortunately, complying is not as simple as using the correct software to build your e-learning program, because the nuances of the software may cause the output to be out of compliance. Many software programs provide a detailed list of the features of their program that are 508 compliant on their websites. However, much of the effort to making the course 508 compliant is left to the developer, who must be familiar with 508 regulations to ensure compliance. In the end, it is worth the effort. Your organization will want to use this best practice to accommodate people with disabilities.

Blended Learning and New Options

Blended learning is the combination of various learning technologies. It is most effective when the best technology is matched with the content and with the learner's needs and availability. It is a natural evolution of e-learning that includes web-based training, CD-ROM courses, videos, webinars, EPSS systems, and simulations. It also includes the less-glamorous media, including classroom training, job aids, books, coaching, and conference calls. When designing a blended-learning solution, consider some of these points:

✔ Blended learning optimizes resources, providing the greatest impact for the least investment. Remember to consider the organizational culture and how receptive it will be to change delivery formats.

✔ The blended-learning solution should be solution focused — what is the business problem you are solving and what is the best way to solve it?

✔ Technology capabilities will drive at least some portion of the blended-learning solution, but remember to include the characteristics of the audience (time available, how motivated, their location) and the characteristics of the content (the subject-matter experts, type of content: skill-based or knowledge-based, and how soon it will be out of date).

✔ Almost all blended-learning solutions will require a communication/marketing plan prior to deployment.

Social media expands T&D's options

Tweet your training? You bet! As social media and smart mobile devices like phones, tablets, and watches firmly establish their place in our society, you can use those resources and let technology make training more effective. Although there are many platforms to distribute the mini-blasts of information to an audience, Twitter is certainly seen as the most mainstream and the system most likely to be approved by your IT team. With the addition of image attachments and its intrinsic limit of the limit of 144 character-messages, Twitter is perfect for concise, relevant training nuggets delivered right to your learners. Here are ten things you could tweet that would enhance either a face-to-face or virtual training program.

✔ Short, snappy description of the training program to potential learners

✔ Reminder of dates and times of program

✔ QR code of the web page with more details on the program

✔ Message from your CEO about the importance of the training

✔ Learning objectives sent one at a time

✔ Images evoking a training class they won't want to miss

✔ Follow up job aids via a mini URL or QR code after the session

✔ Reminders of new behaviors or knowledge you want to make stick

✔ Tips for supervisors to ensure new training behavior is observed

✔ Link to the program evaluation immediately after completion

QR codes, short for *quick response* codes, are handy little tools you can use in multiple ways. A QR code is a matrix of dots or lines that references a specific website containing a set of information. QR codes were initially an alternative to bar codes in the automotive industry. They can be created and read by anyone with Internet access and a reader (a smartphone camera). QRs are an elegant, simple solution to be sure all the training content is always available.

Suppose you need a forklift safety training video accessible to your team 24/7. Simply create the QR code with the URL address of your training video, print the code, attach it to the forklift, and learners can scan and watch the video anytime they need it.

As technology continues to change, more options will continue to be available to you. Near the beginning of this chapter, we expanded the definition of e-learning. Instead of the *e* simply representing electronic, we asking you to consider that it also means *exciting*, *effective*, and even — *easy*. Hopefully this chapter has demonstrated e-learning's ability to be all of those and more.

Developing your skills as an expert online trainer will enhance your entire perspective on learning and ensure that your organization is offering exciting, effective, and easy ways to create a learning adventure for your participants. As Helen Keller said, "Life is either a daring adventure or nothing."

Chapter 7

Being Prepared to Succeed

In This Chapter

▶ Preparing your training environment

▶ Preparing your participants

▶ Preparing yourself for facilitating

▶ Creating a learner-focused attitude

"*P*roper preparation and practice prevent poor performance." As a new trainer in the early 1980s, this was one of the first messages my colleagues shared with me. I later learned that Bob Pike coined and published this statement that he calls the six Ps of an effective presentation. Bob believes that 80 percent of being a good trainer and getting people involved depends upon adequate preparation.

A training session may at times seem like the proverbial iceberg: Participants see only the top 10 percent. And I sometimes think that's how most trainers want to see it too.

In this chapter, you discover how to address the other 90 percent that's below the surface: How do you prepare the environment, the participants, and yourself before the training experience? You know you need to be prepared to succeed, and this chapter gets you there.

Preparing Your Training Environment

When your participants walk into the training session, what do you want them to see? Empty boxes turned on end? Chairs awry? Technicians scurrying about trying to get your PowerPoint up and running? Facilities people moving the refreshment table to the back of the room and bringing extra chairs? You running to and fro trying to find missing materials? Of course not. You're letting them see the other part of the iceberg.

Establishing an environment conducive to learning is a critical aspect of starting a training session off on the right foot. You can ensure that participants walk in to a relaxed atmosphere and an environment that is welcoming and ready. The room says you took the time to get ready for them. You have time to greet them and welcome them to a great training session.

After reading this section you may be amazed at how much time you will spend preparing the environment for your participants. Believe me, it is worth every minute. The more time you spend in the room, the more comfortable you will be during the training session. Make the room yours so that when participants arrive, it will feel as if you're welcoming them to your space.

Know when, where, what, who

It seems logical that you would know the logistics of a training site, yet every facilitator I've met has encountered at least one training nightmare. Some (not all) of these could be prevented by additional preparation. These questions may help you obtain the right information, but it will do you little good if you don't write the answers in a safe place.

- ✔ **When:** When is the training session? Day? Date? Time? Also, do you have enough time to prepare? Is the amount of allotted time for the amount of content adequate?

- ✔ **Where:** Where is the session? On-site or off? If off-site, is it easy to travel to the location? How do you get there? What's the address? Telephone number? Will you need to make travel arrangements? Is public transportation available? How do you get materials to the site?

- ✔ **What:** What kind of training is being expected? What resources are required? What kind of facilities are available? What will you need?

- ✔ **Who:** Who is the key planner? Who are the participants? How many? What's their background? Why were you chosen to deliver the training? Who is the contact person at the training site? How do you reach that person on-site and off?

Lots of answers. Write them down.

Room arrangements

Your room may have significant impact on your training session. Arrange the room to support the learning objectives and the amount of participation you will desire.

Typically you will not have the opportunity to select a room. However, if you do, consider the attributes that will create the best learning environment for your participants.

- ✔ **Size:** Arrange for a room to accommodate the number of participants. Remember that a room that is too large can be as bad as one that may be too small. If it is large, pull the tables together close to the front to create a warm and friendly grouping.

- ✔ **Training requirements:** If the training session entails many small group activities, determine if there is enough space in the room. If not, arrange for additional breakout rooms to accommodate your needs.

- ✔ **Accessibility:** Ensure that the room is accessible to all, including those who have limited mobility.

- ✔ **Location:** If participants need to travel (either by foot or vehicle) to the session, the location should not pose a hardship, for example, walking in rain, or parking difficulty.

- ✔ **Convenience:** Readily accessible restrooms, telephones, snacks, lunch accommodations, and so on help ensure that participants return on time following breaks or lunch.

- ✔ **Distractions:** Select a room that is free of distractions and noise. Thin walls with a sales convention next door may not create the environment you're trying to establish for learning.

- ✔ **Obstructions:** Select a room that is free of structures such as posts or pillars that may obstruct participants' views.

- ✔ **Seating:** Select a location that provides comfortable, moveable chairs. Seating arrangements should further enhance the learning environment you wish to establish. Determine what's most important for the learner. There are probably two dozen ways you could set up the training room The seven seating arrangements in Figure 7-1 are typical. Consider the advantages to your participants for each arrangement. Table 7-1 provides guidance about why you may select each.

- ✔ **Furniture:** In addition to decisions about the seating arrangements and the kind of tables you prefer, you will want a table in front of the room for your supplies and equipment. Don't allow too much space between the table from which you will present and the front participant row. I usually allow just enough room for me to squeeze through when I move from the table to roam about the group. Reducing the amount of space between you and the learners increases the affect level in the room. It closes the distance between you and the trainees both physically and emotionally. The participants feel better about you, themselves, and the training session.

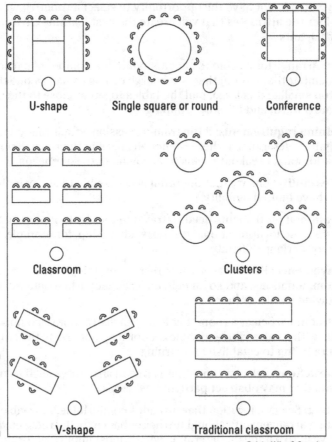

Figure 7-1:
Seating
arrange-
ments.

Table 7-1		Seating Arrangements	
Seating Style	*Number*	*Benefits*	*Drawbacks*
U-shape	Best for groups of 12 to 22	Encourages large group discussion Can push back to form small groups Close contact between facilitator and participants	Difficult to form small groups with those on other side Eye contact between some participants is difficult due to the linear layout

Seating Style	Number	Benefits	Drawbacks
Single Square or Round	Best for groups of 8 to 12	Facilitates problem solving Smaller size increases total group involvement Easy for facilitator to step out of the action	Media and visual use is difficult Limited group size
Conference	Best for 8 to 12	Moderate communication among group	Maintains trainer as "lead" Sense of formality
V-shape (with V pointing to front)	Best for teams of 4 or 5 and groups of 16 to 25	Easy to work in teams at each table No one has back totally to the front of room	Some difficulty to promote teamwork among entire group
Clusters	Best for groups of 16 to 40	Promotes teamwork in each cluster If chairs are placed on only one side of the table, everyone will face the front of the room	Difficult to get those whose backs are to front to participate Some participants may need to turn chairs to face the front of the room
Classroom	For groups of any size	Traditional, may be expected by learners Trainer controls Participants can view visuals	Low involvement One way communication Difficult to form small groups
Traditional classroom	Best reserved for groups over 40	Traditional, may be expected by learners Trainer controls	Low involvement One-way communication Difficult to form small groups

You may also want to consider positioning a table for refreshments in the back of the room. Located there, it can be easily serviced throughout the day. One more thing. Don't forget the wastebasket! In my experience neither training rooms nor hotel conference rooms have wastebaskets. Remember to ask for one.

✔ **Lighting:** Lighting should be adequate. Dimly lit ballroom ambiance will not promote energy in a training session. Is the lighting bright enough? Is it natural lighting? If the room has windows, which direction are they facing? Can windows be darkened, if necessary? A morning sun coming up behind your projection screen will blind the participants and wash out the image on the screen. Know where light switches are located so that you can brighten or darken the room as needed.

✔ **Workable walls:** Most trainers hang flipchart pages on the walls: the session objectives, small group work, and so on. Be sure to use blue painters tape, Some tapes are so strong that they remove the paint from the wall. Is wall space available or do windows surround the room? Does art cover the walls or are they open? Usually the front of the training room should be opposite the entrance to avoid distractions when folks come and go. Is that possible in the room you're considering?

Use markers that absolutely do not bleed through so there is no danger of ruining walls. The only brand that I know lives up to this expectation is Mr. Sketch. Not only that, but they smell good as well — scented like cherry, mint, orange, licorice, and blueberry!

✔ **Climate control:** You will never be able to please everyone in your session. However, if you have the ability to adjust it yourself, you can try. Determine where the thermostat is located and whether you have any control over it. Experiment with it while you set up the room. Does it respond quickly or slowly? Do you need to contact someone to make adjustments? Obtain that person's phone number.

When adjusting thermostats, make changes one degree at a time and give the equipment time to work. Large changes in the thermostat will cause a once too-cool room to become too warm.

✔ **Microphone:** If you have a large room or a large group or the room has poor acoustics or you have a tiny voice, you may need a microphone. Check the room to ensure it is wired for a microphone.

Equipment and visuals

It seems that if anything goes wrong that interferes with conducting the training session, it will have something to do with the equipment.

Your media and visual equipment — DVD player, projector, flipcharts — all help participants understand the message faster and easier. But when something goes awry, it can spell disaster. Preparation can prevent some potential headaches.

How does your training chair stack up?

Have you ever attended a full-day training session sitting on a hard chair that was not adjustable? Most people have, and that's why trainers are interested in providing the most comfort possible to learners. Providing the right chair is critical. If the chair is too small and uncomfortable, participants fidget and get irritable. If the chair is too comfortable, participants may fall asleep.

The chair that you use should allow participants to sit comfortably for six hours. What is the perfect training chair? The ideal training chair should include these features:

✔ Has a back.

✔ Is adjustable in terms of height.

✔ Has adjustable arms to relieve body fatigue by supporting some of the weight. The forearm should be positioned at a 90-degree angle from the upper arm.

✔ Is upholstered in fabric (not vinyl).

✔ Has wheels so participants can move chairs to small groups easily.

✔ Swivels so participants can easily move with the conversation of the large group.

✔ Is at least 20 inches long and 20 inches wide.

Stacking chairs, most often used in training rooms, meet very few of these standards.

Preview one week before the event

✔ Set up the machines and go through all visuals.

✔ Practice with PowerPoint slides to ensure they are in order.

✔ Experiment with dissolve enhancements, animation, and sound effects.

✔ Practice with the equipment you will use, even the flipcharts require you to practice your flipping, ripping, and hanging techniques!

Set up the day before the event

The best thing you can do to be prepared for a training session is to set up the day before it is scheduled. If anything is missing, or if anything goes wrong, you will be happy to have learned about it a day early.

✔ Be certain the equipment works.

✔ Focus all equipment and set the volume level where needed.

✔ Check volume control and know how to adjust it.

If playing a DVD off a computer, be sure to check the quality of the sound, because the speakers on the computer may not be as good as they need to be.

- ✔ Make sure that the projector has the right lens and that it is clean.

- ✔ Mark the projection table placement with masking tape on the floor.

- ✔ Check that the screen is large enough and placed where you want it.

How large of a screen do you need? The distance from the participants should be six times the width of the screen.

- ✔ Tilt the screen forward at the top to avoid keystoning (the image distortion caused when the projector beam doesn't meet the screen at a 90-degree angle).

- ✔ Check the seats (sit in them) to make sure everyone can see.

- ✔ Decide whether you need to dim the lights; do so only if you must.

- ✔ Plan ahead to know where you will be standing.

Prepare for an emergency

Although you can't be prepared for every emergency, you can prepare using these suggestions:

- ✔ Bring an extra projection bulb to the session.

- ✔ Know how to change bulbs.

- ✔ Learn a few troubleshooting tricks for the equipment you use most often.

- ✔ Pack an adaptor plug and perhaps an extension cord.

- ✔ Pack a roll of duct tape to tape down stray cords.

- ✔ Have an alternative plan if the electricity fails — that may mean markers and a flipchart.

Special computer considerations

If you're teaching a computer class or using computers during the training session, take special precautions. Unless you're a computer troubleshooting whiz, have someone who is available when you set up and as you begin the session. Check out a few other things prior to the session.

- ✔ Make sure that you have the name and contact number, including cell-phone number of the person who will assist if you have difficulty.

- ✔ Ensure that the computers have the correct software and version installed.

- ✔ Make sure that you have the log-in ID and password required if necessary.

- ✔ Determine who is responsible for providing and computer supplies.

✔ Supplies you may want to add to the training kits described elsewhere in this chapter include a power strip, remote mouse with extra battery, and a screwdriver (if you're traveling by air, you'll need to place it in checked luggage).

✔ Bring electrical tape, if you will work in a makeshift lab, to tape computer cables and other cords out of the participants' way.

Setup tricks for flipcharts

When your flipcharts are prepared, you will feel more organized and ready to conduct the session.

✔ Use a design you create on paper to guide your writing.

✔ Write on every other page (so you can't see through to the next page).

✔ Use a variety of dark colors; red for emphasis only.

✔ Use numbers, bullets, boxes, and underlining.

✔ Some trainers like to use two different marker colors for every other idea on a list.

✔ Letters should be 1 to 3 inches high.

✔ Pencil cues in the margin.

✔ Print; do not use cursive writing.

✔ No more than ten lines per page.

✔ A misspelled word can be cut out with a razor blade; tape clean paper to the back and rewrite the word.

✔ Bend corners or use tape tabs to find and turn pages more easily.

✔ Adjust the easel to a comfortable height and position it where you want to use it.

Plan flipchart placement so that your back is to the least number of participants. As you face the audience, the chart should be to your non-dominant side if you use it mostly for writing. It should be to your dominant side if you use it mostly for pointing to content. I usually have two charts, one for each purpose, and more if the participants will use them for listing ideas or decisions in small group activities.

✔ Make sure the easel is securely locked and balanced and that the pad is firmly anchored on the easel.

All this equipment preparation may seem like a great deal of work. The first time something goes wrong, however, you will appreciate the attention to details.

Preparing Your Participants

Preparing your participants is tricky. What you think will work to get them involved in the session probably won't. And what you think may be minimal preparation is perhaps the best thing you can do. Imagine that! As you peruse some of these ideas, remember you're working with adult learners. You will see Malcolm Knowles' adult-learning principles are alive and well.

Preparing participants: What works?

How do you help prepare your participants before the session begins? I have found all of these to work:

- Connect with them before the session. An email will do; a letter is better. Let them know what's in it for them (Bob Pike calls this radio station WII-FM) by relating it to their job. Will the session make their job easier? Will it enhance relationships? Will it show them how to manage time better? Tell them about it.

- Send a welcome email stating the objectives of the class. Provide an email address or phone number and welcome them to contact you if they have any questions.

- Send the agenda.

- Send a handwritten note introducing yourself and stating why you're looking forward to working with this group.

- Send a puzzle or brain teaser that arouses their curiosity about the content.

- Send a provocative statement or question that makes them wonder what you're up to.

- Send a cartoon that is pertinent to the session.

- Send the welcome letter in a unique way. One example to send it in a paper bag. I then used the paper bag as a theme throughout the session; for example, participants were encouraged to write an issue on an index card and place the card in a provided paper bag, thus "bagging" their issue until later.

- Send participants a roster of who will attend the session.

- Send them specific logistic information. Where is the training site? What room? Where can they eat lunch? What time will lunch be held? Will they be able to check their emails? Where can they park their cars? What's the closest metro station?

✔ Get them involved early by sending them a questionnaire and using their responses to tweak the agenda and incorporate their needs.

✔ Provide participants' supervisors with a discussion sheet to review. Ask the supervisors to discuss what they hope the participants learn and apply in the workplace.

Unique virtual participant preparation

Connect with your virtual participants several times prior to your session. You can use any of the suggestions in the previous section. In addition, you will want to ensure that they know how to set up their computer, test their connection, and ensure appropriate software is downloaded. Provide them with suggestions about how to create an appropriate learning environment and minimize distractions.

Encourage participants to join ten minutes early. That will give you an opportunity to greet each person by name. If you want, you could turn on your webcam even if you won't use it throughout the session. Invite them to do the same. Can you grab their attention during these ten minutes?

✔ Post a set of rolling quotes pertinent to the content.

✔ Post a rolling set of slides that display the session logistics.

✔ Play music.

✔ Invite participants to connect via chat; the social element is especially useful for ongoing sessions with the same participants.

✔ Show a series of interesting and surprising facts about the session content, such as "Did you know that 9 out of 10 people fear speaking in front of a group more than they fear death?"

In typical face-to-face classes, trainers spend the first session allowing participants to learn about each other. This practice is just as important in an online setting as well. As a first assignment, have participants submit a post to the group outlining their interests as related to the course and outside the course. You could ask that they do this in written or video format.

According to Cindy Huggett, author of *The Virtual Training Guidebook* (ASTD, 2014), virtual trainers are often frustrated because their participants are not engaged. She believes it is because proper expectations have not been established with participants. It is your responsibility to ensure that your participants know that they need to at *least* set up their computers, complete the prework, select a place where they can concentrate, and to minimize distractions.

Darlene Christopher suggests that if you have large files to send to participants, post them online using tools like Google Drive or Dropbox and tell participants how to download them to their computers.

Preparing participants: What doesn't work?

Through many years of experience, I have also found things that do not work. Don't bother with these!

- **Don't send lengthy preread material.** It will only be read by two people and they will complain.

- **Don't send short preread material.** It will be read by 30 percent, ignored by 30 percent, and lost by 40 percent.

- **Don't ask them to write more than a half a page.** Virtual classroom participants recognize that they must complete prework assignments and are more likely to so than those in a traditional classroom.

- **Be sure you have management support.** If participants sense that management is not behind the training, you will expend a great deal of energy on the issue during the session. Participants may be discouraged when they walk into the session,

- **Don't send more than one email.** If you must send an email, be sure that you have included everything and that everything is correct, so that you don't need to send a second email to correct the first!

- **Don't do nothing.** That's right. Nothing doesn't work, either. Make at least one contact with participants prior to the session.

Preparing Yourself

While everything in this chapter is in one way or another preparing you, this section truly focuses on things you can specifically do from thinking through crises that may occur, to practicing your activities, to keeping yourself organized. The better you're prepared, the smoother the session will go.

Prepare to avoid crises

The key to handling crises in the classroom, those unexpected events that crop up at the most inopportune moments, is prevention. The experienced trainer is a close friend of Murphy and his laws of random perversity. A trainer knows that "If something can go wrong, it will." As a result, experienced trainers will take every possible step to ensure a problem can be prevented. Furthermore, they have some contingency plans ready if something actually does go wrong. These pointers will help you prevent catastrophes during the training session.

- ✔ Go through your presentation thoroughly. List every single logistic detail as you come to it. After you have done this for the entire program, create a checklist for yourself. Review this checklist one week before the program, three days before the program, the day before the program and the morning of the program. This ensures that you have thought of every detail on time.

- ✔ Have your handouts and visual aids prepared early enough so that they can be thoroughly proofread and checked to see whether they are in the proper order. If something is wrong, you will have time to correct it.

- ✔ Don't assume that, just because you reserved a room, it will be there waiting for you. Reservations and room schedules have a unique way of canceling themselves. If you're making a reservation at an outside facility, write down the date and time you made the reservation, the name of the person who took your reservation and the confirmation number. If you're scheduling a room internally, write down the date and time you made the reservation and the name of the person who scheduled the room.

- ✔ One week before the program call to ensure the room is still being held. Do the same thing the day before the program.

- ✔ Even if the room is available, don't assume it will be set up as you requested. To help the facilities people arrange the room, provide them with a detailed diagram of how you want the room.

- ✔ The day before the program, you should call to remind them that you want the room set up that day. If that is not possible, get their commitment to have it set up at least two hours before the program is scheduled to begin.

- ✔ Get the name of a contact person who will be at the training site on the day of the training. That person can help you locate any missing materials or fix (or replace) any broken equipment.

- ✔ Arrive at least one hour early on the day of training. This gives you time to set up your own materials as well as time to tend to any last-minute crises. You may be the one who actually tidies the room, arranges (or rearranges) furniture, sets up and tests the equipment, and makes last-minute arrangements.

- ✔ Know how to change the light bulb for any projection equipment and make sure there is a spare available.

Check your room

Even if someone else is responsible to set the room up, check it out. Theoretically, the room should be set up exactly as you requested. Practically, it will not be. Some folks like to make changes because they think they are doing you a favor. For example, I have found that most hotels like to set up the room with extra seats "just in case." Setting up a room for 26 when no more than 20 are expected causes a problem in two ways.

✔ First, the empty seats makes it appear that there are no shows and participants will wonder why that occurred.

✔ Second, the additional chairs mean that people will be farther away from each other, that there may be empty chairs between participants, making it more difficult to encourage interaction and participation.

You may need to do more than just put the extra chairs away. When presenting at a hotel (even when I have had personal discussions and provided detailed drawings), I have had to tear down the table arrangements and redo it. I will call facilities, but they are usually delayed, because of course they think they have completed this job and are off on another. On some occasions I learn when the set up will occur and I try to be present, using the time to complete other setup myself.

✔ Because of the possibility of last-minute crises, have your presentation completely prepared and rehearsed *before* you arrive at the training site. If you plan to do it when you arrive, you may get distracted. Then, when it's time to begin, you will not be prepared.

✔ If you're flying to the training program, either send the materials (insured) well in advance or take them on the plane with you. This will prevent you from having to worry about them getting lost en route.

When I travel to a site, I pack one master set of participant material in my carry-on luggage. If the participant materials are not there for any reason, I can at least have copies made to get the session started.

Of course, no amount of preparation can ensure that your program will go off without a hitch. Use these tips to deal with catastrophes during the presentation.

✔ If equipment fails, calmly look at the equipment and check for obvious problems (accidentally turned off, became unplugged, and so on).

✔ If you're uncertain about how to fix it, ask for volunteers from the participants. There are usually one or two handy people in every program.

✔ If no one can pinpoint the problem, give the group a five-minute break while you find help.

- If help cannot be found or if the problem is not fixable, rearrange your agenda to delete the activity or to have it at a later time when the equipment is fixed or replaced. This requires that you're absolutely prepared, know your program forward and backward and are flexible enough to see new linkages and sequences.

- Use group problem solving or brainstorming to come up with alternatives to any problem (for example, overcrowded room, broken air conditioning, missing handouts).

- Be prepared for any type of participant response. You may have a group that refuses to participate, or you may have one where all the individuals talk at once. Have a plan for facilitating any type of group.

- Use humor to diffuse unexpected situations. Check some of the ways to add humor listed at the end of this book.

- Most importantly, keep your cool. A crisis situation only becomes a crisis when you treat it that way. If you maintain your composure under any circumstance, your participants will assume everything is under control.

Prepare for Virtual ILT

Almost all the advice for physical classroom trainers also pertains to virtual classroom trainers: Know your training style, find out who's in your session, practice, create your personal checklist, and stay organized during the session. A few things are unique, such as:

- Meet with your producer.

- Test your audio.

- Write and post marketing content via your selected method.

- Ensure that the registration and enrollment are tracked.

- Distribute materials via email or a central repository.

- Communicate with participants to ensure that they know how to set up and test their computers, disable pop ups, close their email, post an out-of-office message, and other steps to ensure they can focus on their professional development.

If your organization has a LMS, most of the preparation before the session will be automated and save you time. The drawback, however is what our profession is built on — personalization and connecting with our learners. There may be times when you want to reach out to your learners, especially if some will be new to the technology, if this is the first of several consecutive events, or if your audience is global.

Identifying your training style

Even if you have never trained a day in your life, you have already developed a training style. Like everyone, you have developed preferences in life. How you give directions to strangers. How you explain a task to colleagues. How you clarify information for your spouse. You have developed a preferred way to do each of these and they provide clues about your training style.

Several instruments exist to assist you to identify your training style. You may wish to complete one to determine your style. Most suggest that there are four styles. You may have learned about your communication style, managerial style, or leadership style in the past. The most important correlation between training style theory and other style theories is that all styles are appropriate for different situations. There is no right or wrong style.

What is most important to know about training styles? Consider these elements as you prepare for your training session. Chapter 11 discusses training style in more depth.

- Everyone has a preferred training style that has been developing over the years.

- All styles are appropriate for various situations.

- Each style has advantages and disadvantages.

- Learners each have preferences too, and each of the training styles affects individuals in different ways, some helpful and some less so.

- The most successful trainers will be those who are flexible, that is, they can adapt their training style to meet learners' needs.

When you consider all the information based on the research about training style, one concept remains at the focal point. Trainers must be learner-focused. They must view themselves as facilitators of learning and guides to the learners. The learners are central to the training experience. Table 7-2 clarifies the differences between being learner focused and training focused. Keep these in mind as you move forward in your growth as a trainer.

Most research and common opinion favors a learner-focused approach to training. This is one reason some organizations use learning and development to define their training departments.

What you call yourself is less important than what you do. And what you do as a trainer is to ensure that learning takes place and that the learning is transferred to the workplace, where performance improves.

Table 7-2	Trainer Focuses
Learner Focused	*Training Focused*
Facilitator, guide, coach	Instructor, expert, directive
Learning objectives are flexible	Learning objectives established
Learners influence pace and timing	Trainer follows agenda
Learn by practicing skills	Learn by listening
Elicit examples and ideas from participants	Provide examples and ideas
Assume learners are experienced and knowledgeable	Assume learners are inexperienced and not knowledgeable
Asks more questions	Makes more statements
Learners are primary resource for information; gleans concepts from learners	Trainer is primary resource for information; explains, demonstrates
Activities are primary methodology; Learner is active participant	Lectures and discussion are primary methodology; Learner is passive, absorbing information
Facilitator uses mini-evaluations throughout training session	One final evaluation used

Find out who's in your session

You will want to learn as much as you can about the individuals who will attend your session. You may have already obtained this information when you conducted the needs assessment. And you designed the session based on that information. Now you may want more specifics.

Obtain a roster as soon as it is available and then identify those factors that will help you plan the level, pace, and focus of your session.

- Their jobs in the organization
- Their levels of responsibility and authority in the organization
- Their understanding of the subject matter, any definitions you may need to clear with them early
- The reason they are attending this training that may include: voluntary, mandatory, lack of performance, new skills, new employee
- Their opinions about the training session

✔ Unique personalities that may include informal leaders, outspoken employees, decision makers, experts

✔ Assumptions they may bring with them

✔ Negative concerns: hot buttons, corporate issues, negative experiences

Learn what you can about the participants' schedules. Find out what the group will be doing just before the training and immediately following the training. If the session starts early or runs late, determine whether anyone is in a car pool or on flex-time that will affect their attendance. If the session is off-site, learn what you can about the ease to reach the location, traffic, or parking concerns, and ease to locate the room.

Practice, practice, practice

Master the content of your training session better than you ever imagined. If you were lucky enough to design and develop the session, you have a head start. You were involved in the research and discussions so you have experienced the design and the decisions for what needs to be included. You have read the background information. You know more about the subject than what is included in the training session. Whether you will deliver your content in person or virtually, practice will make you feel more confident.

✔ You may still want to practice some portions of the session. You may want to practice the activities with a small group to determine timing or whether the results garner what you anticipated. This is a good test to find out whether the directions are as clear as they need to be. Perhaps questions arise that you cannot answer. These may still happen during your training session; you can't control that. However, a practice run will still uncover critical flaws or omissions.

✔ Practice the mechanics of the presentation. If you're revealing something to the participants, determine the best time to provide the handout or show the picture or switch to the next slide in your virtual session to maintain the surprise element.

✔ Practice the theatrics. If you're telling a joke or a story with a punch line practice it out loud. If you need to show emphasis through pronunciation, with pauses, or through inflection, practice out loud. If you need to demonstrate something or use gestures to explain something, get feedback from someone.

✔ Practice in the room where you will actually conduct the training. This helps to make the room feel like home.

✔ Video yourself conducting some of the activities or delivering the presentations. Review the recording and decide what you still need to polish. An audio recording works just as well for your virtual session.

✔ Identify questions you will want to ask at specific points of your presentation to elicit another perspective, to check for understanding, or to generate audience participation.

✔ Anticipate questions the participants may ask. Plan your answers to these questions. No, you will not think of everything, but you will think of some and this is a good exercise.

Practice is important and you will want to invest time in practicing. However, what you put in your head is more important than what you put into practice. In other words, know your material. Read as much as you can about the subject. Tap into your subject matter expert (SME) for extra tips. Observe the process. Do the process yourself. Know your material.

Tips for staying organized

Your participants will notice how organized you are. It is a sign of professionalism. Get organized. Stay organized.

Be organized before the session

Create a packing list. I use a generic packing list like the one that follows. This serves as my guide and keeps me organized when I prepare for almost any training session. It is generic enough to use for most sessions. As soon as a date has been established, I begin to complete the information. It is copied on a brightly colored sheet of paper (lime green) so that it is easy to spot among an avalanche of white paper.

Facilitation Training Packing List

General materials:

❑ Trainer's manual

❑ Trainer's kit

❑ Markers for trainer

❑ Masking or blue painters tape

❑ Strapping tape to tape cords to the floor for safety

❑ Bag of creativity goodies

❑ White index cards _____

❑ Index cards: colors _____ sizes _____

- ❑ PowerPoint presentation
- ❑ Computer
- ❑ Backup presentation on memory stick
- ❑ Wireless remote
- ❑ Resources
- ❑
- ❑

For each table:

- ❑ Markers for table tents
- ❑ Sticky-back notes : colors _____ sizes _____
- ❑ Tactile items
- ❑ Prizes
- ❑ Play Doh
- ❑ Crayons
- ❑ Team cards
- ❑ Paper: colors _____ sizes _____
- ❑
- ❑

For each participant:

- ❑ Table tents
- ❑ Participant Manuals
- ❑ Envelopes
- ❑ Books
- ❑ Handouts
- ❑ Evaluations
- ❑ Certificates
- ❑
- ❑

Contact information:

Contact person:	Company:
Telephone (o):	Telephone (c):
Date:	Time:	Number of participants:
Training location:	Building:	Room:
Equipment ordered:	
Travel arrangements:	

Stay organized during the session

The agenda you provide for your participants helps them stay focused on the big picture, the learning objectives, and the sequence of learning events. Your agenda, like the one described in the following section, will be different in a number of ways. The suggestions provided here work for me. You may have other ways for how the agenda will help you stay organized.

- ✔ Add times so that you can tell whether you're ahead, behind, or on time.
- ✔ Print the agenda on bright paper; I use Astro Yellow so that if it becomes lost among other notes on the table, I can easily spot it.
- ✔ For cues, have Activity underlined, PROPS in all caps.
- ✔ Add corresponding page numbers in participant materials.

Use your trainer's manuals or training notes to stay organized. Underline key words and highlight key concepts.

Bring a small travel clock to help you stay on schedule. Even if you wear a watch, get in the habit of looking at the clock on the table. Looking at your watch leads participants to do the same thing. If you glance at it too often, they may begin to get nervous about whether you're still on time. It's not a big deal. It's one of those small things between being a trainer and being a professional trainer.

Train the Trainer Program: Training Agenda

Monday, June 30, 9:00 a.m. to 5:00 p.m.

Overview

9:00	Icebreaker HO <u>Exercise</u> PROPS (your motto); mini-needs assessment (time/experience)
9:30	What We Expect of Each Other <u>Exercise</u>; me/each other/ HOPES on FC; ground rules
9:45	Your Greatest Need: "Bag Your Problem" <u>Exercise</u>
9:55	Training Skills Inventory pp 1–4 <u>Exercise</u>; FC example
10:15	Characteristics and Skills of Effective Trainers pp 5–6 Note: Write directions for eating pie before break
10:30	Break
10:45	Do You Have What It Takes? pp 7–8 (someone don't know well)
11:00	Overview of the Training Cycle pp 9–11

Needs Analysis

11:15	Training Needs: The Whats, Whos, and Hows pp 12–15 <u>Exercise</u> Write directions for eating pie <u>Exercise</u>

Lunch	Prepare for creativity activity; put crayons on tables

Needs Analysis (continued)

1:00	Task Analysis (pie demonstration) p 16
1:20	Developing Learning Objectives p 17

Development and Design

1:30	Adult Learning Theory pp 18–22 <u>Exercise</u>
2:15	Break (candy out)
2:30	Customizing and Tailoring Off-the-Shelf pp 23–24
2:40	Presentation and Activities pp 25–29
3:00	Add Creativity to Your Training pp 30–32 PROPS
3:45	Break
4:00	Creative Activity p 33 <u>Exercise</u>
4:50	Designing Smooth Transitions pp 34–35 FC
5:00	Wrap: Rate 1–7 and why (index cards)

End of Day: Change room arrangement

Books out
Play Doh out
Summarize and post evals on FC

Plan for how and when you will distribute materials. This may not be a problem for a group of 20, but it is for a group of 50, and can be a logistical nightmare for over one hundred.

Packing a trainer's kit

The well-packed trainer's kit includes the following items:

✔ Training supplies

- Masking/painters tape

- Mr. Sketch markers

- Ten sticky-back pads, various sizes

- Push pins

- 3 x 5 note cards

- Blank name tags

- Table tents

- Scotch tape

- Glue stick

- Small stapler and staples

- Zip lock bags

- Small scissors

- Self-adhesive (1-inch wide) correction tape for flipcharts

- Rubber bands

- Paper clips

✔ Emergency items

- Band-Aids

- Tissue

- Sewing kit

- Lip balm

- Cough drops

- Aspirin

Prepare your body and brain

Learn to relax your body. Use whatever technique works for you. Some trainers see a mental image of relaxing each body part from the top of their heads to their toes.

Learn breathing techniques. Slow, deep breathing lowers your heart rate and increases the amount of oxygen flowing to your brain.

Be prepared to give yourself a rousing pep talk. You know ten times more than any other person in the room. You're well prepared. You have memorized your introduction, and your media and visuals are well designed. Your participants are looking forward to being in this session with you. So go out there and let 'em have it!

Prepare yourself by knowing what you will drink before and during the training session.

- ✔ Avoid coffee. If you're new to training, your nervousness may prevent you from counting how many cups you're drinking. Adding additional caffeine to your presentation anxiety may create a bodacious buzz!

- ✔ Avoid dairy products — for example, milk, yogurt — to prevent mucus build-up requiring you to clear your throat.

- ✔ Avoid sugary liquids such as fruit juices and sodas; they coat your vocal cords.

- ✔ Avoid icy beverages because they constrict your vocal cords.

Okay! What's left? Room-temperature or cool water, warm water with lemon, herbal teas, and decaffeinated teas or coffee. Remember this is just to get you through the first few hours. Later, when your nerves have calmed down, you can switch to one of your favorite drinks (nonalcoholic, of course!)

Travel if you must

Travel can be fun and exhilarating or it can be painful and exhausting. This list of tips for preparation will assist the trainer who travels to training sites.

- ✔ **Buy wheels.** You will need to schlep lots of things. Make it easy on yourself and purchase luggage on wheels.

- ✔ **Pack your carry-on luggage as if the rest will not arrive.**

  - The clothes you intend to wear the first day.

  - Personal hygiene supplies.

  - A master of the participant materials and all support supplies.

  - Your PowerPoint presentation.

  - Your trainer's manual or notes.

  - A mini set of the supplies you depend on: couple of markers, pack of index cards, post its packed in a zip-lock bag.

- ✔ **Send participant materials and supplies ahead if you can.** Call several days ahead to ensure that they arrived.

✔ **Personally talk to the contact person for directions** to your hotel and from the hotel to the training site. Email a copy of your flight and hotel information to the person.

✔ **Exchange home and cellphone numbers with the contact person,** especially if you're flying in on a Sunday for a Monday training session.

The procrastinator's checklist

Are you a procrastinator like me? Don't have time to read this entire chapter? Here's a quick-and-dirty checklist of what you need to do when. The following list is particularly good if this is the first time you present. On the other hand, if possible, this is the list I prefer to use each time.

One week before

❏ Practice your session in front of a colleague, asking for input, feedback, and ideas.

❏ Know your subject cold. Your confidence will grow if you're assured about your knowledge.

❏ Memorize the words you intend to use during the first five minutes. The first few minutes of a training session are usually the most nerve-wracking for a trainer.

❏ Make a list of things you will want to remember to do or pack for the session: equipment, supplies, how to set up the room, what you will place at the participants' seats, and names and phone numbers of people who will support the session in any way, for example, the person who has the key to the training room.

❏ If you asked participants to complete a survey or other pre-work, check to be sure you have all the responses.

❏ Confirm all room arrangements, refreshments, equipment, and supplies for the session.

One day before

❏ Run through the entire session, practicing with visuals.

❏ Confirm that you have enough participant materials and all your supplies.

❏ Check that you have your trainer's guide or notes and keep them with you to take to the session.

❏ Check on everything you need regarding the training site including location of restrooms, refreshments, support staff, and so on.

❑ Set up the training room, placing tables and chairs to encourage participation.

❑ Observe the room's mechanicals. Will lighting cause any problems? Windows facing east or west? Determine where the light switches are located. Figure out where the thermostat is located and whether you have any control over it.

❑ Set up your equipment, marking placement of the projection table with masking tape on the floor.

❑ Test the equipment. Run through PowerPoint slides one last time to ensure they are in order. Practice with the actual equipment. Do you know how to use the wireless remote control? Where is the reverse button? Can you roll the pages on the flipchart smoothly?

❑ Arrange the participant's materials on their tables. Place their training manuals, pens, agendas, table tents, markers, and anything else each participant needs neatly at each seat.

❑ Place shared materials participants need for small group activities or exercises in the center of round tables or equally spaced around a U or other linear placement. These items may include post its, index cards, handouts, or paper.

❑ Take one last look around. Empty boxes in the front of the room? Get rid of them. Don't depend on the clean up crew to discard them for you.

❑ Get a good night's sleep.

One hour before

❑ Arrive at the training site at *least* one hour before start time.

❑ Complete last-minute setup.

❑ Organize the space from which you will train. Tools and supplies are where you want them: markers are on the flipchart tray, pencil near your notes, post its and index cards at the side, completed table tent at the front of the table.

❑ Ensure that your notes are in order, turned to the first page, placed where you can stay organized. Check that your visual support is in order and placed where you want it.

❑ Prepare for emergencies. Fill a glass with water. Find a few paper towels for an emergency.

❑ Ensure cords are covered or taped down.

❑ Media equipment placement is correct, test, set to first slide.

❑ Make yourself comfortable: Use the restroom, get a drink of water.

❑ Move around the room and greet people as they arrive up until two to five minutes before start time.

One minute before

❑ Take one more peek at your opening line.

❑ Take a deep breath.

❑ Tell yourself how phenomenal this is going to be.

❑ Find a friendly face.

❑ Smile.

❑ Go for it!

Last-minute virtual session preparation

You have some similar steps to remember as you prepare for a virtual ILT. During the couple of hours before your session starts, you will want to follow a checklist something like this one:

❑ Have two computers set up: one to log into as the facilitator, and one to log in to the class as a participant so you can see what the participants see. The second computer could also serve as a backup if necessary.

❑ Clear the workspace and set it up with everything you need to deliver the training session.

❑ Check in with your producer.

❑ Post an out-of-office message on your email with information about how to reach the producer if someone has technical difficulty.

❑ Review the participant list and have it nearby.

❑ Place your water to maintain hydration on your workspace.

❑ Check all technology connections.

❑ Load polling questions, open whiteboards, check participant privileges or other steps that prepare the virtual classroom.

❑ 15 minutes prior to the starting time, dial into the conference calling software.

Being prepared to succeed

There you have it, the long and the short of preparation — list that is. As a trainer you will find that practice and preparation can make your training session all that you had hoped it would be. And that's something that you knew before you read this chapter.

To paraphrase Bob Pike from the beginning of this chapter, Publius Ovidus (43B.C.–17A.D.) said, "Practice is the best of all instructors."

Part III

Showtime: Delivering a Dynamic Training Session

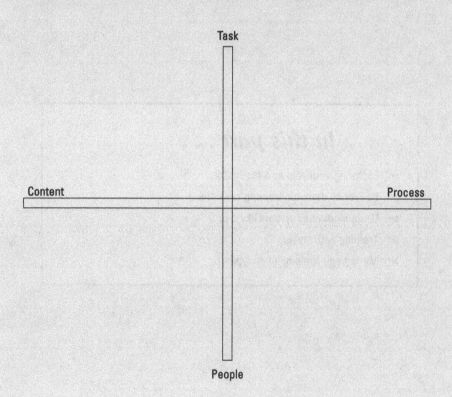

In this part . . .

- ✔ Exploring your role as a facilitator.
- ✔ Delivering dynamic training sessions.
- ✔ Using media and visuals like a pro.
- ✔ Training with style.
- ✔ Managing problems of all types.

Chapter 8

Implementing Training Designs: Your Job as a Facilitator

In This Chapter

▶ Clarifying the terms: trainer, presenter, and facilitator

▶ Identifying facilitation techniques effective trainers use

▶ Introducing, supporting, and processing activities

▶ Determining how to increase participation

*B*uilding on the definitions presented in Chapter 2, I want to further clarify that our profession is about what we *do*, not what we call ourselves. So whether you call yourself a trainer, a facilitative trainer, a facilitator, a presenter, or a talent developer, the title doesn't matter as long as you are clear about what you do to ensure that learning occurs and that the learning is transferred to the workplace to make a difference.

Some believe that all a trainer does is stand in front of a group to lead a learning event. But you know that is incorrect. A professional trainer must be able to conduct every step in the ADDIE model; must know the organization's strategy and goals and how talent development helps achieve them; must be adept at change management, knowledge management, and coaching; and must be on call to advise anyone who may have a question about informal, formal, online, on-the-job, or in the classroom training and development. That's why our job is so much fun — never a dull moment! Chapter 17 discusses our expanding roles.

For a more in-depth discussion about the profession and what's expected of us, be sure to review the Association for Talent Development (ATD) Competency Model. It defines the most recent competencies required for success across the entire training industry. This book is too short to incorporate everything a trainer does, but the certification materials will help. There are ten long volumes of study guides to support you if you choose (and I highly recommend it) to become certified. Becoming certified will help you understand the critical role you play for your organization.

This chapter continues the focus on your role as a facilitator. What does a trainer do? What skills make a great trainer? What's most important about conducting an activity? And if participation is so important, how does a trainer increase it? This chapter answers these questions.

Training, Facilitation, and Presentation: What's the Difference?

I once conducted a training session with a co-trainer, who was upset that I was calling him a trainer. He considered himself a facilitator. Funny thing though; he did the same thing I did: presented information in small doses, facilitated discussion, encouraged participation, conducted small and large group activities, and ensured that participants gained the knowledge and learned the skills the client expected.

You will run into people, like this gentleman, who get wrapped up in words and labels rather than just a clear definition of the actual role. The meanings of words are in people, not in dictionaries. Therefore, I take a pragmatic view of the definitions and begin to make some sense of them.

Note that this chapter focuses specifically on the trainer's role of facilitator.

Are you a trainer or a facilitator?

New trainers sometimes question the difference between the training and facilitating roles when implementing the training design. In *The Winning Trainer,* Julius E. Eitington defines them as follows:

- ✔ **Trainer:** Term used to describe a learner-centered conductor of a course or program. See also Facilitator.
- ✔ **Facilitator:** A trainer who functions in a way to allow participants to assume responsibility for their own learning. The term is in contrast to the more didactic instructor, teacher, lecturer, presenter, and so on.

As you can see, Eitington, for one, believes that the words are interchangeable because the roles are identical. I do as well. In this section, I continue to explore the two terms so that you can understand why label confusion may exist.

Some folks are not aware that the term training brings with it a definition that encompasses adult-learning theory. It assumes that an effective trainer has acquired a certain amount of knowledge and a specific skill set. A manager is a manager. No one tries to tag on another title (well aloud, anyway) that differentiates effective managers from ineffective managers.

There may have been a time when trainers were "tellers" of information, using a didactic model with learners. This was before Malcolm Knowles started to promote the concept of andragogy in the sixties. To add further confusion, some confuse college instruction with training. While it may be true that college professors should base more of their delivery on adult-learning principles, some trainers remember their experiences and want to disassociate themselves from it. Therefore, they give themselves a differentiating title of "facilitator" or "facilitative trainer." A trainer *is* a facilitator. Let me correct that: An *effective* trainer is a facilitator.

Now I add one more dimension: presenter. The definition provided in Chapter 2 states the following definition.

> Presenters: Title given adults who deliver speeches at conferences or to larger groups; minimal emphasis on two-way communication.

Sounds like an ineffective trainer. Wait a minute. Trainers present. They have to present new information in some way, or what would there be to learn? Do trainers only facilitate? No.

Trainers certainly facilitate activities. In addition, they also present information. An effective trainer makes certain that he or she presents this information in a facilitative way. Trainers who are delivering or implementing the training design (sometimes called *stand-up trainers*) must master two key skill sets when they conduct training sessions.

- ✔ They facilitate small-group activities, large-group discussions, and learning in general.
- ✔ They present new information, data, and knowledge.

Both of these skill sets are requirements for the job.

Mystery solved. A trainer is a facilitator *and* a presenter when delivering content, mentoring, coaching, and supporting change efforts. An effective trainer understands both roles and the skills associated with each. An effective trainer implements both roles when delivering training.

If you, as a trainer, believe that

- ✔ Adult learning theory has merit.
- ✔ Adults learn best when they are active rather than passive.

> ✔ Adults learn best when challenged rather than talked at.
>
> ✔ Adults learn best when involved rather than observing.

Then you probably embrace a participative training method, and make an effort to be an effective trainer who models both facilitation and presentation skills. You're an effective trainer.

Use facilitative skills when you present

At some point, trainers need to *present* information. Sometimes, "presenting" is nothing more than having participants learn by reading from a handout. The trainer has *presented* the activity to the learner. Good trainers require good presentation skills. Specific presentation skills such as eye contact, verbal competence, physical control, and others, will be addressed in the next chapter. But for now, think of the one most didactic learning activity you can imagine. Did you think "lecture?" Right!

How can a trainer use a facilitative trainer style to present a lecture? Well, first of all by not calling it a lecture. Try calling it a lecturette or presentation. You may think this is a minor point, but it will help you stay focused on "brief," which is what a lecturette should be.

Besides being brief you can use facilitative methods to obtain a high level of participation during lecturettes. Try these suggestions:

✔ Ask questions during the presentation.

> You probably know that you encourage more dialogue with open-ended questions than closed. However, examine your questions. "Can you identify ideas for how to move forward?" may at first blush sound like an open-ended question, but it really is not. It would be better stated as "What ideas do you have to move forward?"

✔ Answer questions throughout the presentation.

✔ Call on individuals for ideas or predictions of what occurs next.

✔ Conduct round robins to get opinions, ideas, concerns, or questions.

✔ Form small groups to discuss the information presented.

✔ Pause and check for understanding from everyone by creating a conversation.

✔ Take mini polls.

✔ Use humor in the words you use, the examples, or the visuals.

✔ Involve participants in deciding what they need to learn.

✔ Relate ideas from different participants.

✔ Compare or contrast participants' ideas.

✔ Use a parking lot for questions yet to be addressed.

When participants get ahead of you with their questions, create a "parking lot," — a place for participants to "park" their questions until you have provided adequate information to answer them with ease. One idea is to post a flipchart page with a sketch of a parked car on an easel or on the wall. Participants can write their questions on sticky notes and hang them on the page.

✔ Form buzz groups (two or three people who "buzz" for two minutes in response to a question) to identify one concern.

✔ Stop mid-presentation to ask whether everyone is with you.

✔ Reinforce those who ask questions or provide answers.

✔ Integrate quizzes (bingo, crossword puzzles, word completion) within the context of the presentation.

✔ Create a conversation between trainer and participants instead of delivering a presentation.

✔ Intersperse tasks or demonstrations throughout the presentation.

✔ Develop a handout to follow the presentation with key words from the presentation; allow room to take notes.

✔ Design visuals to support the lecturette so that participants can follow your words visually.

As you can see there are many ways to make a presentation interesting and interactive when delivering information through a presentation. Can you do all of these during a virtual ILT? Yes, indeed. Vary how you ask participants to respond. Here are some ideas:

✔ Let me know what you think about this idea through chat.

✔ Give me a green check if you agree with this concept.

✔ If you have used this before, give me a smiley face.

✔ Call on someone specific by saying, "Wisconsin, Mason, what do you predict is next?"

✔ Please raise your hand and give an example of when this happened to you.

You could pose a polling question, ask everyone to elaborate in chat, and then ask someone to unmute and expand on what they think.

Sooner or later trainers need to present information. You will be better equipped to "facilitate" that lecturette if you have mastered both the basic presentation skills as well as basic facilitation skills.

Facilitating Successful Training

Trainers walk a fine line between being proactive and responsive, between being flexible and sticking to the agenda, and between presenting content and facilitating discussion. They must be adaptive to the many learning styles in the room and supportive of the various requirements of all the participants. How do they do all this, act as a role model for the participants, and ensure that the learners have learned all they need to learn?

The 2014 ATD Competency Model identifies *training delivery* as one of the areas of expertise. It is described as delivering "informal and formal learning solutions in a manner that is both engaging and effective."

Throughout this book I have tried to emphasize that training is really all about the learner. Trainers must provide opportunities for actively engaging participants in their learning. Of course the goal is not just activity and participation. The goal is to ensure that the participants gain knowledge or learn skills to effectively improve performance. Active learning may be incorporated in hundreds of methods (some found in the design chapter) such as role plays, simulations, games, and so on. And active learning is also required when you coach a manager to support an employee, create a peer-mentoring group, or follow up with one of your virtual learners to provide additional resources.

It is not enough for a trainer to cover all the content and ensure that the learners are involved. A trainer must ensure that learners practiced the skills, that learning occurred, and the learners are prepared to perform the skills or use the knowledge when they return to the workplace. Learners must transfer the learning to the workplace.

The experiential learning process is often used by facilitators to ensure that learning occurs and that learners are ready to perform on the job. Participants learn inductively, that is, they discover for themselves by experiencing the activity. Other names you may hear used are interactive learning, experience-based learning, action learning, and discovery learning.

Real secrets of successful facilitation

by Sivasailam "Thiagi" Thiagarajan

Twenty-five years ago, I had this get-rich scheme: I will videotape brilliant instructional facilitators in action. I will find common patterns of behaviors and create a training package based on these consistent techniques. Then I will retire to some island in the sun.

I implemented the project by lugging around a heavy video camera and recording ten different facilitators. They were definitely brilliant, but my behavioral analysis was disappointing. I found no consistent common behaviors among these facilitators. To make matters worse, even the same facilitator conducting the same training activity employed different behaviors from one session to the next. To cut the long story short, I did not become a millionaire, but I discovered the real secret of effective presentation: Be inconsistent. In more positive terms, here is the secret: If you want to be an effective facilitator, be flexible, adaptive, and responsive.

To understand this secret, you should understand seven dimensions of facilitation that enhance or destroy a facilitated activity. Because each dimension has two undesirable extremes, I call them the seven facilitation *tensions*. Here they are with their extreme poles.

PACE: Too slow . . . Too fast

INTERACTION: Too cooperative . . . Too competitive

TONE: Too serious . . . Too playful

IMPLEMENTATION: Too rigid . . . Too loose

SHARING: Too intrusive into personal feelings . . . Too protective of personal feelings

FOCUS: Too much focus on results . . . Too much focus on the process

CONCERN: Excessive concern for the individual . . . Excessive concern for the group

Effective facilitation is a balancing act. When an aspiring facilitator asks me, "Should I conduct the activity at a fast pace or a slow one?" I simply answer, "Yes." The appropriate location of an activity along the seven tensions depends on several factors, including the number and types of participants and the structure and purpose of the activity. The secret of effective facilitation is to make these tensions transparent by maintaining a balance between the two extremes. However, "balance" resides in the perception of participants. Thus, the balance along the cooperation-competition dimension may differ drastically between a group from an ashram in South India and a group from a brokerage firm in New York.

How to prevent tension headaches. You can use a variety of common-sense tactics to increase or decrease each tension. For example, to speed up the pace, begin the activity promptly and get it rolling fast. Also announce and implement tight time limits. To slow down the pace, avoid time limits. If a team finishes the task ahead of others, insist on review and revision. Introduce a quality-control rule that punishes teams for sloppy work.

You can figure out your own techniques for increasing or lowering the tensions among the other six directions. To implement these secrets in your next facilitation session, begin your activity with confidence. As your participants work through the activity, continuously monitor the levels along various dimensions. If the seven tensions are at optimum levels, do not interfere with the flow of the activity. If some tension becomes noticeable, intervene with appropriate adjustments. Do this as quickly and as unobtrusively as possible. Continue monitoring the group and adjusting the activity as required.

Do you think I could make my millions by selling this flaky, but powerful, advice?

Sivasailam Thiagarajan, most often known as Thiagi, is well known in the training world as the man who gave games respect in the training room. He considers himself the resident mad scientist at the Thiagi Group. Those of us in the training field have him to thank for designing hundreds of games and sharing both the games and his facilitator concepts in more than a dozen books. Thiagi encourages all facilitators to constantly monitor participant reactions and switch between the passive and active facilitator roles.

Experience is the best teacher

Experiential learning occurs when a learner participates in an activity, reviews the activity, identifies useful knowledge or skills that were gained, and transfers the result to the workplace. An American baseball player, Vernon Sanders Law, stated that "Experience is a hard teacher because she gives the test first, the lesson after." This is the learning process you go through in your day-to-day life—your *life experience*.

Experiential learning activities (ELAs) attempt to duplicate life experience. An ELA is my favorite facilitation technique because participants "experience" what they are to learn before they discuss it, leading to surprises and *a-has*.

ELAs are based on several characteristics:

✔ They are directed toward a specific learning goal.

✔ They are structured; that is, they have specific steps and a process that must be followed to ensure results.

✔ There is a high degree of participant involvement.

✔ They generate data and information for participant analysis.

✔ They require processing or debriefing for maximum learning.

The steps in Pfeiffer and Jones' experiential learning cycle explain what must occur during an activity to ensure maximum learning occurs. The five steps are experiencing, publishing, processing, generalizing, and applying.

Step 1, Experiencing: Do something

This is the step that is associated with the "game" or fun or the experience. Participants are involved in completing a defined task. If the process ends here, all learning is left to chance and the trainer has not completed the task.

Step 2, Publishing: Share observations

The second step of the cycle gives the learners a chance to share what they saw, how they felt, and what they experienced. The trainer can facilitate this in several ways: Record data in the large group, have participants share or interview in subgroups, or lead a variation of a round robin. Questions the facilitator may ask are:

- ✔ What happened? What did you observe?
- ✔ What occurred during the activity?
- ✔ How did you feel about this?

The facilitator typically begins with a broad question and then focuses on more specific questions. The facilitator may probe for turning points or decisions that affected the outcome. This stage is important because it allows the participants to vent or express strong emotions and it allows the facilitator to gather data.

Step 3, Processing: Interpret dynamics or concepts

This step gives the participants a chance to discuss the patterns and dynamics they observed during the activity. Observers may be used to discuss this step. Questions the facilitator may ask are:

- ✔ Why do you think that may have occurred?
- ✔ What did you learn about yourself?
- ✔ What did you learn?
- ✔ What theories or principles may be true based on your experience?

The facilitator will again begin with broad questions and then home in on more specific questions. This stage allows participants to test hypotheses, preparing them to apply what they learned. This stage allows the facilitator a way to observe how much participants learned from the experience.

Step 4, Generalizing: Connect to real life

The key question in this step is "So what?" Participants are led to focus their awareness on situations that are similar to what they have experienced. This step makes the activity practical. Facilitators may ask:

- ✔ How does this relate to . . .?
- ✔ What did you learn about yourself?
- ✔ What does this suggest to you about . . . ?
- ✔ How does this experience help you understand . . . ?
- ✔ What if . . . ?

This stage ensures that the participants grasp the learning that was intended. The "what if" question becomes a bridge to the last step, which is application.

Step 5, Applying: Plan effective change

The last step presents the reason the activity was conducted: "Now what?" The facilitator helps participants apply generalizations to actual situations in which they are involved. The group may establish goals, contract for change, make promises, identify potential workplace changes, or initiate any other actions that result from the experience. The questions that are asked are:

- ✔ What will you do differently as a result of this experience?
- ✔ How will you transfer this learning to the workplace?
- ✔ How and when will you apply your learning?
- ✔ How may this help you in the future?
- ✔ What's next?

Participants frequently follow this step with an action plan or at least spend some time noting their thoughts about how life may be different as a result of the ELA.

The ELA is a powerful tool available to facilitators. It is time-consuming and, therefore, is used sparingly. If you decide to facilitate an ELA, don't take any shortcuts. The value is truly in the process.

Teach authentically in a virtual classroom

by Jennifer Hofmann

The face-to-face classroom is often considered to be the *best* environment in which to deliver training, and when that option isn't logistically or economically feasible, we look to the virtual classroom as the runner-up option.

Well, I've got a secret. Did you know that some performance objectives are best suited for delivery in the virtual classroom? And some performance objectives are best taught in the mobile virtual classroom? Hard to believe, right? Well this is certainly true when you want to facilitate an experiential activity.

Consider teaching a new customer service phone representative how to interact with customers while collecting and inputting data. Traditionally, we would bring the rep into a face-to-face environment — but that's not realistic. The work will eventually be performed at a desk using a telephone to communicate with customers. Using a virtual classroom to deliver this content is much more true to task, allowing individuals to learn in the environment in which they will be performing the work. All required skills can be assessed in the virtual environment: software competency can be observed using application sharing, and incredibly realistic role plays can be conducted in break-out rooms. If the learner can be at his or her own desk while training, using the actual computer, phone, and headset that would be used with a real customer, the training outcome will definitely be more real-work-oriented.

And then there is the mobile virtual classroom. Learners are using mobile devices often because they are, well, mobile. To take advantage of that, be sure to think about what skills they need when they're on the go. For example, if you are teaching a warehouse supervisor how to manage inventory using a tablet, delivering the training via the tablet is a more authentic (real-life/real-work) way of teaching the skill; therefore, the learners will leave the lesson with more skills than they would if training were taught in a less authentic environment. ("If he is going to perform the task that way, then he should learn the task that way.")

This is called *contextual learning.* If we are teaching someone how to create pivot tables in Microsoft Excel, that content should be designed for a virtual desktop environment because that is the environment in which learners will be applying the skill. Learning this skill on a mobile device is not only not contextual, it's difficult to see the detail involved with the tasks.

So the next time you are trying to decide whether using a virtual classroom is a viable option for particular content, take a close look at the desired performance outcome. You might be pleasantly surprised to discover that the virtual classroom is not only viable, it's the best environment for your learners.

Tips for facilitating activities

Activities are excellent learning tools for participants as long as the facilitator is prepared and follows a few suggestions for conducting them. These tips for introducing, supporting, and processing activities will help you think through all the nuances of facilitating activities.

Introducing activities

Ensuring that each activity gets started efficiently is critical. Use these steps to ensure that happens. Note that this is prior to the group's starting an activity or an ELA.

- ✔ Provide brief, general instructions including whether they will need materials, pens, and so on.
- ✔ Establish a clear objective that positions the activity within the context of the training module or session.
- ✔ Don't provide too much information if the intent is for the participants to discover an a-ha!

✔ Use a process to help participants form small groups. Do this before you provide more specific instructions. Otherwise, participants will forget what you told them in the first place!

✔ After participants are settled in their working groups, ascertain that you have everyone's attention. Then provide more specific direction.

✔ Tell participants how much involvement is expected of them. Depending on the activity you may also wish to tell them what will happen after. Will they be expected to share scores with the larger group? Will they be expected to report what happened? Will there be a large-group discussion?

✔ Distribute additional materials that may be required and demonstrate any processes that are necessary.

✔ Announce the amount of time the activity will require. It is a good idea to post the time on a flipchart or on the computer screen for your virtual learners. If the activity has steps within the process, you may wish to post a schedule of how much time should be spent on each step. Suggest any roles that may make the activity move smoothly: timekeeper, recorder, or a spokesperson.

✔ Ensure that everyone knows what to do; ask if anyone has any questions.

✔ Circulate among the groups to ensure that everyone understands the activity.

Supporting activities

Facilitators can be quiet guides to ensure that participants are successful with their activities. Facilitators will walk among the groups to ensure that everyone understands the task, stays on track, and reaches the end. Note that this would actually occur during the activity or step 1 of an ELA.

✔ During the activity, remind participants of the rules, if necessary.

✔ Give a "time is half up" signal and a "5 minutes left" or a "1 minute left" signal. Abrupt commands of "stop" or "time is up" may prevent participants from achieving the goal or bringing closure.

✔ You may need to make suggestions about the process. Take care, however, that you do not give away the answer. Suggesting, rather than commanding, allows participants to maintain control of the situation.

✔ Walk among participants to identify confusion, problems, questions, and time needed to complete the task.

✓ Adjust time, if necessary, and announce to the group, but only if all the groups need more or less time. Allowing some groups to have more time when others finished within the time limit may be perceived as unfair.

✓ Be sure to debrief the activity at its conclusion.

Processing activities

This is probably the most important part of the activity. If you were conducting an ELA, you would be addressing the questions and working through the process included in steps 2, 3, 4, and 5. Otherwise, you will want to assist the learners to understand the implications of what they just experienced or completed. Help them address the importance and the relevance of the activity to themselves personally. Use these suggestions:

✓ Relate the activity to previous as well as future training modules.

✓ Maintain a facilitative role without one-upping participants' experiences. Add information if it is a tip or a technique that will be useful for participants to understand the content or to improve a skill. However, if you can add that information at another time, save it until then.

✓ Share pertinent observations you made during the exercise.

✓ Avoid teaching, preaching, or lecturing.

✓ Stress practical application.

✓ Correct only when participants have obviously come to incorrect solutions, and then use either a questioning technique or participation from other groups to make the correction.

✓ Debriefing is required so that learning outcomes can be discussed. You may wish to record comments on a flipchart.

✓ You may use representatives from each group to conduct the debrief.

✓ Even if participants disagree on the outcome, ensure a common understanding among the group of what occurred before moving on.

Designing your own experiential learning activity

Excited about ELAs? You can design activities that are customized for your participants. Use Table 8-1 to plan your activity.

Table 8-1	Experiential Learning Activity Worksheet

Learning objective _____

_____

Group size _____ Time required _____

Materials/supplies _____

Handouts _____

Physical setting _____ Risk level _____

Process/directions _____

_____

_____

_____

Trainer notes:

   Introducing _____

   Conducting _____

   Processing _____

Participation Prescription: Continue to Increase the Dosage

Participation has been mentioned so often that it may seem as if I am prescribing it as the cure-all for learning. Well maybe so. While a participant may overdose on too much participation, it isn't too likely.

Gotta play the game to perform

In Chapter 2, I ask you to remember something you learned in the past 60 days and *why* you learned it. Now think about *how* you learned what you did. Suppose you selected a game or a sport. Did you select tennis, for example? Perhaps some of these learning activities occurred that resulted in learning:

✔ Someone may have presented you with information and you learned

- Rules of tennis

- How to keep score

- Best kind of racquet to purchase

✔ You read a book about tennis and you learned

- History of the game

- Where the big tournaments are held

- Simple technique to get started

✔ Someone demonstrated techniques and you learned how to

- Properly grip the racquet

- Serve

- Volley

✔ You observed several matches and you learned

- What the courts look like

- Where the players stand to serve

✔ You practiced by hitting the ball against a practice wall and you learned

- Eye-hand coordination

- How to direct the ball

- How to position your feet and body

Well, you get the idea. You have learned information and skills, but knowing the rules and hitting a tennis ball against a practice wall doesn't mean you can play tennis. You need to participate in a game with another tennis player. You need to serve the ball over the net and experience a returned hit. You need to play in a real match with other people to practice what you learned. You've gotta play the game to perform.

Learners need to participate to increase their performance. They need to be involved with other participants to get feedback on what they think they know. In almost all cases learners need to be in the game, practicing and participating to learn.

Participants' expectations of participation

Initially, participants expect you to take the lead in the training session. You will begin to shift the focus away from your role as the leader and to your role as the facilitator as quickly as you can. The key reason why virtual trainers should have the participant list next to them is so that they can begin calling on people by name early. How early may depend upon the experience and the communication skill level of individuals in your group. In most cases you will have a mix that includes at least three participant types:

- Some people will be good listeners, use no more than their fair share of talk time, and contribute when they have something new to contribute. They will be a joy in your session.

- Others will speak often and long, sometimes repeating what was just said by someone else (or themselves). You may wonder if they are speaking just to hear themselves talk. Actually they may just be unfamiliar with having airtime in front of a group, or it may be their rambling style. Whatever it is, you may need to use your facilitator skills to cut them off or to keep them focused.

- The third group will be quiet, cautious about volunteering and getting involved. I generally hold back a bit with these folks. I plan activities that allow them time to reach their participation comfort zone. I push just a bit more each time. The first question might just be a closed-ended question: "Randi, do you agree with what Harvey just said?" Then move to a question that asks for information: "Randi, how have you seen that used?" And finally, a wide-open question: "Randi, how do you feel about that?"

Training remotely

Remote Instructor-Led Training (RILT), where the learners and the trainer are in different locations, continues to be a more common situation. A company in one country buys a company in another, and the new employees need to get up to speed. An organization implements a new procedure or introduces a new product. Employees in other location need to learn about the nuances, but it is not worth the time and cost of travel. What can you expect?

Your voice is your most valuable tool. Without any gestures or eye contact, your voice will communicate everything: urgency, kindness, humor, patience, trustworthiness — everything discussed in this chapter. Your projection, tone, pace, and pitch (and absence of non-word fillers) will encourage participation and engagement.

Your materials will be required to manage the group, define interaction, demonstrate criticality, as well as impart knowledge and skills. Review current visuals and participant

materials with a critical eye, seeing them from the perspective of learning without a leader in the room.

You already have the skills to train remotely — you just may need to strengthen some. For example, asking provocative questions that gain attention quickly or showing empathy to concerns of those in another location. Here are a few quick tips:

- **Practice what you will say.** You probably would anyway, but in this case realize that you need to keep things moving so that things do not fall apart in the other location. You need to be efficient, specific, and organized.

- **Prepare participants.** Use some of the same prework and preparation tactics you use in a virtual setting. Email information early. Create excitement about the content. Use Dropbox or Box.net for sending participant material and document sharing.

✔ **Picture the place.** Ask for a picture of the room where participants will be to help you plan activities or small group arrangements.

✔ **Present a short but robust set of guidelines.** This goes against what I would normally do by allowing participants to set their own ground rules. This is a different scenario. They will have many distractions, which are often curtailed with a simple glance.

✔ **Set expectations.** If this is the first time the participants have experienced a RILT, explain what will happen to address any concerns they may have.

✔ **Connect with individuals.** It is extremely important to use participants' names and understand their unique needs. Create an annotated participant list with names, needs, and interesting facts about each.

✔ **Communicate with confidence.** In order to project your voice and maintain control, I suggest that you stand. This requires that you use a headset so you can move around.

✔ **Have an emissary at the remote site.** Someone who can act as your eyes and ears to let you know when small groups are ready to report out or if someone has a question. The emissary can be a participant, but needs to support you in facilitating.

✔ **Respect the learners' routine and time zone.** That means you may need to conduct training at 6:00 in the morning or 10:30 at night your time.

✔ **Picture who's there.** At least exchange pictures on a group site. Also consider how you can use your webcam and Skype.

To complicate it even more, a special situation occurs when you have participants in the room with you, as well as a remote group in another location. This may be one of the more difficult virtual training scenarios. In this case, I suggest that you have two emissaries, one in each location; they can synchronize between the groups. You may also want to create some friendly competition between the two groups to keep them focused and prevent them from dawdling over activities. Mentally focus on the remote group throughout; you will not need a reminder that you have a group in front of you! As suggested earlier, stand throughout the session. It not only helps you project your voice, it provides leadership for the participants in your room. One last thing, if the organization has access to video conferencing, that would be another option you may want to consider.

Even if you have not conducted remote training yet, you most likely will soon. RILT will continue to grow as our world and the changes in it move faster and faster. Be prepared.

Increasing participation — or why are they called "participants"?

Throughout this book, I use two terms to discuss the individuals in your training session: "learners" and "participants." They are interchangeable, and you will most likely use a term that is most comfortable to you or that is culturally acceptable in your organization.

Though the learner/participant label has switched back and forth based on subtle reasons, emphasis on participation has never wavered. An effective trainer encourages as much involvement and participation by the learners as is practically feasible.

Sometimes, obstacles exist that prevent trainers from providing as much participation as they would prefer, for example, time limitations, facility availability, organizational culture, group size. If those are not a consideration and you're still interested in increasing the amount of participation, examine your competency based on various aspects of delivering training.

Perhaps you have designed the perfect experiential learning activity. Yet participants are not getting involved the way you thought they might. The following areas may give you some ideas of what may inhibit participation and what you need to do to increase participation in your sessions.

Communication

Whether it is a virtual or face-to-face ILT, good communication skills help to encourage participation naturally.

- ✔ **Listen well.** This skill is at the top of almost any good-skills-to-possess list. If you expect participation, this is one you'd better master. You know all the right things to do: Listen to understand, avoid hasty judgment, don't interrupt, ask clarifying questions, and focus on content and intent.

- ✔ **Accept input.** When you receive suggestions, comments, or responses that are not quite right, you need to accept them — at least initially. You of course do not want anyone to leave the session with incorrect information, but you can thank the person, and then ask the group, "What do the rest of you think?"

- ✔ **Project assertiveness.** A trainer needs to be assertive with individuals at times — for example, disruptive participants, argumentative individuals — to ensure participants have the correct information.

- ✔ **Ask questions.** This is probably the most used way to encourage participation. You may ask closed or open-ended questions or rhetorical questions. You may ask for volunteers or call on someone specifically. Allow participants to develop their own answers and accept them.

If you ask participants a question, give them enough time to volunteer a response. If you answer your own question because you're uncomfortable with the silence or because you think participants don't know the answer, then eventually, they will let you answer *all* the questions.

- ✔ **Encourage questions.** If you ask for questions, allow enough time for participants to formulate and ask them. If you find yourself asking people to hold their questions too often, it means the participants are ahead of you. Perhaps there is something wrong with the design. Asking participants to hold questions is one of the biggest deterrents to participation. Use the parking-lot tip found earlier in the "Use facilitative skills when you present" section in this chapter, but don't overuse it.

✔ **Practice silence.** Silence is a way to communicate also. Pause regularly to allow participants to think and process information. They can't talk if you are.

✔ **Check the pulse.** If you just aren't certain about how learners are accepting the content, ask them. Better to catch it early. In a virtual setting, you can take the pulse of the group with a thumbs up or down.

✔ **Use chat.** In a virtual classroom, be sure to attend to the questions coming into the chat feature. It is always a good idea to have a producer to monitor participant comments and questions, but with a large group it is imperative.

Interpretive skills

The ability to read participants' nonverbal messages and to understand the *intent* of verbal messages, as well as the *content* takes communication skills to another level. Learners need to know that you "get it" to increase their participation level.

✔ **Relate to situations.** The ability for a trainer to empathize and visualize from the participant's view increases participation. Participants gain trust and believe that you really do understand.

✔ **Appreciate hot buttons.** Know your participants' hot buttons. If you can ignore them, do so. If you cannot ignore them, prepare your response so that you both save face.

✔ **Be sensitive to nonverbal meanings.** Watch participants and try to interpret the messages their nonverbals are really saying. If you don't understand, don't be afraid to ask. Sometimes, this is better done during a break and away from the rest of the group. In a virtual classroom, follow up after the session to check in with anyone you sense was less than satisfied.

✔ **Translate correctly.** Interpreting what participants say and transferring their thoughts and ideas correctly to the rest of the group verbally or writing them on a flipchart page encourages others to speak up.

Personal traits

Several basic characteristics will encourage participation if they are evident. If they are absent, these may discourage participation faster than any others.

✔ **Sense of humor:** Use humor to lighten the experience. Laugh at incidents. Laugh at yourself. Do not laugh at participants.

✔ **Patience:** Give participants the time they need to learn or practice skills that will make them successful.

✔ **Trustworthiness:** Do what you say you're going to do.

✔ **Openness to ideas:** Be open; at least acknowledge even wild ideas.

✔ **Sincerity:** Sincerity may be one of the most important to encourage participation. People know if you truly want them to participate.

Interpersonal style

The style you exhibit allows participants to trust you and adds to their willingness to contribute to the training session. You display a set of characteristics that are natural to your unique style, yet the most successful trainers are also flexible enough to adapt all the style characteristics required to ensure participation.

✔ **People-oriented and approachable:** Encourage participants to ask you questions. It's a good sign if they are asking you questions at break that have nothing to do with the session. It means they are comfortable asking for your thoughts and find you easy to talk to. Smile.

✔ **Willing to share yourself:** Let people in on who you are. Share something about you. Share your experiences, your successes, and your failures. Be real. They will feel more comfortable about sharing something about themselves.

✔ **Organized:** Participants will trust that you can help them if you're prepared and organized. Being organized also ensures that you have the maximum amount of time to give to your participants.

✔ **Respectful of all opinions:** Trainers can't play favorites if they want to encourage participation. You don't need to agree with all opinions, just respect them and try to understand what it means.

Learning techniques

Effective teaching skills do come into play. Think back to teaching your children or younger siblings. You probably used techniques that continue to work with adults who are learning new skills. An effective trainer will have adapted some of these learning techniques to adult learners.

✔ **Provide clear directions.** Anything that needs to be done correctly needs to begin with clear directions. Don't set your participants up for failure by giving poor directions.

✔ **Catch 'em being good.** Reinforce participants as they achieve success. In addition, provide feedback for the behaviors that contribute to a participative environment, such as volunteering and contributing. Say, for example, "Thanks for doing. . . ."

✔ Allow the learning process to occur even if participants experience some struggles. Survival and learning is often dependent upon the process.

- ✔ **Provide feedback.** Give participants honest feedback about their progress.

- ✔ **Coach.** Coach participants about both the skills they are learning as well as appropriate participation behaviors.

Think through all the techniques you use to encourage learning. Ensure that you remember to use adult-learning principles as the basis for your techniques. Don't destroy the environment for the sake of "the right answer." For example, if you ask participants to identify a list of anything in small groups, don't follow up with a handout of your list of the same thing. Adults may resent it thinking that you could have just given it to them in the first place. Or even worse, that somehow their list was defective in some way and your list is "the right answer."

Attending skills

Sometimes tossed in with good communication skills, attending skills in a training session do much more than open communication. Attending skills help to show that you care about your participants and that you want them to succeed. That's a powerful message when trying to increase participation.

- ✔ **Provide consistent eye contact.** Face the participants; ensure that you make real eye contact so that you can read them. (Don't look at the tops of their heads.) Learn to talk and walk backward. Truly the skill of a gifted trainer!

- ✔ **Balance eye contact.** Scan the group regularly. This will help you know whether anyone is confused, distracted, or focused. This is a critical one for good participation.

I've noticed that trainers (and most speakers) tend to extend the majority of their eye contact to 75 percent of the room to their non-dominant side. To encourage participation of everyone, remember to look at those participants sitting near the front of the room to your dominant side.

- ✔ **Demonstrate attentive moves.** Move around the room as you encourage discussion. Move toward individuals to encourage them to get involved in the discussion or to signal you're about to call on them. Resist the temptation to stand behind a podium or even the table; this creates a barrier between you and your learners.

- ✔ **Provide affirmative nonverbals.** This means body language like nods and smiles.

- ✔ **Stay engaged.** Even while participants are working on activities or small groups, stay engaged. This is not a time to call your office or take a break. Move among the groups, offering assistance, listening for understanding, and answering questions.

Process factors

The process you use to encourage and balance participation is the final area to consider. Participants may interpret a lack of somewhat equal participation by learners as playing favorites or ignoring quieter participants.

- ✔ **Balance participation.** Encouraging the quiet, yet not shutting down the vocal, participants. Reinforcing the correct response, yet not negating the incorrect. Allowing participants to bring up issues, yet staying on track. Balance is the job of an effective trainer.

- ✔ **Maintain flow of interaction.** Observe who speaks to whom and how often. Encourage participants to speak with each other rather than to direct all comments your way.

- ✔ **Build participation.** Consider how you methodically increase expectations. For some individuals you may start by asking for a simple show of hands, requesting volunteers, using a round robin, calling on specific people, being a member in a small group, and eventually acting as the spokesperson for a group.

- ✔ **Create an inclusive environment.** When participants feel psychologically safe in your session, they will want to be a part of it. Encouraging everyone to participate, including quiet learners, demonstrates to everyone (not just those who are quiet) that you value everyone's opinions.

REACTing

There are so many things you may think about to facilitate and encourage participation. Don't worry about learning and perfecting all of them. Many of them will become as natural as good communication skills. That's because many are natural. In effect, it comes down to your reaction to the learners and the learning situation. How do you REACT to ensure an environment that encourages the best opportunities for participation? How do you REACT to create the best learning experience? This *mnemonic,* a tool for remembering, will help you remember the basics for encouraging participation:

- ✔ Relaxed and informal atmosphere
- ✔ Encourage participation
- ✔ Accept them where they are
- ✔ Communication is open, friendly, and honest
- ✔ Take control of their own learning

This quote by Theodore Roosevelt speaks volumes about why some facilitators are successful and others are not. "People don't care how much you know until they know how much you care." Care about your participants and their learning.

Chapter 9

It's Showtime: Delivering Success

- -

In This Chapter

▶ Opening with a BANG

▶ Creating a supportive learning environment

▶ Getting to know your participants and their needs

▶ Using smooth transitions to move from one place to another

▶ Bringing closure to a training event

- -

Showtime! You've conducted a thorough needs assessment, written clear objectives, designed an interactive training program, and developed materials. You're on!

Stage Four, Implementing the Design, illustrated in Figure 9-1, is most likely the part of The Training Cycle that most people think about when they hear any terminology about training. It is certainly the part that everyone sees; now you can see that it is actually the culmination of a huge effort that focuses on the learner and what needs to be accomplished to ensure a successful training.

Now that you've made it to this point, how do you ensure that you deliver successfully? This chapter addresses opening the session with a bang and creating a supportive learning environment. It will share ideas to help you get to know the participants better and about how to continue to address their needs by training like a pro, using questions and answers that lead to learning, and bringing closure to the session.

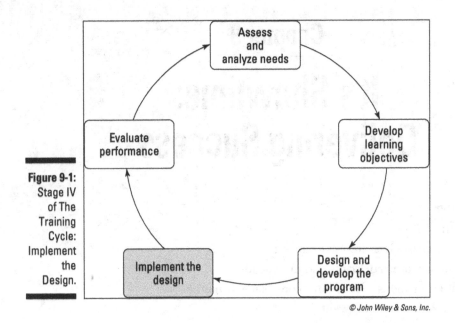

Figure 9-1:
Stage IV
of The
Training
Cycle:
Implement
the
Design.

Opening Your Training Session with a BANG, Online or Off

You completed all the preparation steps to ensure that the room, the equipment, and you are as ready as you're ever going to be. You have arrived an hour early, and you have been welcoming participants as they arrive. It's time to start the session. Many things happen when you deliver a training session, but few are as important as the opening.

Whether virtual or face-to-face, you will want your opening to be informative, yet creative. It should be practical, yet promote excitement. And it should be helpful, as well as enthusiastic. Start your session with a BANG!

Build interest in the session.

Ask what participants know and what they want to know.

Note the ground rules and what to expect.

Get them involved.

In the following sections, I examine each of these.

Build interest in the session

Start the session on time and grab their attention right from the start. Save the ground rules and the housekeeping details for later. Be creative with your opening. You may use props, tell a story, state an unusual fact, ask a provocative question, or make a promise. Participants will want to know what's in it for them: how what they will learn will be useful to them personally or how it will make their jobs easier.

Ask what participants know and what they want to know

Understanding your participants' needs is critical for you, so conduct a mini needs assessment by asking for a show of hands about their experience, expertise, or knowledge. Poll your participants in a virtual session. This also demonstrates that you want to know about them. Ask participants about their expectations. Listen well. You may wish to capture these on a flipchart and then post them on a wall so they can be seen throughout the session.

You may wish to have the "expectations" flipchart page prepped with a title. Although it is a little thing, it sends a message to the participants that you spent time to prepare for them.

Be honest about expectations that are unrealistic for the session or for you. For example, if one of the participants wants to learn about a topic that is too complex or lengthy or will not fit into the agenda, you could say, "We probably won't have time to add that to the agenda, but I would be happy to chat with you off-line or follow up with a reference next week."

Note the ground rules and what to expect

Save time by stating any given ground rules up front, such as start and end time (if they are not flexible.) Ask participants to add others. Again, you may wish to capture and post the ground rules for ready reference. What are the most common ground rules?

Ground Rules for All Classrooms

Stop and start on time	Cellphones on silent mode
Participate willingly	Respect others' opinions
Allow for interaction	There are no dumb questions
Keep an open mind	What's said in here stays in here

Physical Classroom Additions

No sidebars

Timely break

Okay to move around as needed

One person speaks at a time

Virtual Classroom Additions

State your name before speaking

Use chat to ask questions

Avoid the telephone "hold" key

Use mute in a noisy area

Briefly note any administrative details and share what participants can expect beyond the ground rules. Pay particular attention to the word "briefly." Don't dwell on the mundane.

If you must provide a telephone number, email address, or wifi password regarding an administrative detail, post it on the flipchart. If you don't, you will repeat it a dozen times during the day.

Go over the session objectives and the agenda so that participants know what they will learn. Put participants at ease by explaining their role as learners and how you intend to conduct the session. If you facilitate a virtual classroom and you intend to call on participants by name, now is the time to tell them.

I do not put specific times on the participants' agenda. Participants become nervous if they see that you're behind by 30 minutes. They don't understand that you may be currently covering something that was planned for later or that you know that what they are addressing now is much more important than something later and that you can decrease time on another activity.

I print my personal agenda on brightly colored paper. I use bright paper so that I can see it if it gets lost under handouts. I include the timing of activities so that I stay on track. I like to allow flexibility to meet participants' needs, but I also need to take full responsibility for achieving the learning objectives.

Get them involved

Start with a show of hands, and next help everyone get to know each other. Participants learn as much from each other as the program, so start quickly with introductions that are tied to an icebreaker. Knowing something about the other individuals in the session will make it easier for them to listen, to contribute, and to get involved. Several tried-and-true icebreakers are listed in Chapter 21.

The classic four questions answered by participants in a training session include:

- ✔ Who are you?
- ✔ Where do you work?
- ✔ What do you hope to learn?
- ✔ What's something interesting about you?

These four questions are usually embedded in the introductions in some way. Remember that your participants will want to know the same things about you.

Always start on time. Anything else teaches participants that it is okay to be late. You're training them to be late. Waiting for a few stragglers punishes those who made the effort to be on time. If you anticipate legitimate tardiness (bad weather), you can always be prepared to start with something that is interesting but not critical for everyone to know.

Identify all that you want to accomplish in your opening. These things may include:

- ✔ Establish a participative climate.
- ✔ Introduce participants.
- ✔ Introduce the agenda.
- ✔ Clarify the participants' expectations.
- ✔ List objectives of the training.
- ✔ Build interest and excitement.
- ✔ Learn something about the participants.
- ✔ Determine some minimum rules of engagement (ground rules).
- ✔ Establish your credibility.

Plan how you will accomplish what you need to lay the foundation for the rest of the training session. First impressions are critical. A good trainer will catch and hold participants' attention right from the start. That's why it is important to start with a BANG!

Looking at Six Disastrous Debuts

Trainers need to be prepared with an opening — what to say and what to do. If you're unprepared, you may find yourself saying things you didn't mean to say, getting ahead of yourself, forgetting what you were supposed to say, and just generally confusing your audience.

Be prepared so you don't fall into one of these disastrous debuts:

- Asking obvious, contrived questions
- Talking too much, wandering from point to point with no direction
- Telling someone they are wrong
- Making a participant the brunt of a joke
- Forcing your beliefs on the participants, telling them what to do or how to think
- Trying to be funny

Not one of these works. Trust me. I've seen them all. Don't do them.

Creating a Supportive Learning Environment

To successfully create a supportive learning environment you need to get to know your participants, and that means remembering and using their names. It also means that you will want to let them know something about you.

Get to know your participants

If you have opened with a BANG and gotten early participation, learners will expect to be involved in their learning. Don't change the expectation now! Continue to implement activities that encourage discussion and involvement. Begin to call participants by their names immediately to create a supportive learning environment.

I like to use name tents (cardstock folded in half lengthwise) for names. I usually have my name tent completed as a model when they walk in the door. I also place broad-tipped markers around the tables so that their names can be written to be seen from a distance. If everyone has not completed the name tents by the time introductions have been completed, I ask them to do so.

You start to get to know your participants through introductions and by conducting a mini needs assessment during your opening. Select questions that help you better understand the group's skill level, knowledge, experience, and expertise. In the case of a train-the-trainer, for example, I may want to know how long they have been trainers, whether they have ever attended a train-the-trainer, whether they have designed training, and finally whether they thought that training was their destined profession. How do you do this? You may simply ask for a show of hands. If more complex, you may wish to have them complete a few brief questions. (Note, however, that this process doesn't encourage participation, nor does it inform the rest of the participants). If you want to add movement, you may ask participants to stand if their response is yes, or to move to a certain spot in the room based on their response.

Getting to know your participants early in the session is one of the best investments you can make. After you have created a learning environment in which participants feel comfortable to participate, to ask questions, and to learn, the session has the best chance of success.

What's in a name: Five secrets to remembering names

To establish an environment that is conducive to learning, trainers need to build trust and let their participants know that they care about them. Because most people are flattered when someone takes the time to learn and use their names, this is one obvious way to build a positive environment. Oh no! Can't even do that at a party when you meet only one person? Now I'm suggesting that you learn 10, 20, or more participants' names all at once?

 Obtain a copy of the roster prior to your training session. I read it over and try to get a big-picture vision of how many people, men, women, and names. I also look for names that may be difficult to pronounce so that I can take extra care to listen when they introduce themselves. In a virtual session, having the roster in front of you allows you to add notes if participants introduce themselves or it may remind you of a comment or question they had.

These five techniques will help you as the facilitator to learn participants' names in a face-to-face classroom.

Use name tents

Table tents, sheets of cardstock that are folded in half lengthwise and sit on the table like a tent (which is why they are called *table tents*), may have an organization's logos printed on them. Provide fat, dark markers so that you can read everyone's, even of those who sit way in the back of the room. I usually say something like "Use the marker to write your name or whatever you wish to be called for the next couple of days (hours) on the name tent."

I have completed mine, and it is sitting up front as a model. Sometimes this is all participants need. They see the model and imitate it before I even say anything.

 Ask them to print their names on both sides of the name tent so that everyone can see it no matter where they are in the room. This is actually as much help to you as anyone. When you see hands go up to make a comment, a quick glance at the name tent and you can easily say, "Ted, how would you answer that?"

 Be sure you don't have anything in your line of sight between you and the name tent — no glasses, no water pitchers, no props. Otherwise, you will constantly be craning your neck to read names.

 Some organizations insist on preprinting the name tents with participants' names. I oppose this for several reasons. First, there is a chance that a name is misspelled, or worse yet, the person's name is missed completely. Second, it adds a sense of formality that I do not want as a part of my sessions. Third, it adds to the logistic nightmare. Participants need to find their name tents in a stack or someone needs to be available to pass them out. Or a worse solution, they are placed around the tables and participants are not able to select where they want to sit. Fourth, and worst of all, usually the typeface is too small for anyone to read the length of the room, so it is all for naught! The only reason you would want preprinted name tents is if you, the trainer required assigned seating.

Work the introductions

You may think that you can relax a bit while everyone is going around and introducing themselves. Perhaps use the time to get organized for the first information sharing? Not a good idea. Remember these first few minutes are a critical time to build rapport. As people are introducing themselves, listen to what they are saying, look at their names on their name tents, and begin to connect their names and faces. Also, use their names at least twice during the introductions. You can say, "Welcome [name]," or "[Name], thank you for telling us. . . ." Start planting those names in your brain.

Use small-group time

I usually have participants remain in their seats for the first small-group activity. They may either turn to the person next to them or form a group of three or four sitting next to each other. My rationale is that while they are completing the task in the small group, I spend a portion of the time matching faces and names again. If I forget anyone's, the name tent is nearby and provides the cue for me. I set a goal to know everyone's names by the first break. Set a goal for yourself.

Play a game

Several name games work well. If you have time for an icebreaker that focuses on people learning each other's names you may try these. They are fun, and they teach everyone, not just the trainer, the names of the participants. These are worth the time investment for a multiple-day class.

- ✔ **How Many Can You Name?** If your icebreaker includes individuals meeting as many other people as possible, you can let them know that you will "quiz" them on how many people they actually "meet," meaning they remember their names. Before you debrief the icebreaker, ask how many names each participant remembers.

- ✔ **Chain Name:** As you go around the room with introductions, each person reiterates all the people before. For example, person number one only introduces him or herself. Person number two introduces person number one plus him- or herself. Person number three introduces number one, number two, and him-/herself. It becomes more and more difficult, but the rest of the participants begin to help those at the end. The activity establishes a good environment, and everyone learns names.

- ✔ **Doodles:** Have participants add a doodle to their name tent. The doodle must start with the same letter as their first name. For example, Opal may add oatmeal and Dominick may add a dog. The alliteration will help you, and the other participants, remember names.

- ✔ **Name It:** When participants introduce themselves, ask them to add something about their names: the history or meaning of their names, who they were named after, what they like (or dislike) about their names, or any other unique fact about their names. The added discussion about the name itself helps everyone to remember more names.

Cheat

Finally, when all else fails, do what I do — cheat. Before the session starts I draw a sketch of the room and the table arrangement. As participants introduce themselves, I jot the person's name at the corresponding place in the sketch. I can use that later as I practice everyone's name.

Participants feel good when you use their names. Work at remembering them.

Let them know about you

Let participants in on who you are to create a supportive learning environment, both professionally and personally. I tend to be low keyed about my expertise and experience. I may drop subtle hints related to the discussion or the content about who I am. I would not say, "I have published over 60 books." But I would say, "In my last book I interviewed 45 training managers who said. . . ." You do not need to be subtle at all. You do want to establish credibility with the participants.

How about personally? How much you let them in on who you are personally is entirely up to you. I like to get to know participants, so I spend breaks with them as much as possible. I find things out about them that we have in common and then use that information to continue our discussion. Sometimes, as an energizer, I ask participants what they want to know of each other. I get into the fray, and they can ask questions of me as well.

You will want to build professional credibility with your participants. You will want them to know you as a human being as well. Don't keep yourself on a pedestal that prevents you from building rapport with your participants.

Training Like a Pro

As mentioned in the last chapter, trainers have two key skill sets they master when they are conducting training. First, they facilitate small-group activities, large-group discussions, and learning in general. Second, they present new information, data, and knowledge. Both of these skill sets are requirements for the job. I examine the facilitator role in Chapter 8. Now, I examine how trainers can be effective presenters.

Presentation skills

Trainers need to present information. It would be nice to never have to deliver content, but that just isn't going to happen.

Mel Silberman, author and consultant, is well known for his concept of active training. Yet he knew that as a trainer you will need to present information at times. Even, so, Mel believed that participants can be actively involved in the learning. See his "Ten suggestions to turn a lecture into active learning" sidebar.

When you present, whether it is a lecturette, simply describing a concept during a discussion, or responding to a question, the participants will not only hear your content, but they will also "hear" and "see" your presentation style.

It is easier for your participants to learn when your presentation is interesting and even better when it is exciting. This is true whether you are online or in person. How interesting, competent, and exciting do you sound? What do participants infer about you based on your presentation techniques and style?

What do they hear? The Six Ps

Vocal expression adds vitality and energy to your ideas. Several characteristics make up the audio part of your presentation. Think of these as the six Ps of your presentation: projection, pitch, pace, pauses, pronunciation, and phillers.

✔ **Projection** refers to how loud the message is heard. Do you project enough volume? Loudness results when air is expelled from the lungs with maximum force and intensity. The appropriateness of a loud or soft voice depends on the room size or Internet connection, and the need for vocal variety. Variations in volume can be used to indicate urgency, exasperation, and importance.

✔ **Pitch** in a conversation flows up and down the scale naturally. But when some trainers stand in front of a group, their voices become dull and flat. I learned about pitch from Kevin Daley, founder of Communispond. He says picture pitch by thinking of the states of Kansas and Colorado. Kansas is flat; even when you say the state's name, it comes out quite flat. Now picture Colorado with its rolling hills, mountains, valleys, streams — lots of variety. Even when you say "Colorado," your voice can't help but roll up and down the scale. Pitch variety adds interest to your voice, but it also helps you to emphasize important ideas or to signal transitions. Both are important to keep your learner tuned in to what you're saying.

✔ **Pace** is the rate of delivery and is determined by the duration of sound and the number of pauses between sounds. Words can be spoken fast or drawn out. Like projection and pitch, the pace can also signal importance. Try saying $50,000 quickly, as if it is just a small amount of money. Now, say it again, this time slowing your pace and adding emphasis on every other syllable. It can really make a difference.

Select a pace that is comfort for you. Don't try to speed up or slow down. Your brain is accustomed to working with your mouth in a certain cadence. However, if you're told you speak too rapidly, try punctuating your presentation with more pauses. Right. Just snap your jaw closed. If, on the other hand, you're told you speak too slowly, check on a couple of things. First, make sure you're using no fillers. Second, be certain you're not repeating the same information. And third, know your material cold. Practice your content aloud a couple of extra times.

✔ **Pauses** can actually add more emphasis than anything mentioned so far. A judiciously placed pause before and/or after an idea can focus attention right where you want it. Pauses allow you time to think. Pauses also allow you to observe the participants for feedback. Pauses are the sign of a seasoned presenter, because most inexperienced presenters are uncomfortable with silence. Practice your pauses.

✔ **Pronunciation** is critical to make it easy for your participants to understand and learn easily. Speaking articulately, clearly, and distinctly is a sign of a pro. Learn to enunciate clearly. Take care that you do not run words together or let the ends of your sentences trail off so your learners have difficulty hearing.

✔ **Phillers** are those nasty little nonsounds that sneak in when you aren't listening to yourself: Um, ah, and ah, er, okay, ya know, like. All are fillers that can hypnotize your participants into a trance or can grate on their innermost nerves. No matter which occurs, you can be sure that they will not hear your content but may instead be counting fillers. The sad thing is that most people do not hear their own fillers.

The only way I know to eliminate fillers is to hire yourself an Um Counter, someone who will listen to your presentation and provide you with feedback about how many fillers you use per minute and which ones. The shock seems to awaken something so that you can finally hear yourself.

What do they see?

The other half of your presentation is what your learners see. What they see should convey the same interesting, competent, and exciting message.

✔ **Body stance** is one of the first things participants notice. Good posture and poise convey confidence to your message, and your participants will want to know the content. When standing in front of the room, plant your feet and avoid shifting your weight. Moving around and among the participants is good. It uses up some of your nervous energy and helps to create a natural and comfortable environment. However, repetitive moves, such as pacing back and forth in the same spot are distracting.

Try to never have your back to the group. Learn to talk and walk backwards! How about sitting? Sitting certainly changes the tone. It would be rare, but you may sit or even lean against a table. Your stance then says "informal." The tenor of the presentation has changed. In the past I have purposefully pulled a chair in the middle of the room and while sitting had a heart-to-heart discussion with a group that was disagreeable. So the question is, what is your purpose for sitting? What atmosphere do you want to convey?

✔ **Gestures** help to convey enthusiasm and help your participants follow your presentation (first, second). Keep them natural. If you start with your hands at your sides, they will come up naturally. Think about speaking and gesturing to those seated farthest from you. This enhances your gestures, as well as your projection. Avoid crossing your arms, playing with your marker, or touching your head.

How about putting your hands in your pockets? It depends. Are you putting your hands in your pockets because you're nervous or they feel awkward and you don't know what to do with them? Or are you putting your hands in your pockets because you're relaxed and you want to send a message of relaxation to your audience? If you're putting your hands in your pockets for the first reason, then the answer is no, don't do it. Your hands will just get into trouble jangling change. On the other hand, if your reason is to send a message of relaxation, then fine, go ahead.

✔ **Facial expression** should be congruent with your words. In fact, your face can express more than your words! Facial mobility is an indication of a relaxed speaker. Use it to add emphasis to your message and to display energy. Be aware of your expressions and what they may convey.

Early in my career, I was surprised when a participant said to me, "You don't want us to ask questions." This was of course exactly the opposite of what I wanted. I did want them to ask all the questions necessary to understand the skills they were learning. When I asked why she made the statement, she said, "Whenever we ask questions you frown." Wow! I was unaware of frowning. I realized that I was concentrating on their questions, and when I concentrate my face appears to be frowning. It was a great lesson. What are your facial expressions saying about you?

✔ **Eye contact** is important in all conversations. In the United States it represents caring, understanding, and trust. Good eye contact builds rapport with your participants. Avoid looking at the ceiling. Don't just sweep the participants or try to get by with looking at the tops of their heads. People know whether you're making eye contact. Good eye contact means that you see their facial expressions and can tell if they are following and/or agreeing with you.

Be sure to look at all of your participants. I find that most trainers ignore the 25 percent of the people closest to the front on their dominant side. Are you aware of where you're looking? One other thing, I have noticed that good eye contact decreases the number of fillers. Somehow, it's tougher to look someone in the eye and say "um!"

Eye contact is a cultural preference. It is not viewed the same in all cultures. If you're training in another country or training other cultures in the United States, you will of course respect other values. Other cultures view eye contact differently. Some consider it rude or aggressive. Be familiar with the culture of your participants.

✔ **Nervousness** is displayed in numerous ways: pacing or swaying, fidgeting with a pen, jingling change in your pocket, perspiring, shaking, clearing your throat, grimacing, tenseness, and dozens of other things. However, if you have interesting content, your participants will not even notice. The number one rule regarding nervousness is "Do not say that you're nervous." Nervousness is covered in greater depth in Chapter 12. Check it out for additional information.

✔ **See? Online?** You've got to be kidding. Nope. Not kidding. Of course they can't see you in a physical sense, but they can "see" a lack of caring if you voice isn't engaging, or disorganization if you are multitasking ineffectively, or hesitation and nervousness if you haven't mastered your content yet.

Hang a mirror above your computer screen for the times you conduct virtual training. It will remind you to smile. People can hear a smile in your voice.

Ten suggestions to turn a lecture into active learning

by Mel Silberman

Lecturing is one of the most time-honored yet ineffective ways to teach. By itself, it will never lead to active learning. In order for a lecture to be effective, the instructor should build interest first, maximize understanding and retention, involve participants during the lecture, and reinforce what's been presented. There are several options to do just that.

Building Interest

✔ Lead off with a story or interesting visual. Provide a relevant anecdote, fictional story, cartoon, or graphic that captures the audience's attention to what you're about to teach.

✔ Present an initial case problem. Present a problem around which the lecture will be structured.

✔ Use a test question. Ask participants a question (even if they have little prior knowledge) so that they will be motivated to listen to your lecture for the answer.

Maximizing Understanding and Retention

✔ Reduce to headlines. Reduce the major points in the lecture to key words which act as verbal subheadings or memory aids.

✔ Use examples and analogies. Provide real-life illustrations of the ideas in the lecture and if possible, create a comparison between your material and the knowledge/experience the participants already have.

✔ Have a visual backup. Use pictures, brief handouts, and demonstrations that enable participants to see as well as hear what you're saying.

Involving Participants during the Lecture

✔ Spot challenges. Interrupt the lecture periodically and challenge participants to give examples of the concepts presented thus far or answer questions.

✔ Illuminate with exercises. Throughout the presentation, intersperse brief activities that illuminate the points you're making.

Reinforcing the Lecture

✔ Apply a problem. Pose a problem or question for participants to solve based on the information given.

✔ Encourage participant review. Ask participants to review the contents of the presentation with each other or give them a self-scoring review quiz.

How about some feedback?

Feedback is good for learning new skills and improving performance. It is nearly impossible for you to give feedback to yourself. I recommend that you give a copy of the form in Table 9-1 to a colleague or two. Tell them you want honest feedback about what they heard and saw in your training. Then, when they share their observations with you, be quiet and listen. After you have the observations, you can get started on any performance improvements necessary.

Table 9-1	Training Feedback

I am interested in improving my skills as a trainer. Thank you for agreeing to observe my training session. Please provide feedback to me in the following areas. Thank you for your time.

What do you hear (the six Ps)?

Projection:

Pitch:

Pace:

Pauses:

Pronunciation:

Phillers:

What do you see?

Body stance:

Gestures:

Facial expression:

Eye contact:

Nervousness:

What suggestions do you have for improvements I can make?

The participants' materials

Encourage the participants to use the materials provided. First, it will help them to understand the content better. Second, they will more easily find any information should they need to after the training session.

✔ Always refer to every page, even if you won't use it. Tell the participants why it's there, for example, "the resource page is information you may refer to after you return to the workplace."

✔ Decide whether you will have the handouts available as participants arrive, after the session starts, or at the end of the session. Each has advantages and disadvantages. In a virtual setting, you have several choices prior to the session. You can email them or, if there are some unique items such as laminated job aids, you can mail them. If the content is large, you may have the participants download them from a file storage site such as Dropbox or Google Drive.

✔ Remind your participants what page they should be on as you move through the content. This is especially important in a virtual classroom.

✔ During presentations or activities, tell participants whether the information is in their manuals or handouts so they can choose whether to take notes.

Notes: To be or note to be

Whenever I conduct a train-the-trainer session I am asked about notes. Should I use them? Or should I memorize everything? Should I hold them? Should I keep them in the trainer's manual? Should I use an outline? Should I speak from key words? Should I use paper? Should I use note cards? Should I write them in my own words?

My answer is "Yes."

There is no secret about using notes as a trainer. Do what works best for you. My best advice is "Yes, use notes." Your participants are there to see you succeed. They want you to stay on track. They want you to remember everything you're supposed to tell them. They don't want you to memorize a "speech." They want you to converse with them. They want you to be comfortable with the content so that you can interact with them and address their unique needs — even if it isn't on the agenda.

On the other hand, participants *do not* want you to read your notes. This is especially true with a virtual classroom where the participants cannot see you. They can "hear" you reading though.

I cannot advise you of the one way that works best. I can, however, provide you with a few techniques and ideas from experience. I hope you will try a couple and find what works best for you.

✔ **Use the trainers' manual as your guide.** If a trainers' manual has been developed, it is probably filled with most everything you will need to conduct the training session. You may want to go through it crossing off parts you will not be using, or even removing pages that you will not need. If it is an off-the-shelf training program, you may want to customize it for your organization, adding your own examples, questions, and stories.

✔ **Use the participants' manual/materials as your guide.** This is my preferred method. I start with a participants' manual. If it is bound and printed on both sides, I copy it on one side only. I use the information from the trainers' manual (if there is one) and add pertinent notes. I note the time at the top of the page (that it should be when you reach that particular page.) I underline key ideas, add notes about media, props, or handouts, and include special information about putting the participants into small groups.

✔ **Develop your own notes.** Some trainers create their own notes. This of course gives you the maximum amount of creative license to develop your notes so that they work best in your format. Some trainers use an outline, some use key words, and some develop an entire manuscript. I caution you about developing a manuscript. It's a great deal of work. Also, trainers who tend to do this are usually good writers, and after they have written their "good stuff," they want to read it as it is. Be careful. Your learners do not want you to read to them.

Another method is used by trainers who rely on their visuals and media to guide them through the session. They may print the slides four to a page and add their notes or add reminders in the margins of their flipcharts. Some develop their notes using the note feature of the PowerPoint slide presentation and then use the printed pages to guide them.

Experiment a bit until you find the technique that works best for you.

Things I know for sure about notes

Notes will help keep you on track: both time and topic. They are your support system, so use a format that works best for you

Become intimate with your notes. Practice with them and become familiar with what's on each page and where. You should be able to trust that anything you may need will be found in your notes. Therefore, do not write new notes just before your training session. Yes, you practiced with them. They are a little bent and crinkly. You folded them when you didn't mean to. You even spilled a little latte on module three. But don't redo them now. Better that they are well worn and familiar to you than that they are pretty and aren't familiar at all. If you practiced with them, you know where to find the list of five ways to recognize a good leader and the "don't forget to tell the learner."

Number your pages. Whether you use your own pages/cards or modify the trainers' guide, number them. If you use the trainers' guide as a starting point, you may add pages that are more pertinent or delete pages that will not be a part of the training session. Renumber the pages. If you drop them, you will be able to put them in order again. I once sat in the audience and watched a man shuffle his note cards as he delivered his opening lines. The audience did not hear a word he said. We were all aghast at what he was doing. He realized it and recovered by putting us into buzz groups. Fortunately, he had numbered his note cards.

Cue yourself. Whatever technique you use, develop a plan to cue yourself about where to find information. Use highlight markers, underlining, boxes, clouds, arrows, or different colors. You may for example, underline all the places where you need to use a type of media. You may put stars in front of the questions you need to ask. You may draw a miniscreen as a cue to use PowerPoint. You may put red boxes around the times of the session.

If you use the trainers' guide as your notes, it will give the times in some formula that denotes how far into the training you are. For example, 0315 means that three hours and fifteen minutes have passed since you started training. If you actually started at 8:00 o'clock and you have built an additional 15-minute break into the session, you would replace it with 11:30 a.m.

Don't fold or staple your notes. Folding them makes them weak, and stapling prevents you from being flexible with them. I usually keep my notes in a three-ring binder and remove only the page or pages I intend to use during a specific amount of time. When I am finished, I return the pages and pick up the next one or two. I keep the binder at the upper-left-hand corner of the table. I always know where my notes are.

If you create your own note pages, use a heavier stock of paper. It will hold up better. If your hand tends to shake, it won't rattle either! If you use note cards, use larger cards than the 3 x 5 cards. The larger cards will provide you with much more flexibility — and of course room.

One last note: Make your notes work for you, don't be a slave to them.

Asking and Answering Questions

The art of asking and answering questions and encouraging participants to ask questions is a valued skill of trainers. Don't take it lightly. Beyond simply eliciting answers or facts, questions can stimulate interaction and discussion. Questions enable you to assess what your participants know and what they still need to learn. Questions can be used to emphasize and reinforce significant points. Questions encourage participants to evaluate their own knowledge gaps and think about how to address them. Questions encourage thinking.

Encouraging participants to ask questions ensures understanding, enhances interest, increases learning, and prompts interaction.

Encouraging participants to ask questions

Participants may ask questions for different reasons. They may be positive reasons to acquire information. On the other hand, they may ask questions to irritate the trainer or to impress other participants. Fortunately, most often participants ask for positive reasons. So how can you encourage more questions?

✔ At the beginning of the session, encourage participants to ask questions at any time. If you are facilitating a virtual session, encourage participants to use chat liberally.

✔ Kim Seeger, CPLP, likes to ask for a specific number of questions to get things started, "What might be the three most frequently asked questions about our topic?"

✔ Go through your training program. Try to anticipate questions that may come up. During your presentation, pose these questions to the participants if they don't pose them to you.

✔ Stop at natural points in the training and ask for questions.

Have participants work in trios to create a question about the information that you're presenting. Have them write the question on an index card. Collect the questions and redistribute so that each trio has a different question to answer.

✔ If a participant looks puzzled, stop and ask whether there is a question.

✔ If two or more participants are talking among themselves, ask them whether there is something they would like clarified.

✔ Allow time for participants to ask their questions privately. They may be too shy to ask in front of the entire group.

Make it okay to ask questions. Assume that there will be questions. At the same time, convey a message to your participants that you expect questions. You can do this by how you ask for questions. Instead of saying "Are there any questions?" say "What questions do you have?" It may be subtle, but it works.

Guidelines for answering questions

These guidelines provide suggestions as you master the art of asking questions.

✔ Anticipate your participants' questions. Being prepared is always good. If you get the same questions often, you may wish to add the content to the training. Practice answers out loud.

✔ Inform participants of your expectations for asking questions early in the session.

✔ Listen carefully to each question for both content (what is asked) and intent (what is meant). Listen for the emotion that may not match the words of the question. If it seems that the individual's intent doesn't match the content, you may be heading for a let's-see-whether-we-can-irritate-the-trainer situation. If you do receive a hostile question, avoid showing your feelings. Remember, the group is usually on your side.

✔ Treat a "why?" question like a "how?" question. "Why" questions may put you on the defensive because it seems as if you must justify your rationale. However, if you think about it from a "how" perspective, you will respond from a fact basis rather than an opinion basis. For example, if someone asks you "Why do you think your process is better?" respond by stating how your process is better. Do you see the small nuance that will help you maintain your composure?

✔ Paraphrase the question to ensure that everyone heard and that you understood the question. This prevents you from answering the wrong question. You may also choose to paraphrase all lengthy questions to ensure clarity.

Another reason to paraphrase a question is that it gives you time to organize your response before plunging in with an answer.

✔ Take care with how you paraphrase. You do want to clarify what the question was, but you don't want to come across as condescending. Saying "What you mean is. . ." or "What you're trying say is. . ." may come across as insulting.

✔ Keep your answer short and on target. Choose your words carefully. Don't build a watch if the individual has only asked for the time. Avoid using the word "obviously," because this implies that the participant should already know the answer. I also try to avoid "you should," "you must," and other terms that appear to be controlling or moralizing. These words may discourage others from asking questions.

✔ Direct your response to the entire group, not just the person who asked the question. You may start by responding to the person who asked the question, but then look at the other participants during your response. This ensures that the rest of the participants feel a part of the discussion. In addition, it discourages the person from tagging on a second question, which may lead to a conversation between the two of you.

✔ Watch the person's body language. If you're uncertain about whether you hit the mark, verify your response with "Is that what you were looking for?" or "Would you like more detail?"

✔ If you don't know an answer, redirect it to the participants, to another source, or state your follow-up plan for getting the information. In addition, "I don't know" is an acceptable answer. Just be sure to tell the participant what you will do (and by when) to find the information. "I don't know the answer to that, but I can call the office on break to obtain the information." Don't make up an answer. Don't fake it.

✓ If the question refers to something you will cover at a later time, ask the participant to write the question on a Post-It and place it in the parking lot. Address it specifically at the time that the topic is introduced.

✓ I avoid saying "That's a good question" or "Gee, I'm glad you asked that question." If you provide a compliment after every question it may come across as insincere. On the other hand, if you say it sometimes, some participants will wonder if their questions were not "good questions" or if you're not "glad they asked a question." It may seem minor, but if you just avoid the situation, it will be one less concern for you.

Asking questions

Questions are wonderful tools to get participation, to personalize a presentation, or provoke participants to think about the content. To be effective, you will want to think about these.

✓ Plan your questions in advance. When should they appear in your presentation?

✓ Consider your reason for including them. Are you looking for a correct answer? Will the question reinforce a key learning point? Are you trying to initiate controversy? Or are you asking a rhetorical question?

✓ Early on ask the question that will yield involvement by the most participants. For example, if you're asking for a show of hands, ask the question that will cause the most people to raise their hands in response.

✓ Keep questions short and clear.

✓ Ensure that they are relevant to your presentation.

✓ Know whether you want information or opinions.

✓ Go from general to specific when asking a series of questions.

✓ Get participation by asking questions early. Further, be sure to balance to whom you direct the questions.

✓ Be sure that you're asking open-ended questions.

✓ Say the participant's name first, and then ask the question. There is no need to "catch them" in a mini-vacation.

✓ Pause after asking. Too often, trainers are uncomfortable with silence. So they will ask a question. When they do not get an immediate response, they will ask it again. If still no response, they will answer it themselves. This teaches participants that if they wait long enough, the trainer will answer as well as ask all the questions!

✓ Be prepared to take action if you don't get a response.

Asking questions is one of the most used tools you have to encourage participation. Hone your questioning skills.

Questions in action

Think about how you may be able to apply some of what you just read. Think about the next training session you will conduct. Then complete the appropriate information in Table 9-2.

Table 9-2	What Questions Will They Ask?

Anticipate five questions your participants may have in your next training session. List them, and then add your response.

Question: _____

My response: _____

_____

Question: _____

My response: _____

_____

Question: _____

My response: _____

_____

Question: _____

My response: _____

_____

Question: _____

My response: _____

_____

If you anticipate these questions, should you build something into the training that would address them before they come up?

Now think about your use of questions. How could you make your training more dynamic by adding questions? Where? What kind of questions would they be? What would be the purpose? Identify three questions you could ask your participants in Table 9-3.

Table 9-3	What Questions Will You Ask?

Question I could ask: _____

Purpose of the question: _____

_____

Question I could ask: _____

Purpose of the question: _____

_____

Question I could ask: _____

Purpose of the question: _____

_____

Smooth Transitions

Keep your learners in mind as you transition from one topic to the next. Take them with you on a smooth journey as you move through your agenda. Help them see the relevance and the relationships. Help them see the big picture and how things are connected. You will look like the professional that you are. These tips will assist you:

- ✔ **When you're designing the training, make sure it has a logical flow or sequence.** This in itself will enable smooth transitions.

- ✔ **Make sure you properly wrap up the previous topic before going on to the next.** Ask whether there are questions. When there are no more, say "Now let's move on to _____."

- ✔ **Use mini-summaries to transition out of a section.** You may present these summaries, but you do not need to. Ask for volunteers to do this for the group. Or place participants in small groups and ask each group to identify two or three summary statements.

- ✔ **Pick a common theme that relates to both the previous and the upcoming topic.** Address that theme while moving from one topic to the next. Tell them how the role play you just completed is related to the next module.

- ✔ **Use the building-block approach.** In your transition, summarize the concepts from the previous discussion that will be the foundation of the upcoming discussion.

- ✔ **Use visual cues.** If you're following an agenda or a flowchart, show the change from one point to the next. I've used props at times. For example, I used two-by-four blocks to "build" a structure when discussing the Ten Building Blocks of Teams.

✔ **Although it is difficult to practice an entire training presentation, it is very easy to practice transitions.** Go through every lesson of your training, and write down key points for each. Next, look for relationships with the activity or presentation before and after. Last, develop and write the transitions in your training notes. Finally, rehearse them until they are smooth.

Wrap Up an Effective Training Session

Remember that the conclusion should provide a sense of closure for the learners. What are your responsibilities to wrap up your training session? You will need to ensure that expectations were met. You may want to conduct a group experience. Most training sessions end with an evaluation and sometimes ask for additional feedback for improvement. A closing activity may get commitment from participants. You will most likely want to have some final words of wisdom planned as a send-off. The closing is a time to wrap up all loose ends and shift the focus from the training session to the workplace.

This is certainly true with virtual classrooms also. Typically the closure is a little shorter and frequently incorporates the following:

✔ Level 1 session evaluation.

✔ Level 2 knowledge assessment. Many platforms have built-in tools for these assessments and the content is based on the class design.

✔ Follow-up reference materials such as job aid or content that will be helpful once employees return to the workplace.

✔ A send-off that includes information about next steps — this is especially true if the session was a part of a series or a blended learning design.

Ensure that expectations were met

One of the most common ways to address this is to review the expectations that were developed by the participants at the beginning of the session and posted on the wall. You can also conduct a verbal check with participants.

Ensure that you have answered all the questions in the parking lot and that there are no loose ends left undone.

Provide a shared group experience

Many closing activities exist. One of the most creative closing activities I've heard of is to develop a video or a PowerPoint collage. First determine the equipment you will use. Use it to take a video or pictures of the training room before participants arrive. Continue to capture pictures of the group throughout the training session working in small groups, on individual activities, or as a large group. Be sure that everyone is represented in the shots. If you're taking digital shots, put them together in a collage presentation. You may wish to add appropriate music. Then near the end announce that you want to show them all the hard work they have completed during the session. Sit back and enjoy the show. This is a very motivational way to end a session.

I have taken pictures during team-building sessions. Then on the last day I have them developed at a photo shop and share a couple of sets with the participants. Each can take a couple of their favorites. Again, if you do this, ensure that you get everyone in the pictures.

Evaluate the learning experience

All training sessions based on an instructional design model will include an evaluation element. You may evaluate participant reaction, knowledge gained, application of the skills and knowledge, and/or business results. Chapter 13 provides more details about evaluation. You may also consider conducting a feedback session.

You may also wish to request feedback and improvement suggestions for future sessions. One method that works well is to ask participants what went well and what improvements are needed. Use two flipcharts with a "What went well?" heading on one and "What would you change?" on the other. You may alternate making the lists on both flipcharts at the same time.

Summarize the accomplishments and gain commitment to action

You may wish to review the agenda and the objectives. Ask whether everything was covered. Commitment to action can be worked into a closing activity in which you may ask:

- What was the most valuable part of the training session?
- What will you implement back at the workplace?
- What will you change as a result of what you've learned?

You may conduct these discussions in small groups that report out to the larger group. To ensure transfer of learning you may also want participants to pair up with a "buddy." Buddies will support each other after the session has ended. This is a good time for the buddies to exchange contact information and make plans for the first contact. Encourage buddies to record their plans in their participant materials or their electronic scheduling devices.

A favorite activity that I use is to have participants write memos to themselves committing to some actions and/or changes. They put them inside envelopes, self-address, and seal them. I collect the envelopes and mail their commitment memos back to them six to eight weeks later.

Send them off with a final encouraging word — or two

Have your ending designed as tightly as you have your opening planned. Based on this section, you have a number of things to complete. In addition, you will want to have a formal send-off message for the participants. You opened the training with a BANG! End it with the same kind of fanfare.

Help participants remember the experience, give them encouragement, and send them off with something to think about after the session. What could that be? It could be a call to action, a poem, a quote, a moral to a story, an anecdote or illustration, a visual, a reference to the introduction, a rhetorical question, a demonstration, a challenge, a magic trick, or something that makes the point. I will forever remember stabbing a plastic straw all the way through a raw potato, as the facilitator said, "Positive thinking moves mountains. Believe that you will be successful and you will be."

Bob Lucas, author, trainer, and consultant, likes to end day-long training sessions by reading from the Dr. Seuss book *Oh, the Places You Will Go!* The book's message of optimism and reaching goals has high impact. Bob adds his own statement encouraging learners to achieve their goals.

Lastly, stand at the door, shake participants' hands, wish them luck, and say good-bye.

Focusing on the asking-and-answering question section, a quote by my favorite author, e.e. cummings: "always the beautiful answer who asks a more beautiful question."

Chapter 10

Mastering Media and Other Visuals

• •

In This Chapter

▶ Selecting the best media or visual to do the job

▶ Selecting and using visuals

▶ Using powerful visuals that add to the learning

▶ Exploring the possibilities in the other media: social

▶ Looking like a pro using specific media techniques in training

• •

A picture is worth a thousand words. Of course this is a cliché, but it tells you exactly what this chapter is all about. I touch lightly on visuals in Chapter 5, but in this chapter, I focus entirely on visuals: what's available to you, why you should use them, how to design them, and most important, how to use them with your learners.

Before you begin this chapter, consider the expertise you have now by using the self-evaluation in Table 10-1.

Table 10-1	Evaluate Your Audiovisual Expertise

Use this scale to evaluate your expertise when using visuals in the classroom.

1. No expertise; heck, I'm not even sure I know what you mean!

2. Minimal expertise; pretty darn average.

3. Expert; I have mastered this one.

___ I plan the visuals to support the learning objectives.

___ I consider the participants' needs when designing visuals.

___ I design simple and clear visuals.

(continued)

(continued)

___ My visuals speak in headlines, phrases, not complete sentences.

___ My visuals can be seen from the back row.

___ I use san serif typeface.

___ I know exactly when and where to use the visuals for maximum impact.

___ I arrive early to check out equipment and organize my visuals.

___ I do not block the view to my visuals.

___ I maintain eye contact even when using visuals.

___ I avoid reading my visuals.

___ I keep my visuals organized during the training session.

___ I have learned and use tips and tricks that add to my professionalism.

___ I ensure that the visuals support the presentation rather than become the presentation.

How'd you do? Ready for a few tips and techniques?

Select the Best Visual to Do the Job

You have a number of choices available with regard to the type of media — everything from computer displays to paper. The media should support your training session and make it easier for the learner to acquire the skills or knowledge intended.

What's available?

PowerPoint presentations have taken over the training world. They are easy and fast to create. The tools to design them reside inside everyone's laptop. They can be changed or updated on the spot. They add color automatically and may include animation and sound effects, or video clips.

They may, however, also be boring, overused, and less effective than other forms of media and visuals that are available. This list of media and visual support provides an overview of what is available to you.

✔ **Computer projection systems:** This includes PowerPoint presentations and SMART Boards. Both use computer technology to project images. PowerPoint presentations are convenient, and most trainers use the technology. Prezi is being used more. SMART Boards are a combination of a giant computer screen and a whiteboard on which you can write; your hand can act as a giant cursor to move items from one place to another.

✔ **Videos and DVDs:** You may show a video clip to demonstrate a skill, illustrate behavior, or to have an expert deliver content in a way that you could not. You may decide to show a video in its entirety or just a segment that makes the point. You may also use videos to record participants' practice session. This allows them to critique themselves. Most people are their own best critics.

✔ **Participants' Devices:** Participants come to your class loaded with equipment: laptops, iPads or other tablets, phones and watches that connect to the Internet, wearable devices, pens that record action, and many other tools. Tap into this abundance of resources that your participants are usually happy to use.

✔ **Flipcharts:** Flipcharts are large pads of newsprint mounted so that individual sheets can be torn off and hung on the wall or flipped over the top of the pad. The pad is mounted on a large easel about six feet high. Trainers can write on them with chisel-tip markers. Flipcharts work well for creating on-the-spot lists, capturing ideas generated by the group, and creating real-time plans. There is a sense of immediacy and spontaneity to the information presented. Flipcharts are valuable when you're called in to do some spur-of-the-moment facilitating.

Flipchart packs of paper are available in a preglued format that acts like giant post-it pads. Pages stick directly to the wall as opposed to using masking tape.

✔ **Blackboards, whiteboards, magnetic boards, felt boards:** Whiteboards are making a comeback! In fact, you can use a new paint to cover an entire wall that has magnetic properties so that you can use magnets. In addition, some training rooms still have boards on walls or on a movable stand. They are useful for small group recording of ideas.

✔ **Electronic whiteboards:** This type of whiteboard is combined with a copier mechanism. It translates whatever you write on its 3 x 5-foot surface to an 8½ x 11 piece of paper. Participants can each walk out the door with whatever ideas were captured on the board.

✔ **Props:** *Props* usually don't plug in, turn on, make sounds, show animation, or have glitches. They may include samples, models, demonstrations, or any article that a trainer holds to drive a point home. While props have nothing to do with media, they may be great visuals and can capture or refocus attention. They may serve as a metaphor for any aspect of the content. The best prop I use is a $20 bill that I borrow from the leader in the group. I ask whether participants can provide examples of the cost of waste (due to poor communication, poor quality, or whatever the topic is) and begin to rip it up as I restate the examples and throw the pieces on the floor. It drives the point home that waste costs money. By the way, I always return the leader's $20 offline. It's a small price to make an important point.

What are the benefits?

The benefits of visuals to you and your participants are clear. Your participants learn through their five senses. Research suggests that the proportion of learning that occurs visually is much higher than the other four senses combined. Learning that takes place through each sense is approximately as follows:

- **Taste:** 1 percent
- **Touch:** 1.5 percent
- **Scent:** 3.5 percent
- **Aural:** 11 percent
- **Visual:** 83 percent

Most of us have visual preferences for how we learn, which means that adding visual support to your verbal message is a major benefit to your participants. By using visuals in your training sessions, participants grasp the information faster, understand it better, and retain it longer.

Remember some of the key guidance from Ruth Clark in Chapter 5. She states that with regard to visuals, evidence demonstrates that we should

- Use relevant visuals to illustrate your content.
- Keep visuals simple depending on your goal.
- Explain complex visuals.
- Avoid seductive visuals.

Be sure that your visuals add value and make it easier for your participants to learn.

Ensure That the Visual Adds to the Learning

In the "What's available?" section, I list several types of visuals and equipment you may wish to use in your training session. Under what circumstances can you use each? The following lists a number of situations in which each media or visual performs best. You may also decide to use visuals in other situations, depending on your learning objectives and your training session's curriculum.

If you are conducting a virtual ILT, you will be more limited in your options. On the other hand, if you are conducting a video conference, all the options could be used.

Computer projection systems

PowerPoint presentations are useful for guiding your participants through the training session. They will probably be the foundation of your media presentation with others added, as appropriate. You use PowerPoint or Prezi slides for the following, at a minimum:

- Provide the outline to the session
- Cue that you're switching to another module or topic
- Provide introductions to topics
- Present new information in any format
- Present processes in sequential order
- Show relationships; for example, pros and cons, advantages and disadvantages, parts to a whole
- Display charts and graphs; for example, bar graphs for change over time or as a comparison, pie charts to display the division of a whole
- Show pictures of new products
- Illustrate sketches and diagrams
- Diagram organizational relationships
- Give directions to complete an activity during the session
- Offer miniquizzes or challenges
- Show cartoons (with appropriate copyright approval) or mindbenders
- Exhibit video clips of a message from top management or subject matter experts (SMEs)
- Close the session with a statement, call to action, quote, reference to the introduction, or a rhetorical question

Nancy Duarte, author of *Slide:ology* (O'Reilly, 2008) and *Resonate* (John Wiley & Sons, 2010), is recognized as one of the top leaders in presentation design. Her books demonstrate how to create visuals that connect with your learners and graphics that enable them to process information easily.

SMART Boards have a more unique use. They are not appropriate for a large group because most have only a small screen. Still, they may be useful for some of the same things. Due to your ability to interact with them, SMART Boards may also be used to

✔ Create or revise a document as a small group

✔ Brainstorm

✔ Problem solve

✔ Change a process

Videos and DVDs

Videos and DVD presentation work well when it is difficult to re-create a scenario in the training session. You may show a clip to do any of the following:

✔ Demonstrate a skill

✔ Illustrate behavior

✔ Deliver content by an expert

✔ Set up a scenario

✔ Show the wrong way

You may tape participants' practice session to:

✔ Allow participants to review and critique their own skills

✔ Obtain feedback from other participants and the facilitator

✔ Facilitate comparison to later, more improved skills

Participant devices

Participants are going to bring them anyway, so you may as well find opportunities to put them to good use. Personal devices might include laptops, iPads or other tablets, phones and watches that connect to the

Internet, wearable devices, pens that record action, and many other tools. Here are some ideas:

✔ Record a practice session.

✔ Conduct an Internet scavenger hunt.

✔ Allow new employees to locate information on the company intranet.

✔ Download TED Talks or other defined resources as learning tools.

✔ Send twitter follow-up content after the session.

✔ Download tips and hints for ease of implementation after the session.

✔ Encourage participants to take photos of flipcharts or other group work.

✔ Record an activity and encourage critique afterwards.

When facilitating a presentation skills class, a tennis lesson, a debate team, or anything that entails a visible or verbal skill, utilize the recording device that participants have on their tables, phones, pens, or other items. Have someone else record the practice session on the individual's device so they have a record for the future.

Flipcharts

Flipcharts are a reliable, no-computer-glitch, flexible tool that trainers find useful. They are the only practical tool that allows the trainer to display information for a period of time. As information is recorded or discussed, the trainer can remove the pages and hang them on the wall. Flipcharts are portable and an instant resource. One drawback, however, is that flipcharts are best for groups of 40 or fewer participants. Otherwise, flipcharts are useful for many other situations.

✔ Present prerecorded information as you would with any other media

✔ Use for spur of the moment facilitation requests

✔ Capture on-the-spot lists

✔ Record input and ideas generated by the group

✔ Create real-time plans

✔ Track action items and/or next steps generated during the session

✔ Brainstorm ideas

✔ Reinforce or supplement a presentation

✔ Track participants' questions or concerns

- ✔ Display lists or content throughout the session
- ✔ Make a decision by voting with sticky-back flags
- ✔ Prioritize a list of items by having the participants vote with stickers
- ✔ Use in small groups to organize their results
- ✔ Keep as an emergency backup when any technical equipment fails

Flipchart graphics

Adding graphics to your flipchart aids memory, maintains focus, and adds color and fun to the session. The icons in this sidebar get you started replacing words with graphics. Practice with these icons, and then add your own special touch to these or create your own.

✔ A star person indicates people and can show connections between individuals or groups and ideas.

✔ Arrows show movement and can indicate progress or connections. Two arrows pointing at each other may depict conflict.

✔ Light bulbs are used to highlight good ideas.

✔ Thought clouds can refer to reviews or to revisiting a concept. Clouds without the thought bubbles can suggest an idea or vision.

✔ A target can signify a goal or objective.

✔ Dollar signs mean money, and a ribbon can suggest a prize or the best of what has been discussed.

✔ A clock can show time for completing a project or the next steps.

Boards of all types (including electronic)

Whiteboards, magnetic boards, and all other boards can be useful in these situations:

- ✔ Use for same situations as a flipchart
- ✔ Use for building a description step by step
- ✔ Tack up ideas, questions, or concerns
- ✔ Hold, display, and/or move sticky-back notes for discussions
- ✔ Create an affinity diagram
- ✔ Prioritize a list
- ✔ Group ideas into categories

Props

Props include a diverse assortment of three-dimensional items that the participants use to discuss or practice with. They may be used as practical hands-on support to:

- ✔ Display samples of product, errors, and so on for participants to examine
- ✔ Introduce models of actual equipment, locations, buildings
- ✔ Practice skills using actual tools, equipment, or materials
- ✔ Demonstrate a correct process or procedure
- ✔ Use as a metaphor to make a point visually
- ✔ Make a closing statement

Look Like a Pro

A trainer is a professional. Using visuals can enhance your image and increase the confidence participants will have in you. On the other hand, if you don't have professionally designed visuals, if you haven't practiced, and if you don't know the best way to use them, your participants may lose all confidence in you.

Visuals are only effective when

✔ They are relevant to the subject.

✔ They are visible and understandable to the participants.

Use the tips in the following section to ensure you look like the professional you are. First attend to the general tips useful for all visuals and media. Following those tips, you find guidelines for using each of the types of media discussed.

Tips for using visuals in general

Experienced participants have gleaned a number of tips to ensure that they provide the best learning experience for their participants.

Make sure participants can see the visuals

Some of the best presentations are doomed for failure if the participants are unable to see the visuals. These tips will prevent that from happening.

✔ Don't block the view.

✔ Sit in the participants' seats to ensure that they can see the visuals.

✔ Keep a tight focus on what is shown. Visuals must be readable.

✔ Reveal only one point at a time.

✔ Limit the number of ideas on one visual to four.

✔ Use a pointer or laser pointer to focus attention.

✔ Turn projection lights off between visuals.

PowerPoint presentations can dissolve to a black slide so that participants are not distracted. You can also force a black screen by touching the B key.

Orient the visuals for the learner

Imagine that you are one of the participants and are seeing the visuals for the first time.

✔ Tell learners what they are looking at: "Here are four criteria for perception checks."

✔ A good visual may not need words to describe it.

✔ Allow enough time for people to take notes.

Be well practiced

It should be comfortable and natural to use your visuals. That comes with practice.

✔ Charts roll easily (you may need to practice this).

✔ You know how to operate the equipment.

✔ You have prepositioned your equipment and organized your supplies beforehand.

✔ You have arranged the room so that you do not every have to step between a projection light and the screen.

✔ You turn off the projector at the end of the last frame, transparency, and so on.

✔ After its use, leave the equipment alone until after the training session has finished. Don't bother about ejecting a DVD, closing out your PowerPoint slides, or putting equipment or visuals away. You owe your time to your participants.

Ensure that your visuals enhance your performance rather than replace it

Your visuals should not take center stage, but they should help to explain or clarify the concepts you are presenting. This is what Ruth Clark means when she refers to avoiding "seductive" visuals!

✔ Visuals should become an extension of you as you use them to explain the content of your presentations.

✔ Visuals are tied together with a common element; for example, a graphic, a color, or a sketch.

You're prepared for an emergency

Emergencies that occur during the presentation don't have to be a complete disaster. These may help to reduce the effect on your participants:

✔ Have an extra bulb, an adaptor plug, and marking pens.

✔ Know how to change the bulb.

✔ Know how or where to obtain an extension cord.

✔ Have an alternative plan if the electricity fails.

✔ Call a break as you address the emergency.

And finally, in the words of that famous trainer, Anonymous: "Keep it simple, keep it simple, keep it simple."

Guidelines for using specific media and visuals

Perhaps you have read the preceding general tips to ensure success with using the media and visual. How about a few guidelines for each specific media type?

LCD projector guidelines

Keep the limited flexibility in mind when using LCD-projected PowerPoint. It may be difficult to get participants involved in the visuals, so use other media to create and display their ideas. To design PowerPoint slides that incorporate effective techniques, flip to Chapter 5. In addition, try some of these guidelines:

- ✔ Plan ahead to know where you'll be standing.
- ✔ Email the presentation to yourself as a backup.
- ✔ Know the password for the computer you will use.
- ✔ Turn off instant messenger, Outlook, and other communication tools loaded on the computer.
- ✔ Ensure that the computer uses an appropriate screensaver.
- ✔ Ensure that the LCD has the right number of lumens of light for the size of the room.
- ✔ Some LCD projectors identify the life of the bulb; make sure yours has enough life left.
- ✔ Focus and set up before the training begins; on a rare occasion, LCD machines may not be compatible with all computers, especially if you are training globally.
- ✔ Mark the projection table placement with masking tape on the floor in case you need to move it.
- ✔ Use a wireless advance control and try it out ahead; have extra batteries for the control available.
- ✔ Turn off lights immediately in front of the screen but keep them on in the rest of the room.
- ✔ If the projector has an automatic keystoning setting, don't increase the projection angle over 30 degrees.
- ✔ Ensure that both the computer and the projector have proper ventilation around them.

✔ Prepare your participants for what they should be learning and seeing.

✔ Allow an average of 10 to 20 seconds of reading time per slide. Viewers' eyes should have time to move over the entire visual but not become "fixed" on it. Interject your comments accordingly; otherwise, hypnosis may set in.

✔ Set up your computer so that you can *easily* glance at the computer screen, *not* at the screen on the wall.

✔ Speak to the participants, not to the screen.

Video and DVD guidelines

Use video judiciously. Take care that if you include a film clip, it uses up the right amount of time. Also, always preview the tape before showing it in your session.

✔ Never leave videos, CDs, or DVDs in a hot car.

✔ Set up the machine before your presentation.

✔ Practice setting the sound and dimming lights.

✔ Cue the segment and have it ready to play.

✔ Check the sound.

✔ Before playing, provide an introduction that tells why you're showing it.

Trainers sometimes encounter participants who claim they cannot relate to a setting or video because it is not the same occupational setting as the one they are in. Diffuse this issue in your introduction by stating up front that they will see a setting that is different from theirs, but it shouldn't make a difference because the goal is to learn a technique that is transferable to any setting.

✔ Show only the portion that you must to make the point; provide a brief explanation about what happens up to this point.

✔ Before you show the clip, tell participants what to do during the viewing; for example, take notes, look for a specific behavior.

✔ Don't turn off the lights if people will be taking notes.

✔ Follow the viewing with at least one question to get participants quickly involved again.

✔ Allow for discussion and highlight key points.

✔ Ensure that participants are clear about the objectives of the video and what they should have learned..

If you're actually recording, remember these guidelines for a smooth training session:

✔ Test the camera or device beforehand; learn zoom, turning on/off, tripod adjustment, and other techniques.

✔ Determine whether you need an additional person to assist with the recording.

✔ Be prepared for cameras that automatically shut off after a time period.

✔ Adjust the tripod to the appropriate height.

✔ Do a microphone check beforehand.

✔ Test the VCR and monitor beforehand.

Participant devices

What a great way to ensure buy-in from your learners. Encourage them to turn their devices on instead of turning them off. What a novel idea! Here are some tips:

✔ Always ask for volunteers.

✔ Create small groups for activities so that everyone does not need to have a device to use.

✔ Do a spot check to ensure that everyone in the room has access to a device, whether their own or looking on with someone else.

✔ If they will connect with the Internet be certain that you have the password.

✔ Be clear about the directions prior to stating which site they should locate.

✔ Ensure that participants have checklists or guidelines if they are to visit more than one site.

✔ Assign a clear timeline for the completion of the activity.

✔ Post URLs to respond to repeated questioning.

✔ Offer to email all URLs used in the session to participants after the session. If participants identify other sites that are helpful, have them post the URL on a flipchart page hung somewhere in the room so that you can include it in your email.

✔ If follow-up tweets will be a part of the implementation plan, ensure that everyone has an account and knows how to use it.

Flipchart guidelines

Flipcharts may sit patiently waiting in the corner of a training room. When you pull one out, however, be prepared with these guidelines to look like a pro.

- ✔ Charts for displaying information should be to your dominant side; charts for writing on should be to your nondominant side (this ensures that your back is to the fewest participants when you're writing on the chart).

- ✔ Write on every other page so that participants cannot read through to the next page; this also gives a page to absorb pen marks that may bleed through.

- ✔ Select and stage the color of markers you will use before the session.

    Mr. Sketch makes the best markers for flipcharts. They do not bleed through the paper, are washable (even out of your clothes), and, as a bonus, smell great!

- ✔ Printed letters should be 1 to 3 inches high.

- ✔ Use some of the new flipchart stickers and fluorescent tape to highlight words, add borders, or use for emphasis in other ways.

- ✔ Pencil cues in the margin.

- ✔ Bend the lower corners (two pages together if you have written on every other page) closest to where you will stand up so that you can reach down without looking to turn a page.

- ✔ Practice rolling the pages over to the back of the easel.

- ✔ Use sticky-back tabs to locate specific information on predesigned charts.

- ✔ Don't try to talk, write, and spell at the same time.

- ✔ After writing, pause and turn toward your participants before you begin to speak.

    Clear the visual: Tell participants what is on the entire page in one succinct statement before beginning discussion on one individual point. This helps participants stay focused as you explain the content.

- ✔ Stand beside the chart.

- ✔ Talk to your participants, not to the chart, using a *touch, turn, tell* process.

    Lined pads are available if your writing strays from horizontal.

- ✔ Put the marker down when you're not writing.

- ✔ Turn pages out of sight when they are no longer pertinent.

- When appropriate, tear off sheets and hang them on the walls with masking tape.

- Place two-inch strips of masking tape on the back side of the easel to use to tape pages to the wall.

Plan where and how you will hang your charts. Hang them so they can be read left to right. Use the same color marker for charts that belong together.

Hang your charts in a straight vertical line — not going uphill, or downhill. To do this, the first page must be precisely vertical and perpendicular to the floor so that you can use its edge as your guide as you hang the rest. You can accomplish this in at least four ways. First prepare by attaching tape to the top of the chart.

- If wallpaper covers the wall, find the seam and align it.

- If there is a pattern on the wall, use that as a cue.

- If you have time, position two pieces of transparent tape, equal distance from the floor, to serve as a guide.

- When all else fails, grasp the chart with both hands equal distance from the top of the page, stand with your feet flat on the floor, reach the same height with both hands, and attach it.

To complete the task, step back and eyeball the first chart. Make any adjustments. With a little practice you will be able to hang charts perpendicularly without any guide at all.

Blackboards, whiteboards, electronic whiteboards guidelines

Although you may not use them too often, follow this guidance to improve your effectiveness with boards:

- Be absolutely certain that you're using the correct marker; permanent markers or inappropriate markers spell disaster.

- Avoid dark clothing if you know you will use a blackboard; chalk dust will soon find its way to your clothes.

- Star, box, or circle items for emphasis.

- Use the darkest marker if you intend to copy from an electronic whiteboard; even red doesn't copy well.

Use this idea if you don't spell very well and find yourself writing in front of groups. When a participant uses a word that I cannot spell, I print a dozen arbitrary letters in the corner of the board or flipchart, making sure they do NOT spell anything. I then turn to the audience and say, "I am not a very good speller. So if you see that I have forgotten a letter in a word, please just take it from the pile of letters and insert it where it belongs. Thank you."

Props guidelines

Props are used whenever possible to make a point or to give participants hands-on practice. A few tips will make their use easier.

- Keep out of sight until you're ready to have participants interact with them.
- Stretch, be creative, and find the link that allows a prop to be a metaphor for key points in your training.
- Have them readily available for use and touch during breaks.

Take a trip to your local dollar or hardware store to find props and workshop themes that help your participants learn faster and retain longer than any other media or tool you can use.

The Other Media: Social

Maslow had it right when he suggested that people feel safe and secure when they are connected to other people and are included in a group. This feeling of belonging enables participants to more easily face the challenges set before them. When they are learning with others rather than alone, it may seem easier to try something new. Certainly small group activities we use in the classroom or use in breakout rooms in the virtual classroom are social events and the start of social learning.

Web 2.0 technology has sent us in a new direction, using social media tools and social networking activities to learn. What have you observed?

- Growing communities through social networking benefits organizations.
- Employees use social media tools to obtain information straight from the source.
- Trainers use social networking tools to continue the development of employees.
- Social media is extending training and development beyond the virtual and traditional classrooms.
- Social media technology is easy to use.
- Today's tools empower both the trainers and the learners.

What social media tools have you used for learning? There are dozens available: Twitter, Facebook, wikis, LinkedIn, blogs, YouTube, Pinterest, Instagram, and Internet forums on any and all topics.

What can the tools do? The greatest advantage is that the tools bridge geographical gaps around the world. Imagine that Ken Blanchard is visiting your organization to discuss "Ethical Leadership." Skype or Google Hangouts can be set up in conference rooms in Bogotá, Beijing, Berlin, and Baltimore so others can to join in.

Using social media and technology is not that different from creating effective classroom training. Imagine that you are creating a blended learning scenario and you wanted to continue to share data between sessions. Could you

- ✔ Send short messages through your Twitter account reminding participants of individual key points they learned, adding a short tip?

- ✔ Post an article on Facebook and ask participants to read and comment on it before your next virtual session?

- ✔ Ask participants to use Instagram to illustrate how they are doing or what they need help with?

- ✔ Create a post on your blog asking participants to share the most enlightening concept they learned yesterday during the training session?

- ✔ Shoot a one-minute video using their cellphone depicting an example of one of the hazards we discussed yesterday?

Sure you could, and lots more too. Take your ideas into your design plans. And when you think about the AV and media for your learning sessions wherever they may be, remember the "other media," social media and the possibilities for continuous learning.

Looking for more ideas? Jane Bozarth's book, *Social Media for Trainers* (Pfeiffer, 2010) is just what you need to get started.

Identifying ways to use social media tools to extend your participants' learning beyond your ILT classroom is one more exciting role for you to implement.

Social media: your newest training tool

by Jane Bozarth

Since 2009 the proliferation of fun, easy-to-use social tools has brought with it an awareness of how much people value engaging with one another across time and space. This, in turn, has shone a bright new light on ideas around

social learning. Not that social learning is new; we've always learned socially, and it's how we learn most things.

Think about it: As a child you learned your native language by living in the world, engaging with others, and watching others engage with one another. Your parents didn't sit you down with flash cards. Likewise, you learn how to get along in a new workplace by watching and interacting with others. New hire orientation programs cover Internet use policies and insurance forms. But it's by living and moving in the workplace that you learn things like how to get a purchase order cut in a hurry, which boss can't take a joke, and which co-worker has a gift for troubleshooting issues with the printer. The new social media helps social learning happen on a larger scale.

Social tools are constantly emerging and morphing so it's hard to predict what will be next and how people will choose to use them. So when you see a new product or platform, step back and ask, "How can this make the learning in my organization happen better, or more efficiently, or on a larger scale? Can I extend a conversation from my face-to-face classroom?

Can it help connect talent or bits of information across silos? Can it help support a community of learners around a topic or course or practice area? Can it help solve a problem, like reducing duplication of conversations and questions across the organization, or help knowledge workers find an answer more quickly?"

Look beyond the obvious popular use. For example, Pinterest is currently a popular place for shopping and home decorating, sure. But it's also a wonderful visual bookmarking tool, great for amassing, say, reading lists, or images and references instead of a traditional handout, or building a photo-based narrative like "What to Expect Your First Day at Acme." We're great at creating and deploying fabulous, polished instruction. New tools can help us include our learners and support them in becoming contributors to our shared learning rather than just recipients of information we deliver.

Hot Tips for a Cool Ending

The tips listed in this section are ideas I've picked up from the best trainer of all: experience.

- ✔ Practice tearing flipchart pages off the pack with razor-sharp precision. Many trainers yank them off hard or pull them up against the cardboard strip. Both techniques result in ragged edges. Instead, start the chart gently at the perforated tear line, and then continue pulling the page straight *down*. It's like the "Ole!" cape motion of a bullfighter! You'll have a perfect rip nearly every time.

- ✔ When you're given a flipchart that has lots of ragged edges at the top where trainers did not know how to tear off the charts, simply flip the first page to the back to cover all the rough tears.

    Blue painters' tape works better than masking tape; it holds the paper in place and is safe for all surfaces.

- ✔ When conducting a training session at a hotel, be sure to ask whether your room will be used that evening for another group. If it is, recognize that when you return in the morning your visuals and equipment will be moved, perhaps even discarded.

✔ All markers are not created equal. Bring your own; do not depend on someone else's markers.

✔ Ensure that your visuals are the highest quality possible.

If you must apologize for any of your visuals, get rid of them.

✔ Most important: Have a backup plan. The greatest cause of problems in training sessions is something to do with the media and/or visuals. Have a plan if something goes wrong.

Use pictures or charts instead of words whenever possible. Will Rogers stated, "People's minds are changed through observation and not through argument."

Chapter 11

Training with Style

. . . .

In This Chapter

▶ Defining training styles

▶ Understanding group dynamics

▶ Adding energy and excitement to your training

▶ Putting it all together to train with style

. . . .

Chapters 1 through 10 focus on the basics of the training and workplace learning profession: understanding adult-learning theory, learning the steps of the training cycle, practicing good presentation skills, and selecting and using audiovisuals.

This chapter goes beyond the basics to an intermediate level of training skills and knowledge. It covers several topics to explore what it takes to be a skilled professional trainer. It presents four training styles so that you can identify your style and use your strengths to the best advantage for each session. The chapter also explores group dynamics and what it takes to create an energizing and exciting environment.

Understand Your Training Style Strengths

Every trainer brings a unique set of strengths to a training session. The effective trainer recognizes these strengths and builds off of them. To do this it is helpful to have an understanding of the styles and the behaviors that make up the model.

The more you know about yourself and your training style, the better trainer you will be. First, if you know your own style, you will recognize your weaknesses and can make an effort to improve them. Second, knowing other training styles will help you appreciate aspects of training that are important to all participants, thus getting into everyone's comfort zone. Third, the more you know about training styles, the better role model you will be for others.

Even though everyone exhibits characteristics from all style types, everyone has preferences that are ours alone. Ideally a trainer would be balanced among all four styles. However, having a perfect balance is almost nonexistent. Equally as good as a balance is the trainer who is flexible enough to fulfill all roles.

Building the training style model

Remember that every trainer has personal preferences that are based on who they are as individuals. It would be a very boring world if everyone was the same, whether in food preferences or communication styles. Training style is the same. Some training styles will appeal to some learners more than others. Professional trainers adapt their training style to meet the needs of everyone in the classroom.

- ✔ **The training style foundation:** The trainer style model is based on four dimensions of training: content, process, task, and people. These dimensions can be placed on two scales that when combined create a grid displaying four styles.

- ✔ **Content/process continuum:** Trainers may be either content or process focused, so the horizontal scale is a continuum with content at the left end of the scale and process to the right end of the scale as presented in Figure 11-1. Each trainer may be anywhere along the continuum, depending upon their preference.

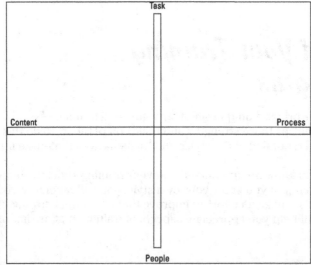

Figure 11-1:
Two training
style
continuums.

© John Wiley & Sons

The content is the purpose of the learning experience. A trainer who is more interested in ensuring that the information contained in the course is delivered accurately to the participants is content focused. Trainers work hard at ensuring that content is accurate and that everything has been put before the learner. A trainer who prefers content over process may try to squeeze everything in. A trainer who prefers this end of the continuum may say such things as "information you'll need" and "other resources available include."

Process is the overall flow of a training program and the flow of events within the program. Process includes such activities as facilitating discussion, forming small groups, and moving from one topic to another. A trainer who prefers process over content may forsake content to ensure a great experience for participants. A trainer who prefers this end of the continuum may say such things as "that discussion went well" and "everything is going smoothly."

Which is better? Neither! You need both content and process in order to have a successful training experience.

✔ **Task/people continuum:** The vertical scale is a continuum with task at the top and people at the bottom as presented in Figure 11-1. Again, trainers may be anywhere along this continuum depending on their preference.

The task dimension focuses on all the "things" that a trainer needs to do to manage a learning environment. The tasks may enable learning such as setting up a simulation, or they may be purely administrative such as record keeping. They may include setup tasks such as rearranging the tables, creating the schedule, and placing materials on the tables. A trainer who prefers tasks over people may forsake discussion or breaks to stay on schedule. Trainers who have a preference for the task end of the continuum may say such things as "I must complete this before" and "we'll need to stop this discussion and move on."

The people dimension refers primarily to the participants and may include others related to the training program. Trainers focus on the people when they do such things as modify the program to meet participant needs, encourage introductions and discussions, and schedule timely breaks. A trainer who prefers people over task may not stay on schedule very well and may need to shortchange some topics to "catch up." Trainers who have a preference for the people end of the continuum may say such things as "what do you think about" and "you will probably enjoy."

Which is better? Neither! You need both task and people in order to have a successful training experience.

All four dimensions are important for a successful training session. How do you see yourself? Perhaps you relate to one end of the continuum more than the other. Perhaps you believe you are balanced between the two ends. You probably demonstrate characteristics at both ends of the continuum. It simply means that you are able to do it all.

Think instead about what you "prefer" to do — those things that come naturally to you. This is important because when you're pressed for time or are under stress, you tend to do what "comes natural." It is at these times that trainers need to push themselves to remember to do it all. Most successful trainers can move easily along the continuum depending upon the situation. Yet each person does have a preferred spot on the continuum when no one is asking you to be anything but who you are naturally. Spot yourself and your preferences on each of the two continuums.

The four training styles

When you superimpose one continuum over the other, you create a grid that displays four different training styles, as pictured in Figure 11-2. When you combine the content end of the horizontal scale with the task end of the vertical scale, you have a trainer who enjoys delivering content, is organized, and in control. I call this training style the *presenting style*.

When you combine the process end of the horizontal scale with the task end of the vertical scale, you have a trainer who states clear expectations, is systematic in presentations, and uses a logical approach. I call this training style the *guiding style*.

When you combine the process end of the horizontal scale with the people end of the vertical scale, you have a trainer who is generally a great listener, encourages discussion among participants, and confirms and reinforces participants. I call this training style the *facilitating style*.

When you combine the content end of the horizontal scale with the people end of the vertical scale, you have a trainer who is motivating, directs participants to the answers, but does not tell them straight out, and who cheers participants on to bigger and greater things. I call this training style the *coaching style*.

Now, before you start reading your personal definitions into the labels for each of these training styles, I am going to caution you to relax. None, let me repeat, *none* of the training styles is any better than any of the others. This information is *only* to help you understand your personal preferences so that you know which areas are your strengths and which areas you need to improve on.

Training Style Preferences

Presenting

Strengths
Delivers interesting presentations
Enjoys being in front of a group
Is a positive center of influence
Is organized and in control
Is comfortable giving information
Is engaging, thinks on his or her feet

Cautions
May not enable or allow participants'
  self-discovery
May have to deal with own ego
May be manipulative or dominating
May be too structured

Guiding

Strengths
States clear expectations and boundaries
Respects participants' active role in learning
May be most appropriate for hard skills
Preempts difficult participants by creating
  ground rules to hold them accountable
Delivers a systematic presentation with a
  logical approach

Cautions
May not be appropriate for soft skills
May be less flexible during the presentation
May not be aware of lagging interest or other
  dynamics
Less ability to "wing it" when mechanicals
  malfunction

Coaching

Strengths
Supports the individual in the process
Motivates and encourages
Heads participants in the right direction
Offers sincere enthusiasm and positive
  attitude
Easily encourages participation
Provides reinforcement naturally

Cautions
May not bring closure to topics or sections
What is taught may not become the
  resource; the coach becomes the
  resource
May not be strong on content details
May lack respect or credibility

Facilitating

Strengths
Encourages active participation
Is a good listener
Tries to be on an equal level with participants
Encourages interaction
Embodies Malcolm Knowles' principles
Draws on and validates experiences

Cautions
May be less focused on content and too
  focused on discussion
May have a short attention span
May not be good with logistics
May lose control and/or lose track of time

Figure 11-2:
Four training
styles.

Remember, no one style is any better than another. So there is no
reason to think that you would want to change your style. It is just
who you are, with your strengths and areas that you need to attend
to more than others.

Using your training style

Even though you have preferences, it is not an excuse for not improving the areas that need to be improved. All of the dimensions are defined by skills — skills that you can learn, abilities that you can acquire.

Take time right now and think about your training style. What are your preferences? Are you balanced in your use of all four dimensions? Or do you have strong preferences? What are your strengths? What areas need improving? What insights have you gained by thinking through this content? What will you do differently as a result of the knowledge you have learned?

If you facilitate mostly virtual learning sessions, does this pertain to you? Yes it does. If this is you, pay particular attention to the "cautions" in Figure 11-2. An inability to overcome these drawbacks will lead to disaster faster than if you are in a physical classroom.

Jean Barbazette is one of the few people who addresses training styles in an orderly way. She developed one of the first trainer style inventories in 1996. Although her model is different from the one presented in this book, her philosophy is similar as presented by her in the following sidebar. Jean has designed and presented train-the-trainer workshops since 1977. The focus of her work in training and development has been to make training programs practical, useful, and concrete. She is the author of *Instant Case Studies: How to Design, Adapt, and Use Case Studies in Training* (Pfeiffer, 2003).

Does one size fit all in training?

by Jean Barbazette

One of the difficult issues trainers and course designers face is to match a lesson to the needs of the learners. Homogeneous audiences make a trainer's task of design and facilitation an easier one. When learners have the same level of experience, interest, and past training, one lesson fits the needs of all the learners. So, what's the best way to design a training session for a diverse audience?

The answer: Design all training using an experiential learning model. Several models with differing numbers of steps have been offered

to trainers over many years to teach through simulations. These models all include

1. Setting up the learning activity

2. Conducting the learning activity

3. Asking learners to share and interpret their reactions to the activity

4. Identifying what was learned through the activity

5. Planning how to use what was learned.

An experiential learning model helps all learners use a shared experience beginning from where they are. Because experiential learning actively involves the learner, it is possible to use the same activity with a diverse audience. Granted, some learners will get more out of an activity than others.

Trainers need a range of skills to facilitate each step of the experiential learning model. In Step 1, setting up the learning activity, adult learners become motivated when they understand the benefits or importance of the activity to themselves and their work. To be successful, set up the activity so learners understand what they are going to do and why they are going to do it. A trainer needs to use Elaine's Presenting Style to give instructions and ground rules for how the learning activity is to be conducted. Setups may also include to:

- Tell participants about the purpose of the activity.

- Divide participants into groups and assign roles.

- Provide ground rules.

- Explain what the participants are going to do.

- Tell participants why they are doing the activity without giving away what they will "discover" as a result of engaging in the activity.

In Step 2, a learning activity is conducted. It will be successful when learners are involved as much as possible. This step may include discussion, case study, role play, simulation or game, inventory, independent study, or reading.

Depending on the activity selected for Step 2, the trainer's style can be anywhere between the Presenting or Facilitating style.

In Step 3, learners share their reactions to the activity by identifying what happened to them and to others as well as how their own behavior affected others. The trainer uses a Guiding Style to ask questions such as these:

- "What was your partner's reaction when you did . . . ?"

- "What helped or hindered your progress?"

- "Summarize the key points from the lecture, role-playing activity, or case study."

Learners in diverse groups learn different things from the same activity. The trainer facilitates a discussion and asks the learners what happened to them (not what was learned) during the activity.

During Step 4, the trainer uses a Guiding Style to help learners discover the idea underlying the activity. This is the "So, what did I learn?" step. Questions that develop concepts may include "What did you learn about how to conduct an interview, discipline a subordinate, teach a new job, and so on."

If this step is left out, then learning will be incomplete. Certainly, participants will have been entertained by the training activity, but they may not be able to apply new learning to similar situations outside the classroom. Indeed, it is only when concepts are inferred from an activity that learners are ready and able to apply them to future situations. Diverse learners can learn different things from the same activity. The trainer's role as a facilitator is to be sure each learner takes away something of value from the activity.

During Step 5, the trainer uses a Coaching Style. This is the "Now what?" step. What do I do with what I learned? During this step, learners use and apply new information learned from the activity to their own situations. It usually involves an action question such as "How will you use this technique the next time a subordinate asks you for a favor?" or "What will you do differently as a result of this activity?"

(continued)

(continued)

Like the preceding four steps, if it is left out, learners may not be able to discern the relationship between the activity and their job (or situation) and may not be able to see how what was learned can be useful to them in the future. Diverse learners definitely take something different from the lesson because different jobs require different applications. The trainer encourages enough discussion so application of the concept is possible for all learners.

So does one size fit all in training? A trainer can use the same activity for diverse learners. A skillful trainer uses a variety of styles — presenting, guiding, coaching, and facilitating — to be sure all learners find value in the same activity.

Group Dynamics

Group dynamics develop when people interact with one another. The study of group dynamics is a more complex undertaking than space allows me to discuss here. Yet understanding group dynamics is important so that you are aware of why your participants are acting the way they are and how it may affect other participants and ultimately your training session. Therefore, I present here a general overview of the kinds of things that can affect group dynamics. This section barely scratches the surface of what many know about the topic. Do group dynamics occur in a virtual classroom? Absolutely. Just ask any experienced virtual facilitator.

Numerous things can affect group dynamics, such as the composition of the group, the atmosphere, the norms under which the individuals operate, the values of the individuals and the group, the communication and participation among the group, the roles that participants play, and the power and influence that exists and is exuded within the group. The following sections examine some of these.

Composition

Composition refers to a number of things. The size of the group may have more effect on team dynamics than on anything else. If the group is too large you may have difficulty keeping everyone's attention and balancing participation. This may be particularly true in a virtual ILT.

Consider the reasons participants are attending the training. Very different dynamics occur when participants believe that they have a choice about attending the training or if they believe they were sent against their will.

The feelings participants have about each other is another composition aspect that can affect the group dynamics. Do they like the other people in the training session? Do all the departments respect each other? Previous as well as current work relationships with each other can affect the dynamics as well.

The formation of subgroups will affect group dynamics. You will want to consider this as you prepare for your session. And you may prepare for the exact opposite, depending upon the situation. For example, if you are teaching team skills, you may want subgroups to form. In that case you will create opportunities to strengthen these teams. At other times you may need to find ways to break up cliques and get the already formed subgroups to split up and work with other participants.

Atmosphere

Begin to examine the dynamics caused by the atmosphere by looking toward the physical setting. Is the room spacious? Too spacious? Crowded? Is the lighting bright? Dim? Natural? Are the tables spacious? Crowded? Are the chairs comfortable? Hard? Is the temperature comfortable? Too hot? Too cold? Can you control it? Guaranteed. It doesn't matter how great your training session is. If the participants are not comfortable it will affect group dynamics negatively. If you are leading a virtual classroom, do participants who are not tech savvy feel comfortable asking for help?

How formal is the training session? Hopefully the timeline is flexible enough to accommodate participants' needs and requests. If it is not, you may influence group dynamics in a positive way by determining how you can build in time for unique participant needs.

The level of interest participants have in the subject will affect group dynamics. The amount of laughter you hear is an indicator of how much fun participants are having. Paired with how interested participants are in the content, both affect the dynamics.

How congenial people are to each other, how they express themselves, and how well they accept others and the session combined are other aspects of the atmosphere that may have either a negative or positive effect on group dynamics.

Norms

When people think about group dynamics, they often think first of norms. Norms are another way of stating what people have grown to expect of each other and the rest of the group. Included in norms are attendance and punctuality expectations. Is it common to show up five or ten minutes late and still be counted as timely? Is that true for some of the group or all members of the group? Is everyone expected to attend fully? How about phone calls? Can participants leave to return messages? Each of these will affect group dynamics — especially if everyone in the session operates under a different set of norms.

Participation has been discussed in other places in this book. The amount and type of participation that is acceptable is a part of the organizational norms. Trainers sometimes stretch individuals, encouraging them to be more participative than they normally would be. That is generally seen as good. Take care that you do not stretch them too much. For example, don't expect introverts or most engineers to enjoy role plays. This is one of the reasons to find out all you can about participants before the training session.

The topics of the training session may affect the group dynamics, but interestingly it may be the topics that are avoided that affect the group dynamics. If participants are listening to content that they believe is good but not displayed within the organization, they may feel the training is a sham. Having an opportunity to express what they are thinking may help the group dynamics.

The norms that individuals operate under when working with the rest of the group are also important. For example, do they treat each other with respect? Do they cooperate during tasks? Are some more competitive than others? Is information shared willingly or withheld? Each of these will affect the small-group exercises in the training session.

Values

The values that individuals bring to the session will affect the group dynamics. Ideally, individual, group, and organizational values are the same. When this is not true, it can affect the interaction negatively. You may see some people stop interacting if certain beliefs are brought up. The direction the group wants to take as a result of differences in values can be a positive experience. In most cases it is wise to allow a discussion of the differences to take place. Unfortunately, it is sometimes difficult to bring closure to these discussions.

Another way values can affect the dynamics of a group is if hidden agendas exist in the group. It may take a while, but generally hidden agendas are uncovered by the behaviors that are observed or the comments that are made. By the way, hidden agendas do not always need to represent a "bad" objective. However, a lack of openness may lead to distrust among the group.

Communication and participation

I have discussed the trainers' role in modeling good communication and encouraging participation. Participants also bring their skills and beliefs into the training session, and this will affect the group dynamics. The degree to which some participants want to be involved may be different from others. This may affect large-group discussions as well as small-group activities. Whether it is a virtual or traditional classroom, the communication and participation aspect of group dynamics is one area over which the trainer has the most control.

Group dynamics will be affected by many things that you do as a trainer. For example, how you handle disagreements and conflicts will be observed by participants. The factors that contribute to the misunderstanding will also affect group dynamics. How you address challenges and how you deal with interruptions will affect the level of trust and respect participants have for you.

Participants will observe how silent members are treated. Are they brought into the discussion slowly, respecting their personal needs? Or are they forced to participate before they are comfortable?

Listening skills of both the trainer and the participants will affect the group dynamics. Participants may have a hard time respecting a trainer who is not a good listener. Training is never one-way communication. On the other hand, a trainer who has a room full of poor listeners will have difficulty in accomplishing the job.

Roles

The roles participants play will affect the team dynamics. Roles are frequently divided into task and maintenance behaviors. Task roles are those things that individuals do to get the job completed. Maintenance roles are behaviors that are completed that ensure a positive atmosphere. Individuals play these roles naturally.

Task roles supply the information, ideas, and energy necessary for the group to accomplish its objectives. These roles get things started and may include asking for information or opinions, clarifying comments, sharing facts or ideas, or suggesting solutions or methods. Task roles may also help to organize by coordinating or clarifying relationships, comparing concepts, defining positions, or summarizing what has happened. Task roles may also focus on action-type events by offering suggestions, prodding the group to take action, or simply keeping the group on task.

Maintenance roles establish and maintain interpersonal relationships and a pleasant atmosphere. They are generally focused on people and the atmosphere. Individuals may play roles to mediate differences or referee disagreements. These roles include searching for common elements in conflicts or offering a compromise. Maintenance roles also include motivators who offer praise and support of others. Maintenance roles include finding the humor in a situation and bringing in participants who otherwise may not speak. Maintenance roles encourage participation, build trust, and relieve tension in a group.

Power and influence

Power and influence are potentially one of the most problematic areas of group dynamics to a trainer. Power is often described as coming from three sources: positional power, informational power, or charismatic power. Each of these three has the potential to affect group dynamics — either positively or negatively. Individuals do not like to feel powerless. Therefore, how individuals use power determines how it affects the dynamics of the group. Using power to lead positively or to contribute appropriately will enhance group dynamics. On the other hand, flaunting power or using it negatively can be destructive.

Individuals who have reporting relationships are often a dilemma for trainers. It may be uncomfortable for a participant to be in a session with the boss present. The subordinate may not feel comfortable contributing during the session.

Rivalry between departments or individuals may also cause group dynamics problems for a trainer. If individuals do not get along outside a training session, the situation can be exacerbated by forcing them to sit in the same room and interact during a training session.

Many things can affect group dynamics during a training session. A good trainer learns as much as possible about the participants and prepares for anything that may cause a disruption. On the positive side, a trainer's knowledge of the participants may also be used to enhance the training session.

Trainers need to be proactive about managing groups and the group dynamics. Should subgroups remain the same for key projects? Or is it better if they change? How do you determine whether the large group is mixing and mingling enough? What do you do to include everyone but not impose on those who prefer to participate by listening? What do you do when you sense tension? How do you deal with someone who may be using power inappropriately? Each of these affects group dynamics and how you address each will affect it also.

This section alerts you to some of the most common aspects of group dynamics. Awareness is the first step. Observe your participants. When you address various aspects be sure to note what happens. Later determine why. You may even want to discuss what occurred with another trainer. Humans being who they are, it is impossible to identify every situation you may encounter. However, your experiences and what you learn from them will equip you to handle most group-dynamics situations.

Creating an Energizing, Exciting, Encouraging Environment

Chapter 2 discusses establishing an environment that is conducive to learning. However, there are times (most times) when you will want to go beyond the basics to create an energizing or exciting and encouraging environment.

How do you do that? You can add energy and excitement to a training session with a little extra planning. Here are some suggestions.

Coloring outside the lines

Remember that old joke "What's black and white and red all over?" As I recall there were a couple of right answers: a newspaper. And an embarrassed zebra. Perhaps others. As a trainer, you need to ensure that you are looking outside the lines, the black-and-white lines, of training and encouraging the colorful, creative world of training.

This book touches on the topic of color a couple of times when I explore media and visuals. One of the advantages of using visuals is that you can add color. However, you can add color in other ways as well.

If you experiment with various colors on visuals, check them out from the back of the room to ensure readability. If you have a virtual class, ensure that the colors on participants' slides are comfortable to look at for an hour at a time.

Color affects everyone, and each color is associated with specific emotions. Marketing folks have depended on color for years to encourage you to purchase one product over another. Trainers can use color to

- Excite and stimulate participants' senses
- Encourage participants to get involved in activities
- Energize participants to retain and apply the knowledge and skills they learn

Consider some of the emotions associated with specific colors, as shown in Table 11-1.

Table 11-1	Color Associations
Color	*Using Color to Evoke Emotions and Energize*
Red	Red says, "Pay attention!" It evokes power, anger, achievement, excitement, and intensity. It tells us to stop. It may send a negative message due to financial shortages. Red should be reserved for highlighting, circling hot spots, or trouble. It can indicate tension or stressful areas also.
Yellow	Evokes happiness, cheerfulness, and warmth. While it can be mellow and indicate optimism, it can also suggest caution. Although it stimulates thinking, it is impossible to see on its own, so use it to fill within the lines. Use it to find ideas and to support creativity.
Blue	Blue creates a feeling of reliability, trust, maturity, authority, peace, and tranquility. Dark blue projects a masculine image, while light blue projects youth. Use blue early in a session to establish trust.
Green	Indicates productivity, growth, youth, and health. Instills a positive image and forward motion, "go." Suggests money or prosperity. Use green branches on a tree to suggest strength or growth. Light green is energizing, but dark green is easier to read. Use it when reaching consensus or finding compromises.
Orange	Stimulates energy, enthusiasm, and positive thinking. This lively color works best for highlighting, but it may be difficult to read in rooms with fluorescent lighting. Use to highlight a subject or create connections.
Purple	Projects assertiveness, boldness, passion, and a power. May be used to signify royalty, richness, or spirituality. Works well with other colors and stimulates ideas during brainstorming.
White	Usually indicates cleanliness, honesty, innocence, or goodness. White space provides visual rest. Use white space to assist with clarity and order.

Color	*Using Color to Evoke Emotions and Energize*
Black	Creates feelings of independence and solidarity. As opposed to red, suggests financial solvency. Has a serious side by representing death, somberness, or gravity of a situation. Easiest of all colors to read by everyone. Usually highlight with a bright color. Because it means finality, it is not the best color to use when brainstorming.
Brown	Indicates strength, support, solidly earthy, and a lack of superiority. It may affect some folks negatively. This is an easy-to-read color but may be depressing or drab on its own.
Pink	Light pink indicates femininity and fun. It is upbeat and youthful. Bright pink creates excitement and passion. Combines well with other colors and may be a good wake-up color after lunch.
Gold/silver	These prestigious hues project elegance and an image of status. May also suggest riches.

So how can you use color in your training? Here are a few things I do to add color.

- Place brightly colored sticky notes in front of participants, that are available for them to jot a note or to mark something in their participant materials.

- Use colored paper for specific activities. For example, I have a page of creativity techniques that has a light bulb in the background that I copy on astro bright-yellow paper. In another training session, I conduct a killer-phrases exercise where the participants list killer phrases on red paper and end up wadding up their pages and throwing them.

- Place a variety of brightly colored sheets of paper in the center of tables for use with small-group activities that require blank paper.

- I frequently place crayons or colored pencils on the tables and may ask participants to complete certain activities using them. A favorite is to use them to decorate their name tents.

- Hang posters that are related to your training session around the room. They may also be posters that encourage thinking positively, that deliver a message, or provide a quote.

- When voting on positive and/or negative issues you can use post-it flags on a wall poster. For example, use a green flag to vote for the characteristic that our team is best at and a red flag to vote for the characteristic that our team needs to improve the most.

- Instead of dark on light, surprise your participants and have them write light on dark. Use white, silver, or gold marking pens and dark paper in red, green, and even navy blue. These things are easy to find in your local office supply store.

Don't use colors willy-nilly. Think through how you will use them. For example, they can be a great way to transition from one module to another. Use highlight to assist learners to note the key areas. Think about which color combinations work best. Use brighter colors to infuse energy after lunch.

Energize the group

Many of things have been discussed in this book that will energize participants:

- Obtaining participation
- Conducting learner-centered activities
- Varying activities
- Creating an active learning environment
- Celebrating success
- Projecting enthusiasm

All of these are important, but sometimes it will take just a bit more. If you see energy waning or enthusiasm wavering, it may be time to move people around the room in the form of an energizer.

Purpose of energizers

Energizers are used to change the mental and/or physical state of participants. They may be used to change the pace of a program; for example, if the session is bogged down in heavy discussion, you can use an energizer to speed up the pace. Or the opposite, you may be able to use an energizer to provide quiet personal reflection after an energetic group activity. Energizers are great to use if participants have been sitting for a while and need to get up and move about.

Energizers are useful for many things:

- Change the pace of the session
- Revive the energy of a group when it is lagging
- Create a transition from one topic to another
- Provide movement for kinesthetic learners
- Subtly break up subgroups that may have formed
- Give everyone a break from listening or sitting for a long period of time

How to determine whether you need an energizer

How do you know whether you need an energizer? There are lots of ways to tell. Try these for starters.

- Participants agree with everything you say.

- Participants are sniffing the scented markers.

- The most interested contributors are reading ahead.

- The doodlers are creating works of art.

- Someone's head thumps on the table, and he or she does not awaken.

- Twenty-five percent of the group has left the room and the rest are wiggling.

- Seventy-five percent of the group is watching the fly circling the donuts.

- Magazines have been pulled out of backpacks.

- Participants are entertained by their watches' second hand.

What do you do? Yes, this is a tongue-in-cheek list. Don't wait until these things are happening. Attend to both participants and the time so that you will sense when a break or an energizer is needed.

Selecting energizers

Use the same common sense for selecting an energizer that you would when selecting an icebreaker. Numerous books have been written about energizers, and sometimes you can adjust an icebreaker to be an appropriate energizer.

- Consider the participants' expectations.

- Consider the size of the group.

- Place the energizer at the appropriate time.

- Have a clear purpose for selecting and scheduling the energizer.

- Initiate appropriate risk, ensuring that it is comfortable for everyone.

Energizer examples

So what does an energizer look like? This list displays the wide range.

- Participants find "their mate" based on anything from clothing to birthday to someone they don't know. Once there, a task is assigned.

- Teams race to complete a puzzle, word game, or "test" related to the content.

- Invite people to write one thing they have learned on a sheet of paper and then turn it into a paper airplane. Fly the planes, and whoever it goes to reads the item on the plane.

- Hold a relay race or ball toss to review content.

- Participants select toys, tools, office supplies, or anything as a metaphor related to the content or to their opinions about the session.

- Lead participants in stretching, relaxing, deep breathing, or "shaking out" exercises.

- Use music: Sing rounds, make up songs, hand out kazoos, or hum.

   For variation, hum using the sounds of various vowels, a, e, i, o, u.

- Sometimes, just a normal break will serve as a great energizer.

Any of the above can be used to energize your group. Experiment with various energizers. You will soon have your own repertoire of energizers.

The Internet opens a whole world of energizers. Search for books from publishers such as the Association for Talent Development (ATD), Bowperson Publishing, Gulf Publishing, HRDPress, Lakewood Publications, McGraw-Hill, and Pfeiffer/Wiley.

Let me entertrain you!

Humor can be the best thing for a training session — or the worst. Especially when it falls flat. A few guidelines will help you to successfully interject humor into your training session. My friend Jeanne builds humor into her presentations in a very natural way. She even calls herself an *entertrainer* and believes that humor adds a great deal to training. What are some of the advantages of adding humor to a training session?

- Can be used to get participants' attention

- Keeps participants interested in content

- Clarifies a point

- Ensures that key points are memorable

- Creates a relaxed atmosphere

- Builds a positive relationship between you and your participants

- Can ease the way through difficult content

Laughing while they learn

Notice that I have not mentioned telling jokes. Some people are good at telling jokes; some are not. If you are in the second category, don't bother. Keep your humor natural and relevant to the content. Know your participants and what will be funny to them.

Natural is best: Humor should fit naturally into the content. Relevance is more important than funny. Do not tell a story or joke that is not related to the content.

Keep a funny file. Build your own list of humorous stories. Keep a file with stories you may use, examples of things that happened to you, jokes, cartoons, and funny quotes. Look for visuals as well. Your file will fill with experiences.

Keep it clean. I shouldn't have to address this, but I will just to be certain. Humor should not use offensive language. Race, religion, sex, stereotypes, and politics are off limits.

What if you don't get a laugh? You have two choices. You can ignore it and move quickly into content, or you can try again with a quip such as "That's the last time I try out my material on a group of trainers" or "That's the last time I ask (name of one of the participants) for new material." Sometimes you can pick up these one-liners watching stand-up comedians on television.

You may wish to check the chapter near the end of this book that provides ten ways to add humor to your training. Many of the ideas are based on things that happen naturally in a training session.

You ought to be in show business

Okay, you've got the general idea. Participants want to have fun. Now how can trainers create their own material?

Write your story in a conversational tone. Keep it short. Practice it out loud. Try it out on someone or two. Rewrite it to clarify or simplify. Make sure the words and timing are right. Be sure your punch line is clear, concise, and of course — funny!

 Customize your joke for your audience. It is guaranteed to get a laugh! You can customize it using names of the people in the organization, competitors of the organization, or the location of your training. For example, the age-old joke "I'm afraid to fly. It's not the plane, it's the drive to the airport," can be customized for the location. If you are in Washington, D.C., you could say, "I'm afraid to fly. It's not the plane, it's the drive to Reagan National!"

Add creativity to training

Creativity is an important aspect of all training, and even if you think you aren't creative, there are little things you can do that will enhance your training style. Try these:

- Promote your next training session in a unique way, for example, by sending the invitation in a paper bag.

- Title your next training session in a creative way, such as "Bag That Problem."

- Hold your next training session in a unique location.

- Introduce new ways to think about the training topic.

- Use themes to energize a session, for example, paper bags, crayons, seeds, hats, maps, airplanes, tools, puzzles, or T-shirts.

- Use at least three different training techniques or methods per hour of instruction.

- Use cartoons that you draw or that have received appropriate copyright approval to use; add the names of managers in your organization.

- Look for double meanings in the words and topics of your training and then play with those double meanings. For example, trainers often claim to have a "bag of tricks." You could play off of the "bag" theme or the "tricks" theme. Use a "bag your problem" activity or use magic tricks as an analogy to some of the knowledge you are training.

- Encourage participants' creativity; engage them in brainstorming.

- Present your participants with challenges, puzzles, and brain teasers.

- Keep a creativity file that you can refer to when you develop your training programs.

- Use energizers often. Be sure they are short, quick, and, of course, energizing! Try to relate your energizer to the course content, like those earlier in this chapter.

- Add planned humor to your next training session. Be sure to use your funny experience as an example.

- End your training session with a story, poem, quote, picture, or gimmick. For example, thrusting a straw through a raw potato to demonstrate the importance of seeing success and following through.

- Read articles and books about creativity to give you ideas.

✔ Shop in toy stores, dollar stores, and children's bookstores for ideas.

✔ Ask participants to evaluate your training program with a limerick.

✔ Take more risks; try things that you have been reluctant to try. For example, I avoided using debates in the classroom for too many years because I was afraid to take the risk. When I did finally use a debate, I was pleasantly surprised about participants' willingness to get involved, as well as the richness of the follow-up discussion.

✔ Trouble getting folks to return after a break? That's probably a good sign that they are communicating during the break. But you do need to start again. Use a cartoon or flick the lights. You may also signal with a noise maker, like a train whistle, kazoo, cow bell, chime, or sleigh bells. Try to vary your approach from one break to the next.

Another way to get participants' attention is to snap your fingers. I begin snapping my fingers and quietly say, "If you can hear me, snap your fingers." Participants in the front can hear it the first time. I repeat myself and eventually the snapping works its way to the back of the room.

✔ Study other presentations you see and identify new approaches to use during your next training.

Take a list of key concepts for your next training session with you to your local dollar store. Compare the concepts and the merchandise in the store to identify themes for your next training session. For example, you can use play money for investing in your future, your health, or your team; puzzles for finding the right fit or everyone has a role; a compass for finding your way, or determining a new direction; rulers for measuring potential, setting goals, or determining growth; or hundreds of other ideas.

Caution: Stick-in-the-muds ahead

No matter what you add to your training design to make it fun, engaging, and to support learning, you must continue to keep the learning objectives in front of you. I purposefully do not call active learning methodologies *games*. Using that term implies, unfortunately, that the training session is all about having fun, not about learning.

Even though you and I know that people do learn and remember when they are having fun, be cautious about the label you use. *Learning activity* just sounds better outside the session to people who weren't there to see all the learning that occurred.

Celebrate success

Remember when you were a kid and your family celebrated all those little accomplishments, like the first time you rode a bike or won a blue ribbon at the science fair? Well, adults like to celebrate success, too. Another way to create an energizing, exciting, enthusiastic environment is to celebrate participants' success.

Use rewards and reinforcement to celebrate success. Trainers use intrinsic rewards such as thank you, feedback on performance, and other verbal recognition. Trainers also use tangible rewards, such as candy, gum, small team prizes, and individual doodads. Or break out a special prize for everyone (a big bag of candy-coated chocolate.)

Check out sources for inexpensive (some as low as a dime each) doodads. Oriental Trading, `www.orientaltrading.com` is a favorite for toys, holiday items, puzzles, key chains, hats, and more things than you ever thought existed. Although it is fun to check that website, it's even more fun to get on its mailing list and have its monthly catalog delivered to your door!

Reinforce what participants learn throughout the session. You could try some of these or make up your own.

- Participants list what they learned on flipchart pages posted on the wall.
- Participants complete a crossword puzzle format or word search.
- Participants stand in a circle, toss a ball, and state one thing each learned.
- Participants write an email to their supervisors stating what they learned and how they would like to implement it.
- Participants write a memo to themselves that the trainer mails later.
- Review key concepts using a game-show format such as *Jeopardy*.

All of these work to enhance and celebrate learning.

Celebrate success at the end of the session as well. Certificates are an inexpensive reward, as is reenacting a graduation ceremony playing "Pomp and Circumstance" or playing any engaging or celebratory tune that brings closure such as "Happy Trails" or "Goodbye, So Long, Farewell."

If you use music in your training session, be sure to get copyright permission from BMI or ASCAP.

Putting It All Together

Many concepts have been presented in this chapter. Can you really do it all? Should you try? Well, that's a trick question. You shouldn't "try" to do anything. You absorb this information and use it when appropriate. Everything presented in this chapter sets a stage for you to add energy, excitement, and encouragement to your sessions. Knowing your training style is the first step to understanding what you will feel comfortable doing.

Training with style means not only ensuring that you get the job done but that you get the job done right — and ensure that you and the participants enjoy everything along the way. You will learn more. Your participants will learn more.

Or as Plato stated, "You can discover more about a person in an hour of play than in a year of conversation."

Chapter 12

Addressing Problems: What's a Trainer to Do?

In This Chapter
▶ Preventing training problems
▶ Dealing with unexpected training problems
▶ Managing disruptive participants
▶ Mastering your presentation anxiety

No matter how well prepared you are, no matter how critical the training is, problems will occur. You simply cannot think of everything — but that doesn't mean you should not try!

Remember, it's not the disaster that matters; it is how you manage the disaster that counts. Your participants will be watching you as a role model, because they may someday be in the same situation.

In this chapter, I introduce you to the COOL technique to manage any disasters that may come your way. Staying COOL makes you appear to be the pro that you are. Most trainers have experienced these problems at one time or another — that's how you know what works best! Your main problems are likely to involve inadequate training facilities, disruptive participants, and your own attack of nerves. What follows is a primer of problems, with the tools you need to cut them off early without losing a beat.

Problems in the Classroom

A host of problems may occur as a trainer. Just when you think you have encountered almost anything that could happen, a new problem will be tossed in your path.

Problems with logistics

Logistics can create big headaches for trainers. Chapter 7 provides guidance for how to prepare and prevent many logistical nightmares from occurring. Here are a few others.

Rooms not conducive to training

You may find yourself conducting training in a room that was never intended to be used for that purpose. You may be in a boardroom with a large table and no room to divide into small groups. You may find a large pillar in the center of the room. You may be in a room that is so filled with furniture there is little space for your participants. You may even find that you have no room at all. I once found myself relegated to the end of a hallway to conduct a training session because the carpeting in the training room was being torn out as I arrived!

In any of these cases, if you do not find out until 60 minutes before the session starts, it is most likely too late to expect a reasonable solution. You should at least ask whether there is a different room available or that could be available at the next break or lunch. If nothing is available, you need to do a quick shuffle in the design and make the most of it. Check for space outside the room for breakout groups.

Furniture is not conducive to training

It may not seem like your job, but ensuring that participants have comfortable chairs and tables that don't fall down is your job. You can tell the second you walk into the room whether the chairs will be comfortable or not. You may even find that the participants will need to squeeze into one-piece desks like those you used in high school.

You will probably want to look for other space for breakout sessions. On these occasions I've even taken participants outside to sit on picnic tables for small-group activities. Participants will appreciate even the smallest things you do to provide additional comfort.

Prevent logistics problems

Preparation is key to preventing logistics problems. You certainly will never be able to think of everything, but the more you plan ahead, the fewer problems you will have. This is true no matter what kind of training you are conducting. Whether virtual, physical, remote, or one-on-one, learn from each experience. Begin to create a generic preparation checklist of items to help you remember what questions to ask, whom to ask, and what to pack.

What can go wrong?

What can possibly go wrong? Try this for a comedy of errors. The address for the community service training session given to the trainer was for 1423 East Oak, but the church was on West Oak. It didn't matter anyway because when she finally arrived, the door was locked and she couldn't get in. She had the director's name and cellphone number, but the director was an hour away and participants started to arrive before anyone could get into the building. Just before the director arrived another trainer showed up who had a key. Unfortunately, this trainer believed that he was assigned the same training room. In fact, they were double booked.

Another room in the basement of the old church was available. Although the trainer was just over five feet tall, she had to duck to miss some of the overhead pipes. Participants jumped in to help her set up and carry her boxes of supplies. When she tried to plug the projector into an outlet, she found that the three-pronged plug would not fit in the archaic, two-holed electrical receptacle. She broke the third prong off to accommodate the electrical requirement.

When the training session started, the overhead pipes began to perspire and drip on the participants' materials, the workshop supplies, and the trainer. The trainer learned that the participants were unaware of why they were attending the training and thought that it was some sort of punishment. The air conditioning kicked in as soon as it was turned on but quickly blew a fuse, and no one knew how to replace it. The receptionist who was supposed to have opened the church never arrived. Therefore, the phone in the room next to the training room rang every few minutes with no one to answer it.

By the way, the good news was that the trainer's suitcase, that was temporarily "lost" by the airline, was delivered just before she left to go to her hotel for the evening.

Yes, this happened to me when I first started training. The funniest thing about the situation is that the participants said it was the best training they had ever attended.

Equipment problems

Nothing can be as frustrating as equipment problems. If something critical is going to go wrong, equipment is the area that will take you down.

What could occur?

Almost anything can go wrong with equipment, starting with it simply not showing up: Someone forgot, it was delivered to the wrong room, or perhaps it is simply not available.

The flipchart pad may be filled with used paper.

In a virtual setting, someone may lose a connection or perhaps a poll question does not load.

You may not have enough copies of the handouts for participants. Perhaps someone did not count correctly. Perhaps more participants showed up than you anticipated.

Prevent these problems

Some problems with equipment can be prevented. Others cannot. But that doesn't mean that you shouldn't try to prevent them from occurring.

Always double-check on your equipment needs. Order it at least a month in advance, follow up one week before your session, and finally, call the day before to confirm date, time, location, and type of equipment.

I obtain the name and office and cellphone number of the person who is responsible for setting up the equipment. This has come in handy more often than I can count.

When you arrive at your room, check the equipment first. Make sure it all works, turns on, and that the cords are taped down. Check to make sure that the flipchart pad is filled with unused paper. If at all possible, have the equipment delivered to your room and set it up the day or night before your session.

In your virtual setting, the best preparation is to practice all the software well in advance. Ensure that you follow all pre-class set-up procedures and make a checklist to follow for each. Be sure that you and your producer practice together as well. And no matter how much of an expert you are, if the session is critical, partner with a producer to manage all the things that can go wrong. One last thing: Ensure that your participants know what to do and whom to contact if they cannot log in. Remember — it can't be you, because you will be facilitating the session.

And when you can't prevent equipment problems . . .

When problems occur anyway (and they will), you can do two things. First, have a backup plan, and second, keep your cool and follow a specific process.

> ✔ **Have a backup plan.** It is almost certain that your equipment will fail at just the moment your presentation is dependent on your visuals. If you're prepared to deliver your presentation without the visuals, all will not be lost. If using slides, have a hard copy so that participants can see anything critical on paper that they would have seen on a screen. I always have a flipchart in the room. It is available for sketching diagrams, creating lists, highlighting key points, or getting your participants involved in the presentation. Besides, your participants will have handouts for most of your events. Facilitate from them. This can work on a virtual session as well. Use audio until your producer fixes the problem.

Remember, you will now be the focal point of your presentation; all eyes will be on you, so you need to attend to your presentation skills: good eye contact, animated gestures, planned body movement, and confident stance. You may also need to use more descriptive language, add more examples, and paint a verbal picture for your participants that they would have otherwise observed visually.

✔ **Follow a specific process.** Know what to try and in what order to try it. Almost everyone uses an LCD projector and laptop computer. Unfortunately, that is one of the most complex problems to uncover. If this equipment malfunctions, ask these questions:

- Is everything plugged in and turned on? Be sure to check extension cords, too.

- Are all the cables firmly connected to the correct input or output ports?

- Are the projector and your laptop set up properly? Be sure that your laptop is selected as the source and that the projector is not in the standby mode.

- Has your laptop been set to display through the external video port? Every laptop computer has multiple display modes and a utility that allows you to toggle among these modes. When toggling between modes, allow at least 15 seconds for the setting to change before trying another mode.

- Have you tried to reset the equipment? Sometimes, simply turning everything off and turning it back on works.

- Have you used your laptop with this type of projector in the past? Some computers are not compatible with some projectors. Although it is rare, it has happened to me.

✔ **Be positive.** If your equipment failure occurs in front of participants, don't complain about the equipment or the situation. Offer a brief apology, take no more than four minutes to fix it and move on. You may wish to call a short break, but don't allow your participants to sit and watch you pull, poke, and prod your equipment.

Yes, equipment can be one of the most frustrating problems a trainer may face. But if you're prepared, it doesn't have to throw you off center. Always learn something from the experience. If you were unable to fix the problem, try to fix it after your participants leave. You may wish to consult with the audiovisual technician. Learn how to fix the problem. If it happened once, it is likely that it will happen again.

Difficult personal situations

Sometimes, things happen to you that create problems. In many cases, it won't seem like a big deal the next day, but that doesn't help when you're in the middle of it. What may happen and what could you do?

You forget what you were going to say

Many trainers are afraid of going brain dead in front of the participants. It happens to everyone during daily conversations with others. However, when it occurs in front of participants, it may be more uncomfortable. You may wish to adapt some of these techniques to your style:

- ✓ Admit that you forgot, just as you would in a typical daily conversation. Continue on and return to the point when you remember it.

- ✓ Take a sip of water that you may have at your table. Often, the 30-second pause will be enough time to recall your train of thought.

- ✓ Try to fill in by repeating the last point in a different way or give an example. Like the sip of water, it will give you a couple of seconds of thinking time.

- ✓ Refer to your notes. Ensure that your notes work for you: You have the information on them that you need, and you have it displayed in a way that you can find what you need.

- ✓ If it is not obvious, shift the attention back to the participants. Ask them what questions they have at this point. Because no one knows exactly what you were going to do or say, it is highly unlikely that anyone will notice the shift.

- ✓ Have a standard phrase that you will use, such as "I lost my train of thought. Perhaps one of you can find it" or "I just went brain dead. Do any of you remember what I was going to say?"

You do not feel well

Unfortunately, there is not much you can do about feeling under the weather. The show must go on, and as a trainer, you rarely have someone to back you up. Certainly, if you have something contagious or if you're so ill that you will be unable to facilitate the session, you may need to cancel. It is difficult to cancel a training session because so many other people are counting on you. At times others may have traveled hundreds of miles for the training event.

If you do not feel well and you're going to continue to conduct the training, consider these suggestions:

- ✓ Don't tell the participants you're not feeling well, or if you do, don't make a big deal out of it. You may get sympathy, but is that what you want?

✔ Shift the session to put more emphasis on participant involvement and activities. You will most likely have participants who have experience and expertise related to the topic. Ask them to assist with delivering information, or leading a discussion.

It is never any fun to work when you do not feel well. Being a trainer is one of those professions, however, that allows little flexibility when illness occurs.

You get off track

It is so easy to get off track. Thousands of detours will cross your path. Sometimes, participants may take you off track with a question. At other times you may take yourself off track because you tell a story or you add information that is nice to know.

As soon as you recognize that you're off track, steer the group back. Try these techniques to help you:

✔ Try to connect what you're saying to where you should be.

✔ Humor may work. Wrap up the topic quickly and say something like, "My, that was a distracting little detour!"

✔ If it is difficult to get back on track, you may wish to take a break.

You're new to the job

Everyone has to start somewhere. Being new to training is not something, however, that you need to announce to the group. Imagine that you were getting on a flight from San Francisco to Frankfurt. You probably do not want the pilot to announce that this is her first flight. Likewise, you do not need to announce that this is your first training session.

In fact, you should never need to make excuses. Using the phrase "bear with me" makes participants feel as if they are putting up with something that is uncalled for. Don't use it. "Bear with me, this is my first training!" may establish a hesitancy from participants right from the start. This is not how you want to start.

Difficult group situations

Sometimes, it may seem that the entire group is creating a problem — and it could be true.

Why may this occur?

Participants' style may not be a match for the training design. For example, if the design calls for a great deal of participation and the audience is made up of participants who prefer an analytical style, you may not get the level of discussion and involvement that is required.

The group may also be preoccupied by other thoughts. For example, if you're training them to learn how to improve processes or make change of any kind, and they know that the company needs to become more efficient, they may be concerned about whether downsizing may occur and how it could affect them. They may also be preoccupied with less threatening thoughts; for example, when training is held to support a change, everyone may feel over-whelmed with the additional work required after the change is implemented. They may simply be concerned with the work that is piling up on their desks while they are attending the training.

Participants may have never been told why they were attending training. Hopefully this happens rarely, but on occasion, participants think that they are being punished because they are not doing their jobs well enough. Participants need to understand how the training affects performance and the vision and mission of the organization, as well as what's in it for them.

It is impossible to identify all the reasons an entire group may be causing dif-ficulty. Techniques exist that help to prevent these problems and to address them when they do occur.

Prevent these problems

You may be able to prevent some of these problems.

- ✔ Focus on participants' needs during the design.

- ✔ Know as much about the participants who will attend the training ses-sion, including such things as their communication style, their attitude toward training, what changes may be going on in their workplace, whether they are all at the same level, and why they think they are attending the training session. You may want to ask what expectations participants are bringing with them to the session or what professional issues participants may be dealing with.

- ✔ Refer to the needs assessment to give you insight about why the training is being held.

- ✔ Interview participants prior to the training to identify concerns and how you will approach them.

- ✔ Connect with the participants' supervisors to ensure that they discuss how the training session relates to the employees' jobs and why they will attend.

- ✔ Be certain that the problem isn't one that you created. For example, you may not have clearly stated how the training is related to the participants — what's in it for them. You may not have established your credibility. Or you may not be providing enough breaks.

If you encounter a difficult group unexpectedly, it is almost always best to address the issue as soon as you're sure. How can you do this?

You may wish to probe a few participants during the first break with "The group seems reluctant to speak up" or "Everyone seems preoccupied, is something happening that I should know?"

You may also just stop the training session and admit that something seems amiss and address it with the group. When I do this, I usually make some dramatic shift that says "We have changed focus." I may pull up a chair in the middle of the room and sit down and begin a discussion. After a hostile or negative statement, I may take a very long pause, cap my pen, and close my facilitator's guide, and say, "Okay, we need to talk." How do I open the discussion? I state the behaviors I have observed and then say something like "It seems to me that we need to address the cause of these behaviors before we can be successful with this training." I then pause and wait for someone to speak up. At some point I may list the issues on a flipchart page to prevent people from repeating what has already been stated.

If you have a group that is not responding to you or the content of the training, it is best to address it as soon as possible. If you do not, you will probably just be wasting time — yours and the participants.

Note: Sometimes, it may seem as if you have a problem group on your hands when in reality only a few individuals may be causing the problem. Managing individual participants who may make the training difficult is addressed later in this chapter.

If training is not the solution

Even though you have conducted a needs assessment and the organization has determined that training is required, you may find that training really is not the solution. There is probably little you can do on the spot except to ensure that you create a meaningful experience for the participants. In many cases you may not change the agenda much, but you may refocus the discussion to topics that provide more usable information.

I was hired many years ago to facilitate a Communications Training — one that I'd conducted many times for this company. I found a group of 20 men who would not speak up, were angry, and obviously did not want to be there. After the introduction module, I quickly called a break and discovered that all of these people had been slated for a downsizing and the training in communication skills was a part of development for outplacement. No one had told me. After the break, we identified some of the issues they were facing, and I adjusted the communication training material, making it as meaningful and useful as I could.

A ten-step solution when training is not

If you're facing a situation where training isn't the solution or perhaps the training isn't the right training, you can follow these steps to make the best of the situation.

✔ Call a timeout. Put the program agenda on hold because the participants are probably not ready to hear or use the information anyway.

✔ Summarize your understanding of the range of viewpoints you've heard expressed.

✔ Use a flipchart and ask participants to help you list all the reasons the program is meaningless (or whatever else their key issue is). Allow enough time for them to list all the reasons they can think of. Post all the responses on a wall.

✔ Explain that if they take a look at their list, they may notice that some of their issues are controllable and some are not. Ask for a few examples about any of the items they believe are out of their control. Allow sufficient "ventilation" time.

✔ Acknowledge that when situations are out of someone's control, there's nothing that can be done to change those situations — for the moment. Explain that the best opportunity for change starts by focusing on what's controllable. Give an example based on one of the items posted on the wall and ask for agreement.

✔ Say something like "So here's the challenge: Look over your list, and let's try to come up with a new list — a list of what you have control over." The group may be slow to start. Don't panic; hang in there and restate the question. When they catch on that you're serious and will stay with the question until it's been answered, you will get responses.

✔ Record their ideas on flipchart paper and encourage input with "Good. How about another one?" As their energy starts to ebb, congratulate them for putting together a great list. Explain that you will give them a break now, and when they come back you'd like them to think about how to apply the balance of the program information they'll be receiving in terms of what's controllable. Check for agreement.

✔ Tell them that you're going to remove the obstacles currently posted on the wall and replace them with the flipchart listing what the group believes is controllable. Do so. Use the break to rethink what you will cover and how you will cover it during the rest of the time allocated for the program.

✔ When participants return from break, explain that it was important to make time to discuss their concerns. Describe your plan for how to proceed and get agreement. Check in with participants toward the end of the session or during another appropriate time to learn their current thinking.

✔ Privately congratulate yourself.

Using a process similar to the one in the "A ten-step solution when training is not" sidebar, I uncovered what communication skills they thought they would need given the situation. I adjusted the program accordingly and salvaged what was going to be a worthless day for the participants.

Take a COOL approach

You may have done everything that has been suggested so far in this chapter, and something may still go wrong. If something happens when you least expect it, you need to be prepared to think on your feet. I suggest you use a COOL approach. Besides, participants often mirror the trainer's emotions. If you're calm, they will be calm.

Calm down immediately

Although it is difficult to do, the first step is to remain calm. Take a deep breath, focus on the situation, and determine the root cause. After the oxygen hits your brain, you're better able to determine what to do next.

Open yourself to all the options

When something goes wrong, a can-do attitude may get you into trouble because you want to charge right in and "fix it." There is no one right answer to any problem, so be open to all possibilities. If someone else is with you (participants or another trainer) ask for their ideas. Do a quick pros and cons assessment of all the alternatives in your mind and select one option.

Optimistically evaluate your options

After you select the solution, move forward, optimistically knowing that you have considered all the factors and have chosen the best alternative. I don't mean be dogmatic about your choice no matter what. I do mean be positive and move forward. Don't second-guess yourself with "should haves."

Look at it from another perspective

A friend of mine taught me to always look at problems from a "What's good about it?" perspective. You could look at any problem from other perspectives as well, such as "What's funny about it?" or "What lesson did I learn from this?" Whether you try to find what's good about the problem or some other perspective, this technique will maintain your professionalism. It will also ensure that you learn from the experience and transfer that learning to future situations.

Using humor to deal with problems

In some cases, humor may be your only option. For example, if you're using a microphone that isn't working, you can ask, "How many in the back can read lips?"

ebb's ten laws of training trip-ups

I work diligently at preparing for and preventing problems that plague trainers. It seems that something new always comes along. I have found a sense of humor to be invaluable. Over the years the staff at my company, ebb associates inc, have created this list of things that can trip up training. Although it is written tongue-in-cheek, at times it is oh so true!

✔ If you're expecting 15 participants, 30 will show up.

✔ If you're expecting 30 participants, 15 will show up.

✔ The electricity will go out exactly when you're ready to show a video.

✔ The only typo in your entire program will show up on the handout about quality.

✔ The day you order fruit in the morning, the group will want jelly donuts with real butter.

✔ The day you order jelly donuts, the group will want fruit with yogurt.

✔ The room reservation you made will cancel itself only on days when there are no other rooms available.

✔ The contact person at your training site will be sick on the day of your training.

✔ If you arrive at the training site early to do some last-minute preparation, the most talkative participant will arrive early as well.

✔ A perfectly open room will sprout a pillar right in the middle of your U-shaped table arrangement.

Humor is not for everyone. If it isn't natural, or if you feel as if you're forcing it, don't use it. Everyone doesn't need to be funny to get through problems. Efficiency, grace, kindness, and a positive attitude work, too.

Maintaining a sense of humor as well as a sense of flexibility is critical to your success as a trainer. Flexibility and humor may also be critical to your sanity, as you can see in the "ebb's ten laws of training trip-ups" sidebar. Although the sidebar humorously suggests that no matter how well you prepare something may go wrong anyway, you still must prepare as well as you can. The key message is to maintain your sense of humor.

Managing Disruptive Behaviors

Sometimes, you can see them walking in the door — the disruptive behaviors. They may be vying for the center of attention, boisterous, or negatively outspoken. On the other hand, they may ignore everyone and refuse to make eye contact right from the start. Disruptive behaviors interrupt the flow of the training session and have a negative effect on the positive climate you're trying to create.

In this book I emphasize the importance of interaction and participative learning in almost every chapter. Of course, most positive things usually have a negative correlation. As you increase interaction and participation among your participants, you give them a high level of flexibility, and you always risk the chance that some participants may get out of hand, easily leading to more active disruptive situations.

Prevent disruptions

The best approach to disruptive behavior is to prevent the disruption from occurring in the first place. Both your attitude and how you manage disruptive individuals will set the stage for the ease with which you manage disruptions.

Create a climate in which participants feel free to give each other feedback on their behaviors: Build trust, reward appropriate behavior, ignore inappropriate behavior, and develop ground rules.

You are the role model for the day. All eyes will be on you and how you handle disruptive behavior.

You will facilitate the group to establish ground rules at the beginning of the training session for both virtual and physical ILT. These ground rules will prevent many problems from occurring — but not all. As you establish the ground rules, ask the participants to help you manage them.

Allowing participants to determine their own ground rules gives them ownership. You can guide them to include rules that address the kind of behavior you want to foster, such as these:

- ✔ **How to address punctuality.** For example, "We will return from breaks on time." Or "We will start and end on time."

- ✔ **How participants will communicate during the training session.** For example, "We will take turns speaking during the session." Or "Questions are encouraged."

- ✔ **The level of participation that is expected.** For example, "Participation should be balanced among participants." Or "We will encourage each other to speak up."

- ✔ **How everyone will demonstrate respect toward each other.** For example, "We will respect each other's ideas." Or "We will not interrupt when someone is speaking." Or "Attack the concept, not the person."

Ground rules should be posted and will serve to guide behavior so that you don't need to be the bad cop in enforcing appropriate classroom behavior. Instead, you can ask, "What did we agree upon in our ground rules?" and allow the participants to police themselves with their answers.

In a multiple-day training session be sure to review the ground rules each morning and ask whether the group would like to add any others or even to rate themselves on how well they are upholding the ground rules. You can use other general strategies throughout your session that will help to manage disruptive participants. For example, you will

✔ Reward and model appropriate behavior.

✔ Show genuine interest in all individuals.

✔ Be open to and invite individuals' comments, ideas, and disagreements.

If someone disagrees with you, be professional and respectful. Acknowledge that there are different ways to think about the topic. Take care that you do not become defensive or that you're not drawn into an argument. Thank the person for offering a different viewpoint and respond appropriately. If you expect a long discussion, you may tell the participant that you're interested in the discussion and request that you continue it during the next break.

These kinds of strategies build trust with your participants and help to make the learning environment one that is productive for everyone attending your training session.

Manage disruptive types

Even after you do all you can to prevent disruptions, disruptions will still occur. In that case, I like to give the disruptive participants the benefit of the doubt. In many cases they are unaware of the disruptions their behavior is causing.

Often, all you need to do is let the disrupters know how their behavior is affecting you and the rest of the class.

Remember, some folks will bring some very heavy baggage into the training with them. A participant may have recently suffered a bereavement or have a child who is not doing well in school. Another may be unhappy on the job or is anticipating a downsizing. Facilitators need to be sensitive to the fact that something may be causing the behavior and they may never know what it is.

Many disruptive behavior types exist. Movie Stars, Deserters, Comedians, Blockers, Attackers, and Dominators are six of the most common. You will experience all of them in all learning settings — virtual or physical classrooms, one-on-one training, or coaching — although they will be the most disruptive in a physical classroom.

Movie Stars

Movie Stars like attention and want to be the center of the action. Sometimes, Movie Stars just have lots of pent up energy and need to focus it in a positive direction. To address Movie Stars you can

✔ Ask them to help with demonstrations or other tasks, thus using their desire for attention to your advantage.

✔ Point out to them that you want to get others' ideas first: "Let's see what others have to say."

✔ Assign a specified amount of time for each response.

Deserters

Deserters come in several models. One deserter may have side conversations that prevent participation; another deserter may simply be reluctant to speak up; still another may have participated earlier in the session but now has pulled out. In your virtual classroom, the deserter is the one who is checking email, revising her to-to list, or viewing a stack of tasks on her desk. The truth is, it is difficult for participants to focus on a learning session when they are surrounded with dozens of other priorities.

Each of these participants has reasons for playing the Deserter role — and some may be positive. For example, the side-conversation deserters may be so excited about the concepts you're delivering that they want to share how they will implement them with their neighbor. (Yeah, that's the Pollyanna in me!) They may not even aware that they are causing a disruption. Some Deserters are reluctant to speak up. Many have told me that they feel they are participating 100 percent. Sometimes, they are merely shy. Others are analyzer types who like to think more than speak.

It is the third type, the Deserter who was a solid participator earlier in the session, but now has pulled out, that concerns me the most. Something has happened that changed the participation level. Perhaps the person received some bad news during a break. Perhaps something happened during the session that upset the participant. It behooves you to find out whether this is the case. To deal with Deserters:

✔ Manage side conversations by casually sauntering behind the two talkers and continuing to present over their conversations. This often works.

✔ Ask a question directly of the Deserter who is reluctant to speak up, starting with easy questions that don't test knowledge. The round robin (going around the group, one person at a time) is a good tool to use with this Deserter. You can also form smaller discussions groups to bring out the shy participant.

✔ The Deserter who was once active but now is not should be a concern to you. Pull the person aside at the first opportunity (perhaps during a break) and ask what has changed. Often, something happened outside the training session. If so, you need not pry. However, sometimes, you may have inadvertently done something that made the participant pull out.

✔ Ensure that the session engages everyone. Make the content relevant to their jobs, use their names, encourage networking, and personalize the learning for everyone. These are critical for your virtual learners.

✔ If you desire participation from everyone, ask the class to write their answers on index cards. This technique gives everyone a fair chance. It keeps the vocal participants busy writing while the quiet participants have a chance to think through their responses.

Comedians

Comedians, the class clowns, may also be looking for attention through humorous remarks. I like to give these folks the benefit of the doubt. They may have a very positive attitude and are trying to add levity to the training session. To deal with Comedians:

✔ Ignore the humor as long as it is not disruptive. Unfortunately most people laugh at the first couple of comments and that keeps the Comedian going.

✔ Ask Comedians to relate their point to the discussion at hand.

✔ Give feedback to the Comedian during the next break if the disruption continues.

✔ Ask Comedians serious questions. If they cannot provide serious answers, you know you have a problem on your hands that probably needs to be addressed one-on-one with the person.

✔ If the disruption spreads throughout the group or if it gets out of hand you may wish to call a break.

Blockers

Blockers are the naysayers in the group. They are the ones who are negative and do not believe anything will work. I give these folks a break because often I find that they have valuable background information, but they have not figured out how to appropriately explain their side of the story. To get them to disrupt less you could

- ✔ Ask what alternative they are willing to propose.

- ✔ Be sure that they do not take the class off on a tangential topic, based on some hidden agenda they may have.

- ✔ Ask the group for other opinions regarding what a blocker may have said.

- ✔ Ask them, "What would need to happen in order for the idea (concept, change, or others) to work?" Expect them to respond with "It won't work." Keep asking what would have to happen and by the third or fourth time a response will roll out of their mouth. In my experience their thoughts are worth pursuing.

Attackers

Attackers toss out barbs directed toward the trainer and other participants. They may call people names and give dirty looks. I've often found that Attackers have never learned an appropriate way to disagree. To deal with Attackers

- ✔ Ask them to confine their comments to the situation, not the people.

- ✔ Refer them to the ground rule that addresses to respect.

- ✔ Some attackers may not be aware of how they come across. In this case, the trainer's feedback may be accepted and even appreciated.

- ✔ Ask other participants whether they agree with the statement.

- ✔ Sometimes it is appropriate to explore their comments further.

- ✔ If not directed at individuals in the room, ignore until a break when you can discuss with the Attacker to identify the root of the problem.

Dominators

Dominators take up much air time by talking, sometimes repeating themselves, and sometimes speaking slowly and in great detail. You can't ignore the dominators; other participants will get frustrated, bored, and lose interest. To address Dominators

- ✔ Break eye contact with them and call on others by name for answers.

- ✔ Consider holding your hand up as if trying to stop a car if they continue to talk without being recognized.

- ✔ Impose a time limit on participants.

- ✔ Break into the middle of a long statement when they take a breath and ask for others' opinions.

- ✔ Assign a gatekeeper role to a participant.

- ✔ To balance participation with a dominator or two in your training session, pose a situation or question and ask people to raise their hands if they have a response. Then call on someone other than the dominators.

- ✔ Create a bin list or parking lot (a sheet of flipchart paper on which you write questions or ideas). Parking lots are used to post comments that are not appropriate for discussion at the current time but will be addressed later in the session. If you have pads of sticky notes on the table, you can have dominators write their comments and post them on the parking lot. This prevents repetition of the same comment.

Although other types of disruptive participants, such as the Rambler, the Clueless, and the Know-it-all exist, knowing how to address these six will prepare you for most situations you encounter. Kim Seeger says that disrupters are great recruiters and often sit next to other disrupters. Consider how you can regroup participants for activities to change the dynamic. In all situations, you would be wise to identify the disruptive person's needs. That may help you determine a solution.

Remember, ignoring a disruptive behavior is one way to address it. I usually ignore most things the first time. It is repetitive disruptions that affect the results of your class. You can always call a break if things get out of hand. Never hesitate to pull the person aside at a break to state the problem and what you may be able to do about it.

On very rare occasions you may need to ask the participant to leave. If you have pulled the person aside and you can't reach a win-win agreement about how to handle the situation, tell the person what kind of cooperation you need. Ask whether the person would be more comfortable staying — and agreeing to your request — or leaving. Reassure the person that you would prefer him to stay and benefit from the session, but you can't allow others' learning to suffer from continued disruptions.

If you have established a climate of trust and support, often the rest of the participants will take care of the disruptive participant for you.

Remember that most of the problems identified are outside your control. You could not have prevented them nor predicted them. Ask yourself whether you could have done something better. If yes, consider it a lesson learned; if not, chalk it up to experience. Accept the fact that people attend training packing their baggage with them. And sometimes, you do the best that you know how and move on.

Sweaty Palms, Parched Throat: Overcoming Nervousness

Stage fright. Presentation anxiety. Nervousness. Platform panic. Pre-performance jitters. Butterflies. Training fear. Nervous tension. Keyed up. Flustered. Whatever you call it, it is normal to be nervous near the beginning of a training session. Several studies show that more American adults are more fearful of talking to a large group than they are of dying!

If you ask other trainers, most will tell you that they experience a bit of anxiety at the beginning of every training session. And they are in good company, too. History suggests that Abe Lincoln shook the first few minutes of every speech. In an interview, Yul Brynner admitted to stage fright after appearing on stage in *The King and I* more than 600 times. Julia Roberts, Jimmy Stewart, Winston Churchill, Warren Buffett, Jack Benny, Jane Fonda, Mark Twain, and Bruce Willis are a few people who have admitted to nervous tension prior to a big gig.

Recognize first that nervousness is a normal response. Almost everyone gets butterflies. The key is to master your nervousness and get those butterflies to fly in formation!

Understanding pre-performance jitters

Where do those performance butterflies come from? They are caused by a natural fear response. Your brain perceives a threatening situation and prepares your body for a flight-or-fight situation. This is the same fight-or-flight mechanism that helped early humans battle rampaging saber-toothed tigers and other ferocious beasts. Adrenalin and thyroxin are dumped into your bloodstream, causing your heart to race, your blood pressure to rise, and your pupils to dilate. Your liver gets busy pumping sugar, and your blood increases its ability to clot. Your body is on red alert — ready for the worst!

Here's the good news. You do not want to eliminate all your nervous energy. Just as the flow of adrenalin gives runners the edge to win a race, this same adrenalin can give you the mental edge to be a dynamic trainer. You want to accept your nervousness as a natural phenomenon, and use it to fuel a more enthusiastic and dynamic training session. As you feel the adrenalin flowing, embrace the energy that it brings.

Accept your nervousness as natural

How can you make nervousness work for you? First and most importantly, *don't* tell your participants that you're nervous. Remember, they are attending because you're the expert. They expect you to succeed, but if you start the training session by saying "Whew! Am I nervous!" they will begin looking for signs of nervousness. If you never tell them, most will never know. Again, don't admit your nervousness to the participants.

Next, know how your body reacts in this situation and accept it. Perhaps your heart races. Maybe your throat gets dry. Perhaps you fidget with things in your pocket. Whatever it is, know how you react, and then accept it as natural. You may even say to yourself, "Oh, my heart is pounding. I knew that would happen." Accept the reality.

Define how your body reacts. Examine the 30 nervous symptoms in Table 12-1 and place a check in the column that describes when this occurs for you: before or during a training session.

Table 12-1   Identify Your Nervous Symptoms

Nervous Symptom	Occurs Before	Occurs During
Voice		
Quivers or crackles		
Speed is too fast/slow		
Monotone		
Change in pitch		
Verbal fluency		
Stammers, halting		
Loss of words, loses place, pauses		
Uses fillers such as "um," "so," "like"		
Mouth and throat		
Excessive saliva		
Dry mouth/throat		
Clears throat repeatedly		
Repeated swallowing		
Breathing difficulty		
Shallow breathing		

Nervous Symptom	Occurs Before	Occurs During
Facial expression		
	Lacks expression, dead-pan	
	Grimaces, tense facial muscles	
	Twitches	
	Limited eye contact	
Arms and hands		
	Rigid or tense	
	Fidgets with _____	
	Grips podium	
	Lack of gestures	
	Waves hands about	
	Shakes	
Body movement		
	Paces	
	Sways	
	Shuffles or taps feet	
	Crosses legs while standing	
Physiological		
	Chest tightness	
	Rapid heart beat	
	Flushed skin	
	Perspires excessively	

Whatever symptoms you experience, these are normal for you. It doesn't matter whether you have checked 2 or 22 items. What is important is that you acknowledge them and that you know how to address them either before or during your presentation.

Master nervous symptoms

Okay, so you have three symptoms before the training begins and three different ones that occur during the training. What can you do about them?

Some symptoms you can do little more than camouflage so that your participants won't notice. Others you can actually learn to change. Here are some general things you can do to physically and mentally prepare yourself for your next training event.

Prepare physically: Relax and be ready

You can do many things to prepare yourself and your surroundings before your session. Most of them relate to relaxing and making yourself comfortable.

✔ **Master relaxation techniques.** Head rolls, shoulder rolls, or dangling your arms at your sides all work well. Practice these techniques as you prepare for your session. Then use those that work best for you just before you begin your session. Even deep yawning helps you relax. A yawn sends a message to your brain that you're ready to relax.

✔ **Use isometric exercises prior to training.** Tightening various muscles, curling your toes or squeezing on a rubber ball before starting the training session works for many trainers.

✔ **Practice deep breathing.** Several deep breaths, in through your nose and out through your mouth, will add oxygen to your brain and clear your brain. This is especially useful just minutes before you start.

I take a couple of deep breaths while the host is introducing me. No one can see what I am doing. I get oxygen flowing and it helps to focus me on the task at hand.

✔ **Arrive early to ground yourself with the room and make it yours.** When participants arrive, greet them. Mingle with as many as you can and learn something about those you meet. Getting to know individuals reduces some of the barriers you may have imagined and decreases some of the fear you may have felt. During the training session, find one or two of the friendly faces you met before the training session started. Return to those friendly faces, but be sure that you do not speak solely to them.

✔ **Don't try anything new.** No new suit, haircut, or shoes. Wear something that you have felt comfortable in before. This is one less thing to worry about. I once saw a trainer who appeared in a new suit — complete with price tags!

✔ **If you have a crutch, use it.** For some their crutch is to use audiovisuals early to divert the participants' gazes. For others it may be to have your notes outlined or highlighted in a particular way. For me, it means having a glass of water nearby. At any time, whether my throat is dry or I forget what I am supposed to do or say, I can reach for the water, take a swallow, and compose myself.

✔ **Organize ahead.** Check out Chapter 7 for specific ways to prepare yourself and the environment. Just knowing that everything is ready to go is relaxing in itself. This is probably more important if you are facilitating a virtual classroom than any other situation. You have a limited span of time with virtually no recovery time allowed.

✔ **Do something physical.** Take a walk just before the session starts. Do some stretches or wall pushups. One trainer told me that he goes into the men's restroom and does a couple of jumping jacks to release pent-up energy.

✔ **During the session, use up excess energy with gestures and your vocal presentation.** Speak and gesture to the person who is the farthest away from you. Move about, as long as it is not distracting or in a repeated pattern. For example, two steps to the left, then two steps to the right, will use up some of your extra energy. However, if the pattern repeats itself too often, participants will be watching your dance instead of learning from you.

Prepare mentally: Psyching up, not out

You can also prepare yourself mentally. Your brain perceives only what you tell it. If you tell yourself that you're going to be nervous, trip over the cord,

A 15-second relaxer

Try this relaxation technique. It takes only 15 seconds and works in almost any situation when you need to reduce anxiety.

1. Lower your head so that you're looking straight down.

2. Squeeze your thumb and index fingertips together on both hands.

3. While squeezing your thumb and finger, inhale deeply while silently affirming "I am calm and relaxed."

4. Exhale slowly, relax your fingers, and tell yourself, "I am prepared and confident."

5. Repeat four times as you visualize a successful training session.

6. Lift your head and smile to whoever is in your eyesight.

and forget what you're supposed to say, you will most likely be nervous, trip over the cord, and forget what you're supposed to say. Get the picture? It takes the same amount of time to paint a good mental picture as a bad one. These ideas will help you psych up for the next training session.

- ✔ **Realize that you will be somewhat nervous.** Accept it as a fact.

- ✔ **Know what to expect when you get nervous and accept it.** When the symptoms occur, say to yourself, "Oh, yes. There it is. I knew my heart would start racing right about now!"

- ✔ **Recognize that the participants want you to succeed.** Forget yourself and put your group first. Focus on the needs of your participants. Think about how important what you have to share with them.

- ✔ **Think of your facilitation as extended conversation.** Imagine that you're talking to your good friend, Dan Greene — except that there are lots of Dan Greenes in the group. Look into their eyes and connect with them on an individual level.

- ✔ **Visualize yourself being successful.** Don't spend energy imagining the worst. Instead, imagine the best. Tell yourself that this is going to be the best darned training these participants have ever attended.

- ✔ **Plan to get your participants involved in the training early.** Ask a question, begin introductions, or start the icebreaker as quickly as you can. After your participants are involved, you will feel more like you're conducting a two-way conversation than a presentation. Going into the training session knowing that within three minutes participants will be actively involved and not staring at you, gives you a real mental boost.

- ✔ **Try appropriate humor early to help you mentally hear approval from your participants.** Humor should not be translated as "jokes." Humor can be many things other than jokes. And jokes are not always humorous.

    Humor can make you feel comfortable in front of a group. Telling a bad joke will not. Although you may see speakers who begin with a joke, don't do it unless you know you can pull it off successfully. To be more successful, the joke must tie to content. The joke must be politically appropriate. You must have practiced it at least three dozen times with success almost 100 percent of the time. If you have any doubts about the joke, don't use it.

- ✔ **Keep your facilitation in perspective.** What if you do something wrong? Can you correct it? Will the participants even know that something was incorrect? And is it the end of the world if you aren't perfect?

And finally: Practice, practice, practice

In Chapter 7, I discuss practicing the mechanics of your presentation and learning the content. Now you want to think about how practice can assist you with nervousness. This includes virtual trainers who should have one or more "dress rehearsals" and run through all of the possibilities. Practice changing slides; practice using the whiteboard; practice what you will say when you place people in a breakout room; practice opening polls. In a physical classroom, there is time to "wing it" when something goes awry; that isn't the case in a virtual classroom. If you are not clear and succinct, you will not come across as the expert you are, and then you will get even more nervous.

As I mention throughout this book and specifically in Chapter 7, nothing is more important to a successful training session than being well prepared. And nothing is more helpful in overcoming nervousness than knowing your material and knowing that you know your material. That takes practice. Use these suggestions to practice your training material:

- **Memorize the first couple of paragraphs you will say.** Nervousness goes away for most trainers after 5 to 15 minutes. If you know what you will say for the first few minutes, you can get to the other side of your nervousness.

- **Practice in front of a mirror.** Many trainers swear by this method. Look yourself in the eye and train away. I must admit that although it works well for many trainers, it doesn't work for me. I prefer several of the next few methods.

- **Record yourself.** Besides hearing the content, a recording allows you to listen to it while you're driving or doing other things. An added benefit of listening to the tape is that you can critique your pace, pauses, clarity, articulation, and other vocal characteristics.

- **Practice activities with your colleagues.** Try the training activities with other people in your department. Practice giving the same directions. Do they understand what you want them to do and the purpose of the activity? I like to ask for a critique as well. What went well? What do they think I could do better?

- **Practice using the visuals.** Practice several times with whatever audiovisual equipment you will use. Practice turning the equipment on and off. Practice with the actual visuals. Being comfortable with the media you will use will reduce your anxiety level. Your visuals should feel natural — almost an extension of yourself.

- **Practice using the wireless remote**. Even just holding it a few times will add to your comfort.

✔ **Practice out loud.** Practice pronouncing difficult words — or find a way to eliminate them. Practicing aloud allows you the opportunity to time your presentation. You may be surprised at how much time it actually takes to deliver some of the training material or how long it takes to tell a good story. Nervousness decreases the more often you hear yourself state the content.

✔ **Present some of the training material to your spouse, significant other, or your dog.** Really! Dogs make great practice participants. They make great eye contact and some will listen forever, giving you only positive nonverbal feedback.

✔ **Get practice in front of groups in other situations as well.** You could try out for a play. You could join Toastmasters, or the National Speakers Association. You could take a Dale Carnegie class or a speaking class at your local university. You could accept a club office or volunteer to give toasts for special occasions. All of these give you opportunities to be in front of a group.

The more often you practice your material, the better you will be prepared for your session. In addition, the more opportunities you have to present in other situations, the better you will understand, appreciate, and improve your training skills. The better trainer you become, the more confidence you will have, which will reduce your nervousness even more.

Tips for specific anxiety problems

Return to the checklist of nervous symptoms you completed in Table 12-1. The ideas in this section refer to specific symptoms you may have checked. In some cases, your only solution is to camouflage the symptom; in others you can actually do something about the symptom.

As you read through these tips, remember that the symptoms occur because your body is readying itself for a fight-or-flight situation. Therefore, you must trick it back into thinking that everything is okay again — which it is!

✔ **Voice:** Few participants will notice any voice symptoms. A crackling voice usually indicates tense neck muscles or inadequate air supply. Stretch you neck or clear your throat. Deep breathing and a swallow of water may also help. Speaking too rapidly may be the most annoying to the listener. Plant pauses at specific points and write a reminder to yourself in the margin of your notes to "slow down."

Grandma's warm tea with honey and lemon is a home remedy that really does work. The honey coats your throat, and the warm tea relaxes your throat muscles. Iced beverages tend to constrict your vocal cords even more. Try to avoid them during the initial portion of your training session.

✔ **Verbal fluency:** Ensure that you know your material completely. Should you lose your place, simply tell yourself that the idea will come to you momentarily and move to another idea. Also, consider some of the ideas in the "Difficult personal situations" section presented earlier in this chapter.

Um, ahh, you know! If fillers are a problem, you will not eliminate them until you hear yourself say them. Appoint an um-counter during your training session. This is typically a colleague, not one of your participants. Making eye contact with the um-counter will remind you to attend to your fillers.

Write UM in large red capital letters on each page of your notes. Seeing the UM has the same effect as making eye contact with the um-counter. It will remind you to listen to yourself.

✔ **Mouth and throat:** Eliminate dry throat by biting on a lemon wedge or spraying with a breath freshener. Have a glass of water available, and avoid taking antihistamines before speaking. Also avoid dairy products for four hours prior to a session to prevent the mucus build-up that requires clearing your throat. You can prevent most breathing difficulties by completing deep-breathing exercises.

✔ **Facial expression:** Make eye contact with people you met before the training session started. Think of them as your friends and smile. If a nervous twitch is something you cannot control, camouflage it until it stops by turning that side of your face away from the participants. Experiment with ways to stop the twitch between training sessions. Sometimes, rubbing a twitch or pressing on it will make it stop. Besides, most participants will not likely notice it anyway.

✔ **Arms and hands:** The more you try to control trembling hands or wobbly knees, the more they seem to shake. Instead, isolate one muscle group and shake out the stress just before you present, much like you see athletes do while waiting for their race. You can also use this technique inconspicuously while participants are working in small groups or while they meet other participants during their warm-up exercise. Until the shaking stops, avoid having your hand in front of audiovisual lights or holding flimsy paper. Use note cards instead. They won't rattle and quiver.

If you're a fidgeter, remove everything from your pockets. Also, place all pens in one place and out of your reach. Participants will be distracted if you're clicking a pen. Get in the habit of using a marker, replacing the cap, and then placing it back in its intended location.

✔ **Body movements:** Start by standing near enough to a table so that you can use it like a touchstone to orient yourself to one place. Plant yourself in front of the group with feet slightly farther apart than normal and with your hands at your sides. In extreme cases you may want to focus on keeping your weight on the balls of your feet. Be sure you have not locked your knees. In addition to making you appear rigid, it also adds tension to your system.

✓ **Physiological symptoms:** Sweaty palms? Try talc or antiperspirant, but experiment a couple days before to determine whether it is comfortable and doesn't rub off on your clothing. Have tissues available nearby. Taking long, slow breaths may slow your heart beat. In extreme cases you may need to hold your breath just before you begin your session. Camouflage your flushed skin by wearing darker-colored clothing next to your skin. White makes your red, flushed skin seem even brighter.

Remember three things about nervousness.

1. **Even if you're very nervous, you will almost always look and sound much better than you feel.**

2. **To make those butterflies fly in formation, you must first recognize that you're experiencing a natural feeling.**

3. **Focusing on your participants and their needs is a helpful way to overcome nervousness.**

It should be somewhat comforting to know that even the most experienced trainers feel some apprehension when stepping in front of a group for the first time. And further, most of the nervousness settles down for most trainers within minutes. Addressing nervousness is not about how to get rid of it but rather, how to manage it. Know how your body reacts to "training jitters" and be prepared to do what it takes to make those butterflies fly in formation.

Problems Can Be Prevented or Resolved

I hope you're feeling that even though problems are a way of life for a trainer, all is not lost. You can do many things to prevent problems from occurring. And when problems do crop up, you can do many things to resolve them.

I can give you but one guarantee in training. You're going to have problems. When it is happening it's not very funny. A lesson that I have learned, however, is that all those problems eventually become lessons learned. I learn something from them every time. Even better, I can sometimes turn these not-so-funny experiences into humorous stories for some later training session. Remember, Will Rogers said, "Everything is funny as long as it is happening to somebody else."

Part IV

It's Not Over Yet: The Follow-Up

Self Memo

Write yourself a memo, committing to at least three things you'd like to do as a result of this training program. Sign it, insert it in the envelope, address it to yourself, and we will mail it back for your review in six weeks.

1.

2.

3.

Name_____

Date_____

Explore how you can use social tools to ensure transfer of learning in an online article at www.dummies.com/extras/traininganddevelopment.

In this part . . .

- ✔ Evaluating your results.
- ✔ Ensuring learning transfers.

Chapter 13

Evaluation: It's Not Over Yet!

*E*valuate performance — that's the fifth and last stage of the ADDIE model discussed in Chapter 3. When you reach this stage, you have made it through the entire Training Cycle, and it is now that you can see the beauty of the complete cycle. You will find yourself returning to the earlier stages during the evaluation stage. For example, you will return to the assessment stage to confirm that you're evaluating what you designed the training for in the first place. You may use the objectives you wrote in the second stage to create specific evaluation criteria. You want the training objectives you write to be specific, measurable, and easily converted to items on an evaluation instrument or performance rating.

The evaluation stage of The Training Cycle, highlighted in Figure 13-1, is important to you as a trainer. It is here that you can prove your value as a business partner to your organization. You will be able to answer questions such as: How has training changed employee performance? How has training increased sales or reduced expenses? How has training reduced rework and defects? How has training affected turnover and employee satisfaction? And ultimately, how is training affecting the bottom line?

In this chapter, I expand on the reason for conducting evaluations, describe Kirkpatrick's Four Levels of evaluation, and provide guidance for how to design your own evaluation plan.

An exciting aspect of this chapter is a sidebar, written by Dr. Don Kirkpatrick in which he describes how the Four Levels came about. Dr. Kirkpatrick died a few years after writing this sidebar and it is a treasure to have his story in his words. His practical and logical thinking process for how he developed

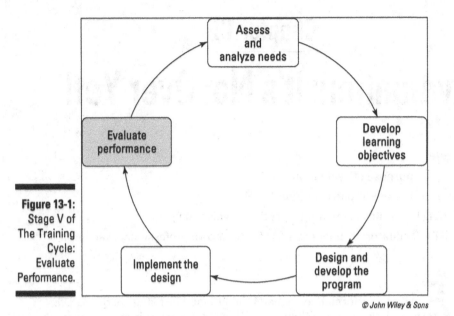

Figure 13-1:
Stage V of
The Training
Cycle:
Evaluate
Performance.

the Four Levels proves that everything doesn't need to be complicated. Sometimes, less is better. This chapter also presents a sidebar by Dr. Jim Kirkpatrick and Dr. Jack Phillips, another leader in the training evaluation arena. We are fortunate to have these gentlemen help us understand evaluation.

Purpose of Evaluations

The purpose of training is to change employees: their behavior, opinions, knowledge, or level of skill. The purpose of evaluation is to determine whether the objectives were met and whether these changes have taken place. One way to consider the importance of evaluations is to recognize the feedback it provides. Feedback can be obtained through self-reporting or by observing the trainee or from business data.

Various kinds of evaluations provide feedback to different people:

- Employees regarding their success in mastering new knowledge, attitudes, and skills
- Employees concerning their work-related strengths and weaknesses. Evaluation results can be a source of positive reinforcement and an incentive for motivation

- ✔ Trainers for developing future interventions and program needs or creating modifications in the current training efforts

- ✔ Supervisors as to whether there is observable change in employees' effectiveness or performance as a result of participating in the training program

- ✔ The organization regarding return on investment in training

The very location of evaluation at the end of The Training Cycle or near the end of this book doesn't mean that you do not think about it until the end. Quite the contrary. You begin thinking about how you will measure the results of the training very early in the design stage — soon after you determine objectives. Decide how you can measure whether the objectives have been achieved.

Review of Kirkpatrick's Four Levels of Evaluation

The concept of different levels of evaluation helps you understand the measurement and evaluation process. Don Kirkpatrick originally developed his Four Levels of training evaluation, reaction, learning, behavior, and results almost one-half century ago. Jim Kirkpatrick has taken up his father's charge to impart the importance of evaluation. He gives it a new slant with Return on Expectations. Jack Phillips approaches evaluation from a return on investment (ROI) perspective. Even with the new evaluation twists, Kirkpatrick's original Four Levels are as applicable today as they were in the 1950s.

As I discuss each of the Four Levels, note the elegant but simple sequence from Level 1 through Level 4. At each level the data become more objective and more meaningful to management and the bottom line. In addition, progressing through each level requires more work and more sophisticated data-gathering techniques.

It is interesting to note that, although there is an increased interest in training evaluation, many organizations still evaluate training at only the first level. It is easiest but doesn't really give organizations what they need to measure the value of training.

Before you decide to conduct any type of evaluation, decide how you will use the data. If you aren't going to use it, don't evaluate.

Level 1: Reaction

Level 1, or participant reaction data, measures the learners' satisfaction with the training. The reaction to a training session may be the deciding point as to whether it will be repeated — especially if it was conducted by someone outside the organization. If the training was presented internally, the Level 1 evaluation provides guidance about what to change. This is true for externally funded training as well, but sometimes, the provider doesn't have a chance to make the improvement. The employee's company will just not attend another training session. Most training efforts are evaluated at this level.

Sometimes called *smile sheets,* Level 1 evaluation usually consists of a questionnaire that participants use to rate their level of satisfaction with the training program and the trainer, among other things. In a virtual classroom, Level 1 data is often collected through electronic surveys.

If you're conducting a multiple-day training session, it is beneficial to evaluate at the end of each day. If you're conducting a one-day session, you may decide to evaluate it halfway through. It benefits the trainer because it provides feedback to you to adjust the design to better meet the participants' needs. It also benefits participants because it allows them to think about what they learned and how they will apply it to their jobs.

Want to measure reaction at the end of day one and you do not have an evaluation form? Try one of these two ways. First, use two flipchart pages. At the top of one write "positives" and at the top of the other write "changes." Then ask participants to provide suggestions about what went well that day, the positives, and what needs to change. Capture ideas as they are suggested. A second evaluation format that I use regularly is to pass out an index card to each participant. Then ask them to anonymously rate the day on a 1 to 7 scale, with 1 being low and 7 being high, and to add one comment about why they rated it at the level they did.

No attempt is made to measure behavioral change or performance improvement. Nevertheless, Level 1 data does provide valuable information.

- ✔ It provides information on the trainer's performance.

- ✔ It is an easy and economical process.

- ✔ If the tool is constructed well, the data can identify what needs to be improved.

- ✔ The satisfaction level provides guidance to management about whether to continue to invest in the training.

- ✔ If conducted immediately following the training session, the return rate is generally close to 100 percent, providing a complete database.

Level 2: Learning

Level 2 measures the extent to which learning has occurred. The measurement of knowledge, skills, or attitude (KSAs) change indicates what participants have absorbed and whether they know how to implement what they learned. Probably all training designs have at least one objective to increase participant knowledge. Many training sessions also include objectives that improve specific skills. And some training sessions such as diversity or team building attempt to change attitudes.

The training design's objectives provide an initial basis for what to evaluate in Level 2. This is the point in which trainers can find out not only how satisfied the participants are, but what they can do differently as a result of the training. Tests, skill practices, simulations, group evaluations, role-plays and other assessment tools focus on what participants learned during the program. Although testing is a natural part of learning, the word *test* often conjures up stress and fears left over from bad experiences in school. Therefore, when possible, substitute other words for tests or exams — even if testing is what you're doing. Measuring learning provides excellent data about what participants mastered as a result of the training experience. This data can be used in several ways:

- ✔ A self-assessment for participants to compare what they gained as a result of the training.

- ✔ An assessment of an employee's knowledge and skills related to the job requirements.

- ✔ An indication of an employee's attitude about the content, if an attitude survey is conducted.

- ✔ An assessment of whether participants possess knowledge to safely perform their duties; this is especially critical in a manufacturing setting.

Level 3: Behavior

Level 3 evaluation measures whether the skills and knowledge are being implemented. Are participants applying what they learned and transferring what they learned to the job?

Because this measurement focuses on changes in behavior on the job, it becomes more difficult to measure for several reasons. First, participants can't implement the new behavior until they have an opportunity. In addition, it is difficult to predict when the new behavior will be implemented. Even if there is an opportunity, the learner may not implement the behavior at the first opportunity. Therefore, timing becomes an issue for when to measure.

To complicate things even more, the participant may have learned the behavior and applied it on the job, but the participant's supervisor would not allow the behavior to continue. As a trainer, you hope that's not happening, but unfortunately it occurs more often than you want. This is when the training department must ask itself whether the problem requires a training solution. Due to the nature of Level 2 evaluation, the measures may include the frequency and use of skills, with input on barriers and enablers.

Measuring Levels 1 and 2 should occur immediately following the training, but you can see why this would not be true for Level 3. To conduct a Level 3 evaluation correctly, you must find time to observe the participants on the job, create questionnaires, speak to supervisors, and correlate data. You can also see that even though measuring at Level 3 may be difficult, the benefits of measuring behaviors are very clear.

- The measure may encourage a behavioral change on the job.
- When possible, Level 3 can be quantified and tied to other outcomes on the job or in the organization.
- When a lack of transfer of skills is clearly defined, it can point to a required training design change or a change in the environment in which the skill is intended to be used.
- A before and after measurement provides data that can be used to understand other events.
- Sometimes, Level 3 evaluations help to determine the reasons change has not occurred that may not be related to training.

Level 4: Results

Level 4 measures the business impact. Sometimes called *cost-benefit analysis* (incorrectly) or *return on investment,* it determines whether the benefits from the training were worth the cost of the training. At this level the evaluation is not accomplished through methods like those suggested in the previous three levels.

Results could be determined by factors such as reduced turnover, improved quality, increased quantity or output, reduction of costs, increase in profits, increased sales, improved customer service, reduction in waste or errors, less absenteeism, or fewer grievances. You also need to determine the other side of the equation, that is, how much the training costs to design and conduct as compared to the results. Identifying and capturing this data are relatively easy. You would account for the cost of the trainer, materials and equipment, travel for participants and the trainer, training space, and the cost of having participants in a training session instead of producing the organization's services and products.

NAMES TO KNOW

Creation of the Four Levels

by Dr. Donald Kirkpatrick

Yes, I am the one who originated and published *Evaluating Training Programs: The Four Levels*. And here is how it came about.

I was teaching at the University Of Wisconsin Management Institute, and I decided to obtain a Ph.D. in the School of Education. My advisor approved my dissertation, which was called "Evaluating a Human Relations Training Program For Supervisors. " I thought that as long as I was teaching in the program, I may as well try to evaluate the effectiveness. These were my thoughts:

If I am going to evaluate, the first thing I am interested in is "How do the participants feel about the program?" After all, they are our customers! I decided to call it REACTION.

My next thought was to try to measure to what extent particlclpants learned the three things we were trying to teach: Knowledge of management principles and techniques; skill in knowing such things as how to motivate and how to train employees. I was also interested in whether or not they had changed their attitudes about their company, their job, or the challenges they face in applying what we were teaching. So I decided to call that LEARNING.

My third thought was to see to what extent they applied what they had learned back on the job. So I called it BEHAVIOR. And finally, I decided to try to measure any results that came because they attended this training program. I called it RESULTS.

The editor of *Training and Development Magazine* from the American Society for Training and Development (ASTD) asked me to write what I had done. I decided to write a series of four articles in 1959, with each article devoted to one of the four "levels," which they were beginning to be called. Professional trainers read the articles, began to try them out, and passed the word on to others in the training profession. Many trainers wrote to me asking for a copy of the articles.

It wasn't until 1993 that a professional friend, Jane Holcomb, told me to write a book because no one could find the articles any longer but many were talking about the "four levels. " The first issue of *Evaluating Training Programs: The Four Levels* was published in 1994 and the 2nd Edition was published in 1998 with some case studies so readers could see how other organizations applied the Four Levels. My first contact was with Dave Basarab, an evaluation expert at Motorola. When I told him who I was, he replied: "Don Kirkpatrick! We use your four levels all over the world!" My response was an unbelieving "You do?"

The book has been published in several languages and I was invited to those countries to introduce the concepts, principles, and techniques and autograph the books. I have been a keynote speaker for numerous national conferences and many in-house programs. People call me a "guru" or "legend," but all I did was come up with four practical and simple ways to evaluate training programs.

Author note: Dr. Kirkpatrick died in 2014.

A cost-benefit analysis may be completed before a training program is created to decide whether it is worth the investment of resources required to develop the program. Return on Investment (ROI) is conducted after the training has been completed to determine whether it was worth the investment.

Measurements focus on the actual results on the business as participants successfully apply the program material. Typical measures may include output, quality, time, costs, and customer satisfaction.

Guidelines for measuring the Four Levels

Before we go further, is it logical to start with Level 1 and move through 2, 3, and 4? Well, not necessarily. Remember that in several places I've reminded you to start with the end in mind. This is certainly true with evaluation. Return to the purpose of the training. What does the organization want to accomplish? What does it expect as a result of the training? Reduced turnover rates? Larger sales? Fewer accidents? This is Level 4. Before you design your training program find out from management what their expectation is. Jim Kirkpatrick, Don's son, calls this Return on Expectation, or ROE.

You will of course still use all four Levels and the chronological order will still be the same. But thinking about Level 4 first — standing Don's Four Levels on their head if you will — gives evaluation a different perspective. Let's examine how you can measure each of the levels. Methods for each level are presented along with guidelines to consider as you develop your evaluation plan.

Measuring Level 1

Level 1, or reaction, can be easily measured during the training event or immediately following it, preferably before participants leave the classroom. A questionnaire, composed of both questions with a rating scale and open-ended questions, is usually used. Some trainers allow participants to take the evaluation with them and/or go online to complete it after the session. The drawback is a lower return rate.

How do you begin?

1. **Determine what you want to learn about the training.**

   You will most likely want to know something about the content, including its relevance to the participants' jobs and the degree of difficulty. You will also want to gather data about the trainer including effectiveness, communication skills, the ability to answer questions, and approachability.

When evaluating training, the end is the beginning

by Dr. James and Wendy Kirkpatrick

While the ADDIE model positions evaluation at the end of the training process, in reality, all four Kirkpatrick Levels must be considered at every step in the program's design, execution, and measurement. Training professionals commonly attempt to apply the four Levels after an initiative has been developed and delivered, but this makes it difficult, if not impossible, to create significant training value. Don Kirkpatrick (1924–2014) said it best in his book *Evaluating Training Programs: The Four Levels:*

"Trainers must begin with desired results (Level 4) and then determine what behavior (Level 3) is needed to accomplish these results. Trainers must determine the attitudes, knowledge, and skills (Level 2) that are necessary to bring about the desired behavior(s). The final challenge is to present the training program in a way that enables the participants not only to learn what they need to know but also to react favorably to the program (Level 1).

Beginning as Don instructed, the expected results must be defined at the organizational level and in measurable business terms so that all involved can see the ultimate destination of the initiative. Only in this way will the learning professional later be able to determine the program's return on expectations (ROE), what a successful training initiative delivers to key business stakeholders. It demonstrates the degree to which their expectations have been satisfied. Stakeholder expectations define the value that training professionals are responsible for delivering. Learning professionals ask the stakeholders questions to clarify and refine their expectations on all four Kirkpatrick Levels, up to the Level 4 Result.

Training events in and of themselves typically produce about 15 percent on-the-job application at Level 3. Although formal training is the foundation of performance and results, creating ultimate value and ROE requires that strong attention be given to Level 3 activities.

To increase application and therefore enhance program results, additional actions must be taken before and after formal training.

Historically, the role of learning professionals has been to accomplish Levels 1 and 2, or just to complete the training event alone. Not surprisingly, this is where learning professionals spend most of their time. To begin creating maximum value within their organizations, learning professionals must redefine their roles and extend their expertise, involvement, and influence into Levels 3 and 4. They must call upon business partners to help design and successfully execute a cooperative effort throughout the learning and performance processes in order to maximize performance and subsequent results.

Before a training event, learning professionals need to partner with supervisors and managers to prepare participants for training. Even more critical is the role of the supervisor, manager or seasoned peer after the training. These people play a key role in reinforcing newly learned knowledge and skills through support and accountability. The degree to which this reinforcement and coaching occur directly correlates to the desired improved performance and positive outcomes agreed upon at the start. As a learning professional, consider these actions:

- Consider each of the Four Levels throughout the training design and development process.

- Determine what information is required to show that the training improved job performance and key organizational results.

- For mission-critical initiatives, focus resources on a strong Level 3 implementation plan and Level 4 tracking and measurement strategy.

- Use evaluation time, money, and resources sparingly in Levels 1 and 2.

Note: For additional information contact inquiries@kirkpatrickpartners.com.

2. **Design a format that will be both easy for participants to complete and presents a way for you to quantify participant responses.**

   Many formats exist, and the design will be a factor of the first question — What do you want to learn? You may choose to have statements rated on a one- to seven-point scale representing strongly disagree to strongly agree (or poor to excellent). You may also wish to ask open-ended questions, or you may choose to do a combination of both types of questions. Even if you develop a format that has questions that are rated on a scale, it is a good idea to add space at the end for comments.

3. **Plan to obtain 100-percent response ratings that are complete.**

   How do you accomplish all that? Most of it is in the timing. Ensure that you plan time into the training design to complete the questionnaire. Twenty minutes prior to the end of the training session pass out the evaluations and ask participants to complete them. It should take only ten minutes, allowing you time to facilitate your closing activity ensuring the learners' last interactions are memorable and positive.

Trainers desire honest responses to their evaluations. To ensure honesty, allow for anonymity. Don't require participants to sign their evaluations. In addition, ask them to drop the evaluations off on a table on their way out versus leaving them at their places. If you have a valid reason for wanting to know who made specific comments, for example, to provide feedback, you may wish to make signing the evaluation optional.

Try SurveyMonkey or another similar format completed at the end of the class on the learners' tablets or laptops. Easy, fast, and still anonymous.

Your training department will most likely have determined an acceptable standard against which you will measure results. For example, 5. 5 on a 7. 0 scale may be considered acceptable by your training department.

If you follow these guidelines, you will be well on your way to finalizing an effective Level 1 evaluation. A comprehensive training-competency checklist can be found at the end of this chapter. You may want to use some aspects of it to create your Level 1 evaluation. You and your colleagues may want to use the evaluation to provide feedback to each other on your training skills.

Some training practitioners snub Level 1 evaluation as too insignificant or perfunctory. Perhaps this is because trainers can conduct more sophisticated evaluations or because it's prudent to tie training to the bottom line. The "smile sheet," as Level 1 is known, has become a pejorative term to some. Don't fall into that way of thinking. Dr. Kirkpatrick's Four Levels are built upon each other. Level 1 is a prerequisite when other levels are used. Even though you're "only" measuring reactions, these are the first-hand reactions of the customers of the training. There are very few more effective and efficient ways for trainers to obtain feedback about performance. You may have the best training design, but if it is delivered poorly, it does affect participants' ability to learn. Level 1 evaluation also serves as a way to focus questions on the content. The key here is to design an instrument that measures the essential foundation elements of the training content and how well it was delivered.

TIP

Hold on to your evaluations. Use the ideas and suggestions they contain to improve your future performance and program designs. The evaluations can also serve as input to your efforts to continually develop your skills and competencies.

Measuring Level 2

Level 2, or learning, can be measured using self-assessments, facilitator assessments, tests, simulations, case studies, and other exercises. This type of evaluation should be conducted at the end of the training before participants leave to measure the degree to which the content was learned. Use pre- and post-test results to compare improvement.

Measuring before and after the training session gives you the best data because you will be able to compare the knowledge level prior to the session and after the training has been completed. This is the best way to determine whether participants gained knowledge or skills during the session. How do you evaluate? Remember KSAs? That's what you will measure: the knowledge, skills, and attitudes that the training session was designed to improve. Use tests to measure knowledge and attitude surveys to measure changing attitudes. To measure skill acquisition, use performance tests, where the participant is actually modeling the skill. Like Level 1, attempt to obtain a 100-percent response rate.

Some trainers use a control group for comparison. And Dr. Kirkpatrick recommends that you do so if it is practical. While this may be the most scientific way to gather data, it may be wasted time. For example, if participants have another way to learn between pre- and post-tests, then don't send them to training. On the other hand, if training is the only way that participants can gain the knowledge, skills, and attitudes, then why bother with a control group? You'll need to be your own judge about whether a control group is beneficial.

Many types of testing formats exist from which to choose, and each brings with it advantages and disadvantages. True/False tests are easy to develop and cover many questions in a short amount of time. The drawback is that if the test is too easy, having superficial knowledge may lead to an inflated score. Be sure to use a subject matter expert (SME) to assist with the design.

Other options that exist include oral tests, essay tests, multiple-choice tests, and measured simulations such as in-basket exercises, business games, case studies, or role-plays. Assessments may also include self-assessments, team assessments, or instructor assessments. A Web-based evaluation may also be created. Although Web-based assessments are cost and time efficient, they bring a couple problems, including guaranteeing that participants are who they say they are when signing in and the ability to protect the questions in the exam banks. Most organizations using Web-based assessments have addressed both of these issues. Whatever testing option you use, be sure that the results are quantifiable.

Create straightforward tests. You're not trying to trip up the participants. You're trying to measure the learning that occurred to ensure improved job performance.

Finally, ensure that testing conditions are optimized by limiting noise, having adequate lighting and comfortable temperature, and eliminating interruptions. Be certain that the test is only as long as it needs to be. Be sure that participants know the rules, such as whether it is acceptable to ask questions during the test.

Pilot any test prior to using it with participants. Return measurement results to employees as quickly as possible. The significance of measurement feedback decreases with time.

Measuring Level 3

Level 3, or behavior, is used to determine the successful transfer of learning to the workplace. Unlike levels one and two, you need to allow time for the changed behavior to occur. How much time? The experts differ, and with good reason. The amount of time required for the change to manifest itself will be dependent on the type of training, how soon the participant has an opportunity to practice the skill, how long it takes participants to develop a new behavioral pattern, and other aspects of the job. So, how long? Anywhere from 2 to 8 months. You will probably need to work with the subject matter expert (SME) to determine the length of the delay required to allow participants an opportunity to transfer the learning (behavior) to the job.

By the way, like Level 2, a pre- and post-testing method is recommended. And again, the question of whether you want to incorporate a control group for comparison needs to be decided.

What do you measure? Each item in an evaluation instrument should be related to an objective taught as part of the training program. Based on the training objectives, you will create a list of skills that describe the desired on-the-job performance. Use a SME to assist you with the design of the evaluation. They will understand the nuances of being able to complete a task. For example, a skill may be "uses the four-step coaching model with employees." A SME will know that even though the four steps are essential, what truly makes the model successful is the supervisor's "willingness to be available to respond to questions at any time. " Knowing this, your checklist of skills will be expanded to include availability.

After you have identified the skills to measure, you select an evaluation method. Evaluation tools may include interviews, focus groups, on-site observations, follow-up questionnaires, customer surveys, and colleague or supervisory input.

Level 3 evaluations should not be taken lightly. It takes a major resource investment. Know what you will measure; know how you will measure; and most important, know how you will use the data.

All trainers should be skilled in Level 3 evaluation methods. The most important reason to conduct training is to improve performance and transfer knowledge, skills, and attitude changes to the workplace. Results cannot be expected unless a positive change in behavior occurs. Therefore, use a Level 3 evaluation to measure the extent to which a change in behavior occurs.

What do you do if the results show that performance has not been changed or skills mastered? You need to go back to the training design. Certainly the first step is to determine whether the skill is required. If yes, examine the training material to ensure that appropriate learning techniques have been used and that enough emphasis has been placed on the skill. Perhaps a job aid is required to improve performance. Sometimes, you may discover something that did not show up in the needs assessment. For example, you may discover that participants are not using the skill because it is no longer important or is not frequently used on the job. In that case you may want to remove it from the training session. This is a perfect example of how the fifth stage of the Learning Cycle feeds back into the first stage.

Getting results that demonstrate performance has not improved is not what a trainer wants to hear. However, it is good to have the knowledge to make an intelligent decision about whether to maintain the training program, overhaul it, or scrap it entirely. Without a Level 3 evaluation, you would not likely be able to make a wise decision.

Measuring Level 4

Level 4, or results, may be the most difficult to measure. Dr. Kirkpatrick frequently stated that the question he was asked most often was, "How do you evaluate Level 4?" Even though Level 4 is the most challenging, training professionals need to be able to demonstrate that training is valuable and can positively affect the bottom line.

One of the issues of evaluating at this level is that you can never be sure whether external factors affected what happened. There is always a possibility that something other than the on-the-job application contaminated the results. Can you really isolate the effects training has on business results? This is one time that using a control group can be helpful to the evaluation results. Yet even with a control group there may be other factors that impact the business, such as the loss of a good customer, the introduction of a new competitor, a new hiring practice, or the economy. Several statistical methods are available to you to consider other evidence. I don't cover them in this book.

So what do you do when management asks you to provide tangible evidence that training is having positive results? A before-and-after measurement is relatively easy because records for the kinds of things you measure (turnover, sales, expenses, errors, grievances) are generally available. The trick is to determine which figures are meaningful.

A second difficultly is predicting the amount of time that should be allowed for the change to take effect. It may be anywhere between 9 and 18 months. Gather the data that you believe provides evidence of the impact of the training. This measurement usually extends beyond the training department and utilizes tools that measure business performance, such as sales, expenses, or rework. Remember, a key issue is to try to isolate training's impact on results. You may not be able to prove beyond a doubt that training has had a positive business impact, but you will be able to produce enough evidence so that management can make the final decision.

You've read in this book and other places that training should align to the business's requirements. How do you do that? Dr. Kirkpatrick suggests that his evaluation levels can be used. Start with Level 4. Determine, with the business managers, what needs to occur (results). What are their "expectations"? Next decide what performance (behaviors, or Level 3) is required to achieve the desired results. Then identify the knowledge, skills, and attitudes (KSAs, or Level 2) employees require to achieve performance expectations. Finally, create a plan to offer the correct training, ensuring employees will be receptive to the changes. Kirkpatrick Partners calls this Return on Expectations.

Which evaluation level to use?

You may choose to evaluate training at one or all levels. How do you decide? Base your decision on answers to the following questions:

- ✔ What is the purpose of the training?
- ✔ How will you use the results of the evaluation?
- ✔ What changes or improvements may be made as a result of the evaluations?

✔ Who are the stakeholders and what do they want you to measure?

✔ What are the stakeholders' expectations?

✔ What business goals will the training impact?

✔ What resources will be required for the evaluation?

Just because there are four evaluation levels doesn't mean that you should use all four. After answering the preceding questions, decide which levels will be the most beneficial for each training program. Evaluation experts agree that Level 3 and especially Level 4 should be used sparingly due to the time and cost involved. A rule of thumb seems to be use Level 4 in those situations where the results are a top organizational priority or for training that is expensive.

Evaluation methods

I have presented a number of evaluation methods in this chapter. In this section, I examine some of the specific tools and discuss the advantages and disadvantages to help you choose the one that will work best.

Objective test formats

This method measures how well trainees learn program content. A facilitator administers paper-and-pencil or computer tests in class to measure participants' progress. The test should measure the learning specified in the objective. Tests should be valid and reliable. Valid means that an item measures what it is supposed to measure; reliable means that the test gives consistent results from one application to another.

Multiple-choice questions take time and consideration to design. However, they maximize test-item discrimination yet minimize the accuracy of guessing. They provide an easy format for the participants and an easy method for scoring.

True/False tests are more difficult to write than you may imagine. They are easy to score.

Matching tests are easy to write and to score. They require a minimum amount of writing but still offer a challenge.

Fill-in-the-blank or short-answer questions require knowledge without any memory aids. A disadvantage is that scoring may not be as objective as you may think. If the questions do not have one specific answer, the scorer may need to be more flexible than originally planned. Guessing by learners is reduced because there are no choices available.

Essays are the most difficult to score, although they do measure achievement at a higher level than any of the other paper-and-pencil tests. Scoring is the most subjective.

Attitude surveys

These question-and-answer surveys determine what changes in attitude have occurred as a result of training. Practitioners use these surveys to gather information about employees' perceptions, work habits, motivation, values, beliefs, and working relations. Attitude surveys are more difficult to construct because they measure less tangible items. There is also the potential for participants to respond with what they perceive is the "right" answer.

Simulation and on-site observation

Instructors' or managers' observations of performance on the job or in a job simulation indicate whether a learner is demonstrating the desired skills as a result of the training. Facilitate this process by developing a checklist of the desired behaviors. This is sometimes the only way to determine whether skills have transferred to the workplace. Some people panic or behave differently if they think they are being observed. Observations of actual performance or simulated performance can be time-consuming. It also requires a skilled observer to decrease subjectivity.

Criteria checklists

Also called *performance checklists* or *performance evaluation instruments*, these are surveys using a list of performance objectives required to evaluate observable performance. The checklists may be used in conjunction with observations.

Productivity or performance reports

Hard production data such as sales reports and manufacturing totals can help managers and instructors determine actual performance improvement on the job. An advantage of using productivity reports is that no new evaluation tool must be developed. The data is quantifiable. Disadvantages include a lack of contact with the participant and that records may be incomplete.

Post-training surveys

Progress and proficiency assessments by both managers and participants indicate perceived performance improvement on the job. Surveys may not be as objective as necessary.

Needs/objectives/content comparison

Training managers, participants, and supervisors compare needs analysis results with course objectives and content to determine whether the program was relevant to participants' needs. Relevancy ratings at the end of the program also contribute to the comparison.

Class evaluation forms

Sometimes called a *response sheet* or *smiley sheet,* participants respond on end-of-program evaluation forms to indicate what they liked and disliked about the training delivery, content, logistics, location, and other aspects of the training experience. The form lets participants know that their input is desired. Both quantitative and qualitative data can be gathered.

Interviews

Interviews can be used to determine the extent to which skills and knowledge are being used on the job. They may also uncover constraints to implementation. Like no other method, interviews convey interest, concern, and empathy in addition to collecting data. They are useful when it isn't possible to observe behaviors directly. The interviewer becomes the evaluation tool, and this can be both an advantage and a disadvantage. Interviews are more costly than other methods, but they give instant feedback, and the interviewer has the ability to probe for more information.

Instructor evaluation

Professional trainers administer assessment sheets and evaluation forms to measure the instructor's competence, effectiveness, and instructional skills. See an example at the end of this chapter.

All of these evaluation methods work. All give you the information you need. Some work better than others for each of the Four Levels. The final decision about which method to use will be yours.

It is easy to grow accustomed to your favorite evaluation method. It is much better to incorporate variety in the evaluation methods used. Gaining expertise with several makes you more skilled in knowing which method will be best for each situation.

Discussions with employees on an individual basis can give insight into the effectiveness of the training session. Are there things you're doing differently as a result of participating in the training program? Have you noticed changes in your attitudes or relationships that may be related to the training program?

ROI for Training

Trainers face a persistent trend to be more accountable and to prove their worth — their return on the dollars invested in training. Dr. Jack Phillips has been credited with the development of Return on Investment (ROI) to evaluate training.

Return on Investment

ROI measurement compares the monetary benefits of the training program with the cost of the program. Few organizations conduct evaluations at this level. The current estimates appear to be somewhere between 10 and 20 percent. Even if organizations do evaluate training using ROI, many limit its use only to those training programs that

✔ Are expensive

✔ Are high visibility and/or important to top management

✔ Involve a large population

✔ Are linked to strategic goals and operational objectives

Although many organizations claim to want to know more about training's ROI, few seem to be willing to make the investment required to gather and analyze the data.

Exploring the ROI process

ROI presents a process that produces the value-added contribution of training in a corporate-friendly format. The ROI process consists of five steps. Note that Kirkpatrick's Levels 1 through 4 are essential for gathering the initial data.

1. **Collect post-program data.**

   A variety of methods, similar to those identified in the last section, are used to collect Level 1 through Level 4 data.

2. **Isolate the effects of training.**

   Many factors may influence performance data; therefore, steps must be taken to pinpoint the amount of improvement that can be attributed directly to the training program. A comprehensive set of tools is used that may include a control group, trend line analysis, forecasting models, and impact estimates from various groups.

3. **Convert data to a monetary value.**

   Assess the Level 4 data and assign a monetary value. Techniques may include using historical costs, using salaries and benefits as value for time, converting output to profit contributions, or using external databases.

4. **Tabulate program costs.**

   Identifying program costs includes at least the cost to design and develop the program, materials, facilitator salary, facilities, travel, administrative and overhead, and the salary or wages for the participants who attend the program.

5. **Calculate the ROI.**

   ROI is calculated by dividing the net program benefits (program benefits less program costs) by the program costs times 100. In this step, you also identify intangible benefits, such as increased job satisfaction, improved customer service, and reduced complaints.

Although it feels like a great deal of work, it will be worth it if you need to provide evidence to management regarding the value of training.

Benefits of planning for ROI

Given the extra effort, it's worth examining the benefits of using ROI in the process.

Probably the most important one is to respond to management's question of whether training adds value to the organization. The ROI calculations convince management that training is an investment, not an expense. The ROI analysis also provides information about specific training programs: Which ones contributed the most to the bottom line; which ones need to be improved; and which ones are an expense to the organization. When the training practitioner acts on this data, the process has the added benefit of improving the effectiveness of all training programs.

ROI provides an essential aspect of the entire evaluation process.

Evaluation in 2015: An interview with Jack Phillips

Q. Jack, it is exciting to be interviewing you. Can you provide our readers with some background on ROI?

JP. We developed a systematic and practical way to show value for learning and development. Value is based on five levels of outcome measures: reaction, learning, application, impact, and ROI. We added a process model to show how data are collected and converted to monetary value and costs are captured to generate the actual return on investment. One of the most important contributions is the variety of methods to isolate the effects of learning on actual business impact data. This is the most critical step to ensure credibility in an impact study.

Initially, the ROI process was developed using concepts from finance and accounting as well as some of the processes from re-engineering and the total quality movement. The ROI was necessary to show the ultimate accountability of comparing the value of learning to actual costs.

Finally, we developed standards for the process and focused on how organizations can implement the methodology, based on the assumption that the best model in the world is not going to be used if it's not feasible, practical, rational, and logical. Much of our work is focused on helping others with implementation--the basis for our certification in the ROI methodology.

Q. How was ROI was developed? What's the real story?

JP. My interest in ROI stems initially from my interest and background in quantitative methods. With undergraduate degrees in electrical engineering, math, and physics and masters in statistics, my personality and interest lie in bottom-line accountability (Myers Briggs is ISTJ). In 1973 I conducted my first impact study as part of my master's thesis where I calculated the return on investment for a co-op program at Lockheed Martin (I was the co-op Director).

My next ROI study (1976) was conducted on supervisor training. I conducted this study in my organization at the suggestion of a senior executive who wanted to know more about training's impact. I continued to use it internally as an HR executive (for two Fortune 500 companies), and ultimately in a banking organization where I served as President and Chief Operating Officer.

Q. What inspired you to develop a process for measuring ROI?

JP. The initial executive reaction from the second ROI study not only inspired me to continue working with the process on my own, but to also spread the word. I began by speaking occasionally, writing articles, and publishing. In 1983 I published my first book, *Handbook of Training and Evaluation and Measurement Methods,* the first training evaluation book in the U.S. I continued to see positive reaction and began publishing additional materials. My Ph.D. dissertation in the 1980s focused on this issue, digging into the issue from a research perspective.

By the early 90s it was clear to me that there was a need for workshops and consulting on this methodology. To our knowledge, there were no one-or two-day workshops on training evaluation. At the end of 1992, we launched the process globally with the ROI Institute, conducting our first two-day workshop in Johannesburg, South Africa. Since then over 1,000 two-day workshops have been conducted with 30,000 participants. In 1995 we launched a one-week ROI certification workshop process.

Since then, 10,000 professionals have participated; 4,000 are Certified ROI Professionals. Its use and adoption throughout the world (in 60 countries) and the continuing feedback we get on this methodology keeps inspiring me and our team to continue our work.

Q. Trainers seem to shy away from ROI. Why does that happen?

JP. The major challenge of L&D teams is to show the business value of their programs. There is both good and bad news here. First, as indicated above, there is a widespread adoption of ROI. In a 2015 study of chief learning officers (CLOs) conducted by *CLO* magazine, 36 percent of CLOs use business impact to data to show business value; 20 percent of CLOs use ROI for that purpose. We think that 50 percent of learning organizations in the USA are using this methodology in some way. Still, that leaves a lot of organizations that do not use ROI. We think the primary reasons are:

There's a fear of ROI because it might expose a program or project that is not working well. If a program is ineffective, the last thing a trainer would want to do is publish a report indicating that it's not delivering the value. The key is to be proactive and use the data to make improvements — not discontinue the program.

Many of the trainers have a fear of mathematics and statistics and equate the ROI methodology with mathematics. (This may be a myth and not necessarily the case.)

This process is very client driven. The trainer must work closely with management groups. Some trainers do not want to do this and will even avoid interaction with the management group.

Trainers do not use ROI because they are concerned about the resources required — both time and money — to make it a reality. (This is often based on a myth and not reality.)

Trainers don't know what ROI is all about and they lack the skills, insight, and knowledge to implement it. The unknown breeds uncertainty, which breeds resistance.

Q. Under what conditions should trainers and training departments use ROI?

JP. Trainers should be concerned about ROI from three different viewpoints:

A defensive posture. You have to be concerned about ROI when there's a need to justify the budget (or avoid budget cuts), or justify a program (or avoid having a program cut). The ROI methodology provides data about value and it's the best way to show the value of learning programs.

A responsive posture. Trainers should be concerned about ROI if they want to be responsible for making a contribution to an organization. Every professional employee should be held accountable for his or her work.

A proactive posture. More trainers these days are concerned about ROI because they want to be proactive, take the lead, and show the value with data that managers appreciate and respect. It's very self-satisfying to see the contribution you've made to the organization, and particularly satisfying for all the stakeholders involved.

Q. Any last words of advice, Jack?

JP. It's important to note that an evaluation should be pushed to the ROI level only on programs that are very expensive, strategic, involve a large number of employees, have high visibility, or attract management interest.

Note: For additional information, contact jack@ roiinstitute.net.

Evaluation: The Last Training Cycle Stage but the First Step to Improvement

Bringing a chapter that could be as big as a book to a close can be difficult. I am delighted that, if you chose to read the entire chapter, you were able to read comments directly from the evaluation experts, Drs. Kirkpatrick and Phillips. Both recognize the value that evaluation holds to making improvements.

You may now be ready to put your evaluation plan together. If so, don't be shy about asking for outside assistance. Statisticians and researchers and other professionals will be able to expedite a process that will meet your stakeholders' needs.

As a trainer, the Level 1 evaluations are important to you. Don't ignore the feedback. Another practice you should consider is to ask a training colleague to conduct a peer review. Do you have a colleague whose opinion you value? Ask the individual to observe one of your programs — even a portion is helpful. Another trainer will observe things and give you feedback on techniques that participants may overlook.

I am delighted to share with you a comprehensive trainer-competency checklist in Table 13-1. Copy it and ask a colleague for input on your next training session. You can also find this evaluation form on the Learning and Development website.

Table 13-1   Training/Facilitating Competency Checklist

Did the facilitator

Skill	Comments
Prepare:	
Adequately prepare participants?	
Appropriately arrange the setting?	
Prepare for the session?	
Prepare notes for the session?	
Demonstrate organization?	
Facilitate Learning:	
Provide an effective introduction?	
Use appropriate group facilitation techniques?	

Did the facilitator

Skill	Comments
Use a variety of visuals?	
Use visuals skillfully?	
Provide ample practice time?	
Use a variety of learning activities?	
Use an appropriate pace?	
Use small groups for learning activities?	
Debrief activities?	
Stay focused on the topic?	
Create a Positive Learning Environment:	
Add creativity to the training?	
Make the learning interesting?	
Share ideas and offer suggestions?	
Use relevant examples?	
Provide candid feedback?	
Handle incorrect answers appropriately?	
Provide time to socialize?	
Reinforce success?	
Encourage Participation:	
Facilitate an appropriate icebreaker?	
Use a variety of methods for learning?	
Establish rapport?	
Make eye contact with all participants?	
Appear relaxed and pleasant?	
Use encouraging body language?	
Provide reinforcement for participation?	
Ask directly for participation?	
Reward risk?	
Share personal examples?	
Exhibit nonjudgmental behaviors?	
Communicate Content and Process:	
Provide an organized delivery?	
Summarize clearly?	

(continued)

Table 13-1 *(continued)*

Did the facilitator

Skill	Comments
Ask thought-provoking questions?	
Encourage questions?	
Answer questions appropriately?	
Create large-group discussions?	
Listen well?	
Check for understanding?	
Make smooth transitions?	
Use appropriate nonverbal skills?	
Speak and enunciate clearly?	
Project voice effectively?	
Display a thorough knowledge of the topic?	
Use appropriate humor?	
Deliver constructive feedback?	
Deal with the Unexpected:	
Handle unexpected events professionally?	
Manage difficult situations or participants?	
Coach those who were reluctant to change?	
Display flexibility?	
Manage time and topics?	
Ensure Learning Outcomes:	
Assess individual learning?	
Provide time for Q&A?	
Confirm on-the-job application?	
Use relevant examples?	
Establish Credibility:	
Demonstrate understanding of the content?	
Display confidence?	
Maintain composure?	
Describe personal experiences?	
Answer questions knowledgably?	

Did the facilitator	
Skill	*Comments*
Evaluate the Training Solution:	
Monitor impact throughout program?	
Ask for feedback?	
Note recommendations for improvement?	
Additional Comments?	

Evaluation is the final stage in The Training Cycle but is certainly only the beginning of improving training. It will be up to you to take your training efforts to the next level, relying on evaluation to help you decide what to improve. In Dr. Kirkpatrick's words, "Evaluation is a science and an art. It is a blend of concepts, theory, principles, and techniques. It is up to you to do the application."

Chapter 14

Transfer of Learning

"**W**ell, that was a great training session; now back to work!" Ever heard a colleague say something like this upon returning from a training session? I have left training with a big binder filled with good ideas. Because work piled up while I was gone, I place the training binder on my desk promising myself that I would look at it later and implement what I learned. Later came and went and soon I moved the binder to a shelf next to lots of other binders filled with good ideas. Why does this happen? And when you are the one in the training role, is that what you want to occur? Of course not! But it takes a team effort to ensure that learning transfers to the workplace.

The supervisors, learners, and trainers form a team right from the start to ensure that learning and skills transfer from the training session to the workplace. You know that the pre-training and post-training activities are as critical as the actual training itself to ensure transfer of learning and performance. That means planning to ensure transfer should occur as soon as possible. Follow-up actions are useful, to be certain. Just remember that even though transfer of learning occurs after the training session, it must start before the delivery of training. This is true in both virtual and physical classrooms.

This chapter addresses the barriers to transfer of learning and the importance of planning for the transfer. It also provides suggestions and tips for what virtual and face-to-face trainers do following a training session.

Make Your Training Memorable: Follow-Up for the Other 50 Percent

An issue cited by trainers since the beginning of time is that the concepts learned in the classroom may not transfer to the job. The training experience becomes a void — an isolated experience that has no practical application in the real world. Some professionals call the follow-up that is required "the other 50 percent."

So what's the "other 50 percent"? You need to look at the entire system from an organizational perspective. The reason that learning does not transfer could be organizational (policies, negative consequences), lack of management support, or the learner may lack the required equipment, supplies, or support system. Therefore, it may not have been a training problem in the first place.

However, assume you conducted a great needs assessment and were correct in identifying a training problem. Yet the training did not transfer. Consider some barriers that may prevent an effective transfer of learning as well as some steps a trainer can take to overcome these barriers during the design phase.

Note: this section could be placed anywhere in The Learning Cycle because transfer of learning starts with the needs assessment to ensure that there really is a training problem and ends with implementation back on the job. I've placed it in this chapter to give it the emphasis it needs. However, because you know there is a need for follow-up at the design stage, be sure to build in strategies you need at that time — early in the process.

Barriers to transfer of learning

It is unfortunate, but true: Many barriers exist that prevent learning from transferring to the job.

- ✔ It is difficult for participants to change their behavior, so they revert back to old habits on the job.

- ✔ Participants may be the only ones practicing the new behavior. Peer pressure may cause them to reject the new learning.

- ✔ The participants' supervisors may not understand the new knowledge, skills, or behaviors; therefore, they do not support or reinforce them.

✔ The participants' supervisors may not agree with the new knowledge, skills, or behaviors; therefore, they may undermine them.

✔ The participants' supervisors may not be proper role models for the new knowledge, skills, or behaviors.

✔ The informal organizational culture may punish the new behavior. For example, I once worked with an organization that made coded locking systems. They found that their return rate was increasing. They found that the returned systems were defective due to production errors; for example, parts were missing, assembly was incorrect. They thought they needed to retrain all their assembly people, when in effect what they needed to do was to change their compensation system. Employees were paid by the number of systems they shipped on a daily basis, not by the quality of the final product. Of course one would expect employees to work as quickly as they could, as opposed to how accurately they could work.

Strategies for transfer of learning

Even though some barriers may be out of your hands, you can do your part as a trainer to ensure transfer of training. Although the transfer of training occurs after the actual session, remind yourself of what can be done before the training occurs and during the training session before reading about what trainers can do after the session. Use all of these ideas for the best assurance of transfer of learning, whether you have a virtual or a face-to-face ILT.

Training isn't just for *learning;* training is for *doing.* That means you are required to ensure that the learning is transferred to the workplace.

Pre-training strategies

Trainers can implement numerous strategies before the training even begins to ensure that training transfers to the workplace.

✔ **Needs assessment:** Make sure the training you provide is derived from a well-conducted and -analyzed needs assessment. Be certain the training is aligned with the organization's strategic plan.

✔ **Coach management:** If managers have requested specific training for their employees, meet with the managers to gain specific information from them, as well as to let them know exactly what their roles will be in supporting and reinforcing the training. This is a good time to "prequalify managers" to determine how supportive they are of the upcoming training session. Encourage them to meet with the learners to prepare them for why attending this training is important. In some cases, you may want to give them a checklist of topics to cover with their employees, or even suggested questions.

✔ **Inform managers about the training:** Provide management briefings about the training. Inform them about how the training supports the organizational goals. Let these folks know the objectives, the expected outcomes, and the expected benefits. Alert management to any organizational barriers that may adversely affect the desired outcome. Engage the managers in problem solving through the barriers and get their commitment to support the group solution.

✔ **Provide pre-training projects:** Get participants and their managers involved in the training concepts before the training begins. You can do this by having them complete instruments or surveys that will, in turn, be used as resource material or data in the actual training program.

For example, the supervisor interview is one of my favorite techniques. I create a list of four to six interview questions that are directly related to the content of the training session. I ask participants to interview their supervisors before coming to the session. When we reach specific topics in the session that are related to the interview questions, I ask participants to share their supervisors' comments. Often the supervisor is as interested in how the information was used as the participant. This creates a good basis for discussion upon the learners' re-entry to the workplace.

Training strategies — during the session

You can utilize numerous strategies during the session to ensure that training transfers to the workplace.

✔ **Practical application:** Make sure that every topic you cover in the training is job related and has a specific "real world" application.

✔ **Use actual examples:** When conducting role-plays, simulations, and other activities, use actual data and experiences. These can come from the interviews you have with managers or participants prior to the session.

✔ **Build in plenty of practice opportunities:** After you know the knowledge and skills required of the learners, design activities that include practice with feedback.

✔ **Poll expectations:** Before conducting the training program, poll the expectations of the participants to assure you are providing them with the skills and information they need. Build in the "what's in it for me?"

✔ **Include transfer to the job in debriefings:** When you debrief on any activity, make sure one debriefing topic is a discussion of how participants can apply the lessons of the activity to their jobs.

✔ **Encourage follow-up actions:** Participants can fortify and augment what they learned by tapping into additional resources from a list that you can provide. They can also schedule an "appointment" with themselves to review their notes. They could plan to discuss with their bosses how they will implement what they learned.

- ✔ **Create a reminder:** Participants can note their primary goals on their tablets, laptops, or other locations where they will see them often. They could also write them on index cards and place them in a conspicuous place at home, work, or in their cars.

- ✔ **Meeting invitation:** Have participants send a meeting invitation to their supervisors to discuss what they learned and what they would like to implement.

- ✔ **Peer transfer partners:** They can be called many things: learning buddies, peer mentors, or learning partners, but the idea is to assign them before they leave the training session. They connect on a weekly basis by email or phone to answer each other's questions and to provide moral support.

- ✔ **Action plan:** After the training has been conducted, have participants list what they are going to do on the job as a result of training. Discuss participant ideas with the entire group.

A *self memo* is a unique action planning tool. I've used this tool for many years and participants still love it. Have participants write themselves a memo during the training session and place it in a self-addressed, stamped envelope. Then mail it back to them in four to eight weeks. See Figure 14-1 as an example.

Self Memo

Write yourself a memo, committing to at least three things you'd like to do as a result of this training program. Sign it, insert it in the envelope, address it to yourself, and we will mail it back for your review in six weeks.

1.

2.

3.

Name_____

Date_____

© John Wiley & Sons

Figure 14-1: Self memo.

Post-training strategies

To transition learners from "I tried it" to "I'll apply it" requires facilitators to design follow-up activities and provide tools to both the learner and the supervisor. In order for learning to transfer, the participant must be committed to the change. In addition, the supervisor must provide the learner with support. As a trainer, you must support both the learner and the supervisor.

These suggestions identify strategies that you can use to ensure that the learners apply what they learn.

- **Follow-up letters, emails, or phone calls from trainer:** A few weeks after the program is completed, you can write follow-up letters or make phone calls. The communication can remind participants of some of the concepts and ask how they are doing in applying them. The phone call has the advantage of being interactive. It allows participants to share barriers they are experiencing and to get ideas from you to overcome them. You can assist learners with dealing with change. See the sidebar.

- **Use m-learning:** Everyone has a smartphone or tablet to receive messages, so determine whether you can put learning in the palm of your participants' hands. Follow up with concise tips and reminders to help your learners stay focused on implementing their new skills.

- **Share the follow-up:** When you follow up with participants, track what you learn. If someone asks a practical question that was not covered in the training, or if the same question comes up several times, take note. Share this information with everyone in the class via an email or a tweet or on a class site that you have established for them.

You may wish to credit one of the participants with follow-up: "Dan brought to my attention that we did not _____." This will encourage others to bring these things to your attention.

- **Support groups:** As a trainer you can encourage participants to form support groups. To do this, a small group of people can commit to meeting after a specified period of time. When they meet they can discuss how they have applied the learning, what problems they have encountered, and what they have done to overcome the problems.

- **Reunion:** If support groups do not appeal to the participants, you can call for a reunion. Have participants demonstrate how they are implementing what they learned in the workplace.

I've heard of some groups who were so dedicated to reconnecting with the other participants that they met after work.

- **Past participants as mentors:** Match participants who have attended the training in the past with participants who have just completed the session. If at all possible bring them into the classroom at some point during the session to meet each other.

- **Twitter Tag:** Before everyone leaves the session, obtain all participants' Twitter user names. Tweet a practical-but-new idea related to the topic to everyone. Name someone at the end as the "Twitter Tag, you're it."

That person tweets something within 24 hours and names another person from the group. Practice this as one of your activities during the session too.

✔ **Practice sessions:** You can encourage participants to plan one or two practice sessions. You can even volunteer to facilitate them. The purpose would be to have participants reconvene after having had some time on the job to practice the skills. They could then practice the next higher level of that skill, get feedback, and make a new commitment to continuous learning.

✔ **Do a quick survey:** Use a tool like SurveyMonkey to conduct a quick survey about how each learner is using the content in the workplace. Compile it and share it with all learners.

✔ **Use other feedback:** Think about other ways to gather data about the success of the session. For example, if you taught a computer class, you can check the help desk calls immediately after the session to determine if there are references to your session. If there are, it means that participants are trying the skills, but still need assistance. Perhaps there is a better method to use next time.

Set up an electronic bulletin board for participants to share successes, ask questions, or just to stay in touch in general.

✔ **Job aids:** Job aids are short, written guides or check sheets that summarize the steps to a task or job procedure. They may also be performance support systems (PSS) or posters that can be taken back to the workplace. They serve as reminders to the participants after the training has been completed. They are especially useful after a skill training program. However, job aids can also be effective in reminding participants of key behavioral concepts.

✔ **Spread the news:** Suggest that supervisors ask their employees to share what they learned with the rest of the department. This could occur during a staff meeting or time could be set aside just for the topic.

✔ **Management support and coaching:** The best way to assure post-training application is to have participants' managers provide support and coaching. You could provide a sheet of coaching tips to managers and then follow up to offer assistance to them in the coaching process.

✔ **Meet with managers:** Three to four weeks following the session meet with the managers in person to determine whether the training addressed the needs and whether the employees are applying the skills and knowledge. You may also use this time to determine what other needs could be addressed in the future.

Assisting learners with change

Remember that adults carry with them strong opinions and points of view. Don't be discouraged when you discover how slowly change occurs. These tips may help you assist learners with change.

- ✔ Listen to the learner's concerns and acknowledge that they are legitimate.

- ✔ Help the learner understand why the change is occurring.

- ✔ Discuss the benefit of the change with the learner.

- ✔ Determine the values held by the learner and, if applicable, demonstrate that these values are not threatened.

- ✔ Problem-solve with the learner to identify choices.

- ✔ Assure learners they will receive encouragement and support in attempting to change — then make sure you live up to your promise.

What Great Trainers Do After Training

Many of the same strategies that you use with participants are things that you can do yourself to ensure continuous improvement. For example, you could write yourself a memo, committing yourself to at least two things you'd like to do better as a result of facilitating your session. Sign it, insert it in an envelope, address it to yourself, and ask someone to mail it back for your review in a month. When it arrives it will be a reminder of what you were supposed to have accomplished.

Make a habit of reviewing your training notes immediately after the session and make additions or changes while it is all fresh in your mind.

Be sure to study the evaluations. What suggestions do the participants have for you? What can you do differently next time, based on the feedback? Review several sets of evaluations to determine if there are any trends. If so, what are they and do they require any changes on your part?

Follow up with the participants, sending them any materials that you promised you would send. This is a great opportunity to find out how they are doing and how you may be able to help them transfer the skills.

If you do not have a Smile File, start one today. A Smile File is a place where you can keep all your kudos. If you did a great job facilitating, you are sure to receive notes, emails, and cards complimenting you on something special or thanking you for going out of your way. Your Smile File will be useful when you are having a difficult day. You can pull it out and read the wonderful things participants have said in the past. That will make it all worthwhile.

Connect with the participants' supervisors relatively soon after the training session. Remind them of how they can support their employees. This may be a time to share a "cheatsheet" with them. You could provide a list of the concepts taught, questions that could be asked, or suggestions for how to assist the learner to implement the skills or use the knowledge.

If the training session will be ongoing, consider conducting a focus group with several key supervisors to obtain feedback before conducting the training again. They can tell you what skills seem to be transferring and which are not. They may also be able to provide you with other insight to improve the training session.

There are many other things you could do following training. I think this is enough to get you started.

Although short, this chapter is a critical consideration for all trainers. Transfer of learning and transfer of skills beyond the classroom are why you are in business. In this fast-moving world, it would be easier to "call it quits" at the end of the training session. A trainer — a great trainer — makes certain that follow-up activities are completed to ensure transfer of learning has occurred.

As you leave this chapter, remember the words of one of the pioneers in the training profession, Robert Mager, who stated in his book *Making Instruction Work* (Center for Effective Performance, 1997): "If it's worth teaching, it's worth finding out whether the instruction was successful. If it wasn't entirely successful, it's worth finding out how to improve it."

Part V
The Professional Trainer

Four Strategies for Your Future Success

- ✔ Refocus development efforts to hone the more strategic, complex critical-thinking skills.

- ✔ Reframe development activities to accommodate the faster-paced VUCA world.

- ✔ Focus less on behavioral competencies and more on complex thinking abilities and mindsets.

- ✔ Emphasize learning agility, self-awareness, comfort with ambiguity, and critical and strategic thinking.

Find out how you can help your organization fast-track Millennial employees to leadership roles in an extra online article at www.dummies.com/extras/ traininganddevelopment.

In this part . . .

✔ Learning, growing, and becoming the best you can be.

✔ Earning your training certification.

✔ Preparing for the future of the profession.

Chapter 15

The Consummate Professional

*W*hat does it take to be a model of success and professionalism as a trainer? Probably the same thing it takes to be a model of success in any vocation, whether it's ballet, soccer, chemistry, plumbing, teaching, or writing. I once read that most people achieve only a third of their potential. Successful professionals in any field achieve more than a third of their potential because they work at it.

How can trainers maintain a professional edge? Professional trainers can continue to grow professionally; they go the extra mile to be better than average; and they give back to the profession. Each of these topics is addressed in this chapter. In addition, you will not want to miss Bob Pike's thoughts about what it takes to be a master trainer.

Grow Professionally

You have an obligation to your participants and employer to continually improve your knowledge and skills. The rapid changes in the world today can turn today's expert into tomorrow's dolt if the person fails to keep up.

Trainers create their own development plan to ensure that they are lifelong learners. Several strategies can be included in a development plan.

Attend formal learning events

Probably the first thing you think about when becoming a lifelong learner is "What class or conference can I attend?" But there is so much more. Check these out.

Go back to school

You may not need an MBA, but courses at the graduate level are critical. Take courses in finance or marketing or organizational development so that you can continue to be a strong contributor to your organization. Take a class to bring yourself up to speed in the technology area. Take an adult-learning class as a refresher or to get another perspective.

Check your local community colleges and universities. Many have continuing education programs that may offer topics to help you grow. I've benefited from programs such as "Dealing with Difficult People," "Project Management," and "Learning to Be More Creative."

Consider certification

Certification confers valuable credibility to anyone in the profession. The Association for Talent Development (ATD) initiated a certification program in 2005. It has constantly been updated to keep pace with the changing profession. Certification benefits trainers by offering a means to prove their value and identify a path of continued professional development.

Seminars and workshops are available to help individuals prepare for certification. The next chapter discusses certification for trainers and others in the broader field of Workplace Learning and Performance.

Take advantage of MOOCs

MOOCs (Massive Open Online Courses) are an emerging format designed to attract thousands of learners and reduce the delivery cost for higher education. Some believe MOOCs will revolutionize corporate learning. If you haven't already registered, you may want to consider it. Sure you will acquire content, but even more importantly you will experience a format that your company may consider in the future.

Attend conferences

At the very least consider attending your professional organization's annual conference. It may seem expensive, but you owe it to yourself to invest in your development. Sometimes local chapters also present conferences or daylong seminars. All of these add to your knowledge and skill base.

To get the most out of these events, network with others. Trade business cards. Offer to exchange information or resources. At least as much learning occurs during the breaks and informal networking as occurs during the formal sessions.

If you network with many folks, jot a note on the back of each business card to remind yourself about the topic, what you were to send, or why you want to stay in touch with the person.

Enroll in a train-the-trainer, preferably one in which you are videotaped and obtain feedback on your training style.

Ask others

Many other learning experiences exist, if you just ask.

Join an association or a group

Toastmasters, National Speaker Association (NSA), ATD, International Society for Performance Improvement (ISPI), The eLearning Guild, and others are great groups for you to join. They provide opportunities for you to learn new skills, stay on top of the latest happenings in the profession, and to network with others in the training profession.

Check out learning organizations' websites. Find a chapter in your area. All will invite you to attend a trial meeting to determine if the group is right for you.

Connect with colleagues on LinkedIn or other social media. By reading their questions and responses, you will grow relationships and learn about best practices and learning opportunities.

Create mentoring opportunities

Identify another trainer whom you respect and would like as a mentor. I've had many mentors in my life. I've learned a great deal and have made many friends. We generally meet for lunch or coffee. Mentors are a great investment.

I am currently searching for someone that I can "hang around" during a custom-designed sabbatical. I am looking forward to pushing myself onto the cutting edge of technology. There are so many opportunities for our profession in the future.

Determine where the experts hang out. Then go there. Sometimes this is a related association or an informal group. More-seasoned people and those with different experiences can offer you priceless advice and knowledge.

Train with a partner

Training with a partner is a unique way to learn from someone else. It allows you to observe another trainer, elicit feedback about your efforts, and learn new techniques and skills. Even if you do not co-facilitate, invite another colleague to observe you during a training session. Ask them to notice specific aspects of your training and solicit their input after the session. You could share the Competency Checklist that appears at the end of Chapter 13.

Do it yourself

You don't have to wait for a class or a conference or a meeting to learn. You can establish your own pace by reading books and journals,

Read

I designed a training certificate program for a client and as a part of my data gathering I asked top training professionals what they did to maintain their expertise. Everyone stated that they read. And they didn't just read a book or two. They read lots! They devoured the printed word. Some subscribed to (and read) dozens of journals and magazines. Others read upwards of 20 books every month. This behavior represents the experts in our profession; they must be onto something!

Subscribe to and read professional journals such as *Training Magazine* and *TD*. Read general business magazines such as *Fortune, Business Week,* and the *Harvard Business Review*. Read the journals published by your company's or your client's industry. And read cutting-edge journals such as *Fast Company*.

Identify resources

Many other resources exist. You can listen to audiobooks while driving longer distances. Organizations sell CDs of conference presentations. Download and listen to podcasts. Electronic newsletters and blogs are everywhere. Subscribe to several until you find your favorites.

You can be a resource to yourself. In fact, you will be your own best critic. Video an actual training session and play it back to identify what you like and what you do not like about your training style. If you think recording the session will be disruptive, you may wish to record yourself during a practice session or just audio record your session using your smartphone. Of course you will not have the visual portion, but you can hear how you sound and will be able to critique the audio portion of your training session.

Learning and growing are ongoing processes, even if you are at the top of your profession. Often it is what you learn after you "know it all" that counts. Aspire to the best of your profession.

Become the professional you want to be

What do you want to do? How do you want others to perceive you? What do you consider your success plan? Do you have one? I only ask because we should all reach our goals and satisfy our desires. Without your personal success plan that's no likely to happen. How do you come across to others?

Body language affects how others see us, but it may also change how we see ourselves. Social psychologist Amy Cuddy has conducted research that demonstrates how *power posing* — standing in a posture of confidence — affects testosterone and cortisol levels in the brain. This is true even when we don't feel confident. In addition, her research shows that how we stand might even have an impact on our chances for success. These are the kinds of things all trainers need to know for two reasons. First, it is knowledge for your own development and success. Even more importantly, this is the kind of information you will want to share with your participants. Check out her TED Talks (search `www.ted.com` for "Amy Cuddy").

Amy Cuddy is just one person who has a provocative message that can help all of us. Who else do you admire? Whether they are in this profession or not, you can learn much from them. Read their books, read their blogs, listen to their podcasts. Then branch out to other people. Smart and successful people always lead you to other smart and successful people.

Sign up for webcasts and webinars. Yes, you can learn something about the topic (one of my favorites is the Zenger | Folkman webinars about leadership), but in addition you will get tips about how to be a better virtual facilitator. ATD offers webcasts from other professional trainers. What a gift that could be for you to gain ideas about how to become the professional you want to be. You will learn both content and delivery techniques. Training is a wonderful profession, but only you can to do what is takes to fulfill your desires.

Go the Extra Mile: Stay on Top of Your Game!

Go the extra mile? Gosh! Isn't becoming a lifelong learner enough? Well, learning new skills is just the beginning. Going the extra mile means that you are looking for ways to constantly improve. How can you be more than a good trainer, a great trainer? In addition, how can you keep your energy up ALL the time? Even if this is the 49th time you have conducted the same session? Is it really possible to be enthusiastic and energetic? Yes it is!

Good to great

A widely read book, *Good to Great,* (Harper Business, 2001) by Jim Collins provides a format to think about how trainers can upgrade their skills (see Table 15-1). The left-hand column in the table lists attributes of good trainers. But good can be great. Several ideas that go beyond good to great are listed in the middle column. Space is available in the right column for you to add your thoughts about what you could do to move from the already good trainer you are to a great trainer.

Table 15-1	Good to Great Trainers	
Good Trainers	*Great Trainers Also...*	*To Be Great I Will...*
Design and deliver training that addresses all learning preferences	Spend quality time with individuals to ensure that each participant's learning needs are met	
Know their content well	Constantly update and improve content based on organizational and industry needs	
Have excellent presentation skills	Seek opportunities for feedback; practice to fine-tune	
Are flexible when difficult situations arise	Have backup plans and options ready	
Are enthusiastic about the training topic	Inspire participants	
Are informed about the most recent developments in their fields	Become experts and contribute to the field by writing articles and books	
Effectively manage the learning setting	Provide feedback and implement improvements	
Ensure that participants learn	Ensure knowledge is applied to the job; follow up after training	
Are good communicators	Are flexible communicators, moving into others' comfort zones	
Are a model of what they train	Ensure participants are models as well	

Great trainers do everything that good trainers do, but so much more and so much better. Invest in yourself. Go from good to great. Believe in yourself. If you don't, who will?

Where's your energy? Stay pumped!

Imagine this. You are about to go into a training program that you have taught countless times. You are starting to lose interest in the topic, and you are wondering how you will get through this without being monotonous and boring. Here are some thoughts about how you can make every training session seem as exciting as your first:

- Recharge your batteries every day. You owe it to your participants to give every session everything you have. Self-talk works well for me: "This will be the best darn training these participants have ever experienced!"

- Even though the topic is not new to you, it is to the participants. Remembering that they may be hearing the information for the first time is exciting. Determine how to have more participant involvement to experience the topic from another perspective.

- Do something that is just a little crazy; for example, if you are showing a video, serve popcorn; ask participants to use crayons for a particular activity; on a nice day hold a discussion outside; in a virtual setting turn the facilitation over to a participant.

- Use previous evaluations for the program to determine an area for improvement. Then integrate improvements into the next program. By striving for continuous improvement, you will never have to train the same program twice.

- A day before the session, examine the part of the program you dislike the most. Chances are it never was right for you. In my case it is usually more presenting and less interaction. Rework that part of the program so that it eliminates why you don't like it. In my case it would be identifying a way to increase participation.

- Observe someone else conducting the session (or other sessions) to identify new presentation or facilitation techniques.

- Page through one of the *Games Trainers Play* (McGraw Hill, 2001) books by Ed Scannell and John Newstrom, one of Thiagi's activity books, ATD's *The Book of Road-Tested Activities,* (Pfeiffer, 2011) or another activity book to add a new or revise a timeworn activity.

- Download the free ATD Trainers' Tool Kit app for new ideas.

- Experiment with activities you have not used before: funneling, an in-basket, or a relay.

✔ Try a new presentation technique or media; for example, use a related TED Talk or conduct a debate.

✔ Conduct research about a topic (Internet, journals, books) so that you have new information to share or so that you feel better prepared.

✔ Invite a guest speaker to conduct the part of the workshop that is most energy draining for you.

✔ Co-facilitate a portion of the session, perhaps role-playing with the other trainer or introducing a "point-counterpoint" type discussion.

✔ Get to know the participants personally. This helps you appreciate how much they need the information you have to give.

✔ Identify new energizers to use with the group each day. Energy is contagious. You will catch it from the participants.

✔ Find cartoons or quotes that relate to the session and introduce them after breaks or as energizers.

✔ The night before the session pull out your smile file that's filled with thank-you cards, fabulous evaluations, special notes, cartoons that make you laugh, clippings, or articles about you. Spend 20 minutes looking through it. What? You don't have a smile file? Better start one today.

✔ Approach every training program as though you want it to be your best ever. Remember how good you feel after you have completed training sessions that the participants love.

✔ Try reverse psychology: Think about the worst job you ever had (mine was making plastic wastepaper baskets on the midnight shift) and compare conducting the training to it.

✔ Determine a reward for yourself following the training session.

✔ Now identify two more things that keep you going and list them here.

  • I could . . .

  • I could . . .

Design

If you design often, take care that you do not fall into a rut of doing the same things over and over. Try something new. It keeps your designs fresh and keeps you inspired and interested.

Plan to include a new type of activity into each program that you design. If you have never used a game show to review material, build one in. If you rarely use guest speakers or role plays, consider them. There is such a wide variety of activities; you may never run out of ideas.

What does professional mean to you?

Every trainer needs to define what it means to be "professional." Take time to determine what it means to you to be a true professional. Write your thoughts out on paper. Share them with others. Consider it for a panel discussion topic at your local ASTD chapter meeting.

Develop your personal training code of ethics; that is, what you intend to live by and honor as a trainer. It could include delivering only the highest quality training, always giving credit to others to whose work you refer, holding confidential information close, and respecting all learners. A code of ethics gives you a guide, something to live by, and on which to base decisions.

To get you started thinking about what it means to be a professional, interview another trainer whose work you respect and who has been around the profession for a while.

Bob Pike has been a part of the training profession since 1969. He has inspired hundreds of thousands of trainers through his Creative Training Techniques workshops and his "Creative Training Techniques Newsletter." Bob is also the author or editor of over 20 books including the best-selling *The Creative Training Techniques Handbook*. The focus of his work is using involvement and participation at all levels to drive greater results. Bob is my model of a consummate professional trainer. He presents ten core skills all professional trainers should live by.

Ten core skills of a master trainer

by Bob Pike

I believe that we make ourselves more valuable when we develop what I call CORE Skills. In management training we often refer to these as *soft skills*, but I think this is a misnomer. Why? Because people are most often hired for the technical skills (their ability to do the job — whatever the job maybe), and they are fired for their lack of personal skills — that ability to work with and through others. These personal skills are the ten CORE Skills I challenge you to master:

1. **Make and keep commitments.** This means that a "yes" is a "yes" and a "no" is a "no." Many people make promises and don't follow through. Or they overpromise and under-deliver. What if you and all the employees in your organization were known as people who made commitments and kept them? Do you think this would help you gain a competitive advantage?

2. **Face each day with a positive attitude.** It's been said that we burn three times as much energy when thinking negatively as when thinking positively. What if you and each person in your organization looked for ways things could be done, instead of reasons why they couldn't? What if we looked at the potentials and possibilities, instead of the problems?

(continued)

(continued)

3. **Persist until you succeed.** Most people quit one step short of success. Thomas Edison, who failed ten thousand times before successfully creating a practical, sustainable light bulb, said most people would not have failed if they had simply tried one more time. He also said that he didn't fail 10,000 times — he simply found 9,999 ways it wouldn't work!

4. **Have a clear positive self-image.** For years, I sold and conducted a program that thousands of others could sell and conduct as well. My price was even a bit higher. There were always those that were willing to cut the price a bit — even a lot — just to make a sale. I didn't. When asked what justified the difference I said, "All other things being equal, you get me with this." I didn't say it to brag or be boastful. What I mean is that I'm committed to getting you results, not just selling you a product. That attitude, that self-concept, that commitment, is worth the difference. I completed a "Faith at Work" program with Ken Blanchard of *One Minute Manager* fame. He talked about **EGO** meaning **E**dging **G**od **O**ut. He pointed out that this could happen with pride, thinking more of ourselves than we ought to — and also with self-doubt — thinking less of ourselves than we ought to.

5. **Multiply your value 100-fold.** Many people focus on the MDR — the Minimum Daily Requirement: what is the least I can do to get by? My focus is on the most we can give to add value to whatever we do. What if we had an organization made up of people who were constantly looking for ways to add value? What power! I consulted for an organization that had been forced to reduce salaries, cut jobs, and faced two years before things improved. We pulled a group of 150 managers together and in small groups led them through a process where they had to find ways to recognize and reward employees without using pay, promises, or promotions. In less than two hours we had a list of over 150 ways that managers could use cafeteria style — picking and choosing those that would work best with their individual employees. Using some of these would help all managers to increase their value by creating a more motivational environment.

6. **Treat this day as if it were your last.** What if everyone in your organization always focused on the highest priorities — both personally and professionally? What if we lived this day in a compartment, not letting yesterday's challenges creep in, not letting tomorrow's problems drain energy — just focusing on doing the absolute best we can right now? What do you need to do today that would cause you at the end of the day to have no regrets?

7. **Master your emotions.** Sister Kenny was founder of the Sister Kenny Institute and originator of innovative cancer therapies even though she was not a medical doctor. She faced harsh criticism for years until her methods finally proved themselves. How did she manage her emotions in the midst of unjust accusations? Perhaps it started at age 6 when she lost her temper over a difference with a playmate. Her mother took her aside and said, "Any one who angers you, conquers you!" Those words must have played back through her adult years until her methods were proven. Look at the work that would have been lost, the tens of thousands that would not have received treatment if she had not known how to rein her emotions in. Her refusal to explode kept her critics from having ammunition with which to destroy her work.

8. **Laugh at the world and yourself.** We take ourselves too seriously. We all make mistakes. Are we going to get down on ourselves or learn from them and laugh at them? Nurse educators have explained to me that often there is laughter in very serious training classes containing life-or-death content. Why? "Because," they say, "What we do is too serious to take seriously all the time." Can you laugh and learn even when things do not go your way?

9. **See a need, take action.** All too often people see a need and say, "That's not my job." Elbert Hubbard wrote a delightful small book over 100 years ago called "A Message to Garcia." It was about an army officer who took a message from Roosevelt to a Cuban revolutionary and emerged from the jungle after three weeks having delivered the message, no questions asked. What if everyone in your organization took action when the need arose, rather than passing the buck? Let's have a renaissance of initiative!

10. **Seek guidance.** Are we willing to ask for help — especially from a Higher Power? Are we willing to ask that we be guided to opportunities to use the talents that we've been given? Are we willing to ask for the wisdom to discern those opportunities that are great rather than those that are merely good? I keep a prayer journal. I spend time praying for world leaders, our nation's leaders, our teachers, our children, my extended family, and so on. As people share needs, I add them to my prayer journal. I pray for the companies that I'm involved in and their employees. And I seek guidance to use the talents and abilities that I've been blessed with.

So now you've had a look at all ten CORE Skills. If you want to put into practice some of these concepts let me offer the following: Read Og Mandino's book *The Greatest Salesman in the World.* This book is less about selling and more about developing the personal skills needed to succeed in any job. In fact, they are really the principles of living life at the highest level. The book still sells over a million copies each year 34 years after its first publication in 1968.

Give Back to the Profession

All trainers receive advice and ideas from others throughout their careers. Therefore, all trainers owe something to the profession. How can you do that?

- **Publish what you have learned or your ideas for others to consider.** *Training Magazine* and *TD* are two publications that print articles by practitioners.

- **Write a book.** ATD Press, John Wiley, Berrett-Koehler Publishers, and HRDQ are all trainer-friendly publishers.

 If you are interested in publishing, contact these publishers and ask for a publication calendar from the periodicals or speak to an editor about the topics they want to publish.

✔ Accept invitations to be a part of a panel discussion, or present at your local professional chapter meeting.

✔ Submit a proposal to speak at a conference.

✔ Be a contributor to your local chapter of NSA or ATD: Present at meetings, volunteer to chair committees, or support the fund-raisers.

✔ Mentor someone entering the training field.

✔ Send a thank-you card to someone who has contributed to the profession.

✔ Present at your local grade school or high school for career day.

✔ Provide pro bono work for a local nonprofit organization.

✔ Start a scholarship fund.

Giving back to the profession is good for the soul. Find a way to volunteer today.

Training is a profession that gives a great deal to its members. Think about how you can give back to the profession, your community, and individuals. Yes, it takes a great deal to be a professional trainer. You can do it. Be all the things that you are capable of being. Thomas Edison believed that "If we did all the things we are capable of, we would literally astound ourselves." Go ahead. What's stopping you? Astound yourself.

Chapter 16

Trainer Certification

Jennifer A. Naughton, SPHR, ATD Senior Director, Competencies and Credentialing, co-author

You may be feeling a bit overwhelmed about the number of skills and the amount of knowledge that trainers and talent development professionals require to do their jobs. It *can* be overwhelming. But support is available. The Association for Talent Development (ATD, formerly ASTD) is the world's largest association dedicated to trainers and talent development professionals. ATD provides trusted, vetted resources to individuals like you who are interested in or work in the field.

Two ATD initiatives are particularly exciting:

✔ The new ATD Competency Model

✔ The ATD Certification Institute's (ATD CI) certification offering, based on that model

Both of these initiatives will continue to have a profound effect on the talent development profession and on each member of that profession.

This chapter provides you with an introduction to ATD and what the association offers. It also provides an overview of the ATD Competency Study, *Training & Development Redefined,* and its value. The ATD Competency Model, in particular, was a direct result of the study. Most exciting, however, is the certification — the Certified Professional in Learning and Performance (CPLP) credential — based on the model and what it means for you.

I am most excited about the topics in this chapter. Jennifer Naughton, ATD Senior Director of both the ATD Competency Study and the ATD CI Certification Program, has graciously given her time to assist with writing this chapter.

The history of the association

The foundation of the organization was created in New Orleans, Louisiana in the early 1940s. The United States was at war, and training was critical to meeting the needs of increased production and replacing workers gone to war. Fifteen people met for the first board meeting of the American Society of Training Directors.

This group helped to convene the membership for the first time in Chicago in 1945. At the 1946 convention, ASTD adopted a constitution that set as its goals: to raise the standards and prestige of the industrial training profession and to further the education and development of professionals in the training field.

Those goals have remained part of the association's purpose even as the profession has evolved. Reflecting that progress, in 1964 the association changed its name to the American Society for Training and Development. As the scope and the impact of the field grew, the profession's focus broadened to link the development of people, learning, and performance to individual and organizational results.

Recognizing the growth, depth, and breadth of the profession, and that the field looks beyond training in its quest to create a world that works better, in 2014 ASTD became the Association for Talent Development (ATD).

All About ATD

ATD is the world's largest association dedicated to those who develop talent in the workplace. ATD members help others achieve their potential by improving their knowledge, skills, and abilities. ATD's members come from more than 120 countries.

Why is ATD's mission important?

ATD's mission is to "Empower professionals to develop talent in the workplace." People are the key to driving an organization's competitive edge. A highly skilled workforce is the primary asset in a fast-paced world where innovation, knowledge, and skills are the currency of success. The best strategic solution to meet these challenges is developing the talent in the workplace through learning initiatives that unleash potential and help people achieve peak performance.

What does ATD do?

ATD is a membership association for professionals who develop talent in the workplace. These professionals have many titles: trainers, instructional designers, talent-development managers, coaches, front-line supervisors, and workplace-learning and performance specialists. ATD creates and curates

Chapter 16: Trainer Certification 333

content, resources, and professional development offerings. The association serves as a convener, bringing people together to learn, network, collaborate, and grow.

ATD provides resources

Through ATD's communities of practice, the association provide resources for professionals in the form of research, analysis, benchmarking, online information, webcasts, books, and other publications. These include the following:

- ✔ **ATD Research** provides benchmarking on trends and topics like coaching, gamification, measuring, and evaluating, and an annual analysis of industry investments and best practices.

- ✔ **ATD Forum** convenes private and public sector organizations from around the world.

- ✔ *TD* **magazine** keeps readers up-to-date on the latest ideas, trends, and best practices.

- ✔ **ATD Press** publishes the best titles on talent development, training delivery, instructional design, learning technologies, performance improvement, talent management, and more.

- ✔ **ATD Online Library** provides access to nearly 3,000 articles, business books, and summaries, plus select content from major newspapers and news sources.

- ✔ *TD at Work* is a series of monthly short format publications on crucial topics in talent development.

Find out what ATD offers firsthand. Check out the association's website at www.td.org.

- ✔ **ATD brings the community together** through content, in conferences, and online.

- ✔ **Communities of Practice** focus on key areas of the field and are led by community managers whose in-depth knowledge ensures that the content, offerings, and resources serve members' needs.

- ✔ **International Conference & Exposition** serves the needs of the worldwide community of talent development professionals.

- ✔ **ATD TechKnowledge Conference & Exposition** focuses on e-learning and the use of technology.

- ✔ **Learning Events and Workshops** address learning and networking opportunities on key topics in the field.

- ✔ **ATD builds member networks** through 120 U.S. chapters, international strategic partners, and volunteer-led international member networks.

ATD offers career development opportunities

- ✔ **ATD Job Bank** and career resources are in the online Career Center.

- ✔ **Certification** is the CPLP credential for individuals in talent development.

- ✔ More than 70 face-to-face and online programs, plus the ATD Master Series, cover the Areas of Expertise in the ATD Competency Model.

ATD recognizes excellence and best practices

- ✔ **Advancing Talent Development Awards** honor individuals' thought leadership in the profession.

- ✔ **ATD BEST Awards** honor organizations that demonstrate enterprise-wide success as a result of employee talent development.

- ✔ **Excellence in Practice Awards** recognize results achieved through practices, interventions, and tools from the entire field of talent development.

- ✔ **ATD Certification Institute Awards** recognize organizations, thought leaders, and credential holders that support the profession through the Certified Professional in Learning and Performance (CPLP) credential.

To be a part of this rewarding profession, become a member of ATD. You will be amazed at what a difference it makes to have the opportunity to grow and network with other professionals. Learn more at www.td.org.

Introducing the ATD Competency Model

The ATD Competency Model provides a strategic model for the profession. With an eye toward the future, the model enables individuals and institutions to be prepared to align their work with organizational priorities. The model's comprehensive view of the field unifies the profession and defines various areas of expertise.

Overview of the model

Having a defined set of competencies is a hallmark of any profession. In simple terms, competencies are what those in the profession collectively need to know and do to be successful. The model, shaped like a pentagon (see Figure 16-1), is comprised of two layers of competencies: foundational competencies and areas of expertise. The following sections clarify what is contained in each of these layers.

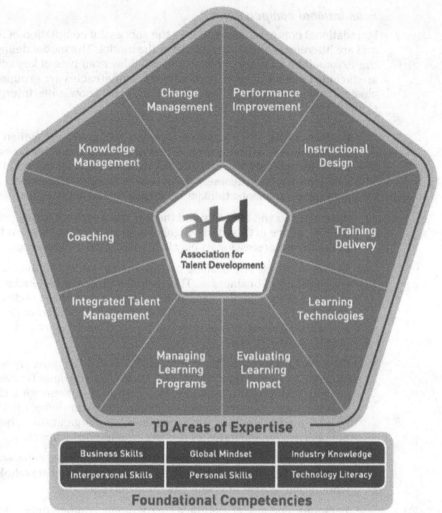

Figure 16-1:
ATD
Competency
Model.

Competencies

In the ATD Competency Model, *competencies* are defined as clusters of knowledge, skills, abilities, and behaviors required for success in all jobs across the talent development profession.

Foundational competencies

Foundational competencies underlie the successful completion of many tasks and are, therefore, found at the base of the model. The model defines each of the 19 foundational competencies and provides examples of key actions that are included in each. The 19 foundational competencies are grouped into six clusters: business skills, global mindset, industry knowledge, interpersonal skills, personal skills, and technology literacy.

- ✔ **Business skills:** The training profession continues to strengthen its role in the boardroom. With that role comes an expectation of business skills. The model includes six business competencies: analyzing needs and proposing solutions; applying business skills; driving results; planning and implementing assignments; thinking strategically; and applying innovation.

  Although you will certainly find these competencies in many professions, their existence in this model highlights the important role that talent development professionals play in helping drive organizational success.

- ✔ **Global mindset:** The training profession must adapt to the increased globalization of businesses. This includes three competencies: appreciating and levering the capabilities, insights, and ideas of diverse individuals; working effectively with individuals from different backgrounds; and working effectively across cultures and borders given the increasingly global workforce.

- ✔ **Industry knowledge:** The training profession often must know other industries or industry sectors. This includes two competencies: being actively scanning and assessing information about current and emerging trends, as well as developing and maintaining knowledge of other industries. A good example of this is a trainer in an organization that serves the pharmaceutical industry or sales training department.

- ✔ **Interpersonal:** The model identifies five interpersonal competencies: building trust; communicating effectively; influencing stakeholders; networking and partnering; and emotional intelligence.

- ✔ **Personal:** The model identifies two personal competencies: demonstrating adaptability and modeling personal development. These two should not come as a surprise, given the emphasis on both throughout this book. Talent development professionals are often expected to model appropriate behavior when change occurs, whether that change is global, cultural, economic, social, or political.

- ✔ **Technology Literacy:** The model identifies one overarching technology literacy competency: identifies, selects, and applies a variety of technologies, matching the appropriate technology to the specific opportunity or challenge at hand. More simply put, this is about using the right technology, not just any technology.

Talent development professionals are role models of the profession. As a talent development professional, you will want to create learning opportunities to upgrade your own knowledge and skills. You must also be in a continuous learning mode for two reasons: first, to serve as role models, and second, because talent development must stay ahead of and on top of new developments in our profession and in the industries that we serve.

Areas of expertise

Areas of expertise refer to the specific technical and professional knowledge and skills required for success in the talent development field. In simple terms, these comprise areas of specialization for the field. Although some professionals are highly specialized and deep in one or two areas, many people aspire to be generalists who can demonstrate deep expertise in more than one area.

Areas of expertise sit above the foundational competencies in the model because both are required. Ten areas of expertise are identified. The ten areas of expertise are listed here:

- ✔ Change Management
- ✔ Coaching
- ✔ Evaluating Learning Impact
- ✔ Instructional Design
- ✔ Integrative Talent Management
- ✔ Knowledge Management
- ✔ Managing Learning Programs
- ✔ Performance Improvement
- ✔ Training Delivery

This book covers almost all from this list.

The value of a competency model

The foundational competencies and areas of expertise provide a model for understanding the requirements of the profession. Among other things, the competency model can be used to

- ✔ Attract people into the profession.
- ✔ Evaluate individuals for selection or promotion.

> ✔ Guide career-planning decisions.
>
> ✔ Assess job performance.
>
> ✔ Establish a foundation for professional credentialing programs.

Although all that is important, the real value of the model is its application to enhance and elevate the profession through certification. It is this last purpose that has created considerable excitement in the talent development field.

If you are serious about being a professional in the talent development arena, you will want to obtain your certification. To get started, obtain your personal copy of *The ASTD Competency Study, Training & Development Redefined* by Arneson, Naughton, and Rothwell (ASTD, 2013).

Certification: What It Means for You

The preceding section discusses the ATD Competency Study and how it provides a road map for guiding professional development and the future of the profession. Here I switch gears and focus on certification and its implications. Before describing the value and components of ATD's certification program, I start with some context.

Certification versus certificate

Certification is a voluntary process whereby a professional body such as ATD recognizes or grants a designation to professionals who have met certain standards. Certified individuals are usually issued a designation recognizing that they have met those standards, often by way of tests and examinations.

Certification and *certificate* are often used interchangeably, but they do not mean the same thing. Certification and certificate programs differ in their criteria and goals. In *certification,* the focus is on assessing knowledge and skills. In a *certificate* program, the focus is on meeting training objectives provided to develop a more narrowly defined knowledge and skill base. Furthermore, certificate programs typically award a document signifying completion, with or without an assessment. Unfortunately, the lack of standardization in terms and inconsistent application create mayhem in the marketplace and really muddy the water.

To determine which is which, ask yourself whether the focus is on the completion of a learning experience (certificate) or the measurement of the competencies and experience you have already attained (certification)?

If you are not ready for a certification program at this time, to help prepare for it, you might consider the ATD Master Trainer, ATD Master Instructional Designer, and ATD Master Performance Consultant programs. The ATD Master programs provide a series of courses as well as examinations, and each results in a Master certificate. More information on these programs can be found at www.td.org.

Certification: Why now?

Ninety percent of the nearly 2,000 academics, practitioners, and leaders in the talent development profession surveyed indicated that they believed an ATD professional credential would be beneficial to the field. ATD then made the decision to move forward with the development of the professional certification program as a direct result. The consensus was that certification would serve as a powerful tool to encourage professional development and a means to prove one's value.

Certification: Show me the value

So, what is the value of certification? In this section, I attempt to answer that question. There are many levels of value — to the individual, the employer, and the profession. I briefly discuss some of the benefits to each group.

Value to the individual

Typically, individuals seek to become certified because it adds to their credibility. It may also provide them with greater opportunities for employment, promotion, and increased earning potential. It can also help to provide a structured pathway for their professional development. Sometimes, certification is even preferred for a given job.

Value to the employer

Certification also provides value to organizations. It can help employers by providing a reference point when evaluating job and promotion candidates. In the January 2005 edition of *Training + Development* magazine, Jamie Mulkey, Ed.D., a test development and security expert from Caveon (a firm specializing in test security), explains that organizations request certification from employees for a number of reasons. "Primarily, organizations want to validate that their workforce is qualified. And a rigorous testing process, such as professional certification, helps them do this." She added that "certification has become the mantra for many organizations who want to ensure individuals in their organization are competent to perform in a given job role."

Value to the profession

Certification helps to establish a set of defined standards for the field. It can help to codify a profession and establish these standards. At the end of the day, certification can serve to raise the bar of professional practice.

In another sense, certification in the training field has intrinsic value. Because competency assessment and people development are at the heart of what people know and do in this field, certification is an important means to an end. In fact, it is often the training and education departments that are the first to outline the requirements for competent practice. Thus, this certification is merely echoing at a macro level what is already being done by those under its umbrella at the micro level.

ATD CI Certification: A Quick Look

The following sections give you a quick look at ATD CI's CPLP credential.

Competencies and certification

So, how is this model linked to certification? And how does it provide a foundation for CPLP certification?

The answer is pretty simple. The model essentially defines the "Which competencies and behaviors to certify?" question. Standards are built later to answer the question "How well does one have to perform these behaviors?" In combination, certification is based on the competencies and performance standards, and certification indicates whether those standards have been met, by way of testing.

Certification design

CPLP certification is comprised of the following elements and requirements:

- **Applicant eligibility:** Five years' experience/ equivalent in profession.
- **Professional conduct:** Signed code of ethics.
- **Multiple-choice exam:** Covering all ten areas of expertise.
- **Work sample assessment:** Covering one area of expertise by way of a submitted project (or work product).
- **Recertification:** Sixty qualifying professional development credits are required every three years to maintain the credential.

Applicant process

The applicant process is described in eight steps:

Step 1: Assess general readiness

Individuals are encouraged to assess whether they meet the eligibility and whether certification (versus some other route, such as a college or university degree or a course or learning event) is right for them.

Step 2: Apply and sign code of ethics

Applicants complete an application, which includes submitting references and signing a code of ethics.

Step 3: Complete practice examination

Applicants can opt to take the pCPLP practice exam to pinpoint areas for development. This step provides feedback about where knowledge gaps may exist.

Step 4: Complete test preparation or course of study

Applicants can choose from a variety of programs to prepare for the CPLP examinations. ATD has a number of instructor-led and online courses to take, called Preparing for the CPLP.

Step 5: Complete general multiple choice exam

After selecting a testing window and test center location, applicants take the 150-item multiple-choice exam.

Step 6: Complete project (work product)

After passing the multiple-choice exam, the performance submission provides an opportunity for applicants to demonstrate their skills in one of several areas of expertise. Depending on the nature of the area selected, the individual will be asked to submit a videotaped submission or a report.

Step 7: Proudly display your designation

After applicants pass the work product, they receive the designation from ATD CI. Applicants then become CPLP certified and have earned their bragging rights.

Step 8: Apply for recertification

In order to keep current and to advance the profession, recertification is required every three years. Evidence of the completion of a variety of types of professional development units are required to maintain the certification. This can fall into a variety of categories:

- ✔ Supplier certificates
- ✔ ATD certificate programs (for example, Human Performance Improvement Certificate)
- ✔ Attending ATD's annual conference (ATD's International Conference and Exposition)
- ✔ Certification in related programs (for example, Certified Performance Technologist (CPT))
- ✔ ATD chapter programs
- ✔ University programs or courses
- ✔ Volunteer services (boards or officer positions)
- ✔ Publications

Consult the ATD Certification Institute (CI) for specific point values and requirements pertaining to recertification.

Be a role model for learning

ATD's leadership in the talent development field goes hand in hand with its leadership in developing certification for the broader profession and the continuous learning that's needed to keep skills relevant. In fact, learning is at the core of ATD's mission and vision. Part of that responsibility includes providing ongoing education and assessment to help keep the profession current.

Failing to keep current can rob an individual of early warning signs that problems may lie ahead. If the demand for some of your skills is starting to increase, you may miss a valuable opportunity to make a course correction.

The ATD Career Navigator

Not certain about your career in talent development? Wondering what roles would be best for you? Need to understand the skills required for each role? Curious about what resources are available to help you build the required skills? Well, ATD's Career Navigator can help. The tool is based on the Competency Model. Once you complete it, you will receive a report that compares your current skills to the skills required for a position.

It gets even better. The Career Navigator recommends developmental activities to help bring you up-to-speed for your chosen role. The tool is an ATD member benefit and can be found at www.td.org/Communities-of-Practice/Career-Development/Career-Navigator. Check it out! It's a great way to start your path toward a satisfied talent development career.

Staying Current

What are your responsibilities as a member of the profession for keeping current? Keeping your certification status current through recertification indicates that you are up-to-date. Lifelong learning and its importance is a popular concept these days. But the real challenge is not just talking about it but doing it, and also serving as a model for others.

You can be a model of professionalism. Start your journey toward certification today. For more information about either the ATD Competency Model or the CPLP certification program, visit www.td.org/model or send an email to competencystudy@td.org.

Your career depends on your continued ability to reinvent yourself and add value. Use the ATD Competency Model, the CPLP certification program, and the ATD Career Navigator as the means to establish the value connection from where you are to where you want to go.

Certification is one of those small steps in your career that may make a huge difference. Achieving certification in your field can be an adventure, one of those life experiences you should not pass up. I live my life by a Helen Keller quote: "Life is either a daring adventure . . . or nothing."

Chapter 17

The Future of the T&D Profession

⬝⬝

In This Chapter

▶ Introducing the VUCA world concept

▶ Understanding the changing T&D environment

▶ Recognizing the expanded roles for trainers

▶ Predicting a vision of the future

▶ Determining how to prepare yourself for the future

⬝⬝

*L*ook around you. Everything is changing: demographics, employee expectations, medicine, technology, the environment, and the global economy. You name it, and chances are it is undergoing change at a dramatic rate. Just keeping up with these changes is challenging. Your job is changing too. Your organization must be agile and adaptable to thrive in this evolving business environment. You support your organization; therefore, you too must be agile and adaptable.

Your organization is becoming more flexible, networked, global, and virtual. Your work as a T&D professional mimics those same requirements. You've seen change coming with virtual classrooms, social and mobile-influenced learning tools, gamification, and your expanded job description.

In his book, *The World Is Flat* (Picador, 2007), Thomas Friedman notes that the rate of change today is much different than in the past. He says that the rapid "flattening process is happening at warp speed and directly or indirectly touching a lot more people on the planet at once. The faster and broader this transition to a new era, the more likely is the potential of disruption."

As a T&D professional, you are feeling this same disruption. This chapter presents how the rapidly changing world affects you and the T&D profession. It explores the changing T&D environment and the expanded roles of the T&D professional. The chapter ends with ideas about how to prepare yourself for the future of your profession.

Blame It on the VUCA World

This rapid flattening, as Friedman calls it, is creating an environment that leaders call a *VUCA world*. Introduced in the late 1990s, the military-derived acronym stands for volatile, uncertain, complex, and ambiguous — terms that reflect the unstable and rapidly changing business world we live in today. This new VUCA environment demands T&D to change its strategy and processes so we can better support our organizations.

VUCA defined

But what exactly does the acronym mean?

- **Volatile:** The "V" in VUCA denotes the speed, volume, and magnitude of change that is beyond a predictable process or design. Think of volatility as turbulence.

- **Uncertain:** The "U" in VUCA represents the lack of predictability in what is happening around us. This makes it difficult for anyone to use the past to predict future outcomes. Forecasting is difficult, causing challenges to decision making.

- **Complex:** The "C" in VUCA stands for the intricacy and complicated factors involved in an issue or planning for the future. Many more dynamics are networked to add to the confusion, making it extremely difficult to know what to do.

- **Ambiguous:** The "A," ambiguity, defines the lack of clarity about the meaning or the causes behind an event, making the "why" hard to ascertain. What really caused a success or a failure? We can't always be certain.

I highly, highly recommend that you read Bob Johansen's book *Leaders Make the Future* (2nd Edition, BK Business, 2012) to learn more about the VUCA environment and Bob's antidote about what we can do.

What does this have to do with me?

Your leaders are operating in a VUCA world. If your organization is struggling, it is at least partially due to VUCA and the speed of change. The new VUCA environment is demanding and challenging for even the best organizations. And all organizations must deal with it. According to Jack Welch, "If the rate of change on the outside exceeds the rate of change on the inside, the end is near."

Recent studies by the Boston Consulting Group, the Center for Creative Leadership (CCL), and others conclude that organizations today must become more adaptive, learning better, faster, and more economically than their competition. Few organizations are "adapting" fast enough or in the right ways to be competitive. Who is adapting? Apple, Google, 3M, Target, and Amazon are often listed as adaptive firms.

What does this have to do with you? As talent development professionals, we must help to position our organizations to be more successful. We must help them learn and develop better, faster, and more economically than the competition. Although your efforts may not be defined in exactly these words, CCL suggests that your over-arching strategy will likely be to:

- Refocus development efforts to hone these more strategic, complex critical-thinking skills.
- Reframe development activities to accommodate the faster-paced VUCA world.
- Focus less on behavioral competencies and more on complex thinking abilities and mindsets.
- Emphasize learning agility, self-awareness, comfort with ambiguity, and critical and strategic thinking.

The Changing T&D Environment

Let's explore the realities we face as we do our jobs. Some of these challenges have been around for some time. They aren't going away, so we'd better get good at dealing with them. Doing more with less, globalization, technology, and multiple generations in the workforce each has a role in defining how we do our work, as well as how we help the workforce do its work.

Entire books have been written about the topics within this chapter. This means that I am barely scratching the surface of the topics as well as how and why they are important to you. You will find experts mentioned throughout the chapter, whose books should satiate your desire for more information. If the chapter sounds as if your job is becoming more business oriented, you are right. Facing business realities is what this chapter and your future work are all about.

Doing more with less

The cry to "do more with less" is nothing new. As trainers, we are tuned into the challenges our organizations face. We understand this business reality, whether it is "new" or a repeated reality of years past. This battle cry is heard in every organization. We need to accept it as a permanent business reality.

Finding ways to continue to provide services to your organizations' growing list of requirements may seem daunting at times. What can you do? Begin by ensuring excellent communication with your organization's leadership. What are their priorities? Where will you obtain the best return on investment? What else can you do? These suggestions are a start:

- **Embrace new roles:** The next section in this chapter talks about the expanded roles indicating that your job is changing. When done well, each of those roles is a good investment because they ultimately save your organization time and money.

- **Prioritize T&D tasks:** You may need to focus on doing fewer things. Trainers may not be able to say, "How do I get these 12 programs delivered?" but instead, "Which of these 12 programs will get delivered?" or "What can we stop doing?" Your job becomes doing the right things with less.

- **Use technology wisely:** Technology options are covered throughout this book. Know what's available and how to use it. If travel budgets are reduced, or time away from your organization isn't as liberal as it once was, think about all the tools you have that weren't available just a few short years ago. Review your most implemented training program. How could you use technology to save resources? Could you:

  - Use Skype or Google Hangouts to reach employees in other cities or countries?

  - Send small nuggets of information, just in time to employees via their mobile devices?

  - Design several short virtual classroom modules to provide the same learning as a physical session?

  - Invite your CEO or a panel of senior leaders to conduct a discussion online in lieu of conducting a training session?

  - Record presentations for future use?

  - Create peer coaching groups or virtual buddies to continue the learning after a shortened class?

  - Deliver job aids using social media tools?

  - Create an online book club?

The ideas are endless. Your resources are not. Tap into technology.

Brain-based learning

Recent evidence in how the brain works confirms what many of us have known for years. Assisting learners to learn faster and retain knowledge longer is one way we help our organizations deal with the VUCA world. As I note in Chapter 2, insights into how the brain learns can help us be better trainers. Your brain doesn't just receive information — it processes it. The brain sorts out all incoming information and tries to make connections. The brain starts learning because it has a question about where new information fits. If adults are invited to ask questions about new information, their brains can do a better job of connecting with information they've already stored. That's because the act of learning begins with a question. If the brain isn't curious about incoming information, it takes the path of least resistance and focuses on something else.

David Rock is the director of the NeuroLeadership Institute and author of *Your Brain at Work* (HarperBusiness, 2009). He uses an AGES model that identifies four requirements to embed ideas:

- ✔ **Attention** must be very high; multitasking dramatically reduces recall. The chemical processes to encode memory are activated when we are very focused.
- ✔ **Generating** a mental map of the new ideas requires participant involvement.
- ✔ **Emotions** need to be high; we only remember things we feel strongly about.
- ✔ **Spacing** learning out into smaller chunks is important.

A high AGES score is required for participants to recall ideas. Attention, generation, emotion, and spacing form the AGES model. Practicing in the form of small group work, gamification, contests, or team teaching can all increase a learning event's AGES score and help to ensure that we provide support to help our organizations' employees learn better and faster.

John Medina, author of *Brain Rules* (Pear Press, 2014), presents 12 entertaining and valuable tools to help you understand how the brain works so you can become a more effective trainer.

Microbursts, capsules, and mini trends

One of the outcomes of the brain-based research is the value in presenting content in smaller chunks — even pill size. In addition, as trainers we are often challenged to present "must know" and not "nice to know" content. Focusing on only "must know" has never been more critical than today. Our learners are swamped by a sea of information every day — or as some call it, *data smog*. We have an obligation to avoid adding to the data smog by identifying only the microbursts of information that are critical for our learners to know and timed close to the time they need to know them. Align these decisions to your corporate strategy.

Technology to the rescue. Mobile learning, social media, job aids — electronic or not, videos, mentoring, coaching, QR codes, podcasts, learnlets, and other options support your delivery of just-in-time capsules of information: what they need, when they need it, and where they need it.

Clark Quinn, author and consultant, writes extensively on topics such as mobile learning, performance support tools, and web-based learning.

It will be up to you to determine the least amount of information your learners need to know and to deliver it in bite-sized, right-sized portions.

Training on the run

What about those times when you are expected to design an interactive training session on short notice? Or when management asks you to condense your session down from a day to two hours? Impossible, you say? You may feel that way, but as the trends clearly show, efficiency and productivity take precedence now. Because this is more the norm than the exception, these suggestions will help you next time it occurs:

- ✔ Conduct a needs assessment that ensures you are training the most important knowledge and skills, and *only* the most important knowledge and skills: Ask a few learners and a couple of supervisors for their thoughts. Then prepare your capsules and microbursts of content.

- ✔ Make use of job aids that can be used during the training session and easily referenced after the session.

- ✔ Use a practical yet simple-to-remember process to teach whatever you need to. Three steps should be the maximum.

- ✔ A shortened time frame does not mean that you turn everything into a lecture. If anything, it is even more critical that participants are involved and experience the skills they must learn. Use a blended learning approach. Direct learners to read content before the session. Spend your time together on role plays or practice activities.

 ✔ Identify how you will follow up with participants. Email the next day with reminders of key concepts. Another email or tweet a week later jogs memories.

 ✔ You may not have much time left for an evaluation, so ask one or two key questions, such as, "What is the most useful concept you learned in this session?" or "What is one thing you wished you had learned but didn't?"

Next time you are asked to do the impossible, just smile and start running!

Globalization

Our organizations become more globalized every day, whether we merge with a company from another country, tap into the workforce on another continent, or collaborate with a foreign organization. Helping our organizations make the adjustment is important. Globalization offers companies exciting growth opportunities; it also introduces a complex array of challenges.

The challenges, often focused on a lack of the right infrastructure, affect the entire organization. Managing global organizations isn't a new challenge, but the accelerating shift of economic activity from Europe and North America to Africa, Asia, and Latin America creates new challenges. Global organizations struggle to adapt to the tension in managing strategy, people, costs, and risk on a global scale. The benefits far outweigh the challenges with the ability to access new customer markets, new suppliers, and new partners.

So how does this create a requirement for trainers? Think about it. The broad supply of skills, knowledge, and experience available within the global work- force represent invaluable assets to your company; however, utilizing these assets effectively is difficult. For example, if your company is like most, it has a vast amount of corporate knowledge gained in various ways. Unfortunately, few companies are good at transferring lessons learned from one emerging market to another. Trainers have the tools to gather, compile, and redistrib- ute lessons learned.

As a trainer, learn about the other culture. If conducting training, learn to pronounce names. Respect personal preferences. If participants have written Ms. or Dr. on their table tents, there is a strong preference to be addressed in the more formal context. Recognize that a highly participative learning approach may be uncomfortable for some cultures. For example, some cul- tures do not view direct eye contact as positively as those who live in the United States.

Diverse cultures require additional effort. A diverse audience requires that trainers speak clearly, are careful about giving feedback, frequently check for understanding, give instructions in the same sequence they are to be followed, avoid single country references, take care with jokes or other potentially offensive remarks, and repeat information when necessary.

Unique differences occur in any language. For example, using the colloquialism of "Are you pulling a fast one?" does not make much sense to someone just learning the language. Say instead, "Are you trying to trick me?" Similarly, sarcasm may be misunderstood or seem too aggressive. "Sure it is!" stated sarcastically will be better understood if you say "I don't think that is correct."

Read a book that identifies common gestures and their meanings in other cultures. For example, a thumbs-up signal that to you indicates everything is okay is a rude gesture in Nigeria and Australia. Or check out LuAnn Irwin and Renie McClay's *Essential Guide to Training Global Audiences* (Pfeiffer, 2008).

Cultural differences make it difficult to tap into talent around the world. Managing workforces that are separated by thousands of miles, international time zones, and diverse cultures can be a challenge. Your organization must be able to create an infrastructure that maintains the diversity of international teams while also empowering local employees. From a positive

Global audience analysis

by Renie McClay

When you design or facilitate global workshops, you should add additional questions to your normal audience analysis. The additional information helps you to plan and deliver more effectively and avoid unexpected things that can derail your plans:

✔ **Classroom sensitivities:** Depending on different countries and cultures, your audience may react to your gender and/ or your classroom management style. It is always good to find out in advance about gender sensitivities and/or management considerations.

✔ **Power and voltage:** Communicate with your contact person about your technology, audio/visual, and power needs. Bring appropriate adapters. Ask if there is anything you should know regarding storms, power outages, or surges. Bring a hard copy and have cloud backup.

✔ **Language skills:** Find out their native language and which language you should teach in and create materials in. Will translation/ interpretation be needed or helpful? If you will not use their first language, you could add more content to slides and handouts and let them review in advance. Learn some greetings in the native language.

✔ **Timeliness:** You, as a trainer, need to be on time. However, some countries are event-focused, not time-focused. Ask when to expect your audience to arrive, take breaks, serve meals, and close the session.

Being sensitive to their culture is of primary importance, both in preparation and in class.

Letting them do as much as possible in their native language can be helpful to them — small group discussions, for example. They will likely already be in an uncomfortable situation, so make it as comfortable for them as possible. Flexibility and adaptability will be two of your most important assets.

perspective, technology has made possible new forms of international coordination within global companies and potential new ways for them to flourish in these markets. Trainers who have experience or expertise in organizational development can be supportive in the VUCA challenge.

The multi-generational workforce

Four generations currently exist in the American workforce: Traditionalists, Baby Boomers, Generation X, and Millennials. What do you need to know about the mix that ensures the best results? As a trainer, you have two issues to address. The first is to ensure the entire workforce appreciates the diversity each group brings. The second is to ensure that the Millennials are developed and ready to take on leadership responsibilities at a much earlier age than was typical in the past.

Generational challenges

You have a great opportunity to bring the generations together through your training efforts. Focus on the similarities rather than the differences among generations. The group that garners the greatest attentions seems to be the Millennials, those employees born between 1981 and 2000.

Complaints from Millennials about the rest of the workforce include that the other generations are not open to new ideas, work in siloes, aren't accessible, are slow to adapt new technology, insist on rigid schedules, and use political games for gain.

Complaints about the Millennials from the rest of the workforce include that Millennials don't follow rules such as dress codes, are not diplomatic, complain too much, do not show respect, expect promotions and incentives without earning them, and do not turn their phones off during discussions.

Certainly there is some truth on both sides. Helping everyone to appreciate the diversity that other generations bring is a first step. Help everyone identify the similarities — for example, everyone wants to do work that makes a difference, desires consistent feedback, and wants to know what is expected of them. The situation is not as bad as some would make it seem. But you can address these challenges by thinking through the differences as you design and deliver training.

Prepare Millennials for leadership roles

Gen X, the generation sandwiched between the Boomers and the Millennials, is half the size of the Boomer generation. This means that as the Baby Boomers retire, only half of the positions vacated will have experienced workers to fill them. Millennials will have early promotion opportunities and will require an accelerated rate of development.

You may use these tips for designing and delivering training to Millennials:

- ✔ **Clarify expectations.** Millennials want to know what is expected of them, how they will be evaluated, and how the knowledge and skills they are acquiring relate to their performance evaluations on the job.

- ✔ **Take advantage of their tech savviness.** Millennials' electronic capabilities are amazing. They have never known an educational environment that was not subject to constant and consistently changing technology. They view learning and technology as going hand-in-hand. In your classroom, use Twitter to share the results of a small-group discussion. Online, provide links to additional resources that learners can access if they want to learn more. Design content so learners can access it on their laptops, smartphones, iPads, or other devices.

- ✔ **Coach along the way.** Millennials appreciate opportunities for coaching, require feedback, and appreciate advice. Use mentors or senior associates during or after training.

- ✔ **Capitalize on Millennials' desire to network.** They are comfortable with teams and group activities, but Millennial employees also like to network around the world electronically. Use social media to continue to enhance their skills fast.

Circumstances are different throughout the world, and what has been successful in the past may not be successful today. About half of the Millennials are currently old enough to have joined the workforce. This means you have some time to gear up, but not much. Your organization expects a plan for how you will address this business reality.

Supporting the C-Suite

Your organization will need your support in this VUCA world, so it's natural to assume that you will be in direct contact with your senior leaders. The greatest skill you will most likely need to develop is the ability to talk C-suitese: to articulate how your achievements impact the organization, state how you've affected profitability, and to express your vision for the future. What does it take to communicate with the C-suite?

Take it from Dianna Booher, author of "Securing Executive Support: Presenting to the C-Suite" in *ASTD Handbook: The Definitive Reference for T&D* (ASTD, 2014): "The first thing you need to do is to understand how members of the C-suite think. Plan your message in advance. Make it concise and to the point. Executives are an impatient lot. They want to know the message first and are happy to fill in with the details later."

Make your message strategic. Strategic ideas get approved and funded. Support the strategy with just enough detail to demonstrate that your plan is sound. Ask provocative questions. Your message should not just "tell" but should also invite thinking from your audience. Booher states that stimulating questions generate more support. What questions can you ask to pique interest from your audience? And can you weave them into a story?

The next time you are invited to the C-suite to present plans for the following year or to justify why a blended learning approach would be better, use Diana's checklist as a reminder of the strategies for success:

- ✔ Open with the big-picture message statement.
- ✔ Select critical information nuggets for a concise message.
- ✔ Deliver a strategic message supported by details that sell the idea.
- ✔ Define several provocative questions.
- ✔ Take a stand on the issue.
- ✔ Create a memorable story.

To summarize this section, you may see these environmental changes as a need to provide better, faster, and cheaper training. And you are right! Each lends itself to your need to produce better training, in a shorter time frame, and at a more reasonable cost than in the past.

Expanded Role for T&D

Yes T&D's roles are expanding again. Depending upon which year you entered the workforce, you may have been called a trainer, facilitator, T&D professional, L&D professional, learning and performance professional, or perhaps something else. These changing role titles indicate the broadening and expansion of the profession. This is also one of the reasons the American Society for Training and Development (ASTD)changed its name to the Association for Talent Development (ATD).

Develop talent. Yes that's what you do. You have accepted the new roles that have been added to your job descriptions over the years. Much of this will not be a surprise. The best part, however, is that these roles are recognized as critical to the entire job of developing employees.

Out of the many new roles, I have selected six to explore more deeply in this section. The first, *onboarding*, is close to the typical "learning event," with the caveat that it is always with your newest employees — the ones you will want to ensure have a good first impression. The other five roles are not usually thought of as typical training or learning department roles. If you begin thinking of your role as a "talent developer," however, you will see how each of these fits into your new job description. Let's examine each of these roles.

Onboarding

How your organization welcomes new employees creates the important "first impression." This is the time to ensure that your company puts its best foot forward. Long-term employee engagement is based on the right fit, starting with your onboarding process. Is it any wonder why this role now falls to you? You understand what it takes to draw people in, to create involvement, to engage employees, and to provide an active learning experience:

- Ensure that new employees receive the information they need to help them integrate into the workforce.
- Ensure that new employees know how their role fits in the organization.
- Build new employees' self-esteem by recognizing the value they bring.
- Introduce new employees to other employees, including management and their department co-workers.
- Ensure that new employees feel welcome and part of the team, and that they leave knowing they made the right decision.

Onboarding is not an event; it is a process. It isn't over after the original event. Assign a "buddy" or "coach" to help new employees find answers and feel welcome. This important new role uses your skills to lead to a higher level of employee engagement right from the start.

Facilitating change

Because organizations are going through massive change, expect to be drawn into the process. You have the kind of skills required for success: knowing about effective communication, understanding motivation, respecting the value of teams, formulating goals and objectives, designing plans, defining performance standards, implementing plans, and dozens of other skills. You also know how important active, involved participation is to the success of any project and how to obtain that involvement. You may even have designed and facilitated change-management training for your organization. This is why your role is critical to helping lead change in your organization.

Ensure that your organization is using a process to guide the change. The key to successfully managing change is strong, effective communication. As your organization moves through a change management effort, you will find many of your skills are critical to its success.

Coaching managers

Have you ever had managers tell you it was your job to develop their people? They are only half right. Developing people, closing the skill gaps in the workforce, and increasing knowledge must be a partnership between you and managers. Managers may not have thought about it this way in the past — you will most likely need to develop and coach them along the way. You will need to clarify their role as a developmental manager and show them how to embed development into the work the employees are doing. You will be "coaching the coaches."

You will help managers be better coaches to support learning and development. But your coaching job doesn't end there. You may also be asked to coach managers to make better decisions, improve their communication skills, design succession plans, and all the other things that define excellent managers or leaders.

Based on ATD's *The Coaching Approach: A Key Tool for Successful Managers* study, coaching is a process that includes three main activities:

- ✔ Proactive listening
- ✔ Asking non-directive and prompting questions
- ✔ Providing targeted, timely, and actionable feedback

As a T&D professional, you know how to do all of those things. Piece of cake! Now you know why this is one of your new roles.

Creating mentoring opportunities

A mentor is a trusted counselor or guide. There are at least two people in a mentoring relationship, and both can gain valuable new knowledge, insight, and skills as a result of participating. Mentoring is not limited to those in a formal program. In our highly connected world of social networking, new mentoring relationships are emerging as a result of savvy employees (and their employers) making connections and joining groups that give them access to potential mentoring matches. Eager learners and seasoned veterans who are willing to be mentors can easily connect and begin a mutually beneficial mentoring relationship. Anyone can start a mentoring relationship.

As a T&D professional, developing employees through mentoring is another role you may be expected to complete. In this role you may:

- ✔ Create a process to locate and match mentor/protégé partnerships
- ✔ Design readiness surveys for mentors and protégés
- ✔ Design and conduct a mentoring training program
- ✔ Determine how to create mentoring opportunities for employees around the globe
- ✔ Identify ways to use social media tools to facilitate mentoring matches
- ✔ Create an evaluation plan to measure the success of the program
- ✔ Determine a balanced diversity approach for the program

Once again, you can see how the skills you honed as a T&D professional provide a practical basis for this role.

Internal consulting

Internal consulting is a unique training and development role. Internal consultants are called upon to facilitate high-level meetings, to master mind change efforts, to take a systems approach for future projects, and execute other exciting high-level projects.

Beverly Scott and Kim Barnes see new internal consulting roles emerging, including performance consultant and trusted advisor. They define them in their book *Consulting on the Inside: An Internal Consultant's Guide to Living and Working Inside Organizations* (2nd Edition, ASTD, 2011).

What does it take to be a successful internal consultant? First and foremost it requires that you gain the trust and credibility of everyone in the organization: leaders and employees. You must be a generalist, competent in a broad range of applications, but you must also be seen as an expert in several areas to ensure credibility. Again, you've been in training for this role!

Building teams

Human beings make up organizations, create the culture, and determine the total effectiveness of their organizations. This effectiveness depends on how well they work together as a group. Indeed, human beings do almost everything in groups. Working as a team is how we get things done, and teams are most effective when they communicate well and function as a cohesive unit. Unfortunately, employees may cognitively "know" the importance of teamwork, but may not practice what they know. We may appreciate good communication, but may not realize how our personal communication may inhibit understanding by our co-workers.

Teams rarely start off great; they learn to be great. And that is what *team building* can do. You can easily "teach team skills," but often a team doesn't request training until it is nearly dysfunctional. At that point, your role changes from facilitating team skills training to facilitating a teambuilding intervention. You may need to work with teams that are less productive and efficient than they should be (sometimes dysfunctional) in order to create a functioning team.

In this role, you will gather information and design an intervention that is customized and unique for every team.

To summarize this section, the effects of the VUCA world require T&D professionals to embrace expanded roles with a broader definition of what trainers do. Working under the banner of Talent Development helps to ensure that you will work hand-in-hand with management to add value to your organization. Change may be huge for some trainers; it is less for others.

Alternative Delivery Options

The future of T&D holds numerous delivery options. Yes, there is virtual training, and we've discussed mobile training. As organizations use employees more efficiently, you may find yourself conducting training as a team. Or if training isn't your primary role, you may be tapped to be a part-time trainer.

Team training

Team training is used in various situations, such as when one is an expert, when content is complex, or when one is a new trainer. It happens in virtual and face-to-face instructor-led training (ILT).

Few things in the training field can be as frustrating and at the same time as enriching as team training. Having the opportunity to train with a colleague is a unique opportunity to grow. Trainers frequently are one-person shows and rarely have the opportunity to work with colleagues and obtain feedback from someone in the same profession. It is also an opportunity to watch another person model new techniques and approaches, tell new stories, and present content from a new perspective.

At the same time, the experience can be very frustrating. The other trainer may take longer on a section, causing you to cut material. The other trainer's style may be the opposite of yours; for example, you keep the front table neat and orderly, but the other person prefers to spend time with participants and doesn't bother organizing until the end of the day. The other trainer presents content in a different way, and you wonder if one of you is incorrect.

The bottom line is that the participants must see you working as a team. They should see nothing but two professionals making sure that they are conducting the best darn training they've ever attended. The suggestions are appropriate for virtual and face-to-face ILT.

Meet prior to the session

Meet at least once prior to the session to review the schedule and content. At that time, assign responsibilities and negotiate ground rules. If it's a virtual ILT, this may occur on a phone call. This may be a good time to use Skype with some show-and-tell for each other. Spend time ensuring clear understanding of your expectations of each other and the outcome of the session. The following suggestions should be considered a minimum:

- ✔ Discuss your training style preference.
- ✔ Discuss the logistics — equipment or room setup, number, and type of participants.
- ✔ Identify any modifications to be made to the design.
- ✔ Walk through the session, making notes about who will do what.
- ✔ Identify where the supporting trainer will be located physically.
- ✔ Request specific feedback from each other.
- ✔ Exchange contact information, especially cellphone numbers.
- ✔ Identify how and when to intervene during the session.

Make each other look good during the session

During the session, both trainers need to work as a team. Even if you are training only half the material, it is still a full-time job. In a face-to-face session, it is unacceptable to read the paper in the back of the room while your partner is training in the front. So what do you do?

- ✔ Remain in the room with your co-facilitator.
- ✔ Stay mentally engaged to ensure that you can assist when necessary.
- ✔ Take notes to provide useful feedback during the post-session debrief.
- ✔ Stick to the ground rules you established, for example:
  - If you want to add something in a face-to-face session, wait for the okay from the lead (the person who is "on" at the time) trainer. In a virtual session when you are in two different locations, create a signal or send a personal message.
  - The lead trainer always makes the final call.
  - Do not correct the other trainer where learners can hear.
- ✔ Assist each other during fishbowls, small-group, or whiteboard activities while the other is facilitating a discussion.
- ✔ Each of you should be responsible for an equal amount of the least-liked or difficult sections.

✔ If individuals are struggling with course content, one of you can provide additional support off-line.

✔ If you are the supporting trainer, stay one step ahead of the other person. What's the next activity? Are all materials available? What's the transition? How can you be helpful?

Learn from your co-facilitator. Take advantage of training with another trainer to build your repertoire of skills. Observe new techniques, ask for feedback on specific skills you want to improve, and pick up stories, examples, and personal touches that seem to work with the participants. This is a golden opportunity — grab it:

✔ Two trainers, working well together, establish a model of cooperation and teamwork for the participants.

✔ Use the advantage of two for modeling, role playing, acting, or debating two points of view. This is a great opportunity during a virtual session.

✔ Carry your fair share, whether you are the lead trainer on the line or the supporting trainer in waiting.

The supporting trainer has a perfect opportunity to watch participants' body language or stay on top of the chat messages. This will provide insight about how well the content is being received and whether adaptations are required.

✔ Show mutual respect, demonstrate listening, and display verbal and nonverbal agreement.

✔ Ensure that both of you have personal time during any breaks.

Provide feedback following the session

Meet immediately after the session to discuss how things went. If you have kept notes during the session, you will be better prepared and organized for the meeting.

If this is a multiple-day session, meet at the end of each day so that you don't lose valuable feedback. The next day will be filled with new experiences and will overtake the previous day.

✔ Provide a professional critique that includes both positive feedback as well as areas for improvement.

✔ Some organizations develop a checklist of skills and attributes they deem necessary. If you have one, use it.

✔ Give feedback on the items the other person has requested. Be honest, candid, sincere, and sensitive.

✔ Use specific examples to make your point.

✔ Identify areas in the training materials, content, or delivery that should be changed or improved; document these to forward to your supervisor.

✔ Use excellent communication, listening, and feedback skills. You will grow professionally and benefit from the opportunity (or even the challenge) to interact with another trainer having a different style, personality, pace, and viewpoint.

✔ Celebrate successes.

Training with a partner can be one of the best experiences you've ever had as a trainer. Use these guidelines to ensure it.

Help for the part-time trainer

The trends in training lead to a need for more trainers. If you're good at what you do, you may be *rewarded* with the opportunity to show others how to do what you do so well. What do you do? Select the sections in this book that you think will be most beneficial to you. Then go out there and try it!

As a part-time trainer, one of the biggest problems you may have is managing both your training responsibilities and your "real" job. These tips will help you:

✔ Accept training projects that are consistent with the objectives of your position.

✔ When you know you will be training, keep a resource file on that topic handy. Clip articles and save other relevant information in these resource files. When you are ready to prepare, all your resources will be in one spot.

✔ Keep a list of points you want to make, things you want to do, or stories you want to tell. Keep the list handy so that when you think of things, you can write them down. When you are ready to prepare, all your thoughts will be collected on your list.

Use index cards to collect your ideas and stories. You can easily track each as you present it.

✔ Keep a training bag ready. Have markers, pens, masking tape, and whatever else you consistently use in training stored in an old briefcase. When it's time to train, just grab your bag. There's no need to scurry around for the things you need.

✔ Keep all your training manuals, handouts, notes, and visuals in one spot. This prevents you from having to assemble everything at the last minute.

Discipline yourself to replenish supplies in your kit immediately upon returning from the current training session; it will always be ready to go.

✔ If you have just completed a program and you know you'll be doing it again, write a summary of what went well and what you'd do differently immediately following the program. Make any changes at that time too. If you do this while the material is fresh in your mind, it will save you time.

✔ Remember that investment pays off. If you spend adequate time preparing for your training the first time you do it, you will benefit every time you train.

Informal learning on the job

Everyone learns on the job. Whether you help yourself, receive assignments from your supervisor, learn from experiences, tap into the Internet, ask a colleague, or join a professional association, every experience that you have — and every experience that you encourage your learners to have — benefits both the individual and the organization.

As a trainer, you can be influential, make suggestions, and help to create an environment that is supportive and conducive to informal learning. These four thought starters provide a few ideas for you:

✔ **Help yourself:** Self-directed learning appeals to most of us because we like to learn on our own. The flexibility allows us to learn when and where we want. This supports most of our natural learning desires. From a learning perspective, how can you reward employees who learn on their own?

✔ **Informal learning:** The unofficial, impromptu, unscheduled way in which most people learn to do their jobs is responsible for 70 or 80 percent of all learning. How can you create an organizational culture that supports informal learning?

✔ **Learn from experiences:** Designing experiential learning activities to fit into classroom activities ensures that learners practice skills. Bringing the real world into the classroom gives learners skills that are required to solve today's problems. Can you also find ways to take the entire learning group to the site? How can you encourage individual learners and their supervisors to learn from experience?

✔ **On-the-job assignments:** Supervisors have many tools at their disposal: rotational assignments, stretch assignments, project-based assignments, and others. Supervisors decide which developmental assignments will be most beneficial for each employee. As an L&D professional, you may need to help supervisors define this important role. How can you coach supervisors to stay in touch with assignments that encourage their employees' development?

Where is this Heading?

The future of learning is here — now. The classroom is no longer bound by walls or calendar dates. According to David Powell of CCL (Center for Creative Leadership) and originator of the Persistent Classroom, the learning future is all around us — wherever our smartphone lies, whenever the time is right, and through whichever mode makes the most sense. In the future, learners will not come to a classroom; the classroom will come to them, bound by neither date nor location.

David Powell, senior faculty and a founding member of the Innovation Lab at CCL, is a member of a team that crafts future scenarios that guide CCL's future strategy for innovation and learning. His concepts are embodied in this section.

David believes that all learning will occur within an *augmented reality* paradigm, and learners will receive a continuous stream of data that can be queried about people, places, and objects as they interact with the world. People will be instantly locatable, and the acquisition of knowledge will occur just-in-time. It will appear when and where you need it.

David believes the learning spaces in the future will be "always on." Everyone will be connected regardless of physical location. We will learn together, but we will be physically apart. We will learn by multiplying and intensifying our connections.

In the future, trainers will be only one source of knowledge. When learners inhabit a radically connected learning space, expert knowledge holders (and what they know) are both student and teacher and are just a click away. When designing a curriculum, content should be broken into a series of bite-sized pieces. Think snacks, not meals. Traditional location-based instructional design needs to be reimagined for unwalled learning spaces, where learners drop in and out of the content stream.

In the future, people will inhabit a personally curated educational world where the curriculum is designed, moment-to-moment, by the participant.

Instructional designers and trainers will work in a world where participants have equal involvement as the trainer.

How to Prepare Yourself

Yes, change is the only constant in today's world. A successful training professional embraces change and welcomes the new roles that come with it. How do you stay on top of this? Beverly Kaye, author *of Love It, Don't Leave It: 26 Ways to Get What You Want at Work* (Berrett-Koehler, 2003), says that you need to be alert to everything that's happening in the world of work. Identify the trends and challenges in the workplace. Talk to people. Find opportunities to enrich your skills. Stay on top of what's happening in your industry. Predict what will happen.

Let's consider some suggestions for how to prepare for your career in the exciting time ahead. Your challenge is to stay in touch with the dilemmas that your leaders and organizations face and to be ready to provide what they need. Let's examine three things you can ponder about your future:

- ✔ Content to support dealing with a VUCA world
- ✔ Future roles that may be required
- ✔ Becoming a lifelong learner

Content

Remember what you read earlier about the VUCA world: The volatility, uncertainty, complexity, and ambiguity inherent in today's business world is the "new normal," and it is profoundly changing how organizations do business.

The skills and abilities leaders once needed to help their organizations thrive are no longer sufficient. Today, more strategic, complex, critical-thinking skills are required. All of us can help our organizations succeed in today's VUCA environment. We can do our part to develop a workforce that counters volatility, uncertainty, complexity, and ambiguity.

Applying the VUCA model as a framework to re-tool employee development models may enable companies to identify and foster the skills organizations need now and in the future.

Pause for a moment and think about it. Even generally, what does it take to work in a VUCA world? Yes, of course the technical and the job-related skills, but what is needed to be successful in a VUCA world? What do your current and future employees need to develop to be successful? What are the "white-space skills" — those skills that are between the job requirements and competencies?

Bob Johansen, author of *Leaders Make the Future* (BK Business, 2012) shares skills that counter VUCA:

- ✔ Volatility requires vision.
- ✔ Uncertainty requires more understanding.
- ✔ Complexity requires more clarity.
- ✔ Ambiguity requires agility.

So imagine that your CEO comes to you and says, "Our employees need more vision, understanding, clarity, and agility." What are you going to say?

I've identified half a dozen skills in each area that I think provide some meaningful topics reducible to KSAs (knowledge, skills, and attitudes), which should be helpful. They certainly aren't all-inclusive, and there is some crossover among them.

- ✔ Volatility requires vision, so what skills do your employees require? How about: strategic thinking, problem solving, integrity and ethics, predictive analysis, scenario planning, and self-awareness.
- ✔ Uncertainty requires more understanding, so what skills do your employees require? How about resilience, managing change, empathy and acceptance, optimism and stress management, discernment, network thinking, and learning to learn.
- ✔ Complexity requires more clarity, so what skills do your employees require? How about critical thinking, teamwork (virtually too), setting priorities, mentoring, coaching, developing talent, managerial skills, communication, and boundary spanning.
- ✔ Ambiguity requires agility, so what skills do your employees require? How about change management (again), accountability and action orientation, fostering innovation and creativity, using technology to be more nimble, time management, and collaboration.

And all of these require complete, concise, and timely communication, and relationship building. That might be a list of "content" we need to deliver— whether formally in a classroom, asynchronously online, in a book, informally through discussions, using our social networks, through coaches or mentors, on apps, in a MOOC, on a webcast, in a brownbag presentation, through a college course. . . . the venue or means does not matter.

Future roles

Now, how about *you?* How do you prepare yourself? Think about your own development and what you need to do to stay ahead. Overall, keep in mind the Thiagi BCF principle — *better cheaper faster.* This is your mantra within the VUCA world. And what will you be doing better, cheaper, and faster?

Here are a dozen roles our profession may see — even within the year. Some are tongue-in-cheek titles, but every role will be necessary soon and describes talent that you should pay attention to. So sit back, relax, and select a new job for yourself!

✔ **Talent Systems Optimizer:** As organizations continue to fold the development function and the HR function under one combined Chief Talent Officer (CTO) hat, all of us need to think "system." From a generalist perspective, you need to learn enough about HR processes so that you can help drive new practices into every part of the organization. Your processes no longer stand alone — they fit together in an integrated Talent System. Remember that your CTO will be expected to lead these efforts and will call on you to support him or her. You'll need to know how to ensure employee engagement — to capture employees' hearts and minds to keep the best people who can create, innovate, and move the organization forward.

✔ **Innovation Implementer:** All companies need to become more innovative. If the C-suite needs to be more innovative, it will require support to implement, inform, deliver skills, share knowledge, and influence attitudes. The learning department is connected to all parts of the organization, and we have better than average communication skills. Our profession encourages creative thinkers more than most professions. Someone else may create the idea, but implementing will be in our hands.

✔ **Corporate Coach:** You may already be a corporate coach, or you may call yourself an internal consultant. Whatever your title, your skills will be necessary. As mentioned earlier in this chapter, there is a new emphasis on coaching managers to develop their people as well as do a better job as managers and leaders.

✔ **Corporate Content Curator:** Content abounds — that's not news, but someone needs to have an eye toward the future to determine what employees "must have" and what is "nice to have." Trainers have faced this question for decades, so that part isn't new. Information is arriving so rapidly and in such large doses that someone in the decision arena must act as the go-between for the C-Suite and the workforce to make these decisions. Once the decision about *what* content needs to be distributed, a plan must be in place for *how* the content is distributed.

✔ **Engagement Planner:** Much like a wedding planner, you will need to be adept at skills that build an engaged and wise workforce. As you are pulled more into talent-management efforts, you will need to ensure everyone understands that training is *not* the answer for everything. The engagement planner role requires skills such as communication, creativity, attention to detail, organization, and resourcefulness.

✔ **The Opportunity Optimist:** F. Scott Fitzgerald said, "The test of a first-rate intelligence is the ability to hold two opposing ideas in mind at the same time, and still retain the ability to function." In the future, to some extent, all of us will be required to view all the uncertain and changing issues that come toward our companies and departments, discern meaning, and plan for a future that others may not be able to understand. Selecting and developing a workforce to be prepared for the future requires the ability to see a problem and implement steps to turn it into an opportunity.

✔ **Data Analytics Team:** As your organization relies more on analytics, it will also require various roles such as these:

- **Data Hygienist** to ensure that data coming into the system is accurate and sanitary.

- **Data Miner** to sift through masses of data to discover what your organization requires.

- **Statistical Architect** to create a taxonomy and organize the data so that it's ready to analyze.

- **Data Engineer** to create sophisticated algorithms and models that can predict customer behavior, pricing strategy, and profitable markets.

- **Marketing Maharishi** to turn the data models and predictions into bottom line results.

✔ **MOOC (Massive Open Online Courses) Master:** Most of the courses currently offered are academic, but more business programs are becoming available daily. Yep, there are lots of problems with partnerships, platforms, cost, and dropout rates. And most organizations are still skeptical about the value of free online courses. Still, the MOOC providers are developing validated certifications. The MOOC Master will need to decide how to use these courses efficiently and effectively.

Yes, these are imaginary roles today, but even without knowing what real roles will exist in the future, you can continue to work on your own development. Share your needs and hopes for continued development. Broaden your skills and knowledge. Learn to be flexible and to watch for opportunities to learn new skills. Learn everything you can about your industry. Set goals and build development plans for your future.

Become a lifelong learner

Finally, stay ahead of the change. To the roles above, add Lifelong Learner Extraordinaire: The profession has used the term *lifelong learning* since the 1990s, but you will be expected to model this to extreme. You will have lots to learn to keep up with your own VUCA world. You will need to be able to immerse yourself in a topic, technique, process, data, whatever, and come up for air with insight for the organization and what it will take to bring the workforce along to accomplish the strategy. Be sure to take the time to keep your skills and knowledge on the cutting edge. Dedicate yourself to lifelong professional development.

Becoming a lifelong learner isn't new to our profession — in fact, we invented the idea. Have you ever thought about all the skills you need to be proficient? I sometimes get exhausted just thinking about everything I need to do my job. This is what makes the job so exciting, but it is also what necessitates becoming lifelong learners.

Sharpen your skills

Develop your skills and knowledge to maintain your place on the cutting edge. By doing so, you are providing the kind of development opportunities your employer and your participants expect and deserve. You owe it to yourself to continue to develop your skills and increase your knowledge. Staying in touch with the changes and the excitement of the profession will keep you enthusiastic and passionate about what you do. We need to learn continuously. Learning is paramount in order to achieve all that you are capable of doing.

Read ATD's 2013 *Competency Study* (available online at www.td.org/Publications/Books/ASTD-Competency-Model) to help you understand and build the required competencies for your professional and career-development journey.

Take stock and take action

Step back and take stock of where you are and where you want to be. Determine some measure of success, drive a stake in the ground, and head for it. You can establish measures that include both knowledge and skills. Next, identify a developmental plan for continued growth. Consider several strategies. Make a list of all the things you would like to learn — professionally and personally. Remember this is an investment in you. If you won't invest in you, who will?

Maintain your personal spark

Yes it is important to maintain your professional spark. It is equally important to maintain your personal spark. How?

- ✔ With physical exercise by gardening, exercising, walking, dancing, playing sports, learning Pilates.
- ✔ With relaxation through meditation, getting a massage, getting enough sleep, listening to music, yoga.
- ✔ Through awareness of your eating habits, drinking enough water, eating nutritious food.
- ✔ With awareness of your emotions by thinking positively, expressing yourself, journaling, having fun, celebrating.
- ✔ By replenishing your mind through daydreaming, reading, learning something new, observing beauty.

Make a list of everything that inspires and rejuvenates you. Put it where you will see it every day. Find the passion in your life. Trainers need to have a spark because we light fires for so many others. Love what you do and do what you love.

Becoming a lifelong learner is exciting. It is sure to put passion back in your life.

As with any profession, nothing is static. Life and our work remind us of the words to Bob Dylan's song, "The times they are a-changing."

Part VI
The Part of Tens

the
part of
tens

Check out how to use humor in training in an extra Part of Tens chapter at www.dummies.com/extras/traininganddevelopment.

In this part . . .

- Starting off on the right foot.
- Warming up learners before your webinar.
- Saving time while training.
- Discovering ten icebreakers that really work.
- Checking out how to be successful using m-learning.

Chapter 18

Ten Tips to Start Off on the Right Foot

First contacts create a lasting impression. Most people have discovered that the first ten minutes of any initial meeting between two people lays the groundwork for almost all assumptions and decisions about the ensuing relationship.

If first impressions are critical, how does a good trainer catch and hold participants' attention from the start? How do trainers start off on the right foot — especially at time when they are facilitating a virtual session? This chapter identifies ten aspects of getting your training session off to a good start.

The Association for Talent Development (ATD) offers a Training Certificate Program — one of dozens. One of the objectives of the program is to teach trainers how to open their training sessions with PUNCH. ATD believes that the opening is one of the most important sections of any training design. Training should open with a purpose, not just open. A training session can open with PUNCH if the trainer accomplishes these five things.

✔ **Promotes** interest and enthusiasm for the training-session content. Participants desire more after the opening. Perhaps there was an element of surprise built into the opening using props or introducing a creative activity.

✔ **Understands** participants' needs — both content as well as personal-esteem needs by learning something about participants' experience and expertise.

✔ Notes the ground rules and administrative needs so that guidelines are established to ensure the training session runs more smoothly: how to use the chat feature, what time lunch will be held, when breaks will occur, and where restrooms are located?

✔ Clarifies expectations by discussing the agenda and the objectives for the session. The opening also identifies other expectations participants have that may or may not be addressed.

✔ Helps everyone get to know each other through the use of icebreakers, discussions, or other activities. Getting participation early sets the stage for full participation throughout the session.

How do you add PUNCH to your training? These ten aspects of starting off on the right foot guide you in the right direction.

Establish a Climate Conducive to Learning

Creating rapport and establishing a climate conducive to learning cannot be overemphasized. This is particularly true when you facilitate a virtual session. When done right from the start it means that participants will be open to and enthusiastic about the learning activities that follow. They will know what to expect. You can set the tone for the rest of the training session by what you accomplish at the beginning.

The opening should indicate whether the rest of the session will have participants up and moving about or sitting or a combination of the two. It should set the tempo and tone of the session. Fast paced? Slow? Jovial? Serious? Interactive? Passive? Creative? Cerebral? Exciting? Calm? All of these describe a potential training climate. Decide what yours will be, and then begin to establish the climate during your opening. Even if participants can't see you in a virtual setting, have a smile in your voice when you open.

If you desire a participative climate, the opening should put people at ease — including the trainer. Participants may be reluctant to get involved unless the trainer provides structure that includes a purpose. They may be shy or may not want to appear vulnerable in front of their peers or strangers.

In a physical classroom, the trainer greets people as they arrive and chats with them. This can occur in a virtual classroom as well. Greet each person individually with a comment such as, "Welcome, Tora, it's 10 below in Madison, Wisconsin this morning. How's Frankfurt?" or "Good morning,

James, did you fix the problem with your computer interface?" Don't delay the training — be ready to start the agenda on time.

Think through the climate that will be the most conducive to learning. Then begin to establish it from the first moment the session begins.

Clarify Participants' Expectations

Participants expect you to ask about their expectations for the session and numerous ways exist for you to accomplish this. Of course the most straight-forward way is to simply ask "What are your expectations for the session?" List them on a flipchart page and post them on the wall. In a virtual class-room, have participants post on the whiteboard. There are other ways to get the same information. You can twist the question a bit to assist learners to get at their questions or concerns from a different perspective. Try some of these:

✔ Ask for hopes and fears. Post on two different flipcharts.

✔ Ask for dreams and desires.

✔ Ask "Why are you here?"

✔ Ask "What questions did you bring with you today?"

✔ Ask "What do you need to happen today for this training to be worth your investment of time?"

✔ Ask "How well do your needs match the learning objectives?" and "What else do you need?"

What if the participants' expectations go beyond the scope of the training design? Better to let them know now how you intend to handle it. You may respond in three ways. First, you can add time to the agenda to address the additional expectations. This most likely means eliminating or shortening something else. Second, if the additional expectation is something that con-cerns only one or two individuals, you may choose to meet with them after the session or during a break to discuss their needs. Third, you may need to tell them that you're not prepared or time doesn't allow for the added con-tent, or whatever is the truth, but that you will follow up with them follow-ing the session. This may mean that you email them additional resources, put them in touch with someone who has the expertise, or whatever will address their concern. In a virtual setting that runs as a series over several weeks, you have the potential to build some of the expectations into future sessions.

Possibly the most important thing you can do for participants, no matter what your format happens to be, is to help them understand "What's In It For Me" (WIIFM). Some trainers describe this as helping participants tune into station WII-FM. Participants who understand why they are involved in a training session, how it will help them do their jobs better and faster, and how the content relates to them will get more out of the training session.

Introduce the Content

Related to clarifying the participants' expectations is introducing the content. You provide an overview for participants by reviewing the agenda and the objectives for the training session. Telling them what's to come provides a foundation for the content and establishes a common starting point for everyone in the room.

Ensure that participants know other aspects of the content as well. They may want to know whether they will be required to take a test, whether they will receive a grade for the course, or whether the grade will affect their jobs. They may want to know what kind of participation will be expected and whether there will be assignments. Model and explain each of these as you walk them through the agenda. In a virtual setting, for example, you can tell them that you will call on them by name periodically, but even better, start calling on them by name while you review the agenda. "Pierre, is that what you expected to see on the agenda?" Some learners may be new to virtual classrooms and not realize that you do expect them to participate.

I generally present the content and then ask participants whether they were anticipating different or additional content. You can do either first. I find my process saves time because I do not have to repeat the content later as I present the agenda. On the other hand, sometimes it is more important for the participants to establish their own agenda than to save time. During instances such as a team-building effort, I facilitate a discussion of their expectations and needs first. It takes a bit longer, but there is more buy-in that leads to better end results. By the way, your icebreaker should relate to the content.

Surprise!

Add an element of surprise right from the start. Add something unconventional to send a message to participants that this session may not be the same thing they have experienced in the past. You may introduce props in your opening or state something unusual or shocking about the topic (that you can prove later, of course). You can also start with an activity first, rather than addressing the logistics of the session.

✔ During introductions most trainers start at the front and go clockwise around the room. Plan to start someplace else, such as the middle back and go counterclockwise. Even better, ask for a volunteer to start, ask for a second volunteer, and select or call on folks all over. This takes a bit of practice on your part to remember who was introduced. When all else fails you can always end by saying "Who has not been introduced yet?" to pick up anyone who was missed in this scatter approach.

✔ Save housekeeping issues until just before break. No one needs to know most of the information until then anyway. Because most sessions start off with a discussion about lunch, parking, and sign-up sheets, you will surprise your participants when you do not begin the same way.

✔ Ask participants to use crayons instead of pens or pencils to generate lists, draw something, write their names on their table tents, or anything else they would typically complete with a pen.

Doing something just a bit differently or in a different sequence introduces an element of surprise that energizes participants, adds interest and excitement to the session, and communicates that this session will not be boring.

Introduce Participants

An opening is not complete unless participants learn who else is attending the session. Whether you use an icebreaker or a quick round of introductions will depend upon the amount of time you have available and how participants will need to interact during the rest of the training session.

Allow participants to become acquainted with one another. Establish a way that they can begin to understand who else is in the training session and what their attitudes, values, experience, and concerns may be. Use this time wisely. Before selecting how participants will meet each other, determine what you want participants to be able to do as a result. You may just want them to be able to match names and faces, but you may want to consider other results that will help to further the training session. What else do you want participants to know about each other? Make a list of what you want to accomplish. These may help get you started.

✔ Have a continuous contact for other content.

✔ Practice solving problems.

✔ Understand attitudes, beliefs, likes, and dislikes.

✔ Practice a creative experience.

✔ Begin to build a team.

Many legitimate aspects exist for what you hope participants will learn about each other and how they will interact later based on this introduction experience. If you use an icebreaker, Chapter 21 is a good place to start. At the least, I suggest that everyone in the group accomplish two things.

✔ All participants hear all other participants' names.

✔ All participants speak up at least once.

In your virtual classrooms, use a participant list as you call on individuals. In a physical classroom, I highly recommend using table tents — the cards folded like a tent that have people's names written on them. They will help you remember participants' names and help participants remember and use each others' names. Have participants place their names on both sides during the introductions. This allows you and other participants to see their names from any angle.

Learn About the Group

Be sure to build time into the opening so that you can observe the group and learn something about the group's dynamics and the individual personalities. Conducting an icebreaker provides you with this opportunity.

It may be tempting to have your head in your notes during the icebreaker to prepare for the next section. If you do, you will be doing participants and yourself a disservice.

Take time to determine how you perceive the group as a whole. Circulate among the participants observing how they work together. Listen to conversations. Who seems to be taking the lead? Who is still reluctant to join in? What strong personalities exist in the group? Who seems to be dominating the discussion?

This time gives you a chance to think ahead to the rest of the design and to be aware of potential difficulties where you may consider changing the process. For example, if you have planned a risky activity and the group appears to be risk-adverse, you may make a mental note about it. It is certainly too early to make the change now, but you may give yourself a personal heads-up that a change may be required.

Obviously, you cannot "see" your participants in a virtual setting, but you can see what they do. For example, if you ask them to write on a whiteboard or engage in any activity, you can tell who participates and who does not.

Make it a practice to use this time to discover as much about the group and individuals as you can.

Establish Ground Rules

Establishing ground rules as a part of your opening shapes the parameters of behavior the participants expect of each other and from the trainer for the session. I generally present the group with a few to get started, or the givens, such as start and end time. (See Chapter 9 for suggested ground-rule categories.) I sometimes make a commitment such as "If we start on time each day (or after each break), I guarantee we will end on time."

Ask, "What ground rules would you like to establish?" Capture the same words that participants have used. You need buy in to the ground rules from everyone, so you may need to modify the list in order to get agreement.

As you facilitate development of the ground rules, be sure to refer to responsibility for them. For example, while establishing ground rules I may make the point that the participants must share in the responsibility of learning, emphasizing my role is to present content and their responsibility is to ask questions if I have not been clear or did not provide enough information.

In a virtual setting, you have ground rules, too, but because your session will most likely not last more than 90 minutes, time allotted to discuss them will be shorter too.

In a physical classroom, post the ground rules in a location where everyone can see them, usually near the front of the training room. This facilitates your ability to reference them if you need to use them to manage disruptions or to use as a reference point to facilitate group dynamics. In your virtual classroom, you can email them prior to the start of the class with other information I like to call "What to Expect." You may also want to post them on the screen prior to the start of the session.

Confront Any Issues

If you know issues exist around the training session, confront them during the opening and plan time to address them. In fact, your icebreaker may incorporate the concerns.

If something is happening in the organization that led to this training session, address it head on. If it is troublesome to participants, allow enough time to discuss. You will find that if you do not address it immediately, participants will not be able to focus on the content you're presenting. And besides, you will most likely address it later anyway.

Establish Your Credibility and Style

Just as you want to know about participants, the participants will be trying to learn something about you, your expectations, your style, and your credibility. You have a number of things to cover in the introduction. How you cover them and in what order will tell the participants as much about your expectations as anything. You will be modeling your style. My preference is to weave them in throughout different parts of the opening.

If participants have not met you before, they will want to know something about you. Begin to share something about yourself during the opening. If you ask participants to divulge something about themselves during an icebreaker, you should divulge the same information. If you ask them to draw a picture that depicts something about them, you should draw a picture, too. This ensures that you share the same information that they do. It also keeps you at a similar level with your participants. Follow Rudyard Kipling's advice: "Don't lose the common touch." Let people know you care about their success and that you're there to guide them; as someone once told me, be a "guide on the side, not a sage on stage." You will be a more successful trainer if you're genuine.

Your expectations for the time together may be covered at the same time that the group establishes its ground rules. Be sure that you build your expectations in as well. For example, if you expect the participants to assist with balancing participation, say so. If you do not, many participants will assume that it is your job to manage all disruptive behaviors. Be sure participants understand your expectations up front.

Your style will come across in the opening — whether you want it to or not. Participants observe how you approach the opening and will make assumptions about your style. Did you take time to listen to participants and clarify what they meant? Did you check your watch?

Some trainers use a bio sketch or have someone else introduce them to establish their credibility. Credibility is a combination of what you know (your expertise), what you have done (your experience), and how you present yourself. Those who present themselves best come across as humbly self-confident. I try to avoid having someone introduce me. If I cannot avoid it, I make sure that it is short and appropriately related to the training I am about to connect. I like to add a personal element or a lighthearted statement that relates to the participants. For example, I may say that I have been conducting training for more years than I want to admit. To establish credibility, I will mention my experience and expertise as introductions to stories. I may say, for example, "One of the things I have learned working in the manufacturing arena for the past 20 years is. . . ." This statement has the same effect as reading it from a resume but is subtler and is positioned where it makes more sense to the participants.

Take a Break!

Yes, take a break. If the opening was an hour in length, take a break. It maintains the energy level, gives participants an opportunity to follow up with other participants, and gives people a chance to take care of personal needs before you begin the content.

Remember, your opening is one of the most important segments of your training session. Be sure it adds PUNCH to the entire design.

Chapter 19

Ten Webinar Warmups

I often ask participants to sign on for virtual training ten minutes early to ensure that they can get a connection. Your participants sign on, their equipment checks as all systems go, they say hi to you, and then what? Most likely learners say to themselves, "Gosh! Ten minutes to get something done! Wow! Let's see what I can do." They look around their desks to find something they can check off their to-do lists. Perhaps they open email (even though you've asked them to close it) and begin to respond to new correspondence. Of course 30 seconds before the class starts they've started a response, are on a roll, and just want to finish it. You start the session with less than everyone's full attention.

What to do? How can you encourage them to continue to sign in early and keep them interested in what's on their screens instead of what's on their desks? And wouldn't it be nice if there was a bonus? How about getting learners involved and participating early? Yes. That'll do it.

The ideas presented in this chapter include ten quick ways to effectively use the ten minutes between sign-in and the actual beginning of a virtual classroom. Some are easy to do; some take a little more preparation. The ideas are meant to entertain, teach, and engage your participants right from the start.

You can certainly have the typical slide up that tells participants what to do while they are waiting to start — for example, give the phone number and code to join the audio portion, ensure they have printed the participant materials, and a number to call if they are having difficulty. But you can certainly get them engaged early by introducing a pre-session warmup.

Use a different warmup for each class. Most of these are quite easy and quick to put together. Soon you will have everyone signing on early just to see what you have created for them each time!

Someone Once Said

Quotation websites are abundant on the Internet. Use one to identify a couple dozen quotes that are related to your topic. Place each quote along with the person who said or wrote it on a separate slide. Add a few graphics, pictures or images, and you have a display that is related to your topic. Display the slides on a continuous loop with appropriate pauses. The slide show should provoke interest and entertain for at least ten minutes.

You can use the quotes to transition into the topic of the virtual session by asking, "Which quote resonates with you as it relates to our topic today?" Don't be surprised if participants ask whether you can make the slide show available to them. I do this in my physical classroom and always receive a request or two.

As an alternative, you could just post one quote and ask participants to post their thoughts in the chat window about the quote and how it relates to the class content.

Test Their Mettle

Create a ten-question quiz that relates to the topic — even vaguely. Pose the questions in a funny, outlandish, or unusual way to get people to break into a smile and stay focused. For example, in a class about strategies to manage globalization, you could pose this true or false statement: "The English invented champagne." Add several more unknown facts, and you have something that will grab their attention.

You can also encourage their creative thinking. You could use brainteasers that may or may not be related to the content. Ask if they can figure them out. For example:

- What do these letters mean? ALPALPALP
- What is unique about these numbers? 8,549,176,320

You can joke later that correct answers are a part of their grade for the class. By the way, the answer to the first question is true. In the sixteenth century, English entrepreneurs imported batches of spoiled wine from the French area of Champagne. As recorded by the British Royal Society in 1662, they added sugar and molasses to ferment and flavor it. And the brainteasers? ALPALPALP means "friends in high places" (a play on the words "pal" and "alp"). The number includes one of each numeral from 1 to 10, placed in alphabetical order.

Chat Away

Post a controversial or debatable statement on the screen. Share how to use the chat feature and invite (via posted directions) participants to respond.

For example, if teaching a teamwork class, you could post a debatable statement such as, "A team needs a strong leader, even if the leader intimidates some team members." Yes, on first read it does seem to be a false statement. Team leaders should not intimidate team members. Yet as wrong as that may sound, there is another side to the statement. Have you ever met someone who was intimidated by everyone? Easily intimidated people need to go halfway and become comfortable with speaking up. The second controversial word in the statement is *strong.* How you define strong depends on your background and experience. Some people see strong as positive; that is, someone who is able to handle any problem with ease or who is strong enough to share the recognition, but accepts most of the responsibility when things go wrong.

Well, this isn't about learning team dynamics, but the example should get you to think of others like it that are related to your subjects and areas of expertise. Again, you can refer back to this exercise at the appropriate time during your session.

Expect Expectations

Ask participants to address one of the topics that is usually covered in the opening of any classroom:

✔ What ground rules do you suggest for our team?

✔ What are your expectations and hopes for this class?

✔ What do you want to know about the other participants?

✔ What questions about the content do you have?

Tell participants to capture their ideas in the chat feature. Open the session by referencing several of the comments and sharing your own input. You could also have participants list their ideas on the whiteboard. Later, you can toggle back to the whiteboard to remind participants of the question and their responses.

At the Movies

Create a couple of short video clips related to the topic of the session and play them on a continuous loop. Ideally they are clips that you can reference during your presentation. Time permitting, you could also video several leaders in your organization who discuss the value of the learning to the organization.

No time to record a video of your own? Post a website URL on the screen that directs participants to use their smartphones or tablets to view a video on the Internet, such as something from TED Talks or other similar sites.

Going Live

There are many reasons why you may not choose to use the webcam during your virtual session, but you may want to consider it during the warmup. As each person logs in, greet them and if possible add a comment about them that is complimentary or informative to the rest of the group. Typically, virtual trainers post their pictures on an opening slide, which is fine. Surprise your participants with a live greeting for a change.

Vote Early, Vote Often

Pose a poll question and ask participants to respond to it. It could be something that asks participants to rate their level of knowledge on a continuum. You could add some humor such as:

1. I'm a star, I know it all.
2. I'm pretty darn average.
3. Wait, what topic? What class is this?

You could also present a poll that asks about participants' opinions of the session or rates how much they think it is needed. When you reach the appropriate place in the session, post the results of the poll and open the discussion for comments.

Show Me the Picture

If your group will meet several times, it is worth it to ask them to send you a picture of themselves (maybe encourage them to send something "in action" or "at work"). Post it with a couple of fun facts about each person. For example, "This is Georgianna, who has worked at the company for six years; she likes to play guitar and read science fiction."

Post the information on slides and use the continuous loop feature.

How Was the Homework?

Most of your virtual classes will have some sort of prework. Invite participants to comment either verbally or in the chat window about the homework. If you do this verbally (or any of these pre-session warmups), be prepared to help them bring closure before the session actually starts. Perhaps you will need to say something like, "Let's hear one last comment before we start our session."

Annotate It

Encourage participants to use the whiteboard and annotation tools to respond in a variety of ways. These suggestions will get you started:

- Post a graphic of a map (the world or country) and have participants annotate where they are located.

- Draw a standard 2 by 2 grid and have participants complete the information requested. For example, if you are following up with a communication styles workshop such as DiSC, ask them to add their name to the quadrant that matches their style.

- Post a timeline and have participants place their name on the line indicating how much experience they have — for example, "How many years have you been a supervisor?"

- Post a picture or a cartoon character in each quadrant and ask participants to place an X in the quadrant that best represents them and their relationship to the topic. For example, in a time-management workshop, you could have pictures of a beaver, rabbit, rhinoceros, and a hamster on a wheel. Ask which animal best represents time management for you. If participants have been together in the past and it would not seem too risky, you could ask them to sign their name in the corresponding quadrant.

Chapter 20

Ten Ways to Save Time While Training

In This Chapter

▶ Identifying ways to save time while encouraging participation

▶ Identifying ways to catch up if you have fallen behind schedule

▶ Determining how to save time without diminishing learning

A s a trainer you will want to keep everything moving along in your session. You recognize the importance of maximizing participation yet are concerned about how much time you have available. This is particularly true in a virtual setting. At times you may need to address issues that your learners are focused on before you move forward with the designed learning experience.

✔ How do you save time while increasing participation?

✔ How do you save time without diminishing any learning experiences?

✔ How do you catch up if you have fallen behind schedule?

Consider the Relationship of Time to Small Groups

If you need to save time during the small group exercise, form more groups with fewer people. A smaller group will accomplish the task faster than a large group. If you need to save time during the report-out stage, form fewer groups with more people. You will have fewer reports to hear.

You could also have groups report just one item at a time in a round-robin fashion. You save time because duplicate ideas are not reported. This works also in your virtual classroom.

Groups may be able to summarize their ideas on flipchart pages posted around the room, or in virtual classrooms, on whiteboards for observation. All ideas can be viewed and discussed by the large group. Depending on the activity, each group could select the one or two best ideas to report on. All ideas on flipcharts are viewed as participants leave for or return from break. In a virtual setting, ideas can be compiled and emailed as a reminder after the session.

One Activity, Two (Or More) Objectives

Time. There is never enough of it. Therefore, way back in the beginning of your training cycle begin to think about how you can save time in the design. One of the obvious ones is to use one activity to achieve two or more objectives. For example, participants may be practicing the skills used to conduct performance evaluations. Observers could be taking notes about how well the process was demonstrated. They could also be observing how nonverbal communication affected the skill practice. The next module may be about communication. Later in the day when you want to discuss feedback, you could ask the folks who received feedback from their observers, "What worked; what didn't?" One activity, three different skills.

You may also save time by using "work" that participants need to complete back on the job. When I work with teams, I use real-life projects that they need to accomplish as the basis for creating experiences in which they can evaluate their effectiveness as a team. In your design consider whether participants could bring projects with them to complete as a part of an activity.

Gentle Prods

When you establish small groups to complete a task or activity, always assign a specific amount of time to complete the task. But no matter what the setting — virtual or physical — people lose track of time. The task needs to be completed in order for the learning to occur. First, be sure that you have designed the appropriate amount of time to complete the task. If you're sure of that, you may do two things to help groups stay on time.

First, you could ask them to select a timekeeper within their groups to manage time.

Second, you may wish to give them time cues throughout the task. Examples may include these:

- ✔ "You should have started the second step."
- ✔ "You should be halfway through the task."

✔ "How much time do you need to finish?"

✔ "The second person in your group should be providing feedback."

✔ "You have about five minutes to go."

✔ "You should be wrapping up."

✔ "Sixty seconds left."

These gentle prods keep the groups moving and on time.

Different Pace for Different Folks

Always plan a reasonable amount of time in a training design so that it can be completed. However, in real life, some participants simply take more time to complete individual projects than others. If you have a design element where you expect that to occur — for example, completing a self-assessment or quiz — schedule it just prior to a break.

Those who finish early can leave and those who take longer have control over whether they would like to continue at the same pace or try to wrap up more quickly. Those who use most of the break time to complete the task may return late to the session. Again, that is a decision they make, and you should not delay the start if they are still out of the room.

Don't forget to also use the gentle prods throughout the activity to keep them informed of how much time is available.

Divvy Up the Work

All work doesn't need to be completed by all people. If a small-group activity is not dependent upon a specific sequence, assign different groups to complete different parts of the activity. For example, if I have given a group a worksheet that has a list of concepts or components, I will ask some of the small groups to start at the top and work down and some of the groups to start at the bottom and work up. Sometimes, just for fun, I ask one of the groups to start in the middle and go either way. This works well in any classroom setting.

All of the concepts or components are addressed by one group or another. Learning is not lost because everyone becomes familiar with all of the components of the activity during the debriefing. During the debriefing I encourage all groups to take notes about what the other groups have produced.

In a virtual classroom, divide a large group of participants into smaller groups when posing a question for the chat box. "If your last name begins A–H, type in the chat box." Keep your responses short. Engage the other participants by asking them to read the responses and choose the most creative, most practical, or some other descriptor.

The Time Is Now

Time cannot be bottled to save for the future, so use it well. You cannot save time. Don't waste it. Use your time resource wisely.

- ✓ Start the session on time.
- ✓ Start on time after every break.
- ✓ Distribute materials and handouts efficiently. If participants are sitting in a U shape, start stacks at both ends and in the back middle. If participants are at separate tables, place the right number of materials for each table in stacks prior to the start of the session or at breaks.
- ✓ Watch carefully the time you spend in large-group discussion. Time can run away from you here. Establish time limits for discussions that are either scheduled or unscheduled.
- ✓ You do not need to hear from every person every time. If you skip a group or individual, catch them on the next question.
- ✓ In a virtual classroom, the big time waster can be in the opening: too much time spent on introductions, logistics, or how to use the tools. No one is suggesting that these are not important, but consider a more efficient way to do it. Can you address all of these before the session begins? Can you contact participants the week before the session to share some of this information? Can you post a video on YouTube about these things and have participants watch it before the session? Heck, you could have participants record 30-second introductions of themselves prior to the session and post them to a group site so others can watch them before starting.

Be Prepared

Examine your behaviors to ensure that you're as well prepared as possible and that you're not the cause for falling behind. This is important for physical classroom, but critical for virtual classrooms. Virtual classrooms aren't nearly as forgiving when something goes wrong.

Preparing for a virtual classroom:

✔ Think contingency planning and have it worked out with your producer. For example, have two computers, one as your main terminal and the other to log in as a participant. Have a plan, in the unlikely event that you lose connectivity, for when you might need to reschedule the training. Have a backup script and your presentation on a memory stick.

✔ Be sure that everything is charged to the maximum degree. Of course, you will probably not need it, but if you do the power supply is available to you.

✔ Do several dry runs to ensure that everything works as it is supposed to. Practice with your producer and if you have a host or co-trainer, practice with them too. Know what everyone will do when.

✔ Finally, it is somewhat acceptable for classroom trainers to stumble over their words; they can recover with a joke or a gesture or a laugh. Stumbling over your words in a virtual setting only comes across as if you are not prepared.

Preparing for a physical classroom:

✔ Provide clear, concise, complete directions. You may be held up by a group that hasn't finished because they did not understand the instructions. If the instructions are complex, put them in writing.

✔ Prepare your flipcharts and other visuals before the session begins.

✔ Be sure you know the objective of the discussion. When the point is made, move on. Don't let discussions drag on.

✔ Test new activities with colleagues to estimate the timing.

✔ If you don't want participants to worry when you're behind, put only general times on their agendas; for example, break the agenda up based on morning and afternoon.

✔ Provide examples that will give small-group discussions a jump-start.

Cut Out the Fat

Examine the training. Understand the objectives and your audience well enough so that you know what information is "must know" and what information is "nice to know." Then be prepared to cut out anything that is "nice to know" when you're short of time. I usually identify the least important activity in each module so that I can set priorities as I go along.

Do job aids exist for some of the content? If yes, you probably can cut some time out in that area by providing the information once and then referring to the job aid for future use.

Often, training materials have lists of things to do or remember. When I get to a page of lists, I ask participants to grab a marker or pen and highlight or circle the ones that I think are essential for them to remember. This provides a quick way to address the list in a time-efficient way.

 When prioritizing what to keep, remember to keep anything that will help them learn more after the session or help them find information later. No one remembers everything they learn in a training session. However, if they know how to find the information later, you will have done your job.

Use Timekeepers

You may wish to act as a timekeeper yourself. Or assign timekeepers to small groups to ensure that the groups finish their tasks on time.

In a face-to-face classroom you can use timekeepers during breaks. Ask for a volunteer who will round up people who have not returned from break. You can offer incentives to those who return from break early or on time. Sometimes, just closing the door to the training room signals those who have lost track of time that the session is ready to start again.

Pre-Training Strategies

Face-to-face time in the training room is getting shorter and shorter. Therefore, you may wish to consider how you can use time before the training begins. You could, for example, assign pre-reading, videos, or exercises to the participants. All these are expected practices in virtual sessions.

Pay close attention to the training assessment to identify skill level, experience, and special needs. Doing so ensures that you're prepared for the variation within the group.

Add techniques to support the training. You may need to develop checklists, job aids, email tips, brownbag sessions, mentors, user support groups, or plan to introduce a buddy system during the training.

Chapter 21

Ten Icebreakers That Work

The room is set. Participant materials are in place. The projector with your PowerPoint presentation is focused, and the participants have arrived. It's time to begin your training session, and first impressions will set the stage for the rest of the time together.

Chapter 18 introduces you to a number of elements that should be included in your opening. One of those is to help everyone get to know each other better. That is the key purpose of icebreakers.

I am convinced that training sessions are better when they start out with an icebreaker. Whether you use icebreakers created by someone else or you design your own, I suggest that you pay attention to some advice based on lessons I learned the hard way.

> ✔ **Never ask anyone to do anything you would not want to do.** This is cardinal rule number one. Isn't it amazing that participants will almost always follow a trainer's direction and do what they are asked to do? They believe that trainers always know what they're doing and that the things a trainer asks them to do will further their learning. If you hesitate for even a moment about conducting a particular icebreaker, don't use it. Your hesitation is a sign that it may not feel good to other participants as well. Participants trust trainers and trust that what we ask them to do is in their best interest. Don't break that trust.
>
> I was once a participant in a training session in which the trainer asked us to get down on our hands and knees, make animal sounds, and find others who were imitating the same animals. As I was on the floor growling like a lion, I spotted the trainer laughing away. I felt duped and had much less respect for that trainer from that point on. Lesson learned? Be careful what you ask participants to do; it should maintain their self-esteem, build trust, and enhance what they are learning.

✔ **Select icebreakers based on the type of group you're training.** The participants who attend your training should help guide your decision. Executives will respond differently than manufacturing employees, and employees in sales will react differently than those in engineering. Ask yourself a few questions about the participants to assist with your choice.

At what level are they in the organization? What jobs do they have? What is their cultural background? What is the age range? What gender? What educational level are they? What expectations will the participants have? What past training experiences have they had? Early in my career I did not take the time to ask these questions. I was asked to provide communications training to a group of engineers. Although I customized the training for the engineers, I used the same icebreaker that I had developed for a communication module for a sales staff. It fell flat. The analytical engineers were the exact opposites from the gregarious sales folks. Lesson learned? Know your audience.

Know whether everyone in your virtual training knows what an icebreaker is. Either define it for them or don't even use the terminology with something like, "We're starting out with an activity that will introduce our topic and help us meet other participants at the same time."

✔ **Relate the icebreaker to the content.** I have always believed that icebreakers should relate to content so that they serve as the introduction to the topic. Today there is a more practical reason for relating the icebreaker to the content: time. In almost all organizations there seems to be more to do with less time to do it. Participants are busy, and it is a good possibility that the organization has asked trainers to squeeze more content into shorter sessions.

This means that it is wise to make every minute of your training session count. For example, if you're conducting a diversity session, select an icebreaker that spotlights differences. If you're conducting a team-building session, select an icebreaker that addresses individual team skills or characteristics. When I relate the icebreaker to the content, the flow of the session is natural. However, when I don't, I create a problem for myself because I must force a connection. Lesson learned? Make every minute in your training sessions count, starting immediately with a related icebreaker.

✔ **Use icebreakers to set the tone and to demonstrate the level of participation you expect.** The icebreaker can set the stage for how much involvement you expect of the participants. If you want them to interact with each other, you can select an icebreaker that gets them out of their seats and moving around meeting as many people as they can. In fact, the number of people participants meet during the icebreaker can be a part of the challenge. If you want participants to work in teams, you may design an icebreaker that encourages teamwork.

I remember using an icebreaker that was so funny it was difficult for any of us to stop laughing. Unfortunately, the topic was a serious one, and it was a challenge to make the switch for both me and the participants. Lesson learned? Select an icebreaker that sets the tone for the environment you're trying to create.

✔ **Observe the group during the icebreaker to learn something about the group and the individuals.** Icebreakers provide trainers with a perfect opportunity to learn about the group as well as individuals. In some cases the group will be outgoing and fun loving. In other cases the group may be defensive and negative. Trainers can observe individuals in the group to determine who seem to be the natural leaders, who has a tendency to dominate, or who is competitive.

At times I have gotten so involved in the icebreaker that I did not take advantage of this opportunity to learn more about the participants in the session. Later when I have had a problem behavior in the training session, I question whether I would have been able to head off the problem earlier if I had given more attention to the right things during the icebreaker. Lesson learned? Attend to the personalities during the icebreaker — the individual participant personalities, as well as the group's personality.

✔ **Watch the time during an icebreaker.** You will have determined how much time you will spend conducting an icebreaker. However, if you have selected an energizing icebreaker, it is easy for time to get away from you in a couple different ways.

First, if you have individual report-outs (as some of the icebreakers in this chapter call for), set a limit on the amount of time allowed for each. If a participant takes too much time, intervene tactfully to get the group back on track. If you have 20 participants and each report-out takes just 2 minutes more than you planned, you will be 40 minutes behind schedule before you have even completed the introduction! Individual report-outs in groups over 25 become tedious and boring. Try another format, for example, individual introductions, but reports by small group. Or you could have the individual report-outs occur in subgroups.

Just recently I had a time problem in a group of 18 in a training certificate program. The final step of the icebreaker involved participants introducing themselves: name, city they lived in, how long in the job, and the slogan that defined them. The first person stood and provided at least 25 percent of his life story. I did not (though I knew I should have) cut him off. His one-minute introduction lasted at least five minutes. Unfortunately, everyone else in the group expanded their introduction to be in line with the first person. At the end of the icebreaker, we were almost an hour behind schedule. Lesson learned? Time can evaporate during an icebreaker. Watch your time carefully.

Remember, an icebreaker's success depends on the trainer in two ways: ensuring that you have established a comfortable climate and that you have selected the right icebreaker. You must be able to quickly establish a climate that gives participants permission to step outside their comfort zone. When you announce that time has been set aside for participants to meet each other, you may look about and see some rolled eyes or hear some groans. That means that a couple of participants would rather sit in their chairs than go out to meet others. Use a tone right from the start to establish a climate that ensures people feel comfortable: a pleasant voice, a friendly smile, welcoming gestures, appropriate eye contact, and short, clear instructions all tell your participants that it is okay to play.

Finally, heed my advice throughout this chapter. It is based on the lessons I've learned over the years. Ask yourself these questions about the icebreaker you intend to use.

- ✔ Did you select one that is appropriate for the participants?
- ✔ Does the icebreaker allow you to establish a climate that gives participants permission to follow your lead?
- ✔ Have you simplified the directions so that everyone will experience success?

If you can answer yes to all of these questions, your icebreaker will achieve the objectives you desire.

Good luck with your icebreakers. May they warm your training sessions immeasurably!

Avoid using the word "icebreaker" when introducing the exercise. Even though that's what it is, remember that the word itself is trainer jargon that may not be understood by everyone. Even more important, however, is that you will appear more professional if you smoothly introduce what you want participants to do and why you want them to do it without labeling it as an icebreaker, an exercise, an activity, or any other "thing" you want them to do. You can say something like, "During the training session, we will be working together and tapping into the expertise in this room. Therefore, it is important that we find out who else is here and what experiences they bring with them."

Bingo

Bingo is probably the most-used icebreaker of all the icebreakers. And the reason is, is that it works. It has been around forever, and I do not know where it originated. Reproduce a Bingo card on a sheet of paper. Instead of having

B-3 or N-13, each square has information written. The information can be so specific that it matches individuals in the group, such as "drives a red Corvette" and "played a saxophone with Kenny G." The information can also be general so that it could match any number of people, such as "likes to drive fast" and "plays a musical instrument." Figure 21-1 provides an example of a Bingo card.

Participants move around the room and find a match to each of the criteria. In the first example they would be looking for a specific person. In the second, several people may match the criteria. Individuals sign the appropriate square that matches their descriptions. It is a great way to meet and greet and learn something about others in the session to encourage additional discussion at the next break.

You can easily tie these questions to the content, if you want. For example, if you're conducting a stress-management class, you could include squares that say "attends yoga classes," "goes for a walk at lunch," or "has used visualization successfully." If you are doing this in a virtual classroom, create a group Bingo card, post it, and have participants annotate their name on a corresponding square.

Drives a sports car	Exercises regularly	Voted in the last election	Has attended a training for trainers	Has season tickets
Plays a musical instrument	Plays poker	Has run a marathon	Likes to ride horses	Enjoys working with wood
Teaches computer classes	Is a gourmet cook	Likes to eat spinach	Has owned a surfboard	Plays golf
Likes to fly	Plays tennis	Collects something	Plays bridge	Painted a house
Has written a book	Is a closet poet	Has a pet	Is counting carbs	Has a garden

Figure 21-1: Bingo icebreaker.

© John Wiley & Sons, Inc.

Expectations

If Bingo is the most used icebreaker, Expectations may very well run a close second. I learned this one from Ed Scannell and John Newstrom, authors of the wildly successful, very useful, and creative *Games Trainers Play* series. Buy any of them; you won't be disappointed.

In Expectations, participants identify what they really want to learn in the training session to make the day (workshop, training, week) valuable and useful to them. After you tell them what the objectives are for the session, have them form groups of two to four. Give the groups five minutes to list two or three on a sheet of paper. As a trainer, you're trying to tap into their initial thoughts. If you allow more than five minutes, they will begin to go beyond the scope of the training. Also as a trainer you need to be prepared to adjust your training session to accommodate those that you can. You may be surprised that most of the participants' expectations will be covered. This works equally well in a virtual classroom.

Hopes and Fears

The Expectations icebreaker taps into the cerebral desires that the participants bring with them to the training session. Hopes and Fears taps into the participants' feelings about the training.

Provide a handout to participants that provides space for them to list their hopes and fears as they relate to the training session. Tell them that whenever people find themselves in a new situation, it is natural to begin thinking about the things they hope will happen and the things they hope will not happen. This exercise is an opportunity to find out how similar everyone is. Allow about three to four minutes for them to complete the handout.

Have participants pair up with someone they do not know or do not know well to discuss their lists. Conduct a round robin obtaining one item from each column from the pairs. You may want to post them on a flipchart. Discuss the items, informing them of the hopes that will occur or what you may be able to do about those hopes that are not planned into the session. Also, reassure them of the fears that are unfounded or quelling fears that are not really going to be as bad as they anticipate. For example, if participants in a speaking class will be videotaped and that is a fear that arises, you can discuss the benefits of the videotaping and let them know that no one will watch it except them (if that is true.) In a virtual setting, have participants respond in the chat box.

Post the flipchart pages on the walls during the first break.

Introduce Me, I Introduce You

It is sometimes easier to introduce others than it is to introduce yourself. In this icebreaker, pair participants up and have each interview the other to learn enough about the person to introduce to the larger group. You may want to suggest the information you would like them to obtain, for example, their names, how long they have worked for the organization, where they attended school, something interesting about them that may be just a little different from anyone else in the room, or what they are hoping to improve as a result of this training session. In a virtual setting, I ask participants to complete this activity prior to the class. It accomplishes two things: First, it saves classroom time. Second, every participant builds one strong bond with at least one other person in the session.

Provide paper for participants to conduct their interviews. After five to ten minutes for the interviews, have participants begin to introduce each other. In an exercise like this, I generally ask for a volunteer to go first as opposed to assigning someone to start. Some people prefer to have a model.

Go to Your Corners

This is another icebreaker that has been around a long time. It is used for discovering participants' common interests. Place four flipcharts in the four corners of the room. On the first page of each write four words or phrases. They should be topics that would generate curiosity and/or tap into the interests of the group. You may use travel, reading, running, and gourmet cooking. Ask participants to choose one. After they select a corner, have them discuss why they chose that corner.

Have someone turn the first page on each chart to reveal the second round. These four pages could include something about the current events of the day. Again, have participants read the charts and select a new corner. Repeat the process.

I generally have the third and fourth pages relate to the content of the session. The third round may focus on needs the participants have and can be stated as "I hope we learn to . . ." followed by four things participants may want to learn. Conduct a short debriefing, asking someone in the group to summarize why they made that choice.

The fourth round can again relate to the content. You may use "I feel good about . . ." or "I think I am pretty good at. . . ." These show the rest of the participants where the experts are in the group.

This activity works equally well for a virtual setting if your platform has multiple whiteboards. It does take quite a bit of time.

This icebreaker can also be used as an energizer if the pace bogs down, such as after lunch in a warm training room. When used as an energizer, identify content items that participants can review in the four small groups.

Little White Lie

Allow participants a couple of minutes to think about this before putting them into groups of three. In the small groups each person makes three statements about themselves: Two are truthful, and one is a lie. For example, my statement may be: I love to drive on icy roads; my hobby is gardening; and I think sleep is a waste of time and do not sleep at least one night each week. The other two individuals guess which one is the lie. After a few minutes the trios introduce themselves, playing off what happened in the activity.

I use this icebreaker to introduce a communication-styles workshop. The relationship is that if you know something about people's styles, you will be able to tell something about their preferences.

Personal Coat of Arms

Creating a Coat of Arms is an icebreaker that is a true classic. Although it has been around for many years, it is just as effective as the first time it was used. Creating a Personal Coat of Arms is more serious than most other icebreakers. In it the trainer asks participants to draw a coat of arms that represents who they are. Participants may want to use words or draw symbols or pictures.

You may want to distribute a shield-like sketch that is divided into four quadrants. Have participants address a different item in each of the four quadrants. For example, participants may identify themselves on their Coat of Arms by answering who they are: at work, at home, at play, and in the future. The Coat of Arms could also display something about what they like to do: at work, at home, at play, in the community. You may request four specific aspects or you may ask for something more generic: "Draw a coat of arms that tells us who you are."

In this icebreaker, it is a good idea to draw your own Coat of Arms and display and explain it to the group. I may share one that looks something like Figure 21-2. I would tell participants that I am a positive person who loves to write. I live on the water and am learning to play tennis.

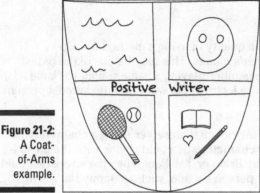

Figure 21-2:
A Coat-
of-Arms
example.

You can do many things with this icebreaker, including relating it to the content or focusing all of the quadrants in the future instead of the present and/or the past.

Autographs

Autographs is one of the most practical icebreakers. It is straightforward and serves as a perfect bridge from introductions to content. You can easily design your own Autographs to match the content in the training program you're designing. I first heard of this icebreaker from Michele Wyman, a colleague and trainer. The goal of this icebreaker is for each participant to meet many participants by obtaining as many autographs as possible.

To customize Autographs for your use, create a handout that lists 15 to 25 questions or statements that can be "autographed" by participants who match the description. Provide a combination of personal statements and content-related statements. Personal statements may include "Has been to Europe" or "Has performed on stage." Content-related statements will match the training topic. A communications training session may include statements such as "Have been told I am a good listener" or "Spends at least 50 percent of on-the-job time communicating."

After brief hello-my-name-is introductions, distribute the handout that you created. Tell participants that they will walk around and meet others in the session. When they meet a participant who matches one of the descriptions, he or she will sign the sheet. To encourage participants to meet as many people as possible, they must have a different autograph after each statement.

Name Association

Name Association has the unique quality of using a method to help participants remember each other's names. This may be one of the oldest icebreakers ever developed. I remember playing a game similar to Name Association — and that was before icebreakers were even invented! I present two alternatives here.

The first is to have participants introduce themselves using a characteristic that helps to identify them. The characteristic could rhyme with the participant's name, such as Lorraine the Brain or Tall Paul. The characteristic could start with the same letter as the person's name, such as Happy Harvey or Timely Terry.

The second association can be related to an imaginary event. Participants introduce themselves and identify something they will contribute to the event that rhymes with their names. For example, if the event is a party, participants may introduce themselves like this:

- ✔ "My name is Ned, and I'll bring the bread."
- ✔ "My name is Mark, and I'll ensure a spark."
- ✔ "My name is Linda, and I'll bring the Splenda."
- ✔ "My name is Maggie, and I'll bring the baggies."

Note that the names do not need to rhyme perfectly and the items don't even need to make much sense. The real reason for using a Name Association icebreaker is to help participants remember the names of the others in the session.

Ask a Question

There may be times when you're looking for something quick and easy. Perhaps you do not have much time up front, but you still want everyone to know something about each other. If the session is only a couple of hours long, you have only a few minutes for an icebreaker. And if you plan for interaction among participants, you may actually save time by conducting a quick icebreaker up front that allows participants to meet each other.

There may be other times when your participants all work together and know each other, and you may want to get them to a similar level of knowledge or take them to a personal level of knowing each other. In these situations you may decide to ask a question of participants. Again, remember you can use this technique and relate it to the content as described in the introduction to this chapter. However, if you're simply looking for a question to ensure that everyone knows something new about the rest of the participants, these questions have worked well for me over the years.

- What do you like to do for fun?
- If you could be any animal, what would it be and why?
- Can you describe your dream vacation?
- What do you like best about where you live?
- What would you do if you suddenly became a multimillionaire by winning the lottery?
- What was the last book you read, and would you recommend it to the rest of us?
- If you could have a party and invite any three people of your choosing, alive or deceased, whom would you invite?
- What historical person could teach you something, and what would they teach you?
- How do you like to spend your Saturdays?
- If you could change the world, what would you do?
- What do you believe was the turning point in your life?
- What opportunity did you miss, and how would it have changed your life today?
- What fictional character do you relate to most? Why?
- Whom do you most admire, and why?
- What's the most unusual thing that has ever happened to you?
- How do you like to celebrate success?
- What do you have in your billfold, pocket, or purse that none of us would expect to find there and why?
- If you were wearing a T-shirt that displayed your life slogan, what would the words on the T-shirt say?
- What is one interesting fact about you that most of the group would not know?
- What is your all-time favorite movie and why?

This is just a small sample of questions you could use. Perhaps this list will start you thinking of others. (I try to tie even these questions to the content, if at all possible.) These questions can be used at other times during a training session. For example, if you need a quick energizer right after lunch, try one of these.

Which icebreaker to use? The decision is up to you. Consider the time you have available, who's in your audience, the content of the training, what you want to accomplish, the location where the training will occur, and what you feel comfortable doing.

What should you accomplish with an icebreaker? There are many things to consider, but I try to accomplish the following as a minimum.

- ✔ Grab participants' attention
- ✔ Establish a participative climate in which everyone is involved
- ✔ Set the pace for the rest of the training session
- ✔ Put people at ease, and this includes me, the trainer
- ✔ Initiate personal interaction between the participants
- ✔ Complete introductions of all participants that goes beyond just their names and where they work
- ✔ Ensure that everyone speaks at least once in the large group
- ✔ Observe the group to define its personality
- ✔ Identify the individual personalities in the group
- ✔ Share enough information so that everyone learns something about the other participants
- ✔ Establish a starting point for or a transition to the content

Create your own list of what you want to accomplish with the icebreakers you conduct.

Chapter 22

Ten Guidelines for M-Learning Success

▶ Reviewing essentials you need to consider to design and deliver m-learning

▶ Discovering ideas to ensure m-learning is useful for your employees

*L*earning in the palm of your hand. What a learning dream! It doesn't get any better than that. M-learning, short for *mobile learning,* refers to content that can be accessed on smartphones, tablets, cellphones, and some wearables. M-learning is most beneficial when you combine a small but critical (because there is either a time or importance requirement) data point with the ability to improve a skill. M-learning also gives you the ability to connect on-the-fly with your learners. This is exciting in our world. This future-leaning opportunity accomplishes several things:

✔ It allows you, the trainer, to provide updates, changes, or new information.

✔ It offers you a chance to deliver small capsules of information, just-in-time and just when the learner needs it.

✔ It provides learners with content on the run and when they need it.

✔ It allows learners to provide you with an update when necessary or if something has changed.

✔ It keeps the relationship between the trainer and the learner active.

Even though m-learning has been a fantasy for trainers for a long time, it was slower to move forward than anticipated. Much of the delay was around "bring your own device," or BYOD for short. The question was how to create learning modules that would be compatible with everyone's device (e-reader, smartphone, netbook, or tablet). That problem has been resolved in most cases. Even so, you should not consider mobile learning as a replacement for classroom training or even for e-learning; it should be a complement to other training formats.

Smartphones are used for many things. In fact, you can do almost everything on your smartphone. You can take videos. You can use it as a level to hang a picture straight. You can use it as a flashlight to light your way in the dark. Why not use it for learning? Some forward-thinking trainers already use smartphones to support learning. They ask learners to play YouTube videos on their smartphone in the classroom and beyond the classroom. They follow up using messages on Twitter. They email just-in-time micro hints when they know the learners really need the information. Job aids can be stored on some devices as quick reminders or checklists to help learners through processes or tasks that are new or not used often.

Be clear that most organizations using m-learning solutions use them as just one part of their entire learning strategy. M-learning is one more tool available to you. One of the best reasons to choose m-learning solutions is the need to deliver content just-in-time or on demand at the place of application. Several professionals, such as sales and service people who spend much of their time in the field or learning professionals — like you — who may travel to other sites, can remain connected to information no matter where they are.

M-learning usually refers to two different ways that mobile devices may be used: training or performance support. Training is formal content that enables users to learn something new they did not already know. Performance support, on the other hand is more like a job aid — informal learning that supports users when they are trying to apply or remember something.

Our learners work on planes, at home, in coffee shops, and at their customers' locations. They work early in the morning, during lunch, and late at night, interacting with people all over the world in every time zone. They need tools at their fingertips to communicate, analyze, and continue to learn. M-learning can be the answer.

Be careful, though. M-learning is not e-learning on a miniature screen. As a trainer, you need to focus on how an effective learning "module" will appear on a mobile device. There are other considerations as well. The user, the purpose, and the environment are different. This means there are some guidelines to remember about the content:

- It should be concise — probably less than five minutes long.
- It should be something that may encourage a response from the learner.
- It should be straightforward and easy to understand because the user will not likely be in a distraction-free environment.
- Ideally it should offer support or knowledge required just-in-time, like an updated policy, a job aid, tips, recent information, or a short communication skill.

So, welcome this tool that you have in your hands — perhaps even as you are reading this sentence. Then heed the advice about how to design learning for it. M-learning is exciting, that's for sure. According to Clark Quinn, author of Desgining mLearning (Pfeiffer, 2011), "Ultimately the 'm' will disappear; learning will be ubiquitous and seamless, taking advantage of where we are and what digital technology is at hand to leverage our actions, add unique value to what we are doing, make us more effective in the moment, and develop us over time. There is, or will be, an app for that, and you should be preparing to capitalize on the opportunity." Are you ready?

Does the Rationale Fit?

Before jumping into the exciting world of mobile, consider whether it is a fit for your organization. First and most important, does your organization allow mobile devices on site? There are still a few organizations that prohibit part or all of their workforce from having mobile devices in the workplace. The reasons could be safety, security, or propriety information. Even if your organization does not prohibit mobile devices, are they ready for m-learning? Consider when and how this solution fits your learners' needs. Use these questions to explore whether the rationale is a good fit for your organization:

- How does a mobile solution meet your organization's goals?
- How would m-learning enhance or expand the options within your other learning opportunities?
- Under what circumstances would mobile learning be the best delivery?
- When would your learners use m-learning most often? Under what circumstances? Why?
- What benefits will the organization derive from an m-learning effort?

Think Small

Consider how much screen space you have and how much information you need to include. Also consider how you can make the application easy to read. If your learners are familiar with designs from other apps, it could be wise to use the same ones. To ensure readability. imagine the smallest device that will be used for the content, such as a smartphone, and design for it. When the content is transferred to a larger device, such as a tablet, the content will still look good. Think in terms of small bursts of information.

Think small as you decide what is included: bulleted lists and highlighting can mean fewer words. Use white space to draw attention as well. In mobile, less is more.

Think Concise

Not only must you think small, but you also must think concise. What's the difference? If you design for a laptop, you probably consider adding everything the learner might need to know. That requires them to page through content to find what they need. A laptop makes it easy to have several documents open or to scroll through a couple of folders. That is not practical on a mobile device, so you need to determine the most concise content that is important to learners at that very moment in time.

Content should be delivered in five-minute or shorter time spans. M-learning is not repurposed e-learning. It must be redesigned. Only include what is absolutely necessary. If you have been asked to repurpose e-learning content, start by creating an outline that will include everything you would like to include in the m-learning content. Then start cutting. Only include what is absolutely necessary.

Mobile learners expect to acquire information quickly and easily, so break the content into small bites that can be digested rapidly. You will hear people talk about *chunking* the content, which means breaking larger modules into bite-size chunks that learners can easily and quickly digest. Your learners want convenience — chunks they can readily find.

Plan for Diversions

Yep! It's going to happen. Your learners will be looking for information between sales calls walking down a street or in the middle of a service call with clients looking over their shoulders. Plan for diversions in the environment. Content should be straightforward and easy to understand because the user will not likely be in a distraction-free environment when reviewing the content. If you integrate multimedia elements, build in the ability to adjust the volume and pause the presentation. Consider adding subtitles in your videos.

Think about safety as well. When and where do you think your learners will access the m-learning content or use the solution? Will the environment be noisy? Will learners be safe wearing earbuds? Document any impediments you anticipate and consider how you can address each.

Create Just-in-Time

Most likely, mobile devices are with your learners almost 100 percent of the time. That can be a huge benefit. It means you can provide content and solutions anytime and anywhere. Ideally, m-learning offers performance support or knowledge required just-in-time, like an updated policy, a job aid, or a short communication skill.

From your learners' perspective, m-learning gives control over when they choose to learn. They can take advantage of downtime. They can tap into the content at the exact point in time when they need it. They can use it on the spot to troubleshoot and generate solutions.

Expect the Unexpected

Need we say it? There may be some technical challenges, things you may never have anticipated. You may also encounter unexpected resistance in your organization.

Your mobile learners are often on a poor 3G connection or worse. Graphics can be slow to load. You need to consider whether even your organization's logo might affect speed.

 Ensure that your content is accessible when technology changes. To do this, use standard file formats that will probably withstand the test of time. Some of these include MP3 for podcasts, MP4 for videos, ePub for e-books, HTML for text and images, and PDF for references or job aids.

You need to ensure that your content can be accessed on all devices. You may need to adjust the setting so that the graphics or other elements are automatically resized to fit the screen. Find a development tool that can support what you need. Ask colleagues and others about their favorite development tool. Finding the one that works best for you is important. For example, gomo by Epic Learning allows you to create a multi-device learning file. It configures the information for all devices, ensuring that the design has the desired aesthetic appeal and that all the text can be viewed.

Extend Learning

Most of us have experienced our organization's requirement to shorten classes. How can we possibly be expected to impart all the content in half the time? You probably had to eliminate some excellent activities that would have given learners an opportunity to practice, discuss, and reflect on the skills and how they would use them on the job. Mobile to the rescue.

You can extend the learning experience in both directions. First of all, you can use pre-assessments to gather learner data. You can assess their knowledge and find out what they think they need in order to perform up to expectations on the job.

You can extend the learning after the class also — whether the class was virtual or face-to-face. By blending a mobile solution with your class, you can ensure that participants learn all they need. After the class, send questions or ask them to describe what happened when they applied what they learned. Based on their response to you, follow up with feedback. Send them links to additional information or a video of the "correct" process.

Extend the learning after the class by sending participants reminders of some of the key concepts they learned in class. If you know they will implement some of the content on a specific day — for example, the first day of performance reviews — send a short list of tips to remember the keys to successful performance review meetings.

You may also want to use mobile devices to encourage peer-to-peer learning. Use one of the social media applications such as Twitter to initiate an implementation round robin as participants share how they are applying what they learned.

Finally, although closer to performance support than training, you can provide a job aid to your learners on their mobile devices. It definitely extends the learning.

Create and Present Videos

Videos are one of the best learning tools at your disposal. New technology makes creating video much cheaper and easier to shoot than ever before. But that does not mean that you can do whatever you want and ignore the basics. Preparation and planning before the shoot ensure a powerful video for your learners. Jonathan Halls, author of *Rapid Video Development for Trainers* (ASTD Press, 2012) believes that at least 40 percent of your production time should be spent on planning if you want a great product.

For m-learning, script it concisely and edit freely. If the video is over five minutes long, consider dividing it. The ideal video for a small device is two to five minutes in length. You may want to consider creating a private YouTube channel for videos to reduce interface issues. In what situations might you use a video?

- Demonstrate how to use a product or how to display its features to a customer.
- Define and communicate changes in the organization.
- Show learners how to complete a complex task.
- Model communication examples in difficult discussions or in a negotiation situation.

You can direct your learners to other Internet resources by embedding a URL in the content.

You've Got the Touch

Ensure that the m-learning design works well with touch. Your learners will need to interact with and provide input to their devices before they can benefit from the learning or solutions it holds. Yes, most devices can connect to external keyboards, but it is not realistic to think that your learners will do that. So you need to design for touch. For example, buttons will need to be large enough for even the chubbiest finger to press accurately.

Clarify Expectations

Laptops. Smartphones. iPads. Android. Galaxy. Kindle. Surface. iPhones. Nexus. iPods. Venue. Everyone has a preferred device they will use for their m-learning. And not everything will look good on all of these mobile devices. At times you may have a file that requires a tablet or laptop, and there is nothing you can do about it. If that's the case, establish clear expectations with your users by informing them up front in the explanation.

Also consider whether the m-learning will be used for training or performance support on a mobile device. Is it new information (training)? Or is it informal learning that support the use of existing skills or learning (performance support)?

What's next? Well, with m-learning — it's in your hands now.

Index

• •

• B •

• W •

• Z •

About the Author

Elaine Biech has been in the training and consulting field for more than a quarter of a century. She is president of ebb associates inc, an organizational development and custom training design firm that helps organizations work through large-scale change. Known as the trainer's trainer, Elaine has been featured in *The Wall Street Journal, Harvard Management Update, Fortune* magazine, *The Washington Post,* and other publications. She is the author and editor of more than 60 books, including *The ASTD Handbook: The Definitive Resource for T&D, The ASTD Leadership Handbook, The Business of Consulting,* and *Thriving Through Change.* Her books have won multiple awards and have been translated into several languages.

An active Association for Talent Development (ATD) member, Elaine served on the National ATD Board of Directors, initiated Consultant's Day at ATD's International Conference and Expo, and helped develop ATD's professional certification. She is a past member of the ISA Board of Directors and the Advisory Council for the Independent Consultants Association. Elaine is the recipient of the 1992 National ASTD Torch Award, the 2004 ASTD Volunteer-Staff Partnership Award, and the 2006 ASTD Gordon M. Bliss Memorial Award. She was selected for the 1995 Wisconsin Women Entrepreneur's Mentor Award. In 2012, ASTD awarded Elaine the inaugural CPLP Fellow Program Honoree from the ASTD Certification Institute. Elaine is currently a member of the Board of Governors for the Center for Creative Leadership.

Dedication

For Shane and Thad, my best development projects.

Author's Acknowledgments

The words in this book were not created in a vacuum. To the many people who were an intricate part of authoring this book: "Thanks!"

Thanks to Dan Greene, my personal and professional support system. Thanks to the generous contributors to this book. You are the Names to Know in the profession: Michael Allen, Jean Barbazette, Jane Bozarth, Ruth Clark, Julie Dirkson, Ann Herrmann-Nehdi, Jennifer Hoffman, Karl Kapp, Jim and Wendy Kirkpatrick, Renie McClay, Jack Phillips, Bob Pike, Becky Pike Pluth, Dana Robinson, and Thiagi.

Thank you to Regina McMichael for your techspertise in crafting Chapter 6 and to Jennifer Naughton for your certification proficiency in writing Chapter 16. Thank you Kim Seeger for your fast and fabulous suggestions.

Thanks to all the ebb associates clients who have challenged me to always design a better training and to conduct it under all kinds of conditions.

Thanks to everyone at the Association for Talent Development (ATD) who allow me to continue to grow and learn, especially Tony Bingham and Jennifer Homer for the special opportunity to publish under the respected ATD brand. Thanks, Tony, for a fantastic foreword.

Thanks to Matt Davis and Stacy Kennedy who agreed it was time for a second edition, and to Corbin Collins for his editing prowess.

All of you deserve much more than the simple thank you that appears here. Thanks for helping me write *Training & Development For Dummies*.

Publisher's Acknowledgments

Acquisitions Editor: Stacy Kennedy

Editor: Corbin Collins

Technical Editor: Kimberly Seeger

Production Editor: Kinson Raja

Cover Image: Robert Churchill/iStockphoto

Apple & Mac

iPad For Dummies,
6th Edition
978-1-118-72306-7

iPhone For Dummies,
7th Edition
978-1-118-69083-3

Macs All-in-One
For Dummies, 4th Edition
978-1-118-82210-4

OS X Mavericks
For Dummies
978-1-118-69188-5

Blogging & Social Media

Facebook For Dummies,
5th Edition
978-1-118-63312-0

Social Media Engagement
For Dummies
978-1-118-53019-1

WordPress For Dummies,
6th Edition
978-1-118-79161-5

Business

Stock Investing
For Dummies, 4th Edition
978-1-118-37678-2

Investing For Dummies,
6th Edition
978-0-470-90545-6

Personal Finance

Personal Finance
For Dummies, 7th Edition
978-1-118-11785-9

QuickBooks 2014
For Dummies
978-1-118-72005-9

Small Business Marketing
Kit For Dummies,
3rd Edition
978-1-118-31183-7

Careers

Job Interviews
For Dummies, 4th Edition
978-1-118-11290-8

Job Searching with Social
Media For Dummies,
2nd Edition
978-1-118-67856-5

Personal Branding
For Dummies
978-1-118-11792-7

Resumes For Dummies,
6th Edition
978-0-470-87361-8

Starting an Etsy Business
For Dummies, 2nd Edition
978-1-118-59024-9

Diet & Nutrition

Belly Fat Diet For Dummies
978-1-118-34585-6

Digital Photography

Mediterranean Diet
For Dummies
978-1-118-71525-3

Nutrition For Dummies,
5th Edition
978-0-470-93231-5

Digital Photography

Digital SLR Photography
All-in-One For Dummies,
2nd Edition
978-1-118-59082-9

Digital SLR Video &
Filmmaking For Dummies
978-1-118-36598-4

Photoshop Elements 12
For Dummies
978-1-118-72714-0

Gardening

Herb Gardening
For Dummies, 2nd Edition
978-0-470-61778-6

Gardening with Free-Range
Chickens For Dummies
978-1-118-54754-0

Health

Boosting Your Immunity
For Dummies
978-1-118-40200-9

Diabetes

Diabetes For Dummies,
4th Edition
978-1-118-29447-5

Living Paleo For Dummies
978-1-118-29405-5

Big Data

Big Data For Dummies
978-1-118-50422-2

Data Visualization
For Dummies
978-1-118-50289-1

Hadoop For Dummies
978-1-118-60755-8

Language &
Foreign Language

500 Spanish Verbs
For Dummies
978-1-118-02382-2

English Grammar
For Dummies, 2nd Edition
978-0-470-54664-2

French All-in-One
For Dummies
978-1-118-22815-9

German Essentials
For Dummies
978-1-118-18422-6

Italian For Dummies,
2nd Edition
978-1-118-00465-4

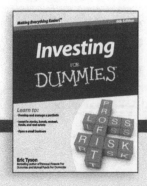

Math & Science

Algebra I For Dummies,
2nd Edition
978-0-470-55964-2

Anatomy and Physiology
For Dummies, 2nd Edition
978-0-470-92326-9

Astronomy For Dummies,
3rd Edition
978-1-118-37697-3

Biology For Dummies,
2nd Edition
978-0-470-59875-7

Chemistry For Dummies,
2nd Edition
978-1-118-00730-3

1001 Algebra II Practice
Problems For Dummies
978-1-118-44662-1

Microsoft Office

Excel 2013 For Dummies
978-1-118-51012-4

Office 2013 All-in-One
For Dummies
978-1-118-51636-2

PowerPoint 2013
For Dummies
978-1-118-50253-2

Word 2013 For Dummies
978-1-118-49123-2

Music

Blues Harmonica
For Dummies
978-1-118-25269-7

Guitar For Dummies,
3rd Edition
978-1-118-11554-1

iPod & iTunes
For Dummies, 10th Edition
978-1-118-50864-0

Programming

Beginning Programming
with C For Dummies
978-1-118-73763-7

Excel VBA Programming
For Dummies, 3rd Edition
978-1-118-49037-2

Java For Dummies,
6th Edition
978-1-118-40780-6

Religion & Inspiration

The Bible For Dummies
978-0-7645-5296-0

Buddhism For Dummies,
2nd Edition
978-1-118-02379-2

Catholicism For Dummies,
2nd Edition
978-1-118-07778-8

Self-Help & Relationships

Beating Sugar Addiction
For Dummies
978-1-118-54645-1

Meditation For Dummies,
3rd Edition
978-1-118-29144-3

Seniors

Laptops For Seniors
For Dummies, 3rd Edition
978-1-118-71105-7

Computers For Seniors
For Dummies, 3rd Edition
978-1-118-11553-4

iPad For Seniors
For Dummies, 6th Edition
978-1-118-72826-0

Social Security
For Dummies
978-1-118-20573-0

Smartphones & Tablets

Android Phones
For Dummies, 2nd Edition
978-1-118-72030-1

Nexus Tablets
For Dummies
978-1-118-77243-0

Samsung Galaxy S 4
For Dummies
978-1-118-64222-1

Samsung Galaxy Tabs
For Dummies
978-1-118-77294-2

Test Prep

ACT For Dummies,
5th Edition
978-1-118-01259-8

ASVAB For Dummies,
3rd Edition
978-0-470-63760-9

GRE For Dummies,
7th Edition
978-0-470-88921-3

Officer Candidate Tests
For Dummies
978-0-470-59876-4

Physician's Assistant Exam
For Dummies
978-1-118-11556-5

Series 7 Exam For Dummies
978-0-470-09932-2

Windows 8

Windows 8.1 All-in-One
For Dummies
978-1-118-82087-2

Windows 8.1 For Dummies
978-1-118-82121-3

Windows 8.1 For Dummies,
Book + DVD Bundle
978-1-118-82107-7

 Available in print and e-book formats.

Available wherever books are sold. **For more information or to order direct visit www.dummies.com**

Take Dummies with you everywhere you go!

Whether you are excited about e-books, want more from the web, must have your mobile apps, or are swept up in social media, Dummies makes everything easier.

Leverage the Power

For Dummies is the global leader in the reference category and one of the most trusted and highly regarded brands in the world. No longer just focused on books, customers now have access to the For Dummies content they need in the format they want. Let us help you develop a solution that will fit your brand and help you connect with your customers.

Advertising & Sponsorships

Connect with an engaged audience on a powerful multimedia site, and position your message alongside expert how-to content.

Targeted ads • Video • Email marketing • Microsites • Sweepstakes sponsorship

Dummies products make life easier!

- DIY
- Consumer Electronics
- Crafts
- Software
- Cookware
- Hobbies
- Videos
- Music
- Games
- and More!

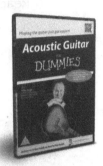

For more information, go to **Dummies.com** and search the store by category.

FOR
DUMMIES
A Wiley Brand